MIRROR MIRROR

The Astrology of Famous People and the Actors Who Portrayed Them

ALEX TRENOWETH

The Wessex Astrologer

Published in 2021 by
The Wessex Astrologer Ltd
PO Box 9307
Swanage
BH19 9BF

For a full list of our titles go to www.wessexastrologer.com

© Alex Trenoweth 2021
Alex Trenoweth asserts her moral right to be recognised as
the author of this work

Cover design by Andy Jay

A catalogue record for this book is available at The British Library

ISBN 9781910531556

No part of this book may be reproduced or used in any form or by any
means without the written permission of the publisher.
A reviewer may quote brief passages.

DEDICATED TO
MR BUBBLES

CONTENTS

Foreword by Julia Parker ... ix
Introduction ... xi

PLUTO ... 1
A Beautiful Day in the Neighborhood ... 2
Al Capone ... 4
Madame Curie ... 7
Schindler's List ... 11

NEPTUNE ... 16
Goodfellas ... 16
Sid and Nancy ... 20
The Pursuit of Happyness ... 24

URANUS ... 27
Amadeus ... 28
The Miracle Worker ... 32
The Story of Louis Pasteur ... 36

SATURN ... 38
127 Hours ... 38
Ali ... 40
Coalminer's Daughter ... 43
Dead Man Walking ... 45
Eddie the Eagle ... 49
Invictus ... 51
Shine ... 55
The Iron Lady ... 59

JUPITER ... 61
Frida ... 62
Lust for Life ... 64
Moulin Rouge ... 66
The Spirit of St Louis ... 69

MARS — 72
- Evita — 72
- James Dean — 75
- Jesse James — 77
- Looking for Mr Goodbar — 79
- Raging Bull — 81

VENUS — 84
- Diamond Jim — 84
- Iris — 87
- Jackie — 92
- Lady Sings the Blues — 95
- My Week with Marilyn — 97
- Stand and Deliver — 100
- The Dolly Sisters — 102
- Wilde — 104

MERCURY — 107
- Bohemian Rhapsody — 108
- Frances — 111
- Grace of Monaco — 114
- Mata Hari — 117
- Young Man With a Horn — 120

MOON — 123
- Chaplin — 124
- Gorillas in the Mist — 127
- My Left Foot — 129
- The Pianist — 132
- The Queen — 135
- Walt Before Mickey — 139

SUN — 142
- Boys Town — 142
- Cry Freedom — 145
- Hotel Rwanda — 149
- La Bamba — 151
- The Elephant Man — 153

NODES — 158
- A Cry in the Dark — 159
- Coco Before Chanel — 161
- Funny Girl — 164
- Gandhi — 166
- Lincoln — 168
- Patton — 170
- Miss Potter — 173
- Ray — 176
- Selena — 179
- The Aviator — 181
- The Buddy Holly Story — 186

CHIRON — 189
- Dance With a Stranger — 189
- Factory Girl — 191
- Judy — 195
- Silkwood — 198
- The Karen Carpenter Story — 200

MULTIPLES — 203
Ted Bundy — 204
- The Deliberate Stranger — 205
- Ted Bundy — 207
- The Stranger Beside Me — 209
- Extremely Wicked, Shockingly Evil and Vile — 212

Thomas Edison — 214
- Young Edison — 214
- Edison, the Man — 216

Elizabeth I — 218
- Fire over England — 218
- Shakespeare in Love — 222

Stephen Hawking — 222
- Hawking — 222
- The Theory of Everything — 225

Harry Houdini — 228
- Houdini — 228
- Houdini (TV Film) — 232

Richard III — **234**
   Richard III (1955) — 234
   Looking for Richard — 236

Dorothy Stratten — **238**
   Death of a Centerfold: The Dorothy Stratten Story — 238
   Star 80 — 241

Queen Victoria — **244**
   Mrs Brown — 244
   Victoria and Abdul — 248

FAVOURITES — 253
   Behind the Candelabra — 254
   Born on the Fourth of July — 258
   Erin Brockovich — 264
   Capote — 268
   Great Balls of Fire — 272
   Hitchcock — 277
   I, Tonya — 283
   Julie & Julia — 287
   La Vie en Rose — 293
   Lawrence of Arabia — 296
   Mask — 300
   Milk — 304
   Monster — 308
   Rocketman — 313
   The Doors — 320
   The Imitation Game — 324
   The King's Speech — 329
   Walk the Line — 334

GROWING PAINS
   Intro — 339
   Jupiter in Aquarius — 344

   Author Bio — 351

FOREWORD

Among the many astrology books published each year – each decade, indeed – how many explore a genuinely new idea? It can safely be said that Alex Trenoweth has achieved that goal in a book which is based on a comparison of the charts of famous film actors and of the personalities they have portrayed for the cinema.

A physical impersonation and spectacular make-up is one thing, but to give the impression even for just 120 minutes, that Mrs Thatcher or Linda Chamberlain are actually on-screen before us requires some kind of indefinable theatrical magic. Magic – or astrology? In her intriguing book Ms Trenoweth examines over a hundred examples of the synastry between actors and their biographical roles. The results are of course variable, as in almost all astrological books concerning synastry, but here, in almost every case, one follows the author's arguments with eager interest.

This is a book not only for the astrologer with a thorough knowledge of the subject, but – spectacularly – for those with a keen, developing interest. A certain amount of knowledge is of course essential when reading, for instance, the separate chapters on the planets – and Chiron and the nodes – but the enthusiastic film-goer will find enormous interest in those which deal, in the core of the book, with the relationship between the actor and his or her subject. The interest broadens when Ms Trenoweth (whose knowledge of astrology and film history run side by side, with neither one in advance of the other) looks at a range of actors who have played the same character – for example, Harry Houdini, Queen Elizabeth I, Queen Victoria and Stephen Hawking.

I must have seen a good dozen Hamlets at the theatre: how I would have liked to read Ms Trenoweth speculate on, say, Peter O'Toole's disastrous performance – what, in his chart, betrays his inability to play the introvert Lawrence with such spectacular insight, when he seemed to have no intuitive connection at all with the introvert Prince? How did the planets at birth encourage John Gielgud to be the finest Hamlet of our time, when that fine actor Jude Law failed to reach the heights? Perhaps another book by another astrologer – but with this book, remember, Alex Trenoweth, comes first. Huckleberry Finn, reading *Pilgrim's Progress*, found 'the statement was interesting, but tough.' This author's statements are interesting and far from tough. It deserves to be the bedside book of the year.

Julia Parker 2021

Julia Parker and Alex Trenoweth

INTRODUCTION

In the summer of 2009, during a visit to my family in Michigan, I persuaded my mother to watch *Julie & Julia* with me. As a kid, I was fascinated with Julia Child and as a six-year-old I'd faithfully watch her on television. I didn't understand what she was doing but I loved the way she did what she did with such passion. As I grew older, I found other interests but I liked to check in on what Julia was doing every now and again. By the time she died, just a few days before her 92nd birthday, I still hadn't understood her unique contributions to fine cuisine. *Julie & Julia* changed all that. I watched the movie completely enthralled by Meryl Streep's performance, marvelling at how the average-sized actress could fill the 6'2" frame of Julia Child.

Reflecting on the film, I realised that I had been so completely absorbed by the actress' performance that I actually forgot she really wasn't Julia Child. Curious, I thought I'd have a look at the real life Child's astrology chart and compare it to Streep's. What I discovered was something that would keep me busy for several years.

Was there something about the astrology that made it easy for the actor to step into the role of a real life person? As I watched more and more biographical films and investigated the astrology, I became very convinced that yes, the astrology tells the story. By the end of 2019, I had watched nearly 200 biopics and set myself the task of writing about these connections for this book.

Some of the films I loved so much that I wanted to write about them in more depth. I was particularly impressed with the actors who learned new skills for their roles, such as Joaquin Phoenix and Reese Witherspoon who sang as Johnny and June Carter Cash in *Walk the Line*, or Rami Malek as Freddie Mercury in *Bohemian Rhapsody*, or Taron Egerton as Elton John in *Rocketman* (also my very favourite film). There was Margot Robbie who spent four hours per day for five days a week learning how to ice skate for her role as Tonya Harding in *I, Tonya*. And I can't leave out Daniel Day-Lewis, who prepared for his role as Christy

Brown in *My Left Foot* by spending most of his time in a wheelchair and learning how to put a record on a turntable with his toes during filming.

Observing how films change through history was also interesting to me. The early biopics of the 1930s – 1950s tended to feature roles of biblical characters which meant the lack of a birth date made them unsuitable for astrological scrutiny. It was from the 1970s that biopics became more popular and films such as Diana Ross as Billie Holiday in *Lady Sings the Blues*, Gary Busey as Buddy Holly and Sissy Spacek as Loretta Lynn in *Coalminer's Daughter* helped to make the genre more popular.

Despite enjoying the majority of the biopics in this book, there were a few I really didn't like and we decided to leave them out. *They Died With Their Boots On* was so historically inaccurate that it put me in a bad mood for a week and *By the Light of the Moon* about the serial killer Ed Gein was never going to go over well with someone who dislikes the horror genre. *127 Hours* I could only watch by peeking out of a blanket but it is included in the collection nonetheless. Speaking of inclusions, the pared-down list of about 100 films came about because the ones that were weeded out were relatively unknown or unpopular, not because the astrology wasn't working. In every single film, the astrology revealed a layer of enhanced meaning and for an astrologer that only heightened the enjoyment.

Once the bulk of the writing was done, I had to think about how I wanted to order the case studies of the films. Chronologically seemed the most obvious but my publisher suggested something more thematic. Would it be possible to categorise them by the planet that showed the strongest synastry between character and actor? I spent a few weeks mulling this over and procrastinating on this re-structure. I shouldn't have worried. In just a few short hours, the job was easily done. There are a few stretches with films that didn't seem to fit in any one category but it was surprisingly easy to find a planetary theme for most of the films.

In terms of methodology, I wanted to keep to a few simple rules. Firstly the films had to be about a real-life person. Secondly, I wanted to keep the orbs of the aspects down to one or two degrees unless otherwise stated. I could have easily taken up a lot of space writing about every minutiae of astrological connection but I thought that would take the fun away. I wanted to stick to conjunctions and oppositions and leave more in-depth analyses to the reader who might even be inspired to write an article for one of the fine astrology magazines currently available. For the charts, I used tri-wheels with the real-life person in the centre, the actor in the middle and the event chart (set for noon in Hollywood unless otherwise stated) for the movie's release. Unfortunately, not all of the precise times of birth were available and in these cases, it is indicated that a noon chart was used with no references to the Moon or angles which would be significantly affected by the time of day. No angles are shown on charts where either or both sets of data have unverified times. Data collection is a moveable feast, so updates are constantly being posted where new information has come to light. As far as we are aware, birth data was correct at time of going to print. All the charts have been created in Solar Fire v8.1.3.

Writing a book can be very exciting but it can also be quite isolating (a bit like studying astrology) so I wanted to thank a few people for going above and beyond for all the support they've given to me. A big thanks to the Cosmic Intelligence Agency's "Astro Babes" Julja Simas, Deb James, Olga Morales, Helen Puckey and Sol Jonassen for all the Zoom laughter during the challenging times of lockdown. Of course my publisher Margaret Cahill deserves a massive shout out for all her patience, good humoured hard work in fine-tuning the book and constant encouragement. A huge thanks to Paul F. Newman for all the double, triple and quadruple checking of data. There was a lot to get through! A massive thank you to Julia Parker for her generosity in writing the Foreword. And I can't leave my furry kitty baby, Mr Bubbles, out of the thank yous. He was both my film-watching and writing companion and we spent his last night together watching *Lawrence of Arabia* curled up on the sofa. I like to think that between his cuddly human and the delectable Peter O'Toole, we gave him the best possible send-off.

PLUTO

In mythology, Pluto ruled the place where souls reside once they become detached from the human body after death. Although not a tormentor of souls, Pluto was still regarded as an enemy to life and he was seen as a powerful god no mortal could escape. He was immune to offerings and sacrifices – unless the person making the sacrifice was seeking revenge or destruction. However, Pluto's habitat was loaded with the rich materials that arouse greed and jealousy in the men who desired to possess such riches.

Astrologically, Pluto is associated with profound changes. Events that change your life completely would have a good dose of Pluto, so actors who are playing the role of a character at the receiving end of such change need somehow to have access to that sense of the phoenix rising from the ashes. The transformation involved with these types of events could eventually bring about a healing. For example, in *A Beautiful Day in the Neighborhood*, a journalist's life is turned around for the better following years of estrangement from his father. An encounter with Mr Rogers (Tom Hanks) changed all that, the film being made all the more powerful by Hanks and Rogers having Pluto contacts both ways between their charts.

Al Capone is definitely not a man to aspire to, and in *Al Capone* we see Rod Steiger's Mars in Gemini tapping straight into Capone's Pluto, enabling him to be depicted in such an unpleasant way we can be assured no one would want to emulate him.

In *Madame Curie*, Greer Garson turned out to be the ideal choice to play Marie. Besides having strong contacts between their charts, Garson also had Pluto conjunct her own MC – perfect for playing the scientist who showed us the power of radioactive elements and the benefits (as well as the dangers) of using them.

Schindler's List is probably one of the most emotionally provocative films in this book. Without question, Liam Neeson's Pluto/South Node conjunction enabled him to tap into Oskar Schindler's Chiron, demonstrating for all of us that as long as there are people around like Schindler there is still hope amidst the depths of such appalling cruelty.

A BEAUTIFUL DAY IN THE NEIGHBORHOOD
Fred Rogers: 20 March 1928, 08:20, Latrobe, Pennsylvania.
A: Steinbrecher
Tom Hanks: 9 July 1956, 11:17, Concord, California. AA:RR
Release date: 7 September 2019

At his sister's wedding, Lloyd Vogel, a new father and an award-winning journalist for *Esquire*, starts a fistfight with Jerry, his father. Lloyd's father had abandoned Lloyd's mother and Lloyd felt his father had disrespected his mother's memory. The following day, he meets up with the legendary television host Mister Rogers, to interview him. Rogers plays down his fame and asks about Lloyd's damaged nose, so Lloyd tells him about the fight and his grudge against his father, whose apology he has rejected.

Lloyd is suspicious of Rogers' nice guy act and is initially interested in exposing him as a fraud. He watches some old episodes of *Mister Rogers' Neighborhood* but can't see anything that could potentially damage the nice guy persona. During a subsequent interview, Rogers reminisces about raising his two sons, takes out two puppets and asks about Lloyd's own stuffed animals as a child, and his father. Lloyd ends the interview early and goes home, only to find that his wife has invited Jerry and his new girlfriend to dinner. Father and son argue again and Lloyd berates his father for abandoning his mother when she was dying of cancer. Lloyd orders him to leave, but his father has a heart attack and the family end up in hospital with him. Lloyd refuses to stay with his father and returns to see Rogers to finish the interview. Emotionally drained, Lloyd falls asleep on Rogers' set and dreams of past childhood difficulties. In his dream, his mother comes to him as she is dying, and tells him to release his anger.

Concerned over Lloyd's condition, Rogers and his wife bring him into their home to rest. Later, Rogers asks Lloyd to think about the people who love him and encourages him to forgive his father. When he returns home, Lloyd apologises to his wife and learns his father has a terminal illness and this was the reason he had wanted to reconcile so badly. Lloyd forgives his father and writes an article called "Can you say. . . Hero?" about the impact Rogers had on his life. The article was *Esquire*'s cover story.

Unsurprisingly, Fred Rogers has a four-planet stellium in Pisces. Although too far out of orb to be a conjunction, they do match Hanks'

Pluto 3

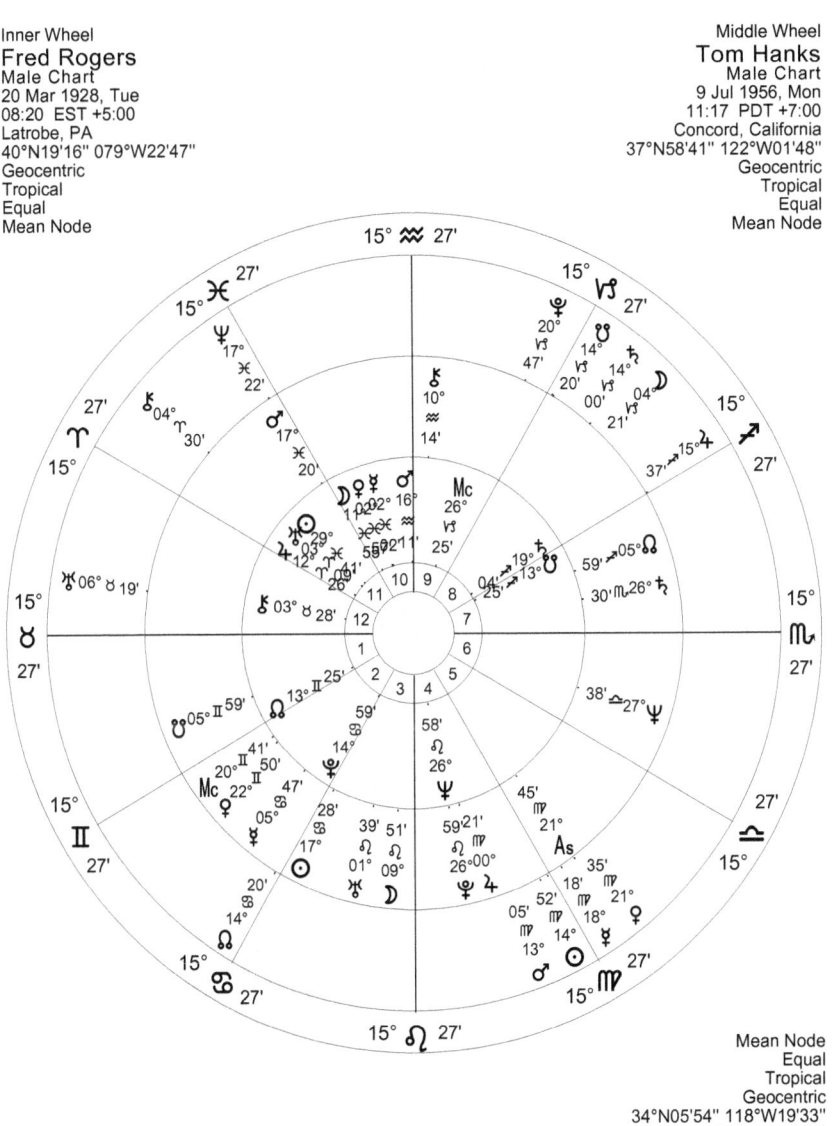

Mars in Pisces nicely. Rogers' Pluto in Cancer is conjunct Hanks' Sun within a few degrees, coaxing further kindness and care from the performance. Hanks' Pluto in Leo is conjunct Rogers' Neptune so here we have a cushion for this powerful planet.

The film was released as transiting Neptune was exactly conjunct Hanks' Mars in Pisces and the planet would have transited Rogers' stellium during filming.

So far, the film has earned $59 million at the box office and was chosen by *Time* magazine as one of the best films of 2019. Hanks has been nominated for a Golden Globes, Critics' Choice, Screen Actors Guild Awards, BAFTA Awards and Academy Awards.

AL CAPONE

Al Capone: 17 January 1899, 09:30, Brooklyn, New York, C: RR
Rod Steiger: 14 April 1925, no time, New York. Source: Wikipedia
St Valentine's Day Massacre: 14 February 1929, 10:30,
A: News reports
Release date: 25 March 1959

Glorifying gangsters and other criminals was banned under Hollywood's 'Production Code' until the late 1950s. Even with the ban lifted Rod Steiger, who portrayed the titular Al Capone, reportedly turned down the script for the film because he felt it glorified the criminality and violence of a gangster. However, the script was given a complete overhaul which the actor accepted. The result was a performance that gave Al Capone absolutely no redeeming qualities.

Set during the time of Prohibition, Capone and other well-known gangsters of the time, began selling bootleg alcohol for ever-increasing profits. Competition between rival gangs led to shoot-outs and intense police scrutiny. With a tip-off from a corrupt journalist, Capone headed south to Florida to avoid arrest. From there, he masterminded the St Valentine's Massacre, resulting in several deaths. He managed to avoid being implicated in the crime but was eventually charged with tax evasion and was sentenced to 11 years in the notorious Alcatraz prison.

Rod Steiger's Mars in Gemini is exactly conjunct Al Capone's Pluto and in opposition to the gangster's Venus. Capone's North Node is conjunct Steiger's Moon in Capricorn which indicates the actor may

Pluto 5

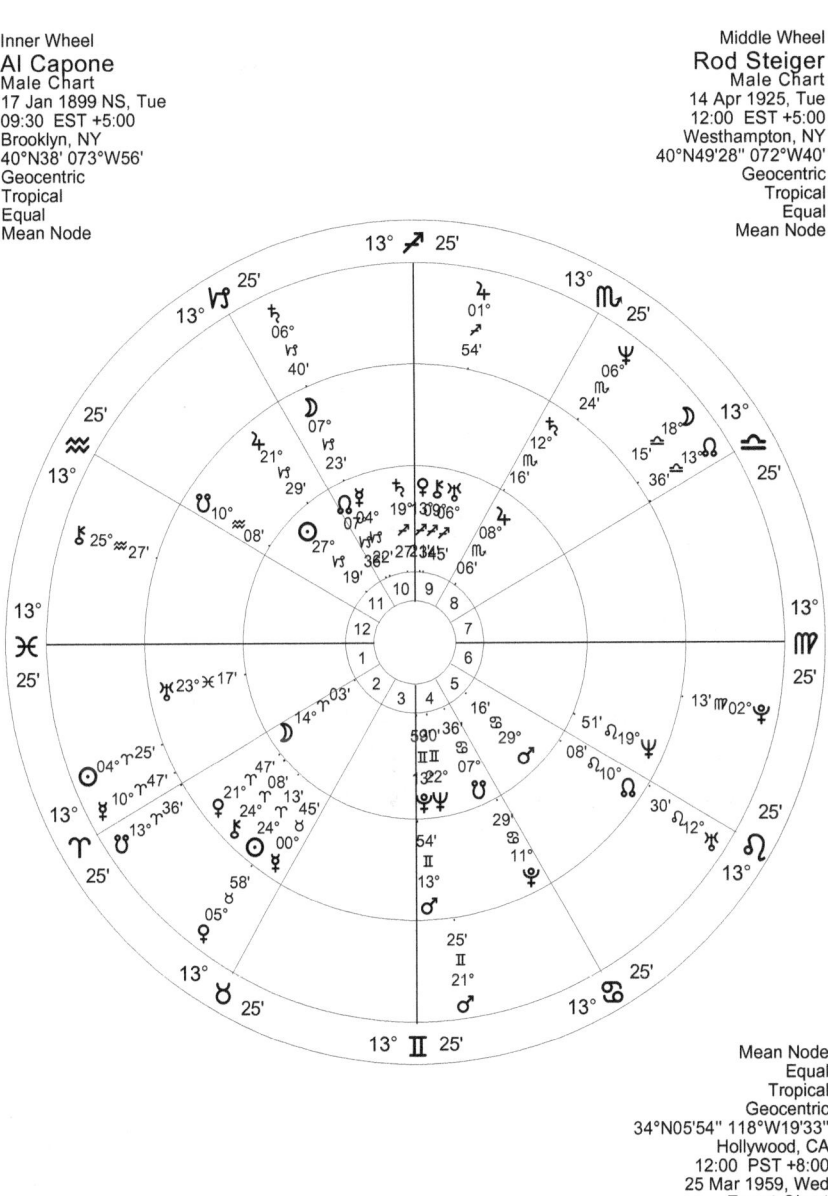

Inner Wheel
Al Capone
Male Chart
17 Jan 1899 NS, Tue
09:30 EST +5:00
Brooklyn, NY
40°N38' 073°W56'
Geocentric
Tropical
Equal
Mean Node

Middle Wheel
Rod Steiger
Male Chart
14 Apr 1925, Tue
12:00 EST +5:00
Westhampton, NY
40°N49'28" 072°W40'
Geocentric
Tropical
Equal
Mean Node

Mean Node
Equal
Tropical
Geocentric
34°N05'54" 118°W19'33"
Hollywood, CA
12:00 PST +8:00
25 Mar 1959, Wed
Event Chart
Al Capone release
Outer Wheel

6 Mirror Mirror

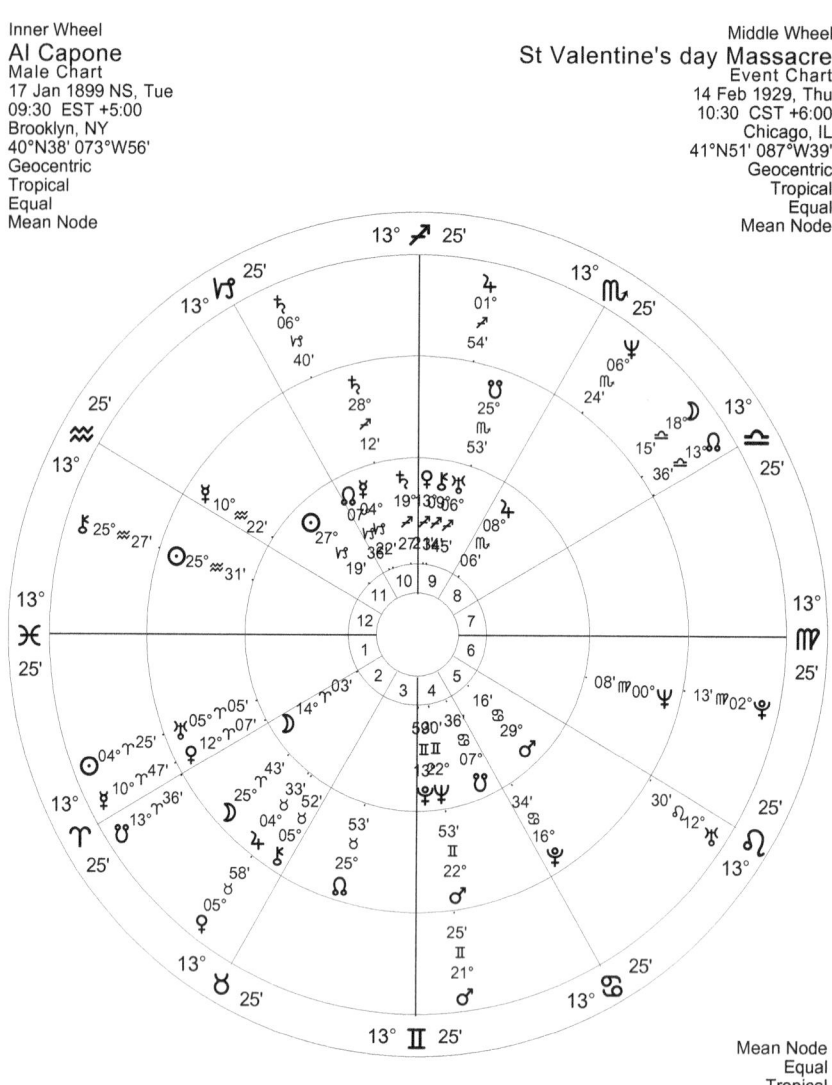

have felt he was born to play the part. *Al Capone* was a film filled with crime, corruption, blackmail, murder and other acts of violence associated with the underworld of The Mafia.

Perhaps the worst of the crimes was Capone's masterminding of the Valentine's Day Massacre from his hideout in Florida. The real life event of the St Valentine's Day Massacre had transiting Mars in Gemini conjunct Capone's Neptune. This was a crime tangled with lies, disguises and deception. However, the film did end with Capone in prison for tax evasion so perhaps this showed justice being served with transiting Saturn conjunct the gangster's North Node in Capricorn when the film was released.

The film was criticised as being just another film about Capone but it was generally well received and was named "Sleeper of the Year". However, citing invasion of privacy, some of the surviving members of the Capone family tried to sue the filmmakers but a judge ruled against them.

MADAME CURIE

Marie Curie: 7 November 1867, 12:00, Warsaw, Poland. AA: RR
Greer Garson: 29 September 1904, 04:45, London, England.
C: Scholfield
Pierre Curie: 15 May 1859, 02:00, Paris, France. C: March
Walter Davis Pidgeon: 23 September 1897, no time, Saint John, New Brunswick, Canada. Source: Wikipedia
Release date: 15 December 1943

Marie Curie's (neé Sklodowska) timed birth chart reveals that she is a Capricorn ascendant. Generally speaking, this would indicate a hard-working and serious approach to life. Before her marriage, Marie is studying in Paris, living in quite poor conditions and working harder than her body will allow. One day, she faints in class and a professor sympathises with her situation and invites her to a party his wife is putting together for other professors and their wives.

It is at this party that Marie meets her future husband, the somewhat shy and absent-minded Pierre, whose ascendant is conjunct Marie's Moon and South Node in Pisces. He allows her to share his laboratory and discovers her gift for science. Her ruling planet Saturn is conjunct her

8 Mirror Mirror

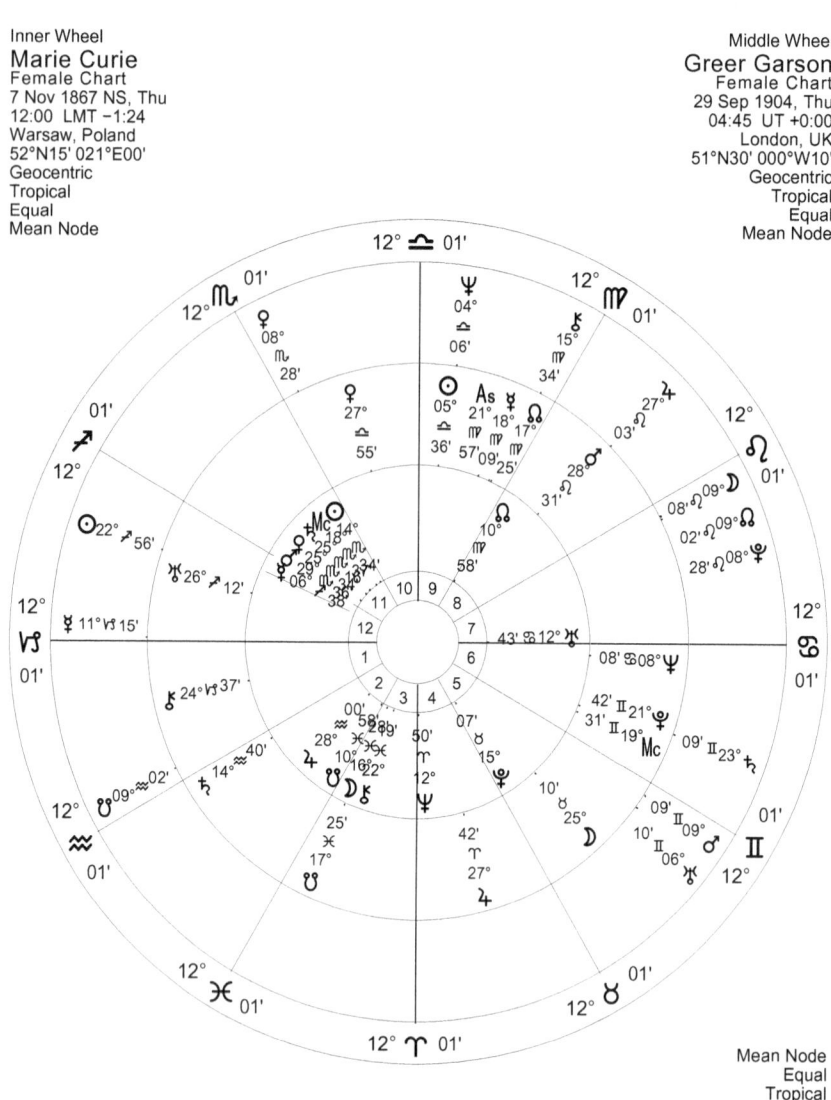

Pluto 9

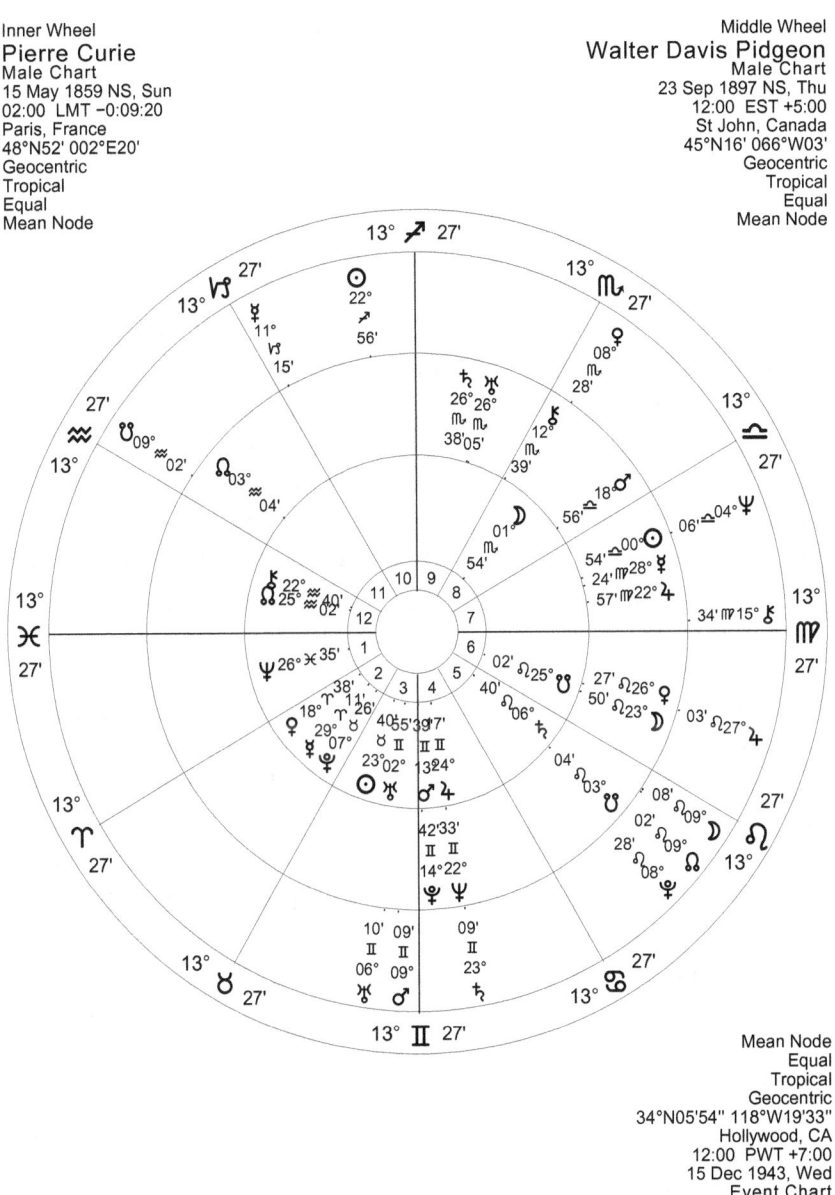

Venus and MC in Scorpio and her Uranus is conjunct her descendant. So it makes perfect astrological sense that it takes a long time for her to realise she has fallen in love with Pierre after years of working in a lab with him. After he discovers that she intends to return to her native Poland following graduation, he takes her to meet his family. He proposes marriage and she accepts.

The couple begin experimenting with radioactive elements and make several ground-breaking discoveries together. After achieving world-wide fame, they receive the Nobel Prize and visit Paris again after their many press conferences.

While walking back from buying Marie a pair of earrings, Pierre absent-mindedly steps in front of a delivery wagon and is killed. Although in deep shock and grief, Marie remembers that they had previously agreed that if one of them died, the other must carry on their work. Many years later on the twenty-fifth anniversary celebration of the discovery of radium, she gives a speech saying that science is on the path to making the world a better place. It's wonderful to note the astrological symbolism of her having Pluto in opposition to her Sun in Scorpio by an orb of less than one degree.

Marie Curie was portrayed by Greer Garson who had her natal ascendant, Mercury and North Node in opposition to the scientist's Moon in Pisces. The actress' Pluto was conjunct her own MC, making her an appropriate choice to play someone who experimented with radioactivity. The discovery of the outer planets (Uranus, Neptune and Pluto) coincided roughly with the discovery of radioactive elements, and both science and astrology were forced to accept these new energies into their individual systems.

Pierre Curie was portrayed by Walter Davis Pidgeon who had his natal Venus conjunct Pierre Curie's South Node. Curie was a devoted husband and it is no astrological surprise that his Mars in Gemini was conjunct the actor's Pluto.

The film was released as transiting Jupiter in Leo was conjunct Pierre's South Node, Pidgeon's Venus, Greer's Mars, and all opposing Marie's natal Jupiter in Aquarius.

Pidgeon and Greer were nominated for Academy Awards and the film is listed in the AFI's 100 Years...Heroes and Villains, and 100 Years...100 Cheers categories.

SCHINDLER'S LIST

Oskar Schindler, 28 April 1908, no time, Svitavy, Czech Republic.
X: RR
Liam Neeson, 7 June 1952, no time, Ballymena, Northern Ireland.
X: Starkman
Amon Göth: 11 December 1908, no time, Vienna,
Austria-Hungary. Source: Wikipedia
Ralph Fiennes, 22 December 1962, no time, Ipswich, Suffolk,
England. Source: Wikipedia
Release date: November 30 1993 (Washington, D.C.)

In Krakow, Poland during World War II, Jews are forced into an overcrowded ghetto by Germans. Oskar Schindler is an ethnic German from Czechoslovakia who had hoped to make his fortune by using Jewish workers in his factory. He bribes the Nazi Party to acquire a factory to make enamelware and has maintained a friendly relationship with its members. He hires a Jewish official with contacts to marketers and other members of the Jewish business community to help him run the business with cheap Jewish labour. This ensures as many people as possible are deemed essential to the German war effort so they're not sent to concentration camps.

Amon Göth, an SS officer, arrives to oversee the construction of a new concentration camp and orders that the ghetto be emptied upon its completion. Schindler is deeply upset by the subsequent massacre. When he sees a young girl in a red coat (the film is otherwise black and white) hiding from the Nazis and then later sees her body in a wagon full of corpses, he knows he cannot continue to stand by and watch the extermination. In the meantime, Göth treats his Jewish maid and other prisoners in the ghetto with shocking brutality. To keep Göth on his side, Schindler lavishes gifts on him whilst planning to build another camp to keep as many people safe as possible.

Eventually, Göth is ordered to ship the workers to Auschwitz. However, Schindler pays a huge bribe and he and his Jewish official secretly create "Schindler's List" to transfer people to a safer place to work in a munitions factory.

At one point, the train carrying women and girls is accidentally redirected to Auschwitz, and Schindler has to bribe the commandant of Auschwitz with a bag of diamonds to have them released. In time, Schindler uses up all of his money bribing Nazi officials. As he is a member of the Nazi party, Schindler has to flee the advancing Red Army to avoid capture. His final act is to persuade the SS guards not to murder the prisoners but to return them to their families as free men rather than as criminals. When he leaves to surrender to the Americans, he is given a signed statement from his workers attesting to the role he played in saving their lives. They also give him a ring with a quote from the Talmud: "Whoever saves one life saves the world entire." Oskar Schindler is comforted by this, feeling guilt only for the lives of those he couldn't save. The next morning, the workers are liberated.

The epilogue reveals that Göth was tried and executed for his crimes against humanity. Schindler's marriage failed as did his future business attempts, however he was honoured for his efforts to save his workers from being put to death. In an incredibly moving scene, surviving workers place a stone on Schindler's grave (a sign of respect in the Jewish custom) and the final visitor, the actor who played Schindler (Liam Neeson), places two roses.

Schindler and Göth were born the same year and so their outermost planets were similar. But of course there are revealing differences. Schindler had a natal Venus/Pluto conjunction in Gemini. Let's face it: he led an incredibly intense double-life and had this been discovered, he would have been in very deep trouble.

Neeson has a natal Pluto/South Node conjunction in Leo opposing Schindler's natal Chiron. *Schindler's List* brought recognition to a previously unsung hero and Neeson, already a well established A-lister, was integral to bringing his story to light in this powerful film. Schindler's Mars in Gemini is conjunct Neeson's stellium. His story was of a man who essentially lived two partitioned lives: one as a member of the Nazi party and one as a man who lost his fortune saving the lives of Jewish prisoners who would have died in concentration camps had he not risked everything to save them. Schindler's Neptune in Cancer is exactly conjunct Neeson's Uranus. The final scene of the film (when Neeson places two roses on Schindler's grave) beautifully demonstrated the profound impact this role had on him. The film was released as Saturn transited Schindler's Chiron and Neeson's North Node in Aquarius.

Göth's North Node and Pluto were also conjunct Schindler's planets

Pluto 13

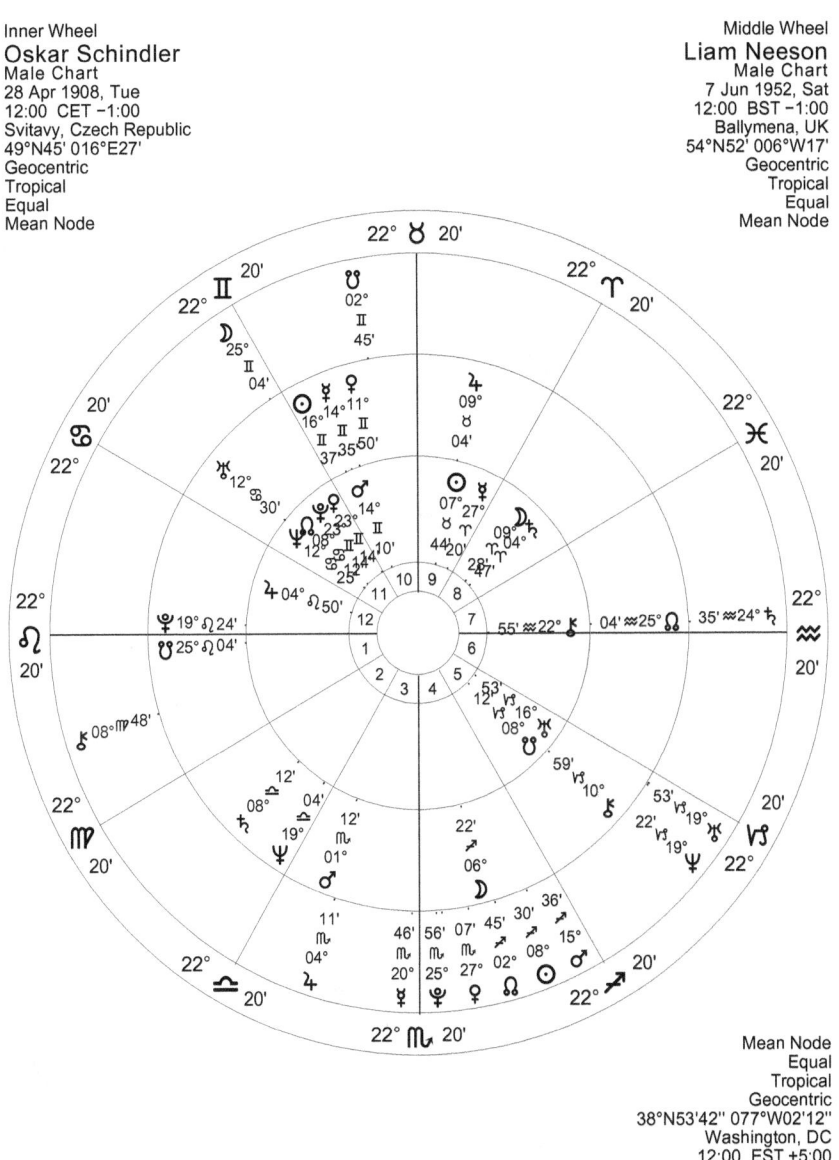

14   Mirror Mirror

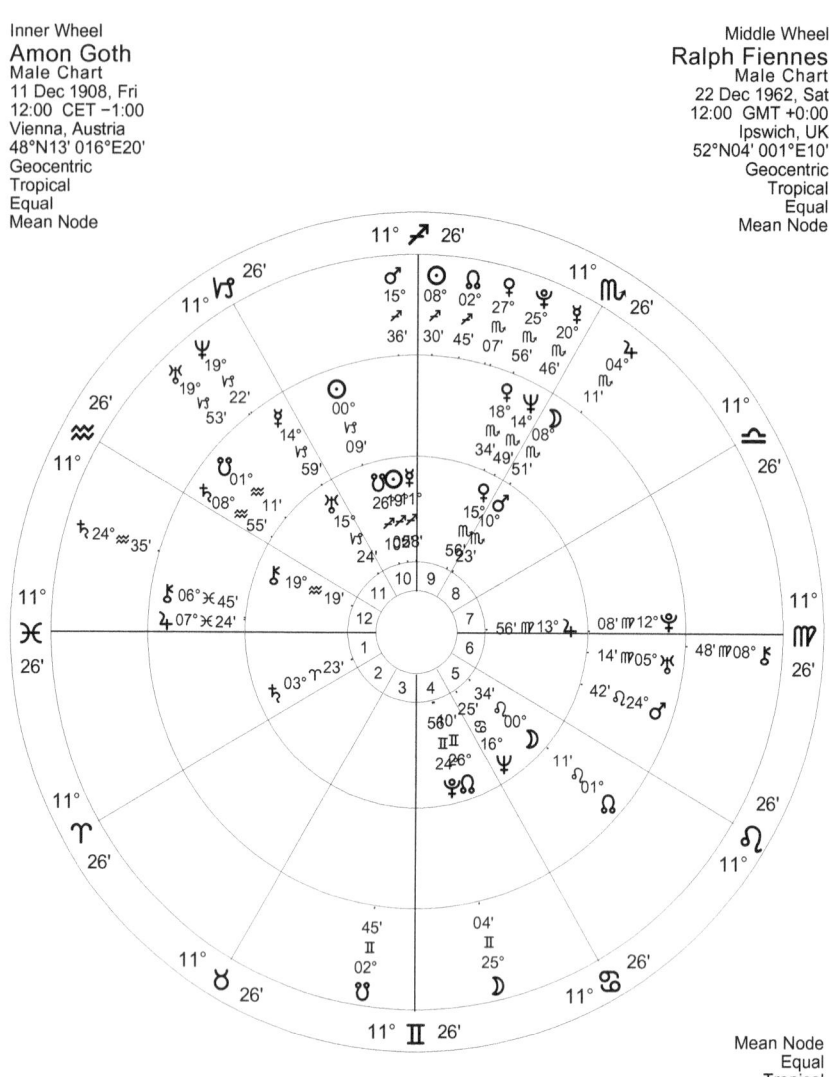

in Gemini. That he assumed such a vile position of power and was in such intense secret conflict with Schindler is not very surprising when viewed astrologically. Pluto is the modern ruler of Scorpio and the traditional ruler of Scorpio, Mars, is in its own sign and conjunct Venus. Given the right, perfect storm conditions, this indicates a desire to seize power. And Göth was in that perfect storm. He also had Uranus in Capricorn exactly sextile Venus so he would not have been immune to shady business deals either. Göth's Uranus is conjunct Fiennes' Mercury and his Venus/Mars is strongly connected to the actor's Venus/Neptune conjunction in Scorpio. As an actor, playing a villain can be very tricky – especially if it concerns the Holocaust. It may be assumed Fiennes wanted to be bad but convincingly so, and yet respectful to the people who were touched by the film. Fiennes' Neptune is the astrological cushion that allowed him to step into the part without being completely absorbed into it. This in turn allowed him to plug into Amon's imagination to understand his motives safely. Chiron transited Fiennes' Uranus/Pluto conjunction in Virgo within an orb of four degrees when the film was released.

Mars in Sagittarius transited Göth's Sun and Mercury in the days following the film's release and the transiting Uranus/Neptune conjunction in Capricorn was in opposition to his natal Neptune in Cancer. Although the Oscar glory went to Neeson, Fiennes must be praised for his careful portrayal of Göth: it was a delicate balance that never strayed into glorifying villainous acts.

The film won an Academy Award, a Golden Globe and a BAFTA for Best Picture. Neeson was nominated for the same awards in the category of Best Actor. Ralph Fiennes was nominated for an Academy Award for Best Supporting Actor and won a BAFTA in the same category.

NEPTUNE

Like his brother Pluto, Neptune was given a third of the natural world and his dominion was the seas and their storms. Astrologically, Neptune is associated with confusion, dreams, addiction, psychic insight and the imagination.

In *Goodfellas*, amongst other contacts, Ray Liotta's MC is exactly conjunct Henry Hill's Neptune in Virgo, so Liotta's mission was to bring the sleazy, violent, drug-fuelled culture of the film to the public's attention. The fact that the film is widely regarded as one of the best ever made shows he pretty much achieved it.

In *Sid and Nancy* Gary Oldman's North Node is conjunct both his own and Vicious' Neptune on the ascendant. Who better to portray such a sad descent into addiction?

Neptune doesn't always have to involve addiction though – it is also the planet of aspiration and inspiration, and in *The Pursuit of Happyness* Will Smith uses his Venus/Mercury conjunction in Libra to perfectly capture Chris Gardner's Neptunian dream of a better life. Neptune also figured strongly in the chart for the film's release; it netted millions at the box office and brought accolades for Smith's performance.

GOODFELLAS

Henry Hill: 11 June 1943, no time, New York City.
Source: Wikipedia
Ray Liotta: 18 December 1954, 06:07, Newark, New Jersey.
AA: RR
Karen Hill: 16 January 1946, no time, New York City.
Source: Wikipedia
Lorraine Bracco: 2 October 1954, no time, Brooklyn, New York.
Source: Wikipedia
Release date: 9 September 1990

As a teenager, Henry Hill becomes enthralled with the Mafia and begins working for the local *caporegime* Paulie, and his associates Jimmy and Tommy. After successfully running errands for a time, Henry is given more lucrative jobs and he, Jimmy and Tommy, spend a lot of their time at a nightclub, drinking and chasing women. Henry eventually falls in love with Karen, a Jewish woman, and although she is troubled by his criminal activities, she too becomes enamoured by the glamorous lifestyle.

They marry despite her parents' disapproval and the couple become a part of the Mafia family. Henry opens his own nightclub and one evening an associate of the family insults Tommy, so Tommy and Jimmy kill him. The problem is, the murdered man was part of the Mafia and thus his associates will be forced to take revenge. Once Tommy and Jimmy realise this, they cover their tracks by burying the body far away. However, several months later there's a danger it might be dug up as the area is scheduled for re-development, and they are forced to exhume the decomposing body and re-bury it at another location.

Karen discovers Henry has a mistress on the side – she begins harassing the mistress and even holds Henry at gunpoint. Henry moves in with the mistress and only moves back with his wife when Paulie insists he must. However, Jimmy and Henry are arrested after collecting on a debt from a gambler and in order to support his family from inside prison, Henry begins to sell cocaine. Once released, he expands his drug empire against Paulie's orders and recruits Tommy and Jimmy to help him.

A highly successful raid organised by Jimmy nets over $6 million but the hired crew behave in such a suspicious manner that Jimmy has them killed. As bodies are found all over New York City, only Henry and Tommy are spared. However, Tommy is shot in the face as a reprisal for a previous murder.

Henry becomes more and more paranoid from drug use and is eventually arrested on drugs' charges. Karen is forced to flush away what remains of his stash and is consequently left penniless. Paulie ends their association and after it becomes clear Jimmy can no longer be trusted, Henry has no alternative but to enter into the witness protection program. He testifies against Paulie and Jimmy and the film ends with him saying he is now forced to live his life "like the average schmuck".

Henry Hill's Neptune in Virgo is exactly conjunct Ray Liotta's MC and his Jupiter in Cancer is exactly conjunct the actor's Uranus/Jupiter conjunction. Transiting Pluto was conjunct Liotta's Saturn, and Uranus was conjunct his North Node. Also transiting Saturn in Capricorn was conjunct Lorraine Bracco's Mars when the film was released.

18 Mirror Mirror

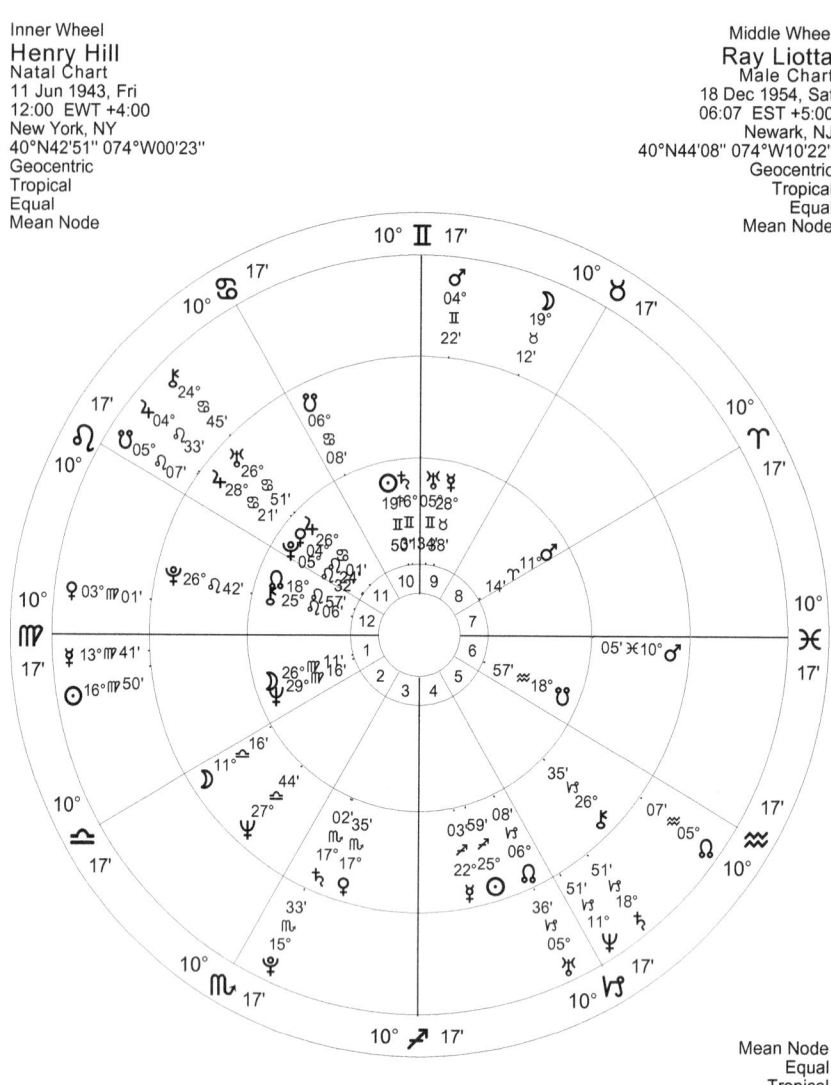

Neptune   19

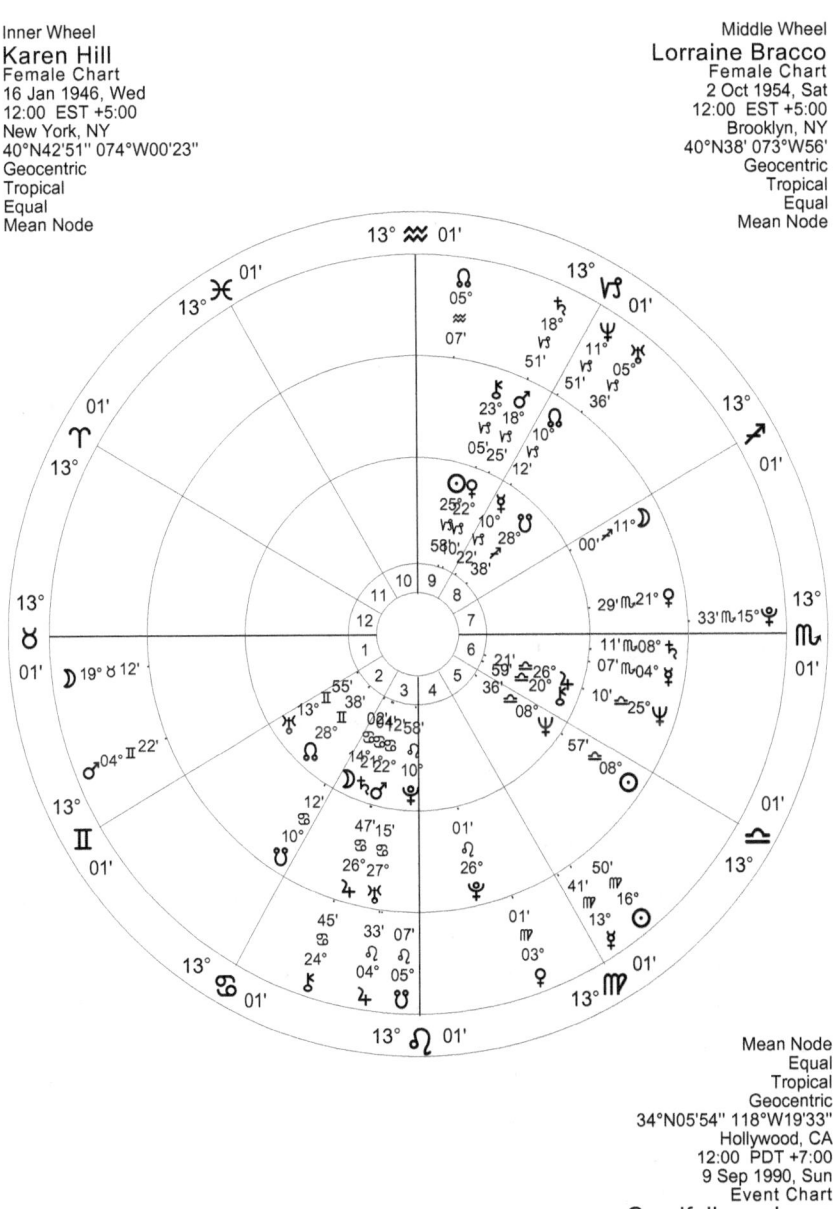

Lorraine Bracco's North Node in Capricorn is exactly conjunct Karen Hill's Mercury and transiting Neptune was on this point when the film was released. Lorraine's Jupiter/Uranus conjunction in Cancer opposes Karen's Sun within one degree of orb. Additionally, the actress' Sun in Libra is exactly conjunct the mobster wife's Neptune. The film was released when transiting Chiron in Cancer was conjunct Lorraine Bracco's Jupiter (as well as Ray Liotta's Uranus/Jupiter). Transiting Jupiter in Leo was conjunct Henry Hill's Venus and also the South Node was conjunct his Pluto.

The film was nominated for Academy Awards and Golden Globes for Best Picture and Actor. *Goodfellas* is widely regarded as one of the greatest films ever made. It won a BAFTA for Best Film and Robert DeNiro was nominated for Best Actor. Joe Pesci won an Academy Award for Best Supporting Actor.

SID AND NANCY

Sid Vicious, 10 May 1957, 19:09, London. A: RR
Gary Oldman: 21 March 1958, 21:55, London. C: Lepoivre
Nancy Spungen: 27 February 1958, 06:52, Philadelphia, Pennsylvania. B: RR
Chloe Webb: 25 June 1956, no time, New York. Source: Wikipedia
Nancy's death: 12 October 1978
Release date: 8 May 1986

The film begins on 12 October 1978, with several police officers dragging Sid Vicious out of the Hotel Chelsea following the death of his girlfriend, Nancy Spungen. Sid is driven to a police station and upon arrival is asked to describe what happened. Police officers become frustrated when Sid is visibly troubled and unable to speak.

The year before this, Sid Vicious and Johnny Rotten, band members of the punk band The Sex Pistols, meet groupie Nancy Spungen, a heroin addict who has come to London with the express intention of sleeping with them. She is too forward and they ignore her. After feeling guilty for being rude to her, Sid begins dating Nancy and it is implied she introduces him to heroin. Although they are in love, their relationship is tightly entwined with their deepening addiction, which causes problems

Neptune 21

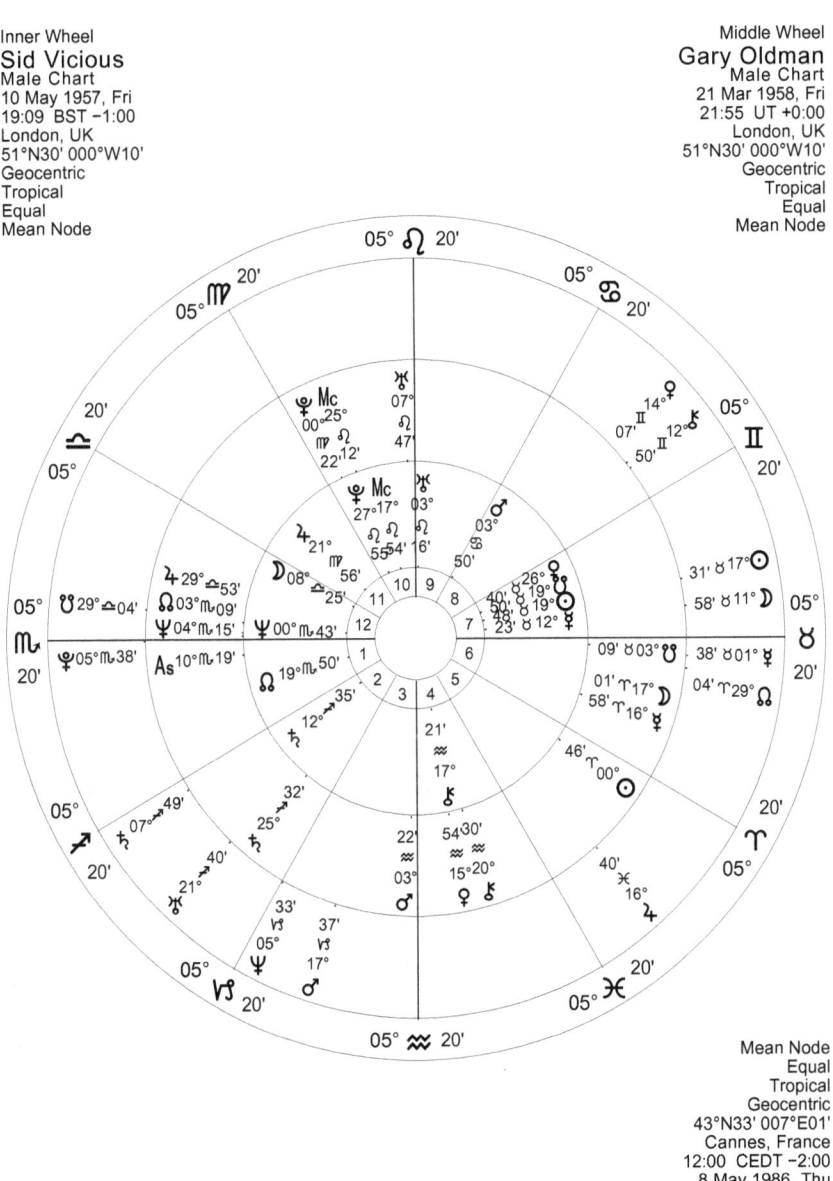

22 Mirror Mirror

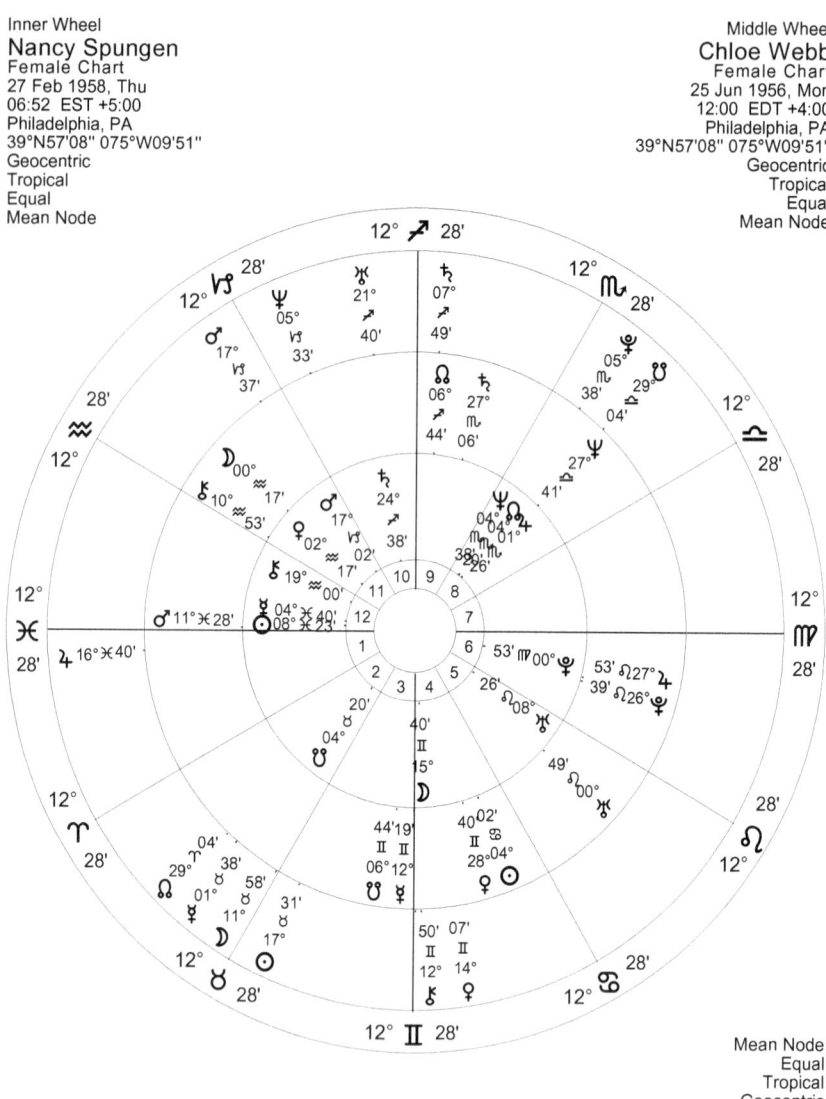

within the band. The band break up shortly afterwards (in early 1978) during a disastrous American tour because Vicious is incoherent and often violent. Although friends have warned him of the negative effect Nancy is having on his life, Vicious ignores them.

In New York, with Nancy managing him, he is dismissed by audiences who have seen too much of him. Nancy goes into a deep depression and the couple make a suicide pact. However, later Sid loses sexual interest in her and wants to call off the pact. He also wants to return to London, get clean and re-start his life. Nancy begs him to kill her and in a drug-induced fight, he stabs her, although it's unclear if it was deliberate or accidental. When she regains consciousness, Nancy staggers into the bathroom and dies.

Sid's mother, also a heroin addict, bails him out of jail. In the final scene, Sid is in a taxi, believing Nancy is alive and beside him. The couple embrace as the cab drives off and the audience is told that Sid later died of an intentional heroin overdose.

Vicious had Venus conjunct the fixed star Algol so he would have been attracted to intense women. Spungen's Neptune was conjunct Vicious' ascendant in Scorpio and her Venus in Aquarius opposed his Uranus in Leo so the addiction and the instability of the relationship makes astrological sense. Oldman and Vicious had similar ascendants with the actor's North Node and Jupiter pulled into the mix either side of Vicious' Neptune. His Pluto was on the actor's MC in Leo, which brought intensity to the role. By a wide orb, Oldman's Sun in Aries was in opposition to Vicious' Moon in Libra. Chloe Webb, who plays Nancy in the film, has Mars in Pisces which was conjunct Spungen's Sun and ascendant, so she would have been 'plugged into' her addiction.

Transiting Pluto was exactly conjunct Vicious' ascendant during the week of the Cannes Film Festival when the film was released. *Sid and Nancy* is an uncomfortable depiction of the destructiveness of addiction and the consequential deaths of two young people.

Although the controversial film was passed over for Academy Awards nominations, film critic Roger Ebert gave it four-out-of-four and the film has become a cult classic.

THE PURSUIT OF HAPPYNESS

Christopher Gardner: 9 February 1954, no time, Milwaukee, Wisconsin. Source: Wikipedia
Will Smith: 25 September 1968, 21:47, Philadelphia, Pennsylvania.
A: RR
Release date: 15 December 2006

Chris Gardner invests his entire life savings in selling portable bone density scanners, the sales for which are supposedly going to make him wealthy. Unfortunately, the pictures they produce are only slightly better than a standard X-ray and he has trouble selling the machines. Although he does very well in selling the majority of them, the slow sales cause financial problems in his marriage, and his wife, who has been working double shifts as a cleaner, walks out on him and their five-year-old son.

By chance, Gardner meets Jay Twistle, a manager for Dean Witter Reynolds, who inspires him to become a stockbroker. Twistle tells him about an opportunity to become an intern for his company and arranges an interview for him. While he is talking to Twistle, a homeless man steals one of the scanners.

As sales of the scanners are so slow, Gardner has little money and has to agree to paint his apartment in lieu of payment or be evicted. In the middle of the job he is arrested for unpaid parking tickets and is ordered to spend the night in jail. He has to call his wife to beg her not go to work so she can take care of their son for the night.

The following morning, he turns up for his interview without having showered and still in his painting clothes. However, he manages to impress the interviewers and is offered an internship – a single unpaid position which is open to nineteen other people.

His estranged wife becomes angry and tells him she's going to New York to find work. After further arguing, they agree Gardner will care for their son because she doesn't have the means to look after him. After she leaves, Gardner's bank account is frozen by the Internal Revenue Service for unpaid taxes and he is evicted from his apartment. He and his son are forced to sleep rough or, if they can, sleep at a homeless shelter. In the meantime, Gardner continues to attempt to sell the remaining scanners while his son is at day care, as well as maximising his client contacts as

Neptune 25

Inner Wheel
Chris Gardner
Male Chart
9 Feb 1954, Tue
12:00 CST +6:00
Milwaukee, Wisconsin
43°N02'20" 087°W54'23"
Geocentric
Tropical
Equal
Mean Node

Middle Wheel
Will Smith
Male Chart
25 Sep 1968, Wed
21:47 EDT +4:00
Philadelphia, PA
39°N57'08" 075°W09'51"
Geocentric
Tropical
Equal
Mean Node

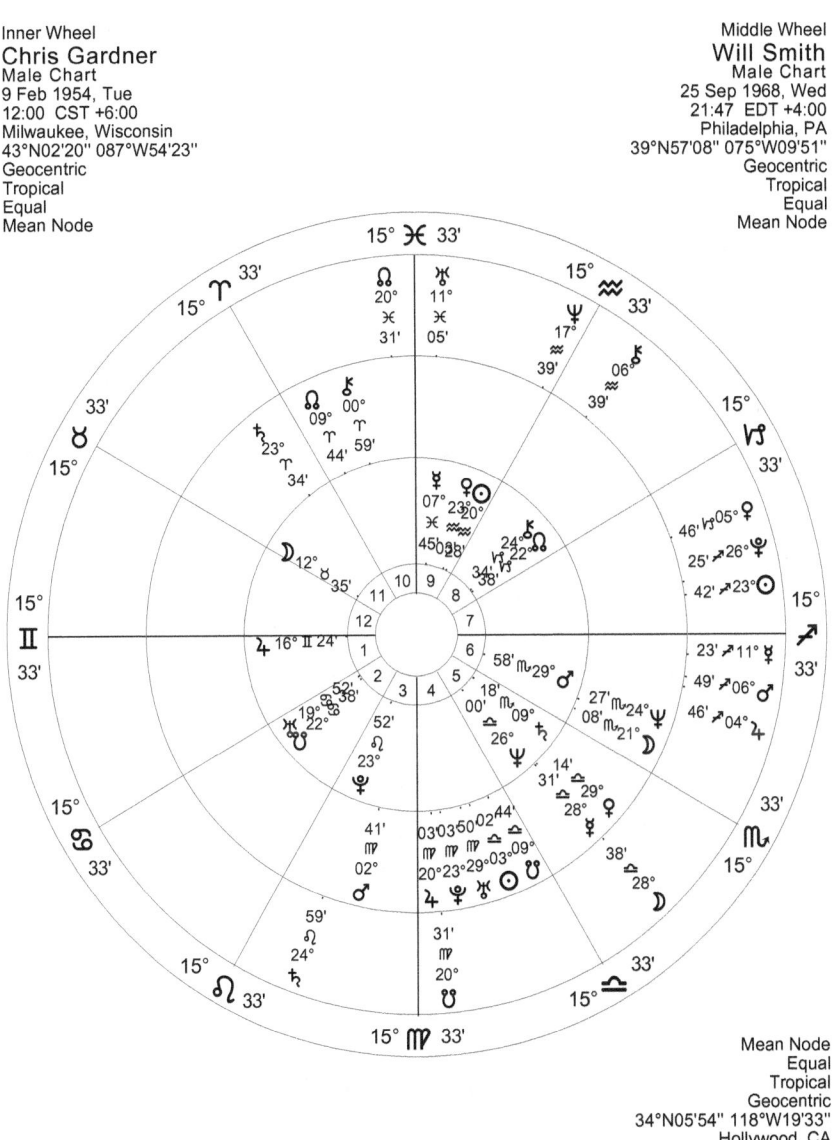

Mean Node
Equal
Tropical
Geocentric
34°N05'54" 118°W19'33"
Hollywood, CA
12:00 PST +8:00
15 Dec 2006, Fri
Event Chart
Pursuit of Happyness release
Outer Wheel

part of his internship. He recovers the stolen scanner and fixes it. He says the sale of the scanner is "pure oxygen" to his dire circumstances.

Despite all his difficulties, Gardner never reveals his sad state of affairs to his potential employers and even loans his last five dollars to one of his bosses. After concluding his six-month internship, he is told he's beaten all the competition and his boss repays the five dollars he borrowed. Overwhelmed and tearful, Gardner shakes hands with his new bosses then collects his son from day care. As they walk along telling each other jokes, they pass the real Chris Gardner, who appears in a cameo role.

The epilogue reveals that Gardner went on to huge financial success.

Even without a timed chart, it can be seen that Chris Gardner had the Moon in Taurus opposite Saturn in Scorpio and the Sun in Aquarius opposite Pluto in Leo. These aspects can be tough on the finances until the native learns how to manage them. What Gardner had in his favour was a sense of humour and charm and we see this in Will Smith's Venus/Mercury conjunction in Libra conjunct Gardner's Neptune.

The movie was released as transiting Neptune was conjunct Gardner's natal Sun and transiting Saturn was conjunct his natal Pluto. This is the glamour of Hollywood portraying a story of hard graft, bad luck but ultimate success. Transiting Neptune would have passed over Smith's MC during filming and it has to be said that he made the struggle look good.

The film grossed over $162 million at the box office. Smith was nominated for an Academy Award, a Golden Globe and a Screen Actors Guild Award for Best Actor.

URANUS

In astrology, Uranus is associated with upheavals, particularly those that come from people coming together to bring about revolution.

Wolfgang Amadeus Mozart turned the world of music upside down. His rebellious and extraordinarily talented Uranian influence has affected generations of composers right up to the present day. In *Amadeus* his total irreverence for the morals and starched etiquette of the court is perfectly captured by Tom Hulce, who also has Uranus conjunct the South Node. It clearly takes one to know one.

Sometimes, it just takes a bit of Uranus to bring about a miracle. In *The Miracle Worker* we see an important breakthrough in the life of young blind, mute and deaf girl, Helen Keller (Patty Duke), brought about by her teacher Annie Sullivan (Anne Bancroft). Astonishingly, Duke's ascendant is conjunct Keller's Uranus and Bancroft's Uranus was in orb of the planets in Sullivan's stellium in Aries. Bancroft clearly succeeded in her quest to reach into the inventiveness of this teacher, and indeed she was highly praised for her performance.

Uranus is also about invention and we are treated to a glimpse of it not only in the subject matter of *The Story of Louis Pasteur*, but also in the skill of the actor. Paul Muni's Mars in Libra is square Pasteur's stellium (which includes Uranus), enabling him to make a tough job look easy. His efforts more than paid off as he won an Academy Award for Best Actor.

AMADEUS

Wolfgang Amadeus Mozart: 27 January 1756, 20:00, Salzburg, Austria. AA: Schofield
Tom Hulce: 6 December 1953, no time, Detroit, Michigan. Source: Wikipedia
Antonio Salieri: 18 August 1750, 22:00, Legnago, Italy. B: Scholfield (Chart not shown)
F. Murray Abraham: 24 October 1939, no time, Pittsburgh, Pennsylvania. Source: Wikipedia (Chart not shown)
Release date: 6 September 1984

The film opens with Antonio Salieri, in an asylum recovering from an attempt to cut his own throat, confessing to a priest that he has killed Mozart.

Salieri tells his tale in a series of flashbacks. As a child, he promised total devotion if God would grant his wish to become a famous composer – something that was against the wishes of his father. When his father died shortly afterwards, Salieri assumed this was God's way of telling him his wish would be granted, so he became a devout Catholic.

In time, Salieri begins working at the palace of Emperor Joseph II in Vienna where he meets the young Mozart, who is at the same court function. Salieri quickly discovers his incredibly talented rival is also immature and offensive and has an obnoxious laugh. He is unable to understand why God would give such great talent – better than his own – to such an unsuitable person. Thinking God is mocking him, Salieri renounces his promise to Him and, in revenge, sets out to destroy Mozart.

Mozart's alcohol-fuelled antics continue to cause offense in the court, but because he is producing such brilliant work his behaviour is overlooked. However, his health begins to decline through over-working and over-drinking, and Salieri hatches a plot to push Mozart over the edge. Salieri hires a young girl to pose as a maid in order to spy on him. She tells Salieri that Mozart is working on a composition that has been forbidden by the Emperor. However, when summoned to explain his actions, Mozart manages to convince the Emperor to attend the concert where the composition will be performed.

When Mozart's father dies, he composes another opera and Salieri realises Mozart has created an imposing, dark character that symbolises

Uranus 29

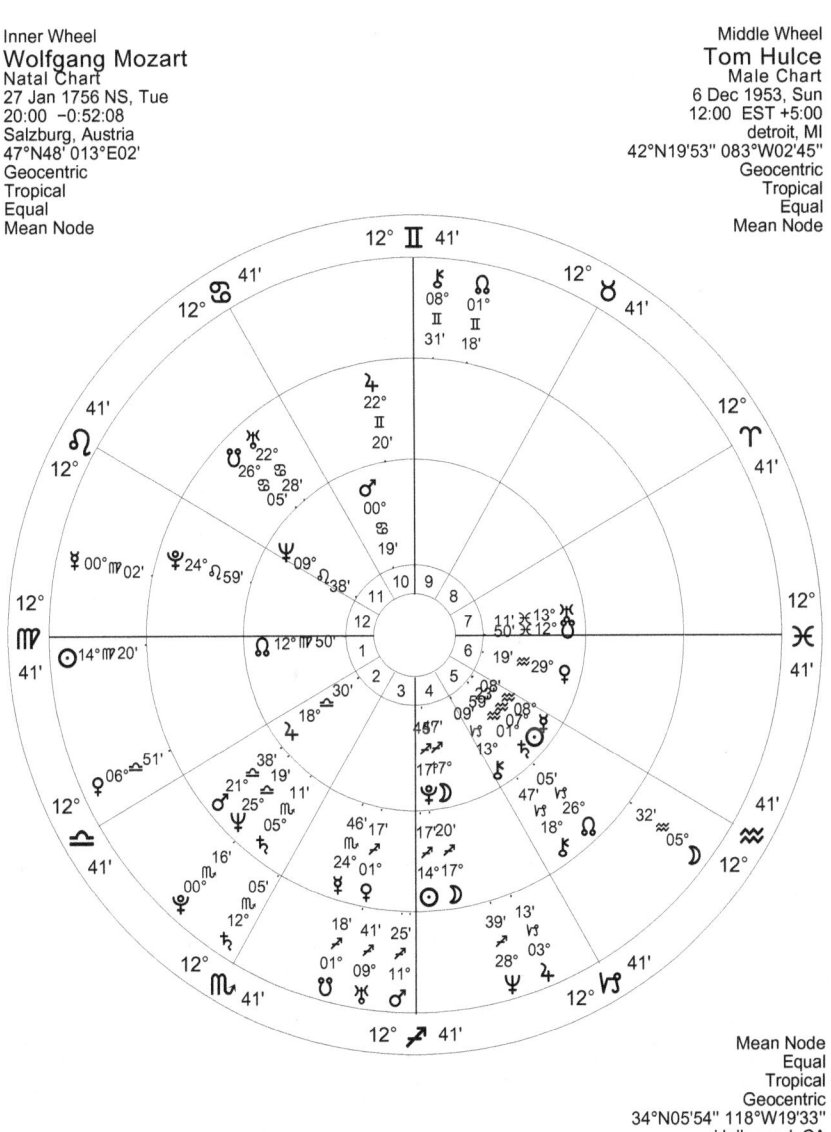

his dead father. Salieri dresses as the terrifying character and tricks Mozart into agreeing to write a requiem with the idea he will steal it, present it as his own and play it at Mozart's funeral. However, Mozart is unable to concentrate on finishing the requiem and accepts a lesser-paid commission to write a different opera. Furious with his decision, Mozart's wife leaves home with their son, leaving him more vulnerable to Salieri's schemes.

Mozart eventually works himself to death while composing the requiem which has been finished with Salieri's help. Realising Salieri's involvement with the death of her husband, Mozart's wife hides the requiem and Mozart's body is buried in an unmarked grave.

The film circles back to Salieri in the asylum confessing to the priest. He refuses to absolve Salieri, who concludes that God has taken Mozart so he will not have to share God's glory with such an inferior talent such as himself. Salieri then sarcastically absolves the priest and as he is wheeled away says that mediocrity is their patron saint.

Mozart's laugh is heard as the film fades out.

Mozart's natal Moon was conjunct Pluto in Sagittarius and with his Uranus and South Node in Pisces conjunct Salieri's Moon, it is easy to see how Salieri would have found Mozart a little hard to take. Even with an untimed chart, the actor F. Murray Abraham would also have the Moon in Pisces as well as his Mercury in Scorpio conjunct Salieri's descendant. Abraham also had his Chiron in Cancer exactly conjunct Salieri's Venus, showing an empathy with his pain.

Like Mozart, Tom Hulce also had Uranus conjunct the South Node but in a different water sign, in his case Cancer. The actor's Sun in Sagittarius was also within a couple of degrees of Mozart's Pluto/Moon conjunction and the transiting Sun during the film's release was trine to this, illuminating the power of the connection.

Transiting Neptune in Sagittarius was exactly conjunct Salieri's North Node and transiting Pluto in Scorpio was within one degree of his Chiron and Abraham's Sun when the film was released. Additionally, transiting Saturn in Scorpio was within one degree of Abraham's Mercury.

Uranus 31

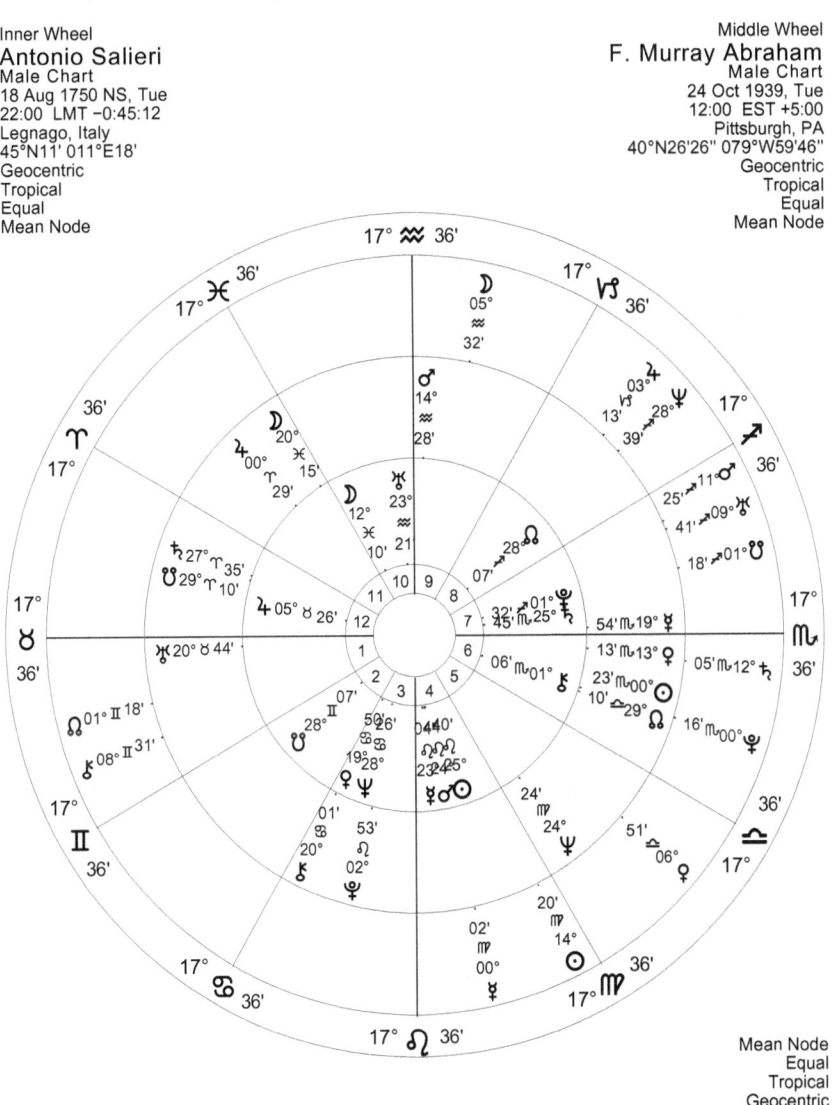

Transiting Chiron in Gemini was exactly conjunct Mozart's MC when the film was released. Transiting Mars and Uranus in Sagittarius were also close to conjunctions in the charts of Mozart and Hulce at that time.

The film won Academy Awards for Best Picture and Best Actor (for F. Murray Abraham) and was nominated for several BAFTAs and Golden Globes which Abraham won. Hulce was also nominated for several awards but came away empty-handed.

THE MIRACLE WORKER

Helen Keller: 27 June 1880, 16:02 (unverified), Tuscumbia, Alabama. DD: RR
Patty Duke: 14 December 1946, 22:39, Manhattan, New York. AA: RR
Anne Sullivan: 14 April 1866, no time, Feeding Hills, Agawam, Massachusetts. Source: Wikipedia.
Anne Bancroft: 17 September 1931, 11:50 (unverified), Bronx, New York. DD: RR
Release date: 28 July 1962

Helen Keller's world is a dark and silent one. As a baby, she caught a fever and lost her sight and hearing, so the only way she can communicate is by taking what she wants or by throwing a violent tantrum until her parents concede. As she grows bigger and the tantrums become more violent, her parents seek help from a school for the blind.

Anne Sullivan, a newly-qualified teacher from the school and half-blind herself, arrives to help Helen's parents deal with the young girl. She's shocked to see that Helen is allowed to do just about anything she wants to, including grabbing food from other people's plates. Through sheer force of will, Anne begins to teach Helen some basic manners and eventually makes a breakthrough in teaching her how to communicate.

Within an orb of one degree, Sullivan's natal Uranus was on Keller's Venus in Cancer. Their relationship consisted of communicating through pressing sign language letters into the other's hand. All the planets in Sullivan's stellium in Aries – Sun, Mercury, Neptune, South Node and possibly the Moon – are within orb of conjunction to Keller's Jupiter.

Helen Keller's Uranus in Virgo was conjunct the actress Patty Duke's ascendant within an orb of four degrees. Keller's Mars was conjunct

Uranus 33

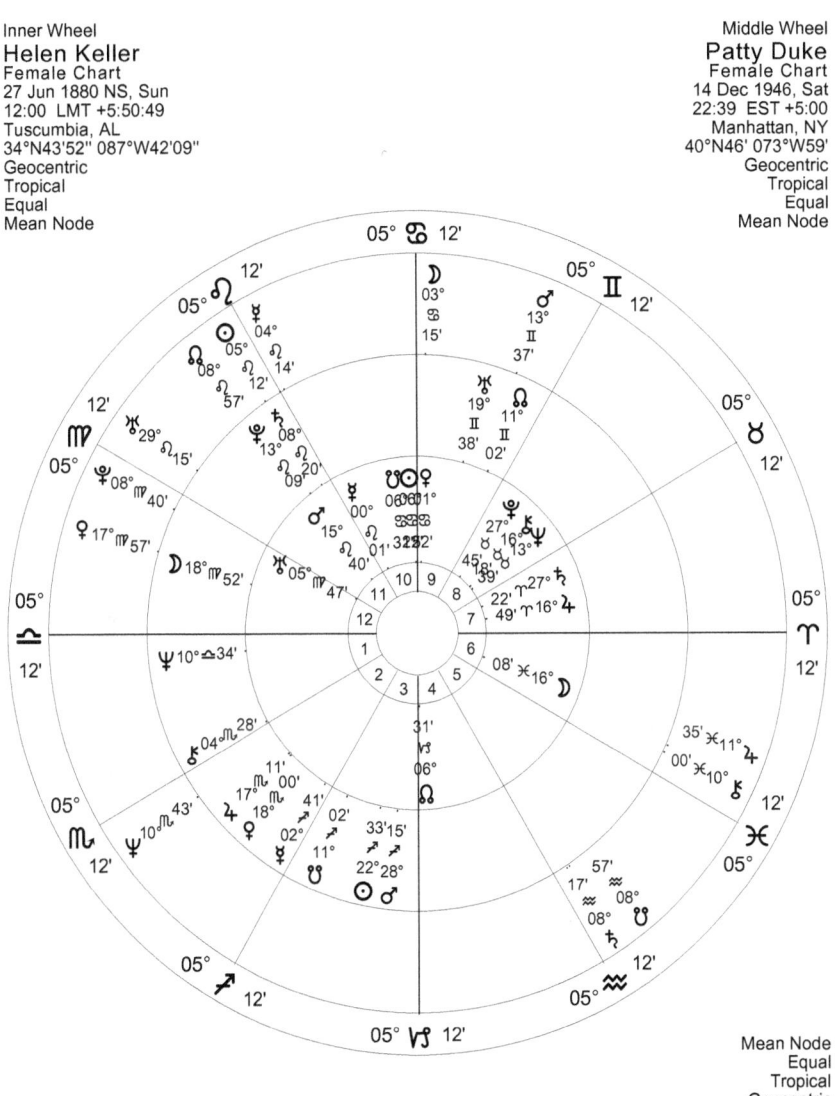

34   Mirror Mirror

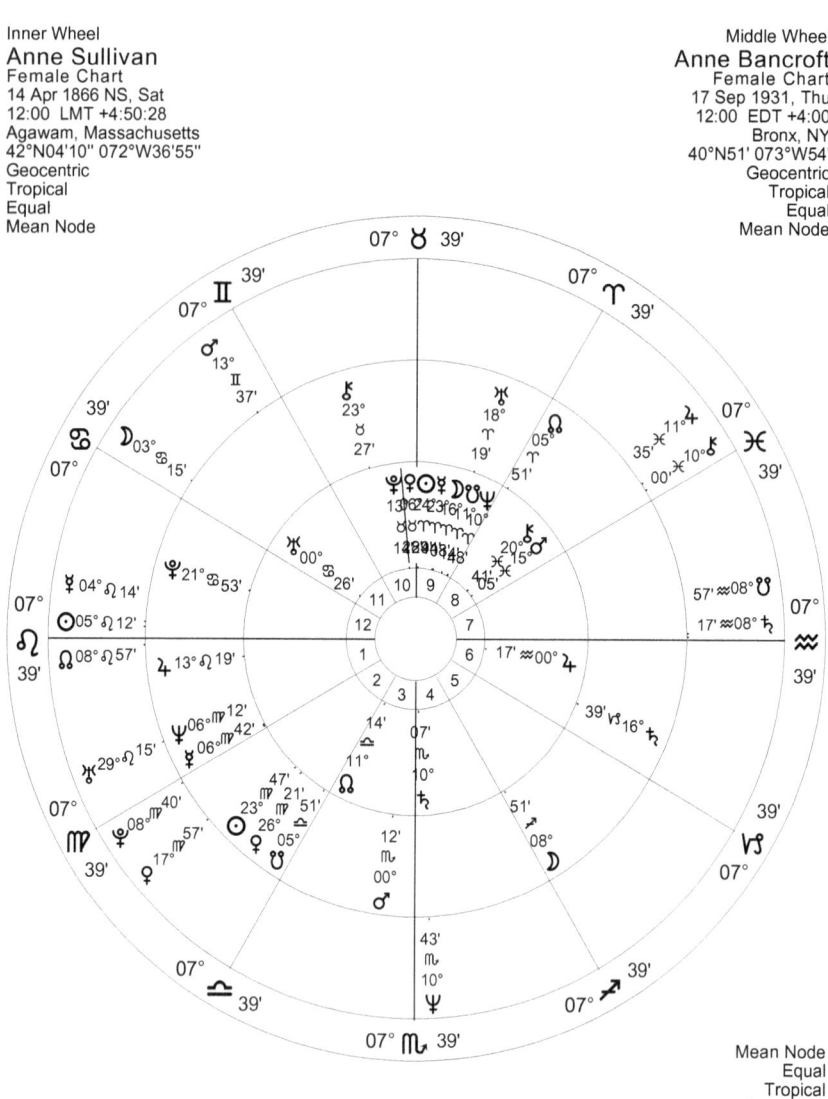

Duke's Pluto in Leo, perhaps giving those tantrums a particular boost in explosiveness. Even using a noon chart for Keller, actress and subject have a Moon opposite Moon in Virgo/Pisces.

The actress Anne Bancroft's Uranus was in orb of the planets in Anne Sullivan's stellium in Aries (which means Keller and Bancroft had a Jupiter/Uranus conjunction too). Bancroft was trying to reach into the inventiveness of this teacher, and indeed she was highly praised for her performance.

Duke's Pluto was conjunct Bancroft's Jupiter in Leo. Their performance was highly physical and they were both probably full of bruises and various aches and pains after filming. It was an uncomfortable film to watch with all the pushing and grabbing that went on – some viewers felt that the physicality of the role went too far. However, what the audience could not have known is that Bancroft's Sun and Duke's Moon were in conjunction in Virgo. There is an intuitive, precise way of "fighting" that made it look convincing without causing injury.

The Miracle Worker was released as Pluto transited Duke's ascendant and Jupiter and Chiron transited her descendant. It cannot be denied that this role changed her life and launched her career as an actress. Pluto also would have transited Bancroft's Mercury/Neptune conjunction: she was portraying a teacher who taught a blind and deaf girl how to speak.

The Neptune of the film's release was in opposition to Keller's natal Neptune and, within a four degree orb, it was Keller's Mercury return too. This was a film about the miracle of a deaf and blind girl learning to communicate and it won the young Patty Duke an Academy Award for Best Supporting Actress.

The Neptune of the film's release was conjunct Anne Sullivan's natal Saturn. Who was it that had persisted and worked towards this miracle? None other than Anne Sullivan, and the actress who portrayed her won the Academy Award for Best Actress.

THE STORY OF LOUIS PASTEUR
**Louis Pasteur: 27 December 1822, 02:00, Dole, France.
AA: Gauquelin
Paul Muni: 22 September 1895, 05:00, Lviv, Ukraine. C: RR
Release date: 22 February 1936**

An astrologer might expect Uranus to be prominent in the chart of a scientist, and we are not disappointed with Louis Pasteur, who was born with Mercury, the Sun, Neptune and Venus all conjunct Uranus within seven degrees in the sign of Capricorn.

Pasteur was famous for inventing vaccines and encouraging better hygiene practices by sterilising medical equipment to prevent patient contamination. This film chronicles Pasteur's struggles to persuade the general public that vaccines could prevent anthrax in animals, and protect humans from contracting rabies.

As in the case of *The White Angel*, actors have a way of making the messy medical profession look glamorous. Paul Muni's Neptune is conjunct Pasteur's Moon within one degree and his Jupiter is conjunct the scientist's MC. Muni's Mars in early Libra is square Pasteur's Mercury, Sun, Neptune, Venus and Uranus in Capricorn, and his Sun in late degrees of Virgo is trine Pasteur's Mars. Muni may have found it difficult to work with the animals he was inoculating but he somehow managed to make it look like he knew what he was doing.

Within an orb of eight degrees, Chiron the Wounded Healer was transiting their Moon/Neptune conjunction when the film was released. Additionally, transiting Saturn was exactly conjunct Muni's North Node in Pisces. How fitting that Muni brought Pasteur's work to the silver screen.

Muni and the film were nominated for the AFI's 100 years...Heroes and Villains, and 100 Years...100 Cheers categories. Muni won an Academy Award for Best Actor and the film was nominated for Best Picture.

Uranus 37

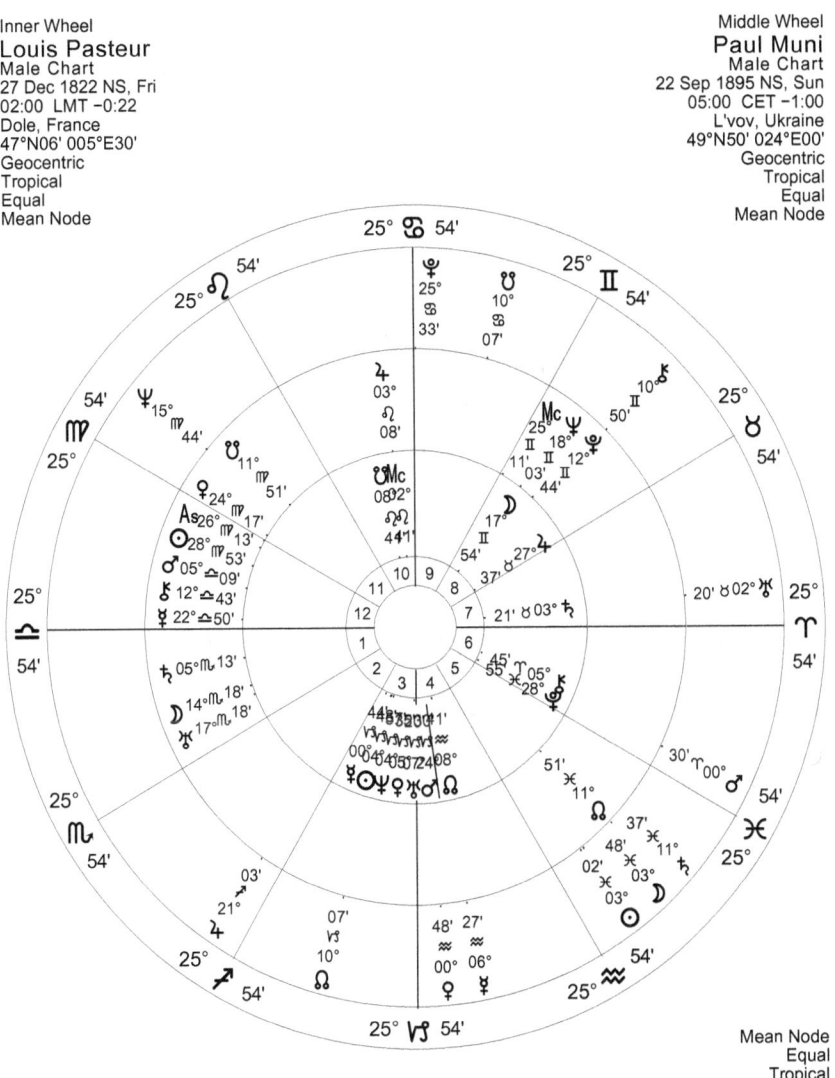

SATURN

To astrologers, Saturn is related to boundaries: being strong enough to make solid decisions, follow rules and understand limitations. When we feel pain, we usually stop whatever we are doing that causes the pain. But what if you had to choose between unimaginable suffering or death? This question was one faced by Aron Ralston (James Franco) in *127 Hours*.

Saturn is also about discipline as would be employed by elite athletes – or in the case of Eddie the Eagle (Taron Egerton), not-so-elite athletes who find themselves at the Olympics. Sometimes it also takes tremendous discipline for actors to transform themselves for their role as in the case of *Ali* where Will Smith put on masses amount of muscle to portray Cassius Clay/Muhammed Ali and indeed Saturn was transiting the actor's ascendant when the movie was released. Geoffrey Rush, who learnt to play the piano in *Shine*, had his Moon conjunct David Helfgott's Saturn in Leo. It is striking that Sissy Spacek's Saturn was just two degrees away from the ascendant of Loretta Lynn. Punishment and consequences are also key concepts of Saturn. *Dead Man Walking* was about a nun Helen Prejean (Susan Sarandon) and a man (Sean Penn) facing the ultimate punishment. When we understand our Saturn, we are deserving of respect or gravitas as we see in Morgan Freeman's portrayal of Nelson Mandela in *Invictus*, or Meryl Streep as Margaret Thatcher in *The Iron Lady*.

127 HOURS

Aron Ralston: 27 October 1975, 21:58, Marion, Ohio. AA: Viktor
James Franco: 19 April 1978, 19:04, Stanford, California.
AA: Viktor
Release date: 4 September 2010

Ralston goes hiking alone in Utah without telling anyone where he is heading. Whilst climbing, he slips and falls, dislodging a boulder, which traps his right hand against the canyon wall. He calls for help but realises he is completely alone.

Ralston begins a video diary and does his best to keep warm at night and ration his food and water. When his water runs out, he has to resort

Saturn 39

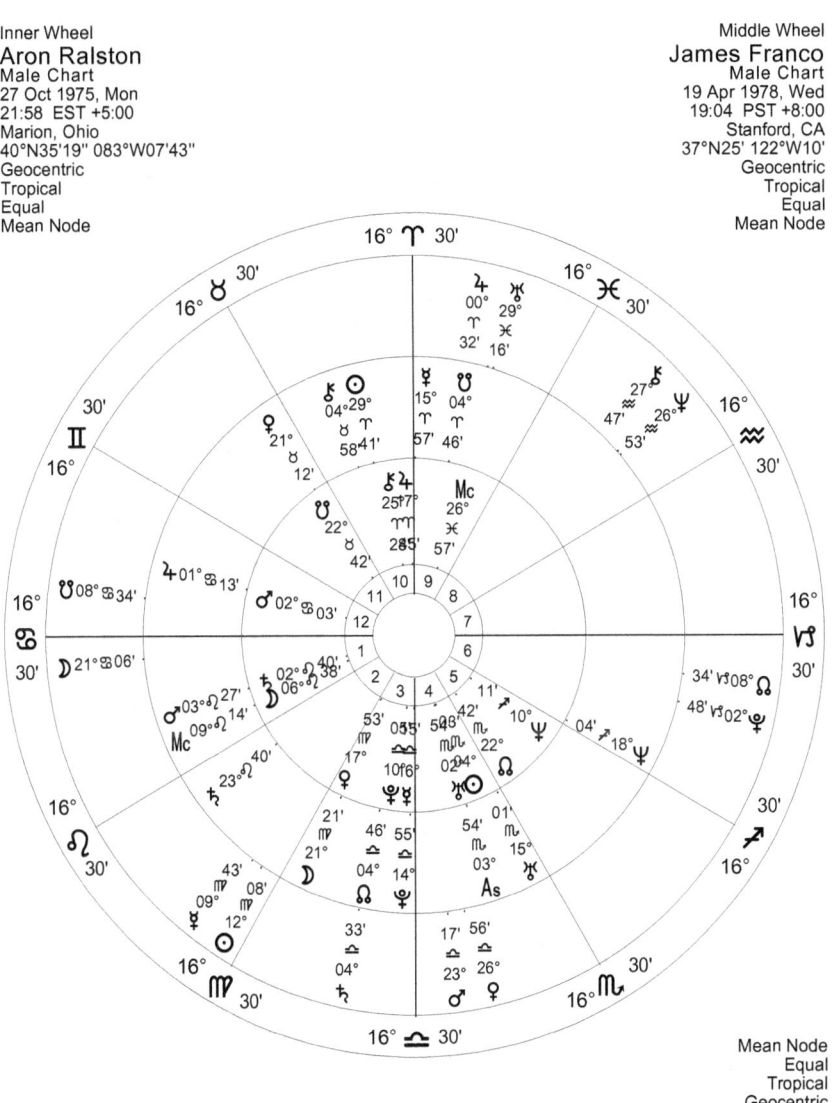

to drinking his own urine. After a few days, he realises the only way to free himself is to cut off his arm, but his knife isn't sharp enough. Falling into depression, he begins to hallucinate about escaping and relives past experiences, including the obsessive thought that he should have left a note to tell someone where he was going. A vision of his future son prompts him to take drastic steps to survive. He breaks the bones in his arm and slowly amputates his hand to free himself. He then uses his remaining hand to rappel down a cliff and seek help.

Ralston's tendency for obsessive thoughts can be seen with his Pluto/Mercury conjunction in Libra which, as they were born only a few years apart, is also conjunct Franco's own Pluto. Franco's Venus in Taurus is conjunct Ralston's South Node and the actor's Jupiter in Cancer is within a one degree orb of Ralston's Mars, both trine to Ralston's Uranus/Sun in Scorpio and Franco's ascendant. This is remarkable because this is a very tense story about survival and overcoming insurmountable odds. Ralston also has Saturn and the Moon in Leo within four degrees of orb which are in turn conjunct the actor's Mars and MC.

Transiting Uranus in Pisces would have been conjunct Ralston's MC during filming and transiting Saturn in Libra was exactly conjunct Franco's North Node and is within orb of conjunction to Ralston's Pluto.

The film was nominated for Academy Awards, Golden Globes and BAFTAs for Best Film and Best Actor, among several others.

ALI

Muhammad Ali: 17 January 1942, 18:35, Louisville, Kentucky.
A: Steinbrecher
Will Smith: 25 September 1968, 21:47, Philadelphia, Pennsylvania.
AA: RR
Release date: 25 December 2001

The film begins with Cassius Clay's victorious win over Sonny Liston, making him the second youngest heavyweight boxing champion at the time.

Clay spends time talking with the Muslim minister Malcolm X, and is invited to the home of Islam leader Elijah Muhammad who gives him his new name, Muhammad Ali, of which his father disapproves.

Clay marries his first wife, an ex-Playboy bunny who is not only a

Saturn 41

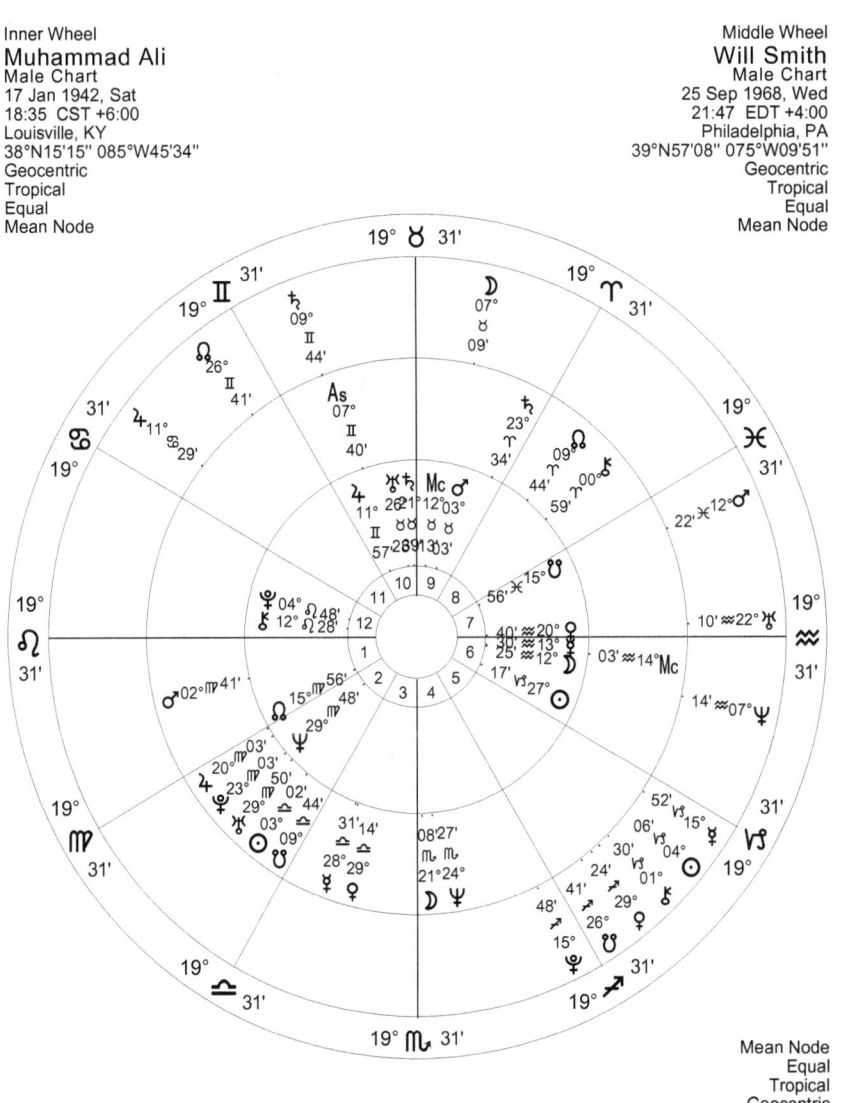

non-Muslim but she also refuses to follow the gender segregation codes of Islam. After spending time with Malcolm X in Africa, Ali is again invited to the home of Elijah Muhammad and agrees not to speak to Malcolm X again. When Malcolm X is assassinated, Ali is devastated.

Returning to the United States, Ali fights Liston again and knocks him out in the first round. As his wife still refuses to follow the obligations of a Muslim wife, Ali divorces her.

Ali is drafted for the Vietnam War but refuses to enlist – so his passport, boxing licence and championship titles are stripped from him and he is sentenced to five years in prison. Following his release he re-marries, and after a few years his conviction is overturned. In his comeback match, he wins by a technical knockout after three rounds.

In what was labelled as "The Fight of the Century", Ali experiences the first loss of his career against Joe Frazier. In Zaire for the "Rumble in the Jungle" contest, Ali has an affair. When his wife reads about it in the newspaper, she flies out to Africa to confront her husband. He tells her he isn't thinking about love and just wants to win the fight. In the fight against George Foreman, who had beaten Frazier, Ali uses his "rope-a-dope" technique which means he leans against the ropes and lets Foreman tire himself out. The film finishes with him knocking Foreman out and regaining his heavyweight championship title.

The end credits mention that Ali requested that proceeds of the film go to a friend who had been a long-time supporter.

Although a very fine athlete, Ali was also a showman as his ascendant in Leo attests. His defiance of authority and use of unusual boxing techniques can be found in his stellium in Aquarius conjunct his descendant. For the heavyweight title, we can look at the heaviest planet, Saturn, in the heaviest sign, Taurus. Like many men of his generation he also had Uranus conjunct Algol but his strong principles kept him from the horrors of Vietnam that many of his peers had to face. Uranus transited Ali's stellium and descendant in Aquarius during filming and when the film was released, Uranus was within two degrees of his natal Venus and within one degree of his natal Saturn. Boxing is not a pretty sport but Ali brought grace, good humour and obviously the strength of Saturn to every fight. Smith's Moon in Scorpio was exactly opposite Ali's Saturn in Taurus showing the actor's emotional connections to the boxer.

Within a two degree orb, Will Smith's MC in Aquarius is conjunct

Ali's Moon and Mercury. It's almost like Ali was whispering in his ear for this career-changing role. Smith also had to gain a substantial amount of muscle for the role, a dedicated regime which was aided by Saturn transiting his natal ascendant during filming.

Smith's portrayal of the great man earned him his first nomination for an Academy Award for Best Actor. Jamie Foxx was nominated for Best Supporting Actor at the Academy Awards.

COAL MINER'S DAUGHTER
Loretta Lynn: 14 April 1932, 16:00, Van Lear, Kentucky.
C: Przybylowski
Sissy Spacek: 25 December 1949, 00:03, Tyler, Texas.
AA: Steinbrecher
Release date: 7 March 1980

Coalminer's Daughter is the rags-to-riches story of one of Country & Western's legends, Loretta Lynn.

Loretta is one of eight children growing up in a rural community in Kentucky. The family are poor and conditions are harsh but they pull together to survive. By the time Loretta is fifteen she is married and by the age of nineteen she has four children. The young family move to Washington where the husband has found work in the forest industry. Loretta occasionally sings at a local "honky tonk" club and eventually makes a debut appearance on local radio.

In time, she is discovered by a small record label and invited to cut a demo tape in Los Angeles. In the big city there are many misunderstandings between urban and country dwellers especially as Loretta begins to do interviews and answers questions about her early life as a coalminer's daughter in the backwoods of Kentucky. After the death of her father, Loretta and her husband embark on an extensive promotional tour, visiting radio stations throughout the south and distributing their handmade marketing material.

The couple are so naive about the music business that they don't notice that Loretta's first single, *I'm a Honky-Tonk Girl* is in the charts. She is invited to sing at the Grand Ole Opry in the summer of 1961, and then at even bigger venues. That summer, Patsy Cline is in hospital after a serious car accident. Loretta dedicates a performance to her as a musical

44 Mirror Mirror

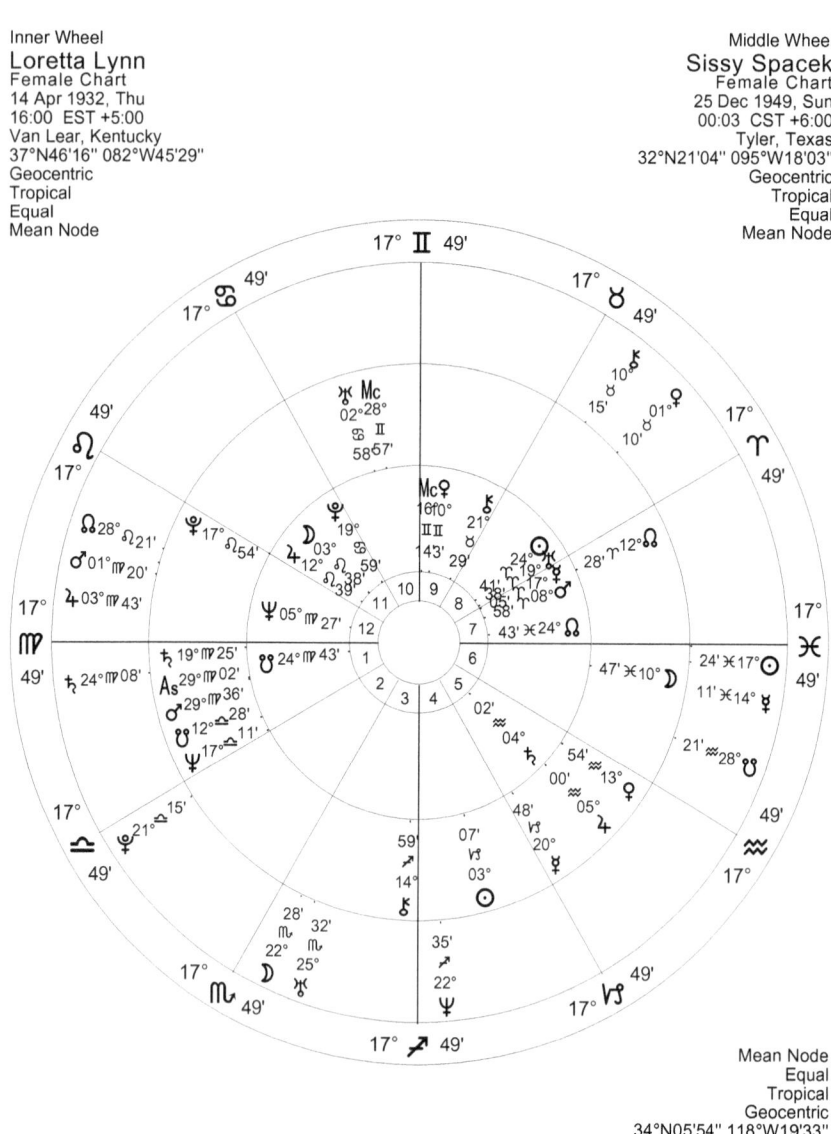

get-well card and Cline sends her husband out to find her so they can meet. The two singers form a close friendship that ends when Cline dies in a plane crash a few years later.

As Loretta becomes more famous, the pressure of touring, performing and trying to hold her marriage together causes her to have a nervous breakdown just before an important performance. She takes a year off from performing and recovers on a Tennessee ranch before returning to the stage as the "First Lady of Country Music".

The film ends with Loretta singing her 1970 hit song *Coalminer's Daughter* to a packed audience.

Lynn's chart is notable for its Saturn in Aquarius opposite her Moon in Leo. Saturn brings heaviness, responsibility and hard work and with its connection to the Moon, the emotions and memories of the past can be very serious. Lynn's descriptions of her poor upbringing are symptomatic of this harsh aspect. Sissy Spacek's portrayal of Lynn won her much praise. Within an orb of one degree, her Jupiter in Aquarius is conjunct Lynn's Saturn. This is taking something tragic and making it work. Lynn's nodal axis is very close to Spacek's ascendant/descendant axis and many of her planets in Aries are close to the actress's North Node. It's worth noting that coal is ruled by the planet Mars and Spacek has this planet conjunct her ascendant.

Coal Miner's Daughter was released as Jupiter transited Lynn's Neptune in Virgo and Saturn was transiting her South Node in Virgo.

The film won Academy Awards and Golden Globe Awards for Best Picture and Best Actress.

DEAD MAN WALKING

Helen Prejean: 21 April 1939, no time, Los Angeles, California.
Source: Wikipedia
Susan Sarandon: 4 October 1946, 14:25, New York. A: RR
Matthew Poncelet (based on Robert Lee Willie): 2 January 1958 – 28 December 1984
Sean Penn: 17 August 1960, 15:17, Los Angeles. California.
AA: RR
Release date: 29 December 1995

Matthew Poncelet has been on death row in a Louisiana penitentiary for six years for killing a teenage couple. He committed the crime with

46 Mirror Mirror

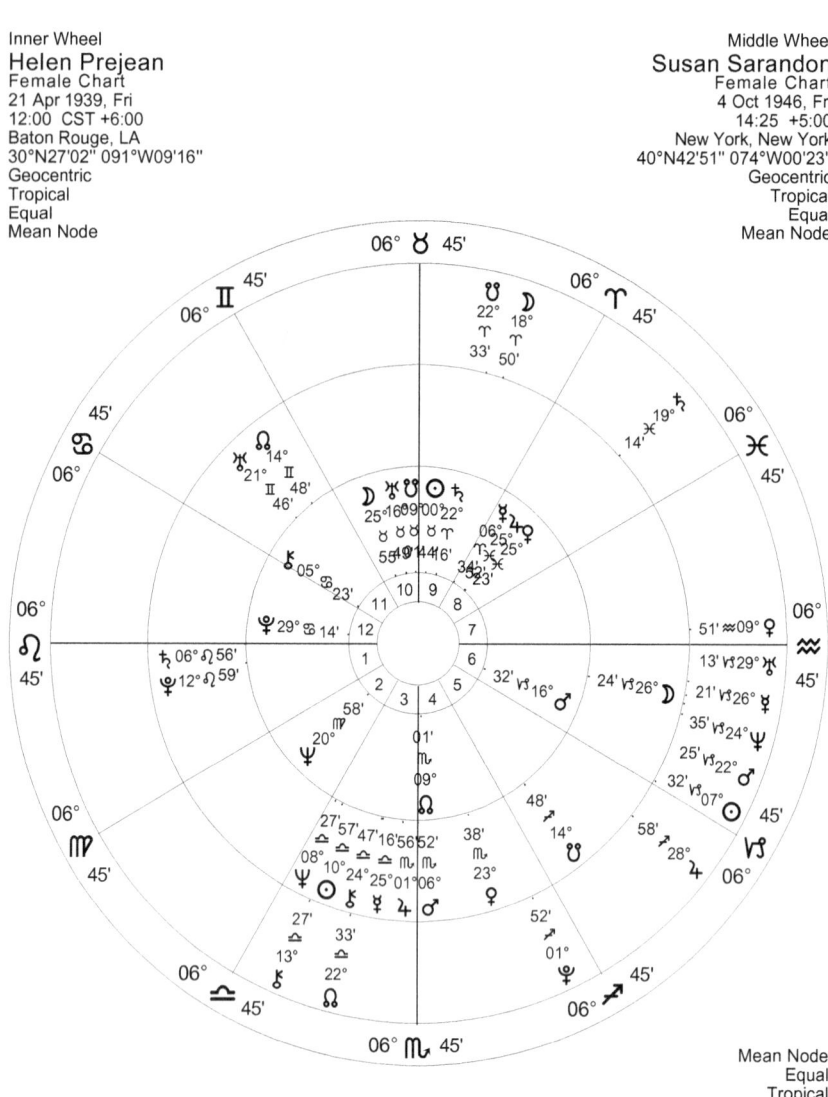

Saturn 47

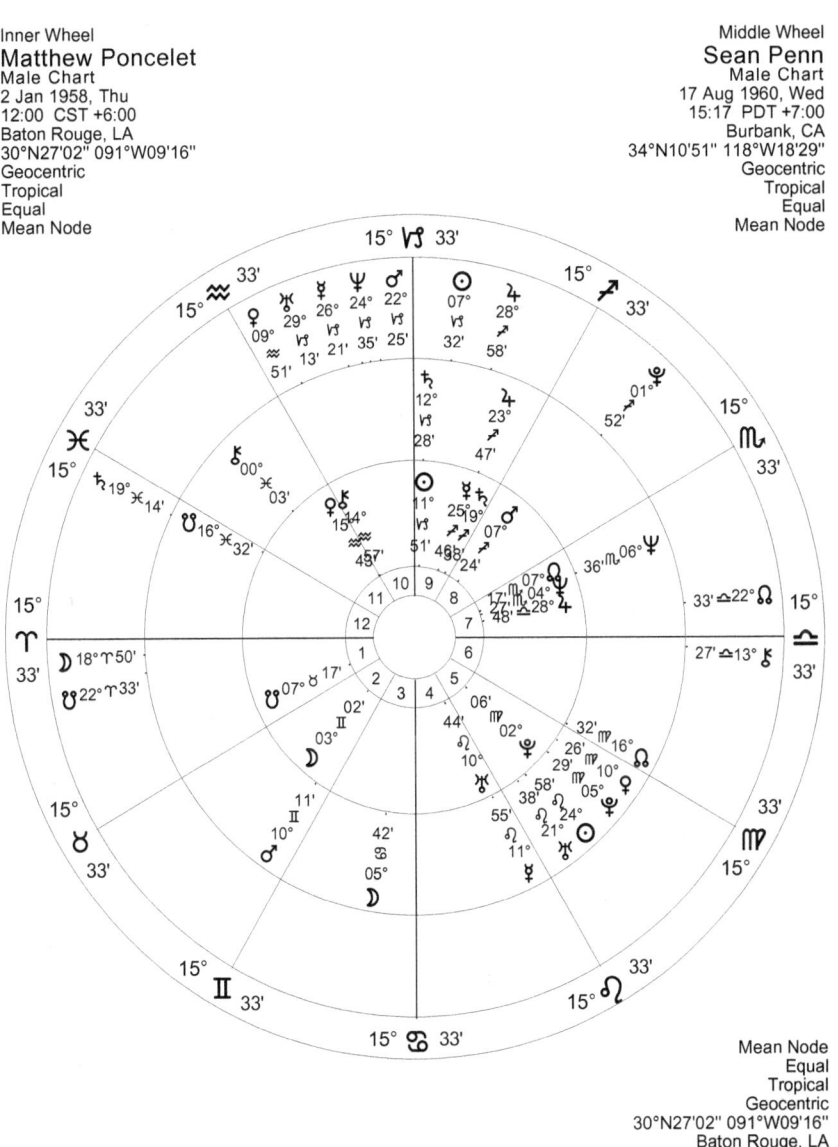

another man who was sentenced to life imprisonment. Sister Helen Prejean, a Roman Catholic Sister, has been corresponding with Poncelet and as the day of his execution draws closer, he asks her to help him get a final appeal.

Sister Helen could not have been prepared for meeting Poncelet. Deeply unpleasant, menacing, remorseless and worst of all, racist, he maintains his innocence by blaming the other man for pulling the trigger that killed the victims. Nevertheless, she convinces an experienced attorney to take Matthew's case and establishes a relationship with Poncelet and his family. She also forms a relationship with the families of the victims, who don't understand why she is trying to help the killer of their children.

The appeal is declined and Poncelet asks Sister Helen to be with him through his execution – she agrees. She tells him the only way he will find redemption is to take responsibility for what he did and ask for forgiveness. As he is taken from his cell, he tells Sister Helen that he killed the boy and raped the girl. As the lethal injection is prepared, he asks the boy's father for forgiveness and tells the girl's parents that he hopes his death will bring them peace. The boy's father attends Poncelet's funeral and later prays with Sister Helen.

Helen Prejean's Pluto is exactly on Susan Sarandon's descendant in Cancer and within a few degrees of opposition to the actress' Moon in Capricorn, which seems appropriate for the role of a woman who helped a condemned man find redemption. The movie was released when there was a four planet in stellium conjunct Sarandon's ascendant and opposite Prejean's Pluto.

Matthew Poncelet's Saturn in Sagittarius is within three degrees of Sean Penn's ascendant which seems appropriate for a man awaiting execution. Poncelet's Sun in Capricorn is conjunct Penn's Saturn and the transiting Sun was within orb of a conjunction when the film was released.

The movie was released the day after the anniversary of Poncelet's execution.

Sarandon won an Academy Award for Best Actress and was nominated for a Golden Globe. Sean Penn was nominated for an Academy Award and a Golden Globe Best Actor.

EDDIE THE EAGLE

Eddie (Michael Edwards): 5 December 1963, no time, Cheltenham, England. Source: Wikipedia

Taron Egerton: 10 November 1989, no time, Merseyside, England. Source: Wikipedia

Release date: 12 December 2015, Austin, Texas.

Like many children, Michael "Eddie" Edwards dreams of competing in the Olympics. He was never terribly athletic and wears thick glasses. Whilst his mother indulges and encourages him, his father does the opposite. While still a teenager, Eddie decides he wants to participate in the Winter Games and takes up skiing. Rejected by the British Olympic officials for his lack of athletic professionalism, he realises there is one sport that has not had any British participants for six decades: ski jumping. With no other competitors in that sport, Eddie sees his opportunity; he goes to Germany to train and is continuously picked on by more seasoned jumpers.

Eddie is initially self-trained but then manages to find a coach of sorts in an alcoholic snow-groomer, Bronson Peary. After Eddie severely injures himself, Peary tells him to give up. However the two form a bond of shared ostracism and Peary ends up employing all manner of unorthodox methods to improve Eddie's form. Eddie eventually qualifies even though Olympic officials decide to change the rules to prevent him from competing. Peary realises that Eddie is going to make a fool of himself and his country if he represents the British team. Undeterred, Eddie says that he only wants to compete in the Olympics, not win medals.

Eddie is picked on by the other Olympic athletes for his obvious lack of ability but his over-the-top-celebrations for setting a British record (but still coming in last in the competition) are a crowd pleaser and the media embrace him as "Eddie the Eagle". Peary continues to criticise Eddie over the phone for not taking the sport seriously. After apologising to the press for his lack of professionalism, Eddie decides to enter the competition for a jump length he has never attempted before. Admiring Eddie's determination and courage, Peary has a change of heart and goes to the games to encourage him. After an uplifting conversation with a fellow competitor he idolises, Eddie fails miserably at the jump.

50 Mirror Mirror

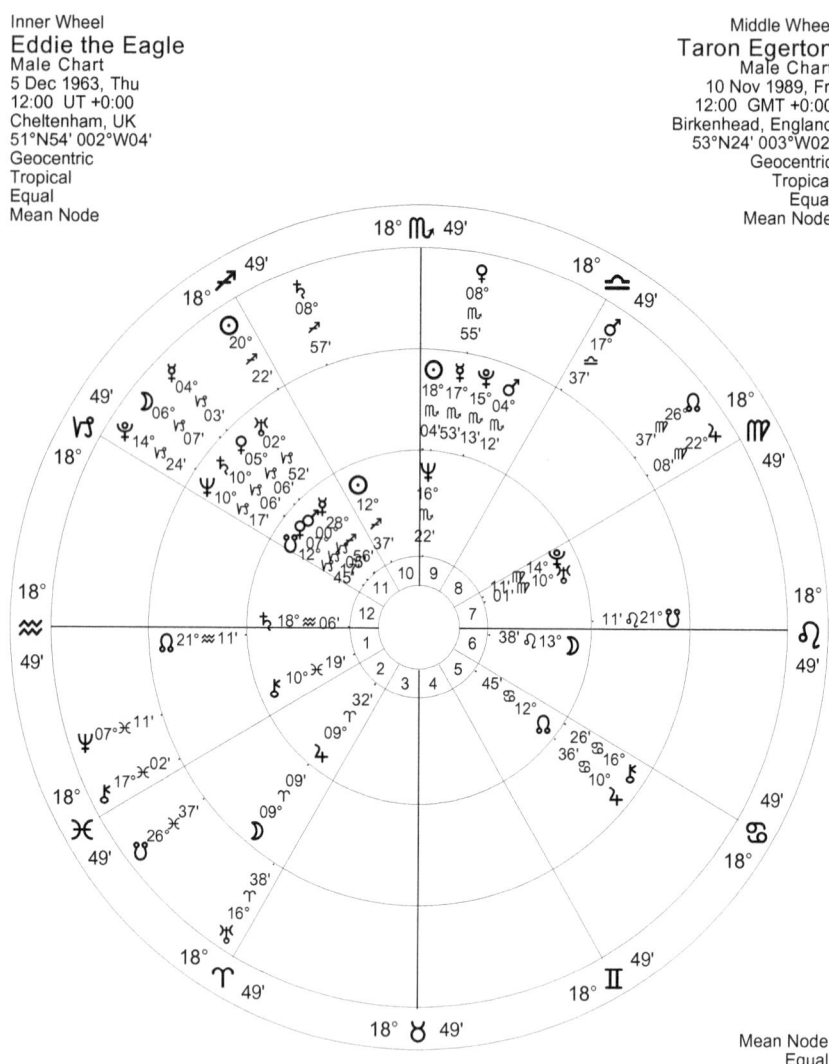

Although he scores last in the competition, crowds from around the world cheer for him and the press refer to him as "Eddie the Eagle". Eddie is even included in the closing speech of the Olympic Games: "You have broken world records. You have established many of your own personal bests and some of you have even soared like an Eagle".

Eddie the Eagle returns to his hometown as a record-breaking hero. His mother warmly embraces him and his father's T-shirt proudly proclaims: "I'm Eddie's Dad".

Even with an untimed chart, Eddie has the Moon in Leo, an indication that he would enjoy the spotlight. Both he and Egerton have a stellium of planets in Capricorn which pretty much ensures a strong work ethic and a determination to succeed. Additionally, Egerton has three planets within two degrees of Eddie's Neptune in Scorpio so the actor was well attuned to the dream mind-set of a champion athlete. The film was in production talks when transiting Pluto was on their stelliums in Capricorn and then finally released as transiting Saturn was within four degrees of Eddie's Sun in Sagittarius.

The film was generally well received and had nominations for minor awards.

INVICTUS

Nelson Mandela: 18 July 1918, 14:54 (unverified), Mvezo, South Africa. DD: McEvoy
Morgan Freeman: 1 June 1937, 02:00, Memphis, Tennessee. A: RR
Jacobus Francois Pienaar: 1 January 1967, no time, Vereeniging, South Africa. Source: Wikipedia.
Matt Damon: 8 October 1970, 15:22, Boston, Massachusetts. AA: McEvoy
Release date: 11 December 2009

Nelson Mandela is released after spending twenty-seven years in prison. Four years later, he is elected as the first black President of South Africa and faces substantial difficulties in the post-apartheid era. Mandela's greatest concern is the divide between black and white South Africans, which has a history of leading to violence. Even amongst his own security staff, distrust is evident. This extends to black South Africans cheering for England at rugby games rather than their own team. Mandela recognises that this is because to many blacks, the mostly white South

52 Mirror Mirror

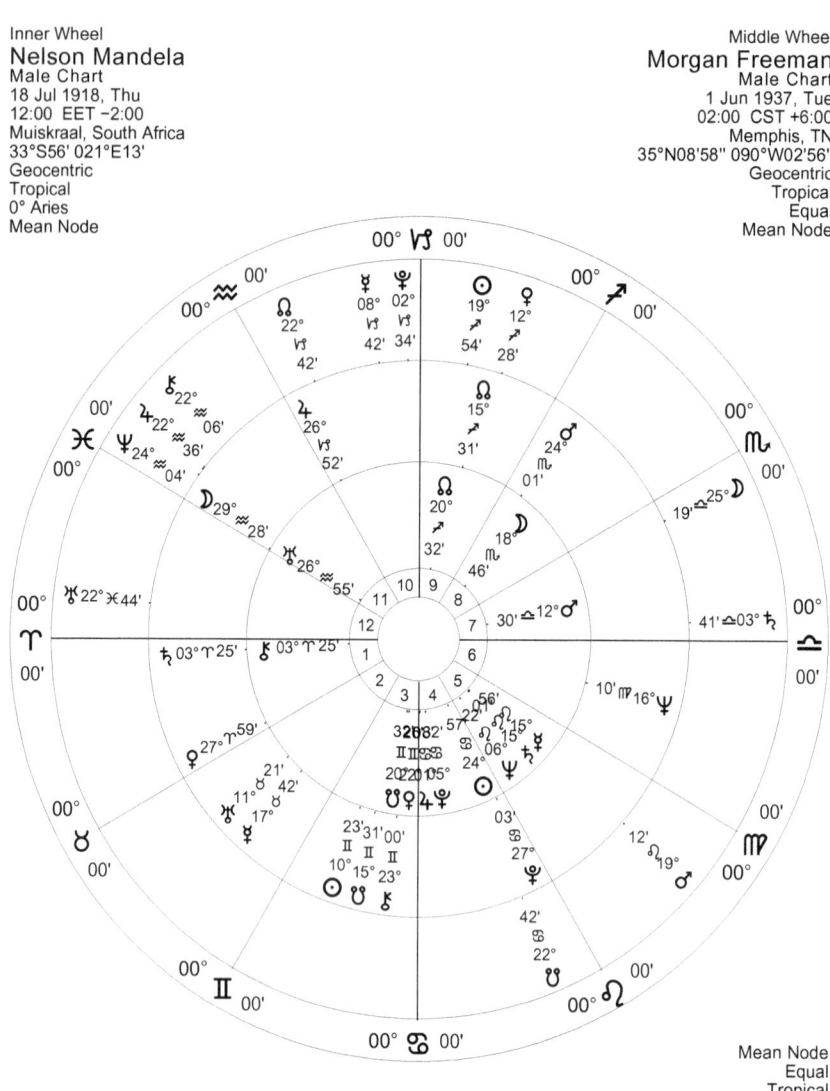

Saturn 53

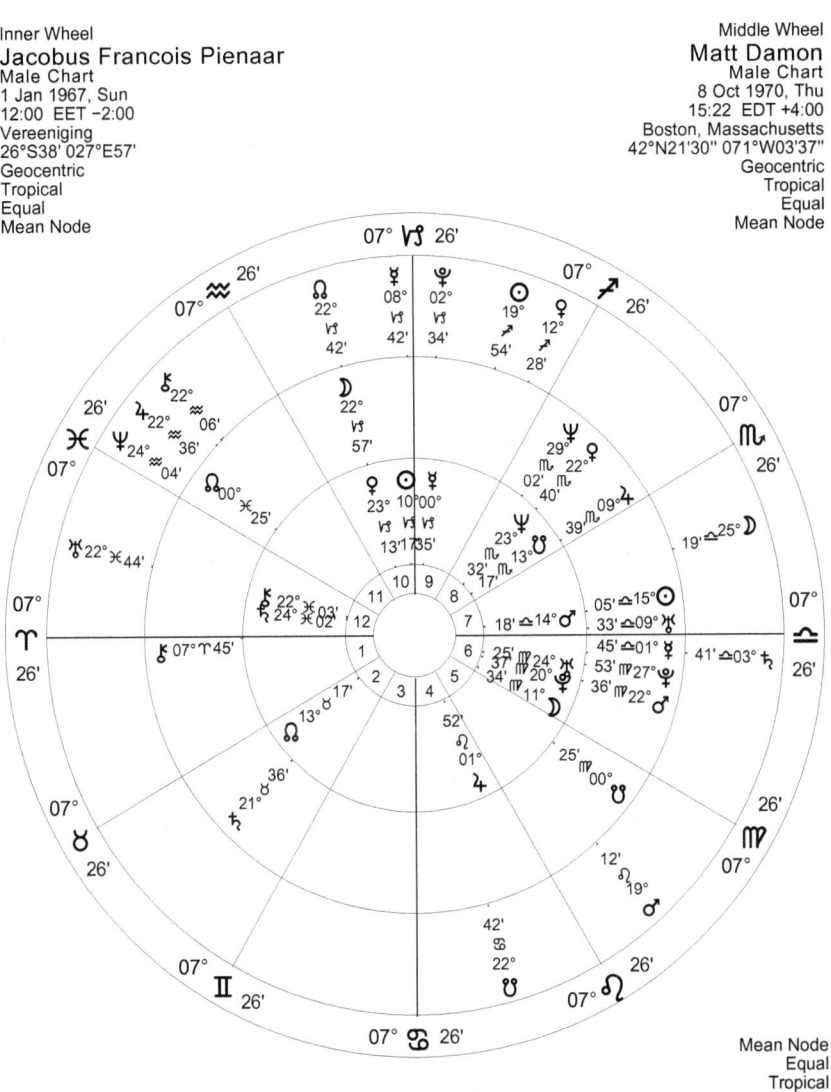

African team represents apartheid. With the Rugby World Cup being hosted in South Africa, Mandela works on persuading the all black sports committee to support the South African team, the Springboks. After meeting the captain of the Springboks, François Pienaar, he implies that a victory could lead to uniting and inspiring the nation. He shares the poem *Invictus* which had been a source of inspiration to him while he was imprisoned. This leads to a firm friendship between the two.

The Springboks begin to interact with their fans and, with friendships being established, support for the Springboks grows. Even Mandela's security staff begin to soften towards each other. The South African team continues to defeat rivals and just before a big game, the team visit Robben Island where Mandela had spent many years as a prisoner. Pienaar expresses his astonishment that Mandela "could spend thirty years in a tiny cell, and come out ready to forgive the people who put [him] there".

At the final of the Rugby Cup, Ellis Park Stadium in Johannesburg is packed with Springbok supporters. A low-flying 747 jetliner causes a security scare but as it flies over the stadium, the message "Good Luck Bokke" (the Afrikaans nickname for the team) is revealed on the undersides of the wings. Before the match, Mandela arrives on the field wearing a Springbok cap and a replica of Pienaar's jersey.

After the Springbok win, Mandela and Pienaar meet on the field to celebrate the victory. As Mandela is driven away from the stadium, he watches South Africans celebrating their victory and a recording of his voice reciting *Invictus* from earlier in the film is played again.

Freeman's Chiron in Gemini was within one degree of Mandela's Venus: here we have two men whose voices are listened to. Freeman's Saturn in Aries is exactly conjunct Mandela's Chiron and the film was released when Saturn opposed this point. Freeman's Moon in Aquarius is within three degrees of the politician's Uranus. Transiting Pluto in Capricorn opposed Mandela's Jupiter and Pluto, signalling the deep and profound political changes depicted in the movie.

Pienaar's Neptune in Scorpio is within one degree of Damon's Venus and his Venus in Capricorn is within one degree of Damon's Moon. Most striking though is that Pienaar's Uranus/Pluto conjunction in Virgo are two degrees on either side of Damon's Mars. Transiting Uranus in Pisces opposed this conjunction and was exactly conjunct Pienaar's Chiron when the film was released. The voice of a generation spoke through a man portraying a sportsman. Damon, who had to master the difficult South Africa accent, had transiting Saturn in Libra conjunct his natal Mercury – and with a perfect line up of Pienaar's Venus, Damon's Moon and the transiting North Node in Capricorn, it seems it was a role literally made in heaven..

Morgan and Daman were nominated for an Academy Award, a Golden Globe and a Screen Actor Guild Award but did not win. The film was nominated for several other awards.

SHINE

David Helfgott: 19 May 1947, 08:24, Melbourne, Australia.
C: March
Geoffrey Rush: 6 July 1951, no time, Toowoomba, Australia.
Source: Wikipedia
Gillian Helfgott: 10 December 1931, 05:04, Melbourne, Australia.
A: RR
Lynn Redgrave: 8 March 1943, 08:15, London, England. A: RR
Release date: 25 January 1996

The film opens with a distraught man taking refuge from a rainstorm by wandering into a restaurant. The restaurant employees can't understand him very well, but learn his name is David and that he is staying at a local hotel, so one of the waitresses helps him to get back there. He tries to indicate that he's a musician but she doesn't understand and leaves.

As a child David was taught how to play the piano by his father, Peter, and showed great talent. However, Peter is highly competitive and intolerant of mistakes or what he sees as disobedience. The father becomes more abusive as the son becomes more proficient.

As a teenager, David wins a prestigious scholarship and is invited to the US to study. Although the rest of the family is supportive, Peter becomes abusive and tells David he can't go. David continues to study and is eventually offered another scholarship, this time to the Royal College of London – but again his father forbids him from taking up the offer. Encouraged by a friend to run away, David leaves for London and begins to study with a prestigious professor. When a concerto competition is announced, David chooses to play a very demanding piece that he had attempted to learn as a child. As he practises, his behaviour becomes

56 Mirror Mirror

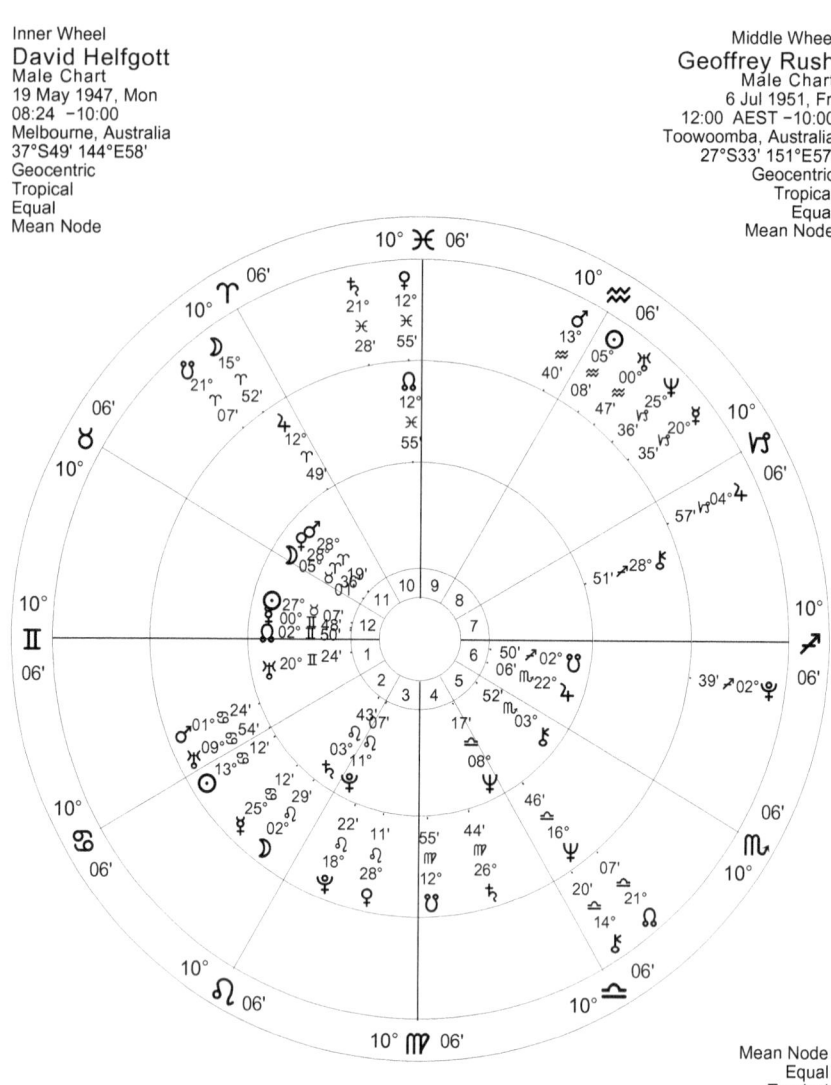

Saturn 57

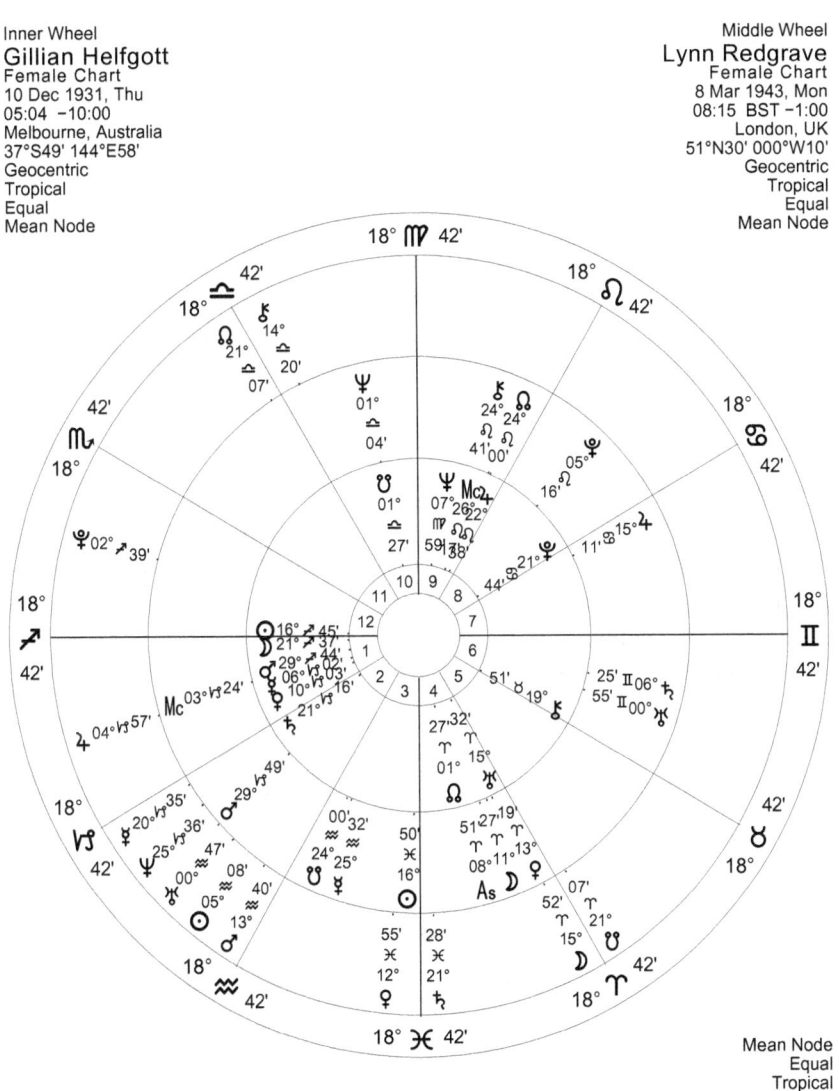

more manic and although he wins the competition, he has a nervous breakdown after his performance. He is admitted to a hospital where he receives electric shock treatments.

When he recovers, David returns to Australia but his father refuses to speak to him and David relapses. He is in and out of various mental institutions until he wanders back to the restaurant where we first see him at the beginning of the film, and astounds everyone with his piano playing. The owner of the restaurant begins to look after him and to repay her kindness, David performs for the guests. An astrologer(!) friend of the owner takes an interest in David and they end up falling in love and eventually marry. His new wife helps him cope when his father dies, and supports his return to professional performing.

Geoffrey Rush's Saturn in Virgo is conjunct Helfgott's IC and so the actor could understand the effect a tyrannical father would have had on the piano prodigy.

The film was released as transiting Mars in Aquarius opposed Helfgott's Pluto in Leo. Venus in Pisces transited Rush's North Node by exact degree and Chiron in Libra transited the actor's Neptune within an orb of two degrees.

Redgrave's Chiron and North Node in Leo are conjunct Gillian's MC and Jupiter as well as the actress' Neptune on the astrologer's Venus, giving a sense of healing and destiny. They also have a Venus and Uranus conjunction that nicely demonstrates the depiction of an astrologer falling in love with a prodigious yet troubled man. Jupiter in Capricorn was transiting the actress' MC and Gillian's Mars when the film was released.

Although the Helfgott family disputed the depiction of Helfgott's father, Rush won an Academy Award, a BAFTA, a Screen Actors' Guild Award and a Golden Globe for Best Actor. *Shine* was nominated for an Academy Award, a BAFTA, and a Golden Globe for Best Film and the cast was nominated for their performances at the Screen Actors Guild Awards.

THE IRON LADY

Margaret Thatcher: 13 October 1925, 09:00, Grantham, England. A: RR

Meryl Streep: 22 June 1949, 08:05, Summit, New Jersey. AA: Steinbrecher

Release date: 26 December 2011

Margaret Thatcher's life is shown in flashbacks, from working in her father's grocery shop and the difficult relationship she had with her mother, to her announcement that she had won a place at Oxford. Her struggles as a young lower middle class woman to break into the male dominated Conservative Party are portrayed along with her marriage to Denis Thatcher. She undergoes voice coaching and an image change in order to secure her position as Leader of the Conservative Party.

Key events during her time in office such the 1979 general election, the Brixton riots of 1981, the miners' strike in 1984/85 and the bombing of the Grand Hotel during the 1984 Conservative Party conference (when she and her husband were almost killed) are also shown in flashback. The sinking of The Belgrano during the Falkland Islands conflict and her emergence as a world leader are also covered.

Thatcher is shown in later life, aging but still authoritative and even aggressive. Eventually she loses her party's support and has to leave 10 Downing Street with her husband. The final scene of the film shows her packing up her late husband's belongings and tearfully telling his ghost it's time to go. When she tells him she wasn't ready to lose him, he replies: "You're going to be fine on your own... you always have been".

Streep's Saturn in Virgo is within two degrees of Thatcher's MC and her South Node in Libra is within one degree of Thatcher's Mercury. Additionally, Streep's Chiron in Sagittarius is within two degrees of Thatcher's Venus and the actress has her Moon in Taurus conjunct Thatcher's descendant. Most impressively, Streep's Jupiter in Aquarius (which is also conjunct her ascendant) is exactly conjunct Thatcher's South Node.

Transiting Uranus in Aries was exactly square the actress' natal Sun and Uranus in Cancer and transiting Jupiter in Taurus was exactly square the nodal axis of Thatcher when the movie was released.

Meryl Streep received her 17th Oscar nomination and won Best Actress for the 3rd time, a full Saturn cycle after she last won the award with her leading role in *Sophie's Choice*.

60 Mirror Mirror

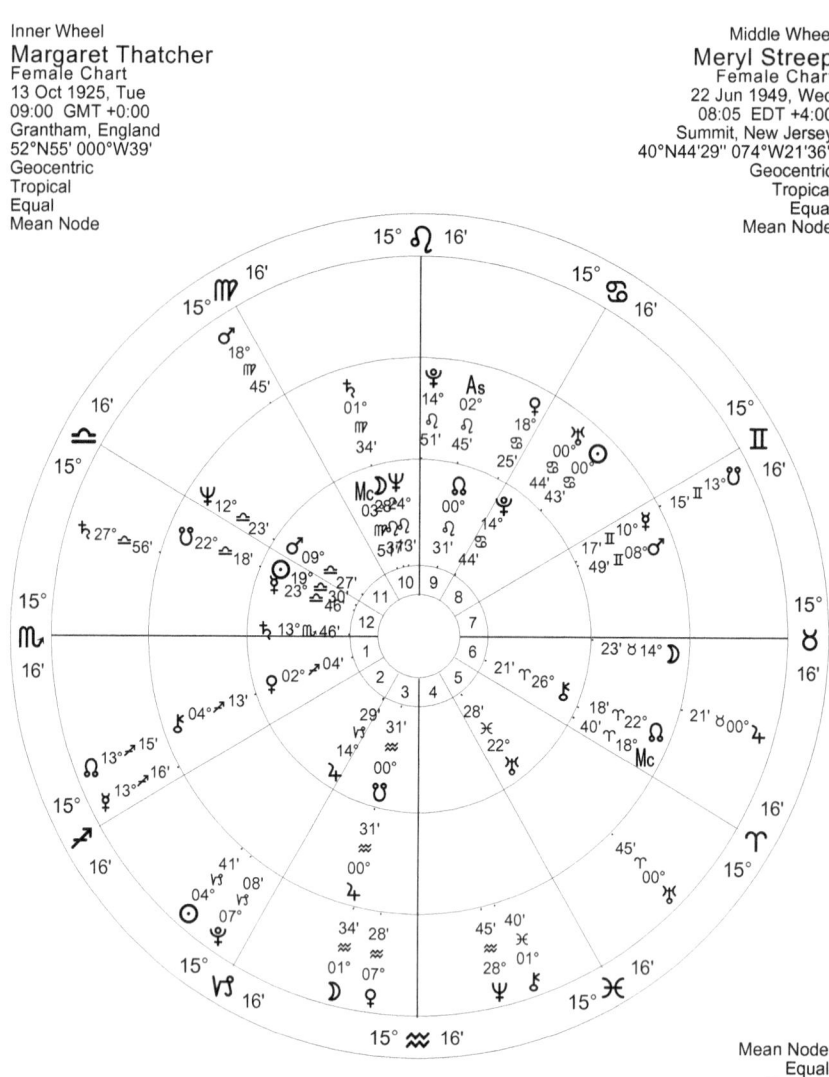

JUPITER

In mythology, Jupiter was a sky god whose unique perspective allowed him to enjoy omniscience, omnipotence and omnipresence. Jupiter was in charge of law and order but that didn't stop him from taking advantage of the opportunities that found their way to him. His adventures and restlessness caused his long-suffering wife Juno continual great concern.

In astrology, Jupiter represents our need to explore, learn and grow. In *Frida*, Salma Hayek's Jupiter connection with Frida Kahlo's North Node allows her to tap into and express the artist's vision, while in *Lust for Life*, Kirk Douglas' Mercury in Sagittarius was within a one degree orb of Van Gogh's Jupiter/South Node – the perfect combination with which to express the artist's frustration at not being able to capture the visions in his mind.

Long distance travelling and risk-taking are also a part of the Jupiter experience which was very much seen in the story of Charles Lindburgh's (James Stewart's) marathon solo flight across the Atlantic in *The Spirit of St Louis*. The conjunction between Lindbergh's Jupiter in Capricorn and Stewart's Moon allows the actor to express the sheer optimism and hard work that went into making the flight.

However, Jupiter can also represent our excesses as experienced by the tragic artist Henri Toulouse-Lautrek (José Ferrer) whose excessive drinking contributed to his demise in *Moulin Rouge*. Ferrer's Venus/Jupiter conjunction in Sagittarius conjunct the artist's three-planet stellium allowed him to tap straight into the deepest feelings of the student of life, desperate to properly express himself as he continually searched for meaning in his life.

FRIDA

Frida Kahlo: 6 July 1907, 08:30, Coyoacán, Mexico, AA: RR
Salma Hayek: 2 September 1966, no time,
Coatzacoalcos, Veracruz, Mexico X: Wikipedia
Release date: 29 August 2002

The film begins with the artist Frida Kahlo being carried on her bed through the streets to her first solo art exhibition in her home country of Mexico. The film then flashes back to her life as a school girl, meeting the muralist and political commentator Diego Rivera as he sketches a nude woman, despite his wife's obvious annoyance.

Frida is a passionate young woman, fiercely independent and sensual. A horrific bus has accident left her with injuries that will trouble her for the rest of her life. Encased in a full body cast, she is encouraged to begin painting by her father, as she suffers through the painful convalescence. Eventually she heals enough to be able to walk again and asks Rivera to assess her potential to make a living from her artwork. He encourages her and the two begin a dysfunctional relationship, marrying shortly after. However, they both have multiple affairs, including one with the same woman.

The couple travel to New York City, where Rivera has been commissioned by the Rockefeller family to complete a mural, *Man at the Crossroads*, in the Rockefeller Center. Owing to his political beliefs and his refusal to compromise his work, Rivera loses his commission and the mural is destroyed. Kahlo suffers a miscarriage and persuades her reluctant husband to go back to Mexico with her. However, when she discovers he is having an affair with her sister, Kahlo leaves him and returns to her family home, where she sinks into alcoholism.

Kahlo and Rivera reunite at the celebration of *Dia de los Muertos* where he implores her to help look after Leon Trotsky, who has been granted political asylum. Trotsky and Kahlo begin an affair after he reveals he admires her work, but he has to leave the safety of her home when his wife finds out. Rivera also discovers the affair and although he doesn't seem to mind about the others, the one with Trotsky eventually leads to their split. Kahlo travels to Paris and when she returns to Mexico, he asks for a divorce.

Trotsky is murdered and Rivera is the prime suspect. As the police

Jupiter   63

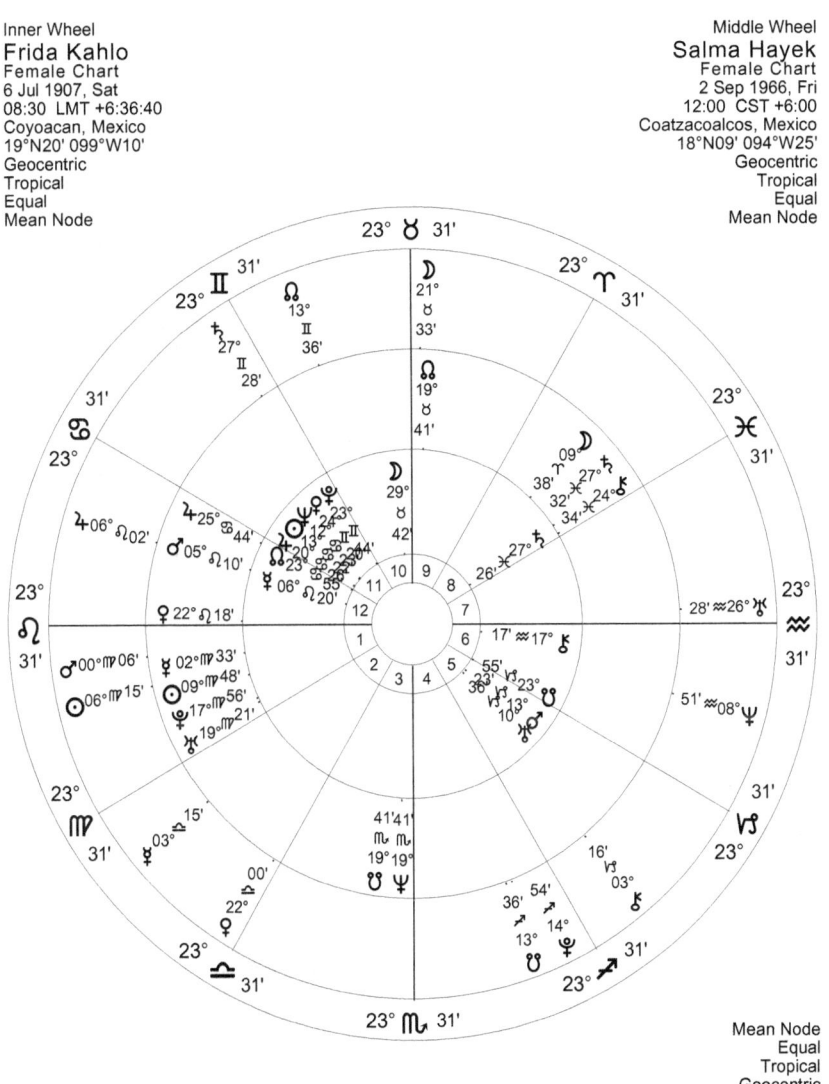

can't find him, Kahlo is placed under house arrest until her sister arrives to escort her away, telling her Rivera has arranged her release. The couple are reunited and re-marry.

Sadly, Kahlo's health continues to deteriorate and she has to have a partial leg amputation. By the time of her first solo art exhibition in Mexico, her bronchopneumonia is so severe that her doctor forbids her from going. Determined, Kahlo is carried – in her bed – to the museum where she is honoured by her husband and many distinguished guests.

Kahlo and Hayek were born exactly two Saturn cycles, both having Saturn at 27 degrees in Pisces. Within one degree, Hayek's Venus in Leo was conjunct Kahlo's ascendant, the actress' Mars in Leo was conjunct the artist's Mercury and her Jupiter in Cancer was in two degrees of Kahlo's North Node.

The film gave a new generation the opportunity to see and appreciate Kahlo's quirky work as Uranus transited her descendant during filming. Kahlo had Mercury at 6 degrees Leo, just a degree away from Hayek's Mars. This is a feisty, passionate connection giving the actress a deep understanding of the artist and this conjunction was transited by Jupiter in the same sign when the film was released.

LUST FOR LIFE
Vincent van Gogh: 30 March 1853, 11:00, Zundert, Netherlands.
AA: Gauquelin
Kirk Douglas: 9 December 1916, 10:15, Amsterdam, New York.
AA: Steinbrecher
Release date: 17 September 1956

Like his father, Vincent trained to be a clergyman but he was found to be unsuitable. After pleading to be given some sort of role, the Church placed him in a poor mining community and he casually began making drawings about everyday life in the village.

Vincent is eventually completely rejected by the Church and he returns to his father's home where he falls in love with his cousin and begins obsessively pursuing her. Trying to prove his love and impress her, Vincent holds his hand over a candle flame – but disgusted by him as well as his inability to support himself, she tells him she never wants to see him again.

Jupiter 65

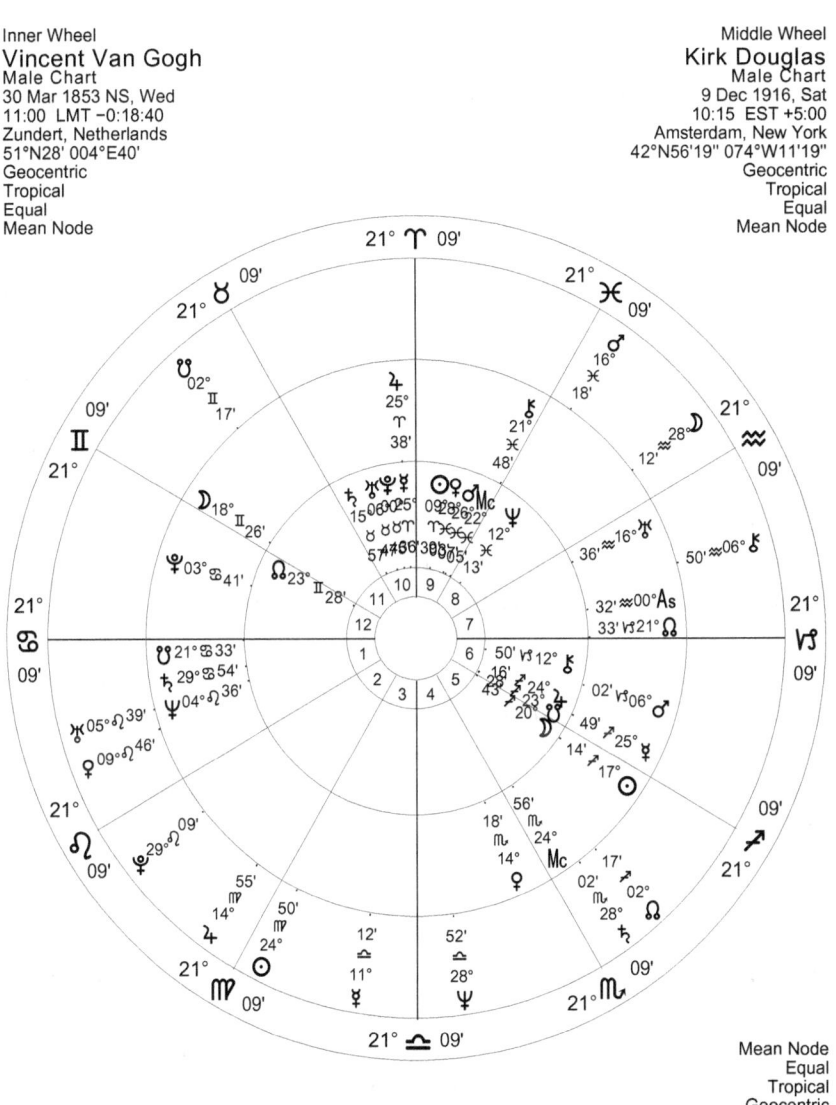

Thus rejected again, Vincent goes to Paris where he forms a relationship with a prostitute. She too is put off by his inability to support himself and leaves him. Vincent then meets the French artist Paul Gauguin who gives him a set of paints when he sees Vincent's talents. Financially supported by his brother Theo, Vincent constantly worries that he can never paint what he sees in his mind.

Vincent has an argument with his friend because Gauguin can't tolerate Vincent's obsessive tendencies. In despair, Vincent cuts off his own ear and also begins experiencing hallucinations. He voluntarily signs himself into a mental institution but with Theo's help recovers enough to return to painting. However, he shoots himself in the head in frustration because he can't replicate on canvas what he sees in his imagination. He dies shortly afterwards.

Douglas' nodal axis was exactly on Van Gogh's ascendant-descendant in Cancer and his Mercury in Sagittarius was within a one degree orb of Van Gogh's Jupiter/South Node. If that weren't enough, they had a Sun/Moon conjunction in Sagittarius, Douglas' Jupiter in Aries was exactly conjunct the artist's Mercury, and Chiron was within one degree of Van Gogh's MC.

Transiting Uranus in Leo was conjunct Douglas' Neptune, and transiting Chiron in Aquarius was in opposition to this when the film was released. Douglas won a Golden Globe for his performance and Anthony Quinn won an Academy Award for Best Supporting Actor for his role as Van Gogh's friend, Paul Gauguin.

MOULIN ROUGE
Henri Toulouse-Lautrec: 24 November 1864, 06:00, Albi, France.
AA: RR
José Ferrer, 8 January 1912, 22:10, San Turce, Puerto Rico.
AA: Palmer
Release date: 23 December 1952

Set in the middle of a Moulin Rouge night club scene, the film portrays Henri Toulouse-Lautrec finishing a bottle of cognac after sketching the club's dancers. Paid for his art with free drinks, he waits for the club to clear before his disfigured body is revealed to the cinema audience. As

Jupiter 67

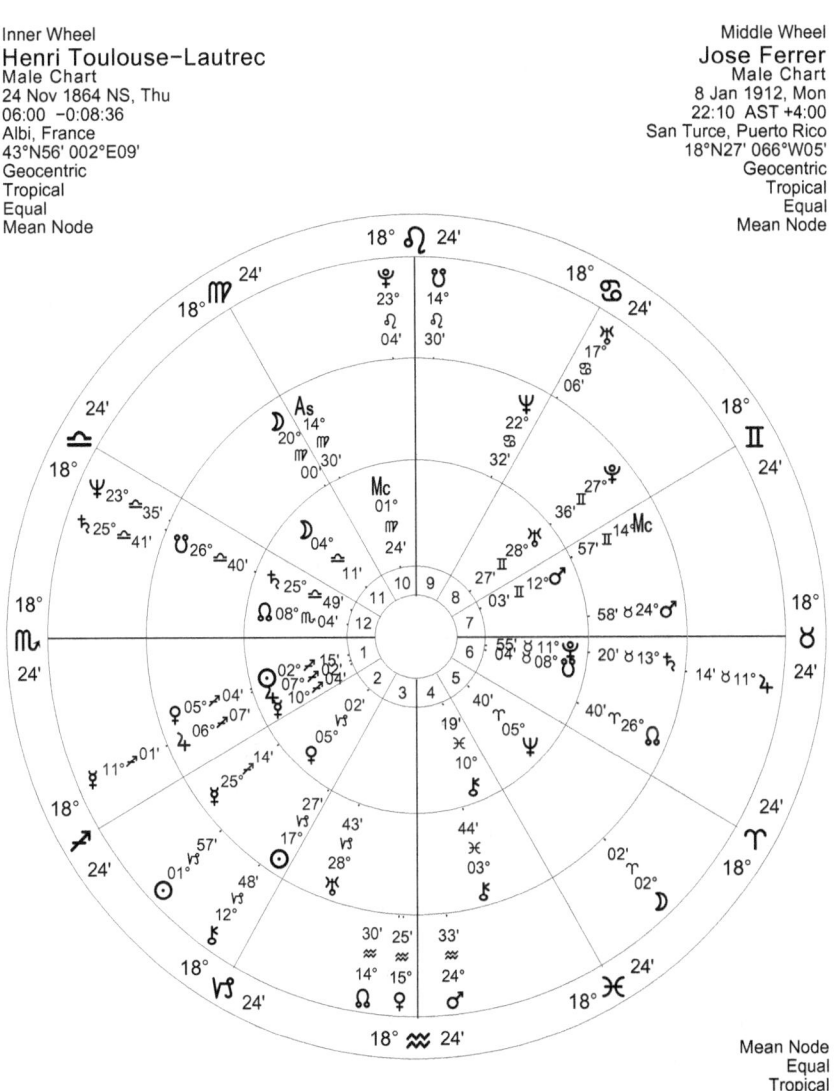

he is shown walking to his apartment, we are told that he fell down a flight of stairs as a child and as a result of a genetic difficulty, his legs had never healed. Henri became an artist to escape the pain of his injuries and to forget that his parents did not want more children in case they turned out like him.

As Lautrec grows into a young man, he suffers continued rejection in love despite his obvious talents as an artist. Women declare their love for him, only to cruelly take his money and tell him he will never find a woman who loves him because of his deformity. His preoccupation with relationships can perhaps be explained by his Moon in Libra in opposition to Neptune in Aries. It may also explain why he found solace in alcohol.

Lautrec eventually finds success in painting although his father denounces his work, implying it is beneath his aristocratic upbringing. However, the painter also begins to realise that the Moulin Rouge has become a respectable place and not just a club for the misfits of society. He eventually meets a woman who asks him if he loves her, but as he has been so wounded by other women he lies and tells her he doesn't. She sends him a letter, saying that she loves him but can't wait any longer. Although he searches for her, he can't find her and he ends up in a run-down tavern drinking heavily while reading her letter over and over.

Weeks later, in a state of the delirium tremens, he thinks roaches are crawling all over him. Trying to get them off, he ends up falling down a flight of stairs. He is transported back to his family home where his father begs for forgiveness and tells Henri his paintings have been displayed in the Louvre. As Henri dies, the figures from his painting come to life in his imagination and bid him farewell.

José Ferrer, the actor who played Lautrec, had a Venus/Jupiter conjunction in Sagittarius conjunct the artist's three-planet stellium. Sagittarius is the sign of the student of life who continually searches for their truth. In life, despite his pain and suffering, Lautrec was able to bring the vivid adventures in his mind to life on the canvas. Ferrer's South Node was conjunct Lautrec's Saturn, so as an able-bodied actor he was able to understand Lautrec's limitations. When the film was released, both Saturn and Neptune were transiting this conjunction in a tribute that is fitting to the life of an artist with such difficulties. Transiting Jupiter, the ruler of Sagittarius, was transiting Lautrec's Pluto and Ferrer's Saturn and we can see how Ferrer's work as an actor helped keep the genius of the artist in public memory.

This version received seven Academy Award nominations, including Best Picture, Best Director (John Huston), Best Actor and Best Supporting Actress (Colette Marchard), but only won two for Best Art Direction and Best Costume Design.

Baz Luhrmann also released a film about the Parisian cabaret on 1 June 2001 starring Nicole Kidman and Ewan McGregor. Although the plot lines are very different, it is worth noting the newer film was released as Uranus in Aquarius was conjunct the Mars of the 1952 version.

THE SPIRIT OF ST LOUIS

Charles Lindbergh: 4 February 1902, 01:30, Detroit, Michigan.
AA: RR
James Stewart: 20 May 1908, 07:15, Indiana, Pennsylvania.
AA: Scholfield
Flight Take-off: 20 May 1927, 07:52, New York
Release date: 21 February 1957

On the eve of his historic non-stop flight from New York to Paris, aviator Charles Lindburgh lies awake and unable to sleep, in his hotel room near Roosevelt Field. He reflects on his career as a pilot.

There have been several attempts at the transatlantic flight. Two pilots have already died attempting the feat but Lindbergh has an idea to build a stripped-down, single engine aircraft. He had proposed the idea and has received financial backing, but there was one problem: the backers wanted to choose their own pilot to fly the plane.

Lindbergh finds a company based in California to build the plane he needs and they promise to build it in just 90 days. To decrease the weight of the plane, it will be stripped of all heavy equipment – including the radio and parachute. Lindbergh intends to make the 40-hour flight without a co-pilot and by using 'dead reckoning'. The plane is named "The Spirit of St Louis" and he flies it to St Louis to show the investors. Just before he takes the plane to New York to begin his flight to Paris, a young woman gives him a compact mirror to help him read the compass. The mirror is stuck to the instrument panel with chewing gum and a friend gives him some sandwiches along with a St Christopher's medal.

70   Mirror Mirror

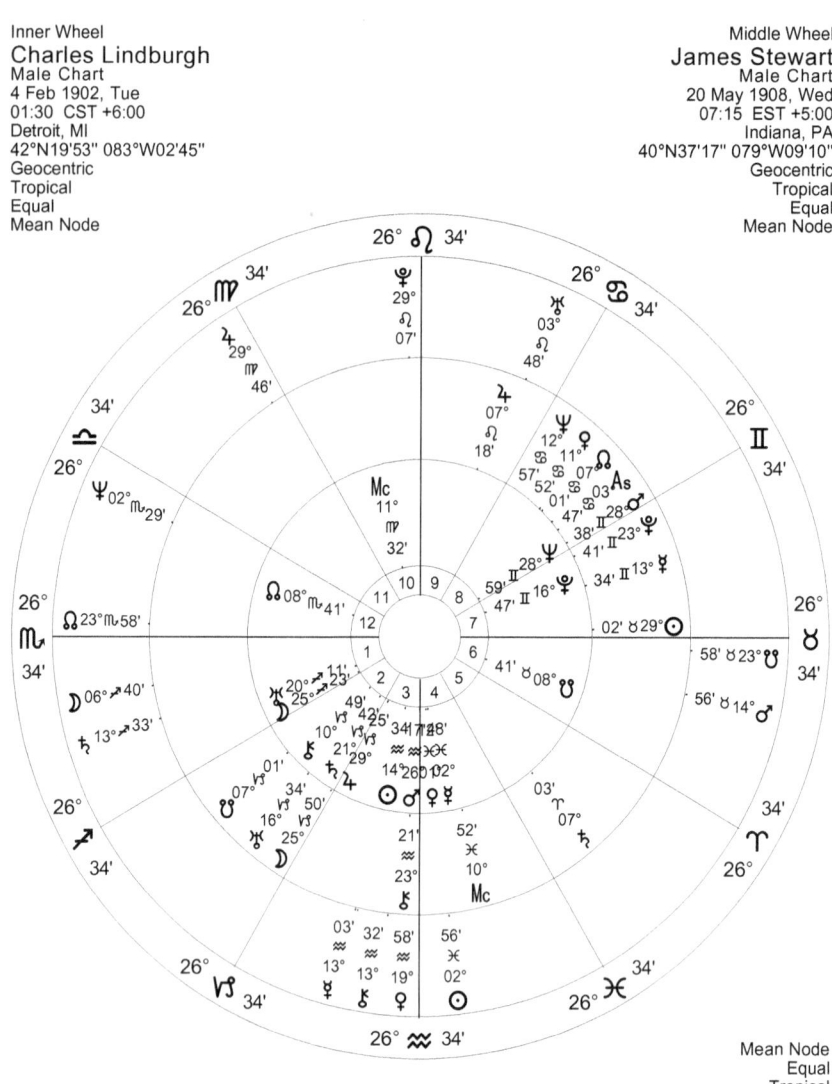

The scenes of Lindbergh in his plane – with the near misses and the small miracles – are quite beautifully captured by James Stewart. The struggle to stay awake in particular makes an impression as Lindbergh suffers from hallucinations from lack of sleep. The plane lands safely in Paris and Lindbergh receives a Congressional medal of honour for his accomplishment.

Stewart's Moon was conjunct Lindbergh's Jupiter in Capricorn, perhaps representing the long distance, arduous travel across an ocean. Stewart had his Sun in Taurus conjunct Lindbergh's descendant and his Mars in Gemini conjunct the aviator's Neptune. Here we have a stubborn man acting out the ambitions of another person – who wasn't allowed to sleep!

The chart for the take-off of the flight shows transiting Mercury and the Sun conjunction in Taurus on the conjunction of the Sun and descendant of the actor and aviator.

When the film was released, a Chiron/Mercury conjunction was transiting Lindbergh's Sun in Aquarius and transiting Saturn was opposing Stewart's Mercury.

Stewart's performance and the special effects of the film were praised although the film itself received mixed reviews.

MARS

Mars was the god of war to the Romans; astrologically, Mars is our aggression, temper and passion. *Evita* (Madonna) was about a woman's short but triumphant life that she described in her final broadcast to her people as like the "brightest fire." Quite amazingly both women have their natal Mars within one degree. The fight to discover one's purpose is often a feature of Mars and we see this in *James Dean* with James Franco portraying the legendary actor. They too have a Mars conjunction. It is no astrological surprise that Tyrone Power was able to understand *Jesse James* as the actor and the outlaw have a Mars/Sun conjunction. *Raging Bull* is uncomfortable viewing because of its violence. Natally Robert DeNiro has his natal Mars conjunct the dreaded fixed star Algol which is square Jake LaMotta's natal Venus. *Looking for Mr Goodbar* was a disturbing film to many people because it was about the murder of a young teacher for deaf children and her double life as a nighttime bar fly, a combination that was viewed as progressive when the film was released in the late 1970s. The film was released during Diane Keaton's Mars return.

EVITA

Eva Perón: 7 May 1919, 05:13 (unverified), Buenos Aires, Argentina. DD: Penfield
Madonna: 16 July 1958, 7:05 (unverified) Bay City, Michigan. DD: RR
Release date: 14 December 1996

The film opens with the funeral of Eva Perón, the first lady and spiritual leader of Argentina, then backtracks ten years to recount her incredible rise from humble beginnings as an illegitimate child born into a lower-class family, to her ascension as a (controversial) heroine. The story is told by a member of the public called "Che" who uses different disguises to represent the different people who play important parts in Eva's life.

Longing for a better life in a bigger city, at the age of fifteen she persuades a tango singer to take her to Buenos Aires. After he abandons her she has several affairs with influential men before meeting Colonel Juan Perón at a fund raising event following the San Juan earthquake

Mars 73

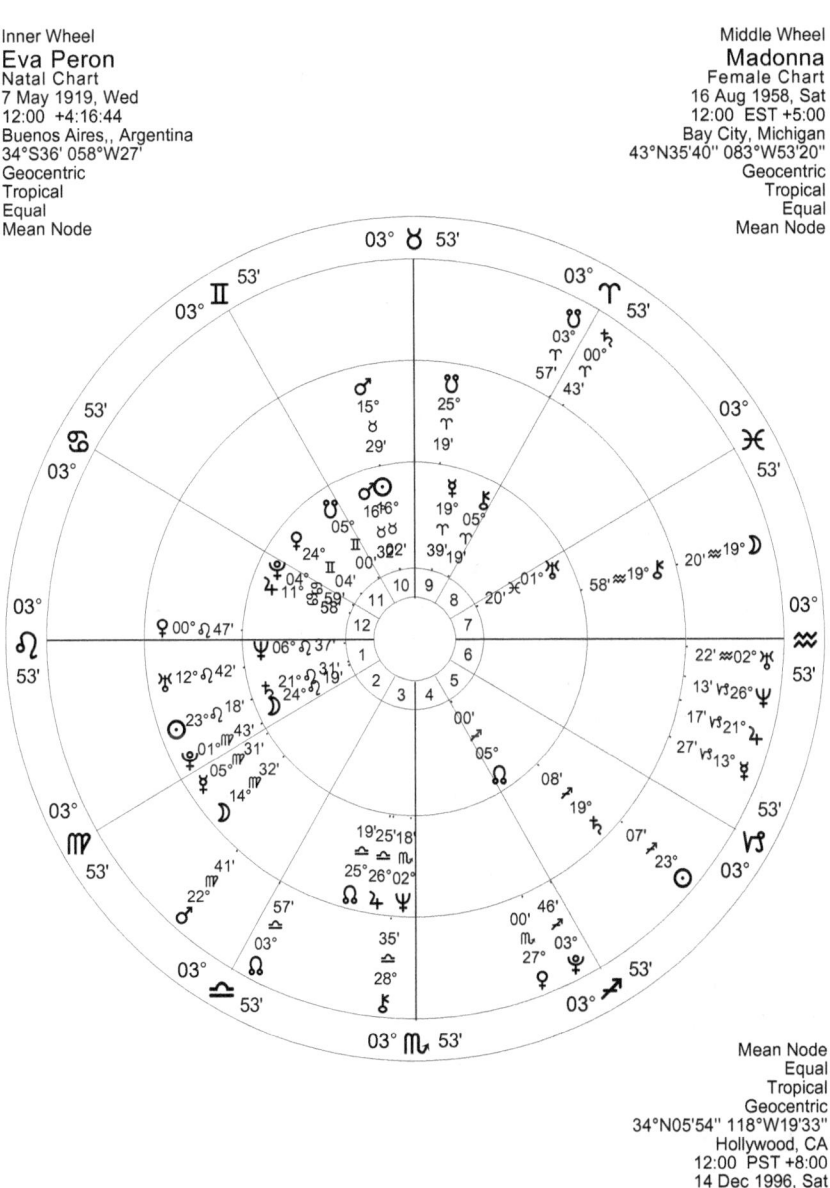

of 1944. By this time Eva has become an actress, a model and a radio personality. Using all of her skills to promote Perón's election to presidency, they both receive support from the people as they share the common trait of being working class. Her skills at promotion are so impressive that her supporters force the government to release Perón from jail where he had been imprisoned to prevent him from winning the presidency. Eventually, he runs for and then wins the presidency and marries Eva when he realizes the formidable force they have become.

Eva plays the role of First Lady with style. However, her visit to Europe receives a decidedly mixed reception: she is adored in Spain and intensely disliked in Italy (where the Pope gives her a small, meagre gift). She returns to Argentina and sets up a huge charity to help the nation's poor, the money from which the film conveys would have otherwise been plundered by corrupt politicians. She is adored by the millions of people she's helping, who have now given her the nickname of Evita.

Evita's health begins to fail and she is diagnosed with terminal cancer, forcing her to decline the Vice Presidency. In her final appearance, she tells the people that her life has been short because she lived it like the brightest fire. Large crowds gather outside the hospital and hold a candlelight vigil for her recovery. Her death is signalled by the light being turned off in her room.

Madonna's Sun in Leo is within two degrees of Eva Perón's Saturn, indicating how the actress was able to understand the First Lady's public work and subsequent acceptance by the public.

Madonna's Mars conjunction with Peron's Sun/Mars was in trine with transiting Mercury in Capricorn on release – literally giving them both a voice. Madonna had to fight for the role of Perón because it was assumed she had become too tarty to do it respectfully. Indeed, it may be argued that the role showed Madonna's talents in a completely different light as many people reckoned they had seen all they had wanted to see of her. Peron's Saturn (and possibly her Moon) was conjunct the singer's Sun. The film brought a degree of respectability to both Madonna and Perón.

Madonna won a Golden Globe for Best Actress and the film received several awards for Best Song.

If you are a fan of Madonna, you might like to check out *Growing Pains* to read a fuller interpretation of the transits for her success.

JAMES DEAN

**James Dean: 8 February 1931, 09:00, Marion, Indiana.
AA: Przybylowski
James Franco: 19 April 1978, 19:04, Stanford, California.
AA: Viktor
Release date: 4 August 2001**

Dean is orphaned as a child when his mother dies and Winton, his estranged father, sends him (and his mother's dead body) on a train from California to Indiana to his aunt and uncle.

After high school, Dean moves back to California and discovers Winton has remarried. Dean begins taking acting lessons and is encouraged to move to New York to pursue an acting career; he is eventually accepted into the Actors Studio. He receives critical acclaim in Broadway theatre productions and also lands a role in a television movie drama – however none of this impresses Winton, who continues to reject his son.

Dean's first Hollywood role in *East of Eden* is so successful that Jack L. Warner, the President of Warner Bros. wants to turn him into a movie star. However, Dean's off-screen behaviour raises suspicions about his private life, but he's able to quell rumours of bisexuality by becoming romantically involved with Pier Angeli.

The two set up home together and Dean is cast in *Rebel Without a Cause*. When he doesn't show up for the premiere of *East of Eden*, Warner is furious and threatens to shut down production of *Rebel Without a Cause*. However, the reviews of Dean's performance are so good that the idea is dropped. In the meantime, Angeli leaves Dean and marries another actor. Dean signs a one million dollar contract for Giant but his emotional fragility is revealed as he has conflicts with the director, George Stevens.

Eventually Dean confronts his father about his disinterest and learns that his real father was a man his mother had an affair with, and the man Dean had thought was his father didn't have the courage to raise him as his own. The truth is a comfort to Dean, who settles into a happier life, resolving his conflict with Stevens.

Shortly afterwards, Dean is killed in a car accident that shocks the world. Returning Dean's body to Indiana, the man who had rejected Dean all his life sits with his body all the way home.

76   Mirror Mirror

Inner Wheel
James Dean
Natal Chart
8 Feb 1931, Sun
02:11 +6:00
Marion, Indiana
40°N33'30" 085°W39'33"
Geocentric
Tropical
Equal
Mean Node

Middle Wheel
James Franco
Male Chart
19 Apr 1978, Wed
19:04 PST +8:00
Stanford, CA
37°N25' 122°W10'
Geocentric
Tropical
Equal
Mean Node

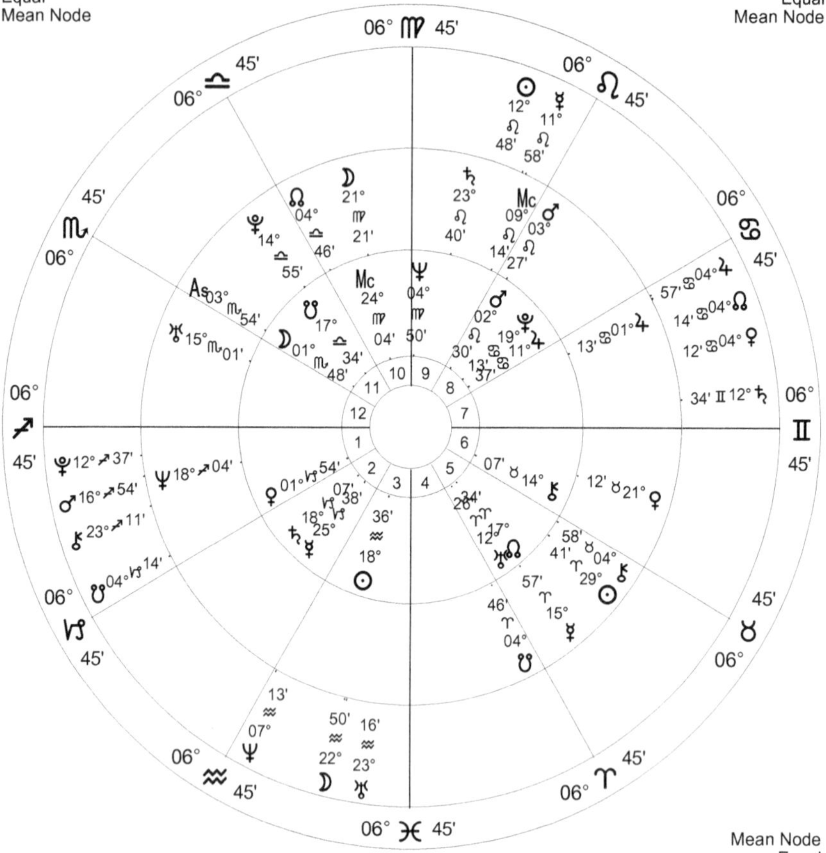

Mean Node
Equal
Tropical
Geocentric
34°N05'54" 118°W19'33"
Hollywood, CA
21:00 PDT +7:00
4 Aug 2001, Sat
Event Chart
James Dean release
Outer Wheel

Within an orb of one degree, both actors have Mars in Leo and Franco's ascendant in Scorpio is conjunct Dean's Moon. Franco's Mercury in Aries opposite Pluto in Libra is on Dean's nodal axis within in two degrees.

Although their natal Jupiters in Cancer are too far out of orb to be considered a conjunction, the transiting Jupiter/Venus conjunction on the day the film was released was within orb to both.

Franco received a Golden Globe for his performance as well as a nomination at the Screen Guild Awards for his portrayal of James Dean.

JESSE JAMES

Jesse James: 5 September 1847, no time, Kearney, Missouri.
Source: Wikipedia
Tyrone Power: 5 May 1914, 17:30, Cincinnati, Ohio.
B: Scholfield
Release date: 27 January 1939

1939 was a bumper year for movies. *Gone With the Wind*, *Goodbye Mr Chips* and *The Wizard of Oz* were all released in this year and these movies were the top three. In the wake of their popularity, *Jesse James* is often overlooked but as it was the fourth highest grossing film, it surely is worthy of attention.

Tyrone Power plays the eponymous outlaw. It is quite likely that Power had grown up hearing about the legend and his exploits, which were no doubt garnished with more admiration than a criminal should receive. James was born with his natal Sun in Virgo opposing Saturn in Pisces within an orb of three degrees. This aspect can make the native feel that they constantly have to fight with authority or adjust rules to their liking because they are not comfortable with the restrictions imposed on them. The lawlessness with which James operated seems to confirm this tendency. Tyrone Power had his nodal axis on this opposition so perhaps the actor was quite literally able to understand where the outlaw was coming from. James' Sun is in an exact trine to Mars in Taurus which can be notoriously stubborn and difficult to shift. It seems that once he got something in motion, he may not have been able to change direction. Power had his Sun conjunct the outlaw's Mars.

78 Mirror Mirror

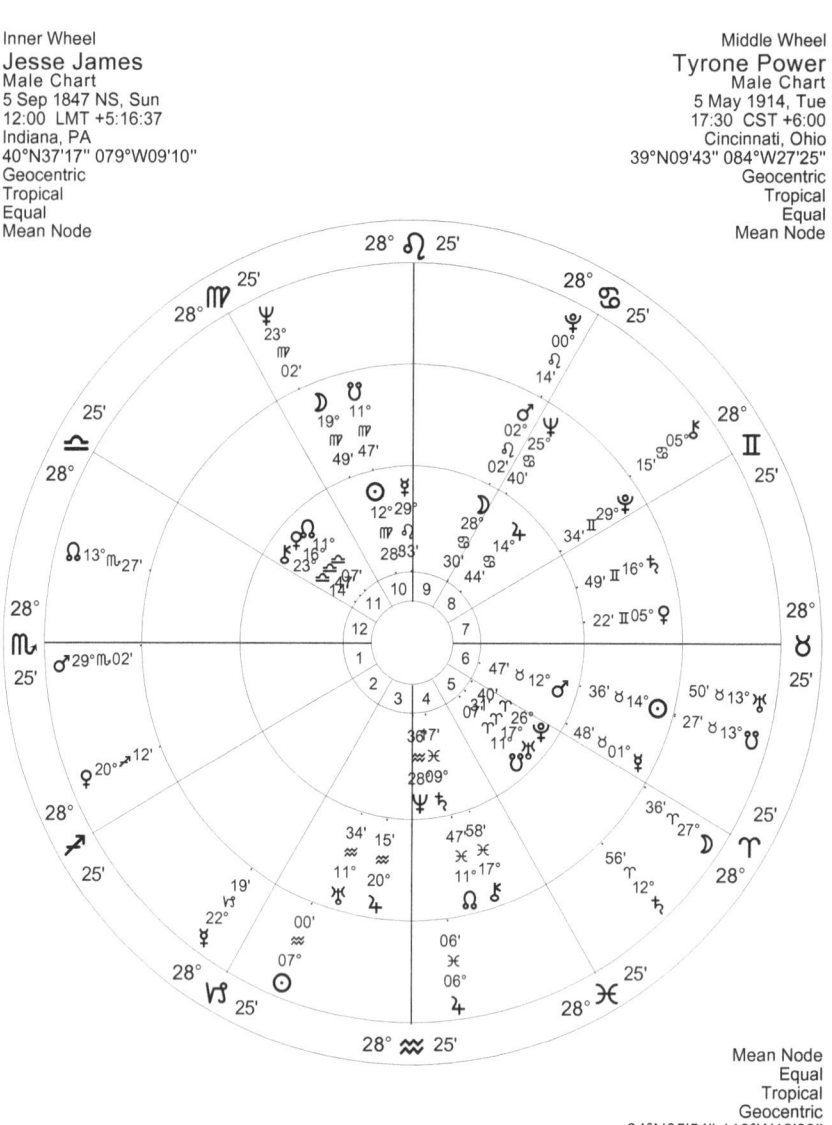

The movie centres around James' singularity in getting revenge on those who had killed his mother.

The movie was released as Saturn in Aries was conjunct Jesse James' South Node.

As a point of interest, the death of a horse during filming meant that the American Humane Society would begin overseeing all films involving animals. At the time of the film's release, Venus was transiting through the sign of Sagittarius. As Sagittarius is represented by the centaur, a bi-corporal animal that is half-man, half-horse, it seems only fitting that the message of treating animals with more respect was made during this time.

LOOKING FOR MR GOODBAR
Roseann Quinn: 17 November 1944, no time, New York.
Source: Wikipedia
Diane Keaton: 5 January 1946, 02:49, Los Angeles. AA: Wilsons
Murder: 2 January 1973 (early hours)
Release date: 19 October 1977

Roseann Quinn had the Sun conjunct natal Mars in Scorpio and Judith Rossner's best-selling novel is based on her murder. Quinn had grown up in a repressed household and by the time she was ready to explore her sexuality, it was the so-called Swinging Sixties.

Looking For Mr Goodbar has the feeling of a cautionary tale. It tells the protagonist's story (her name was changed to Theresa Dunn in the film), moving from virgin and caring schoolteacher by day to promiscuous lush by night. By the end of the film, she has been murdered by one of her one-night-stands.

Diane Keaton, who plays Theresa Dunn in the film, had her ascendant at eighteen degrees Scorpio, conjunct Quinn's Mars/Sun conjunction within eight degrees. It must have been a challenge to play a character with such extreme sides to her personality. The conjunction may have enabled Keaton to step into the role of Quinn's seedier side but the actress also had a Mars/Saturn conjunction in Cancer on Quinn's North Node, which must have helped her understand the character's caring side as

80   Mirror Mirror

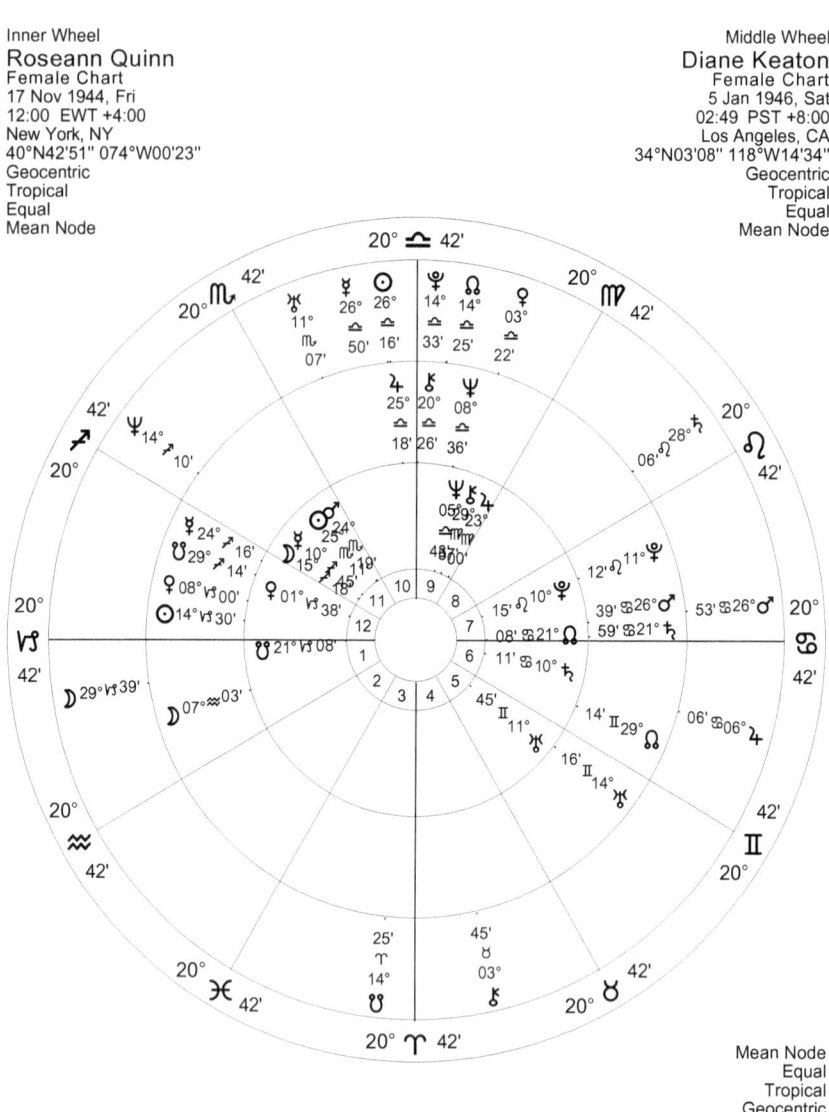

well. The manner in which Keaton kept both sides so well balanced was what made the film intriguing and successful.

The movie, and its title with overt sexual overtones, was released on Keaton's Mars Return and Venus was transiting the Neptune of both the actress and the character to within a few degrees.

Keaton was nominated for a Golden Globe Award for Best Actress.

RAGING BULL
Jake LaMotta, July 10, 1922, no time, The Bronx, New York.
Source: Wikipedia
Robert DeNiro: 17 August 1943, 03:00, Brooklyn, New York.
A: RR
Release date: 14 November 1980 (New York City)

Jake LaMotta, an overweight Italian-American, rehearses his comedy act while the story of his career as a professional boxer is told in flashback. Robert DeNiro famously piled on 60 pounds of weight for this role.

As a boxer, Jake suffers his first loss in a fixed fight against Jimmy Reeves. Jake's brother (and fight organiser) Joey reassures him that Salvy, one of his Mafia connections, can help Jake win the middleweight title.

A short time later, Jake spots Vickie, a fifteen-year-old girl in the neighbourhood swimming pool. Despite already being married, he seduces and eventually marries her. In the meantime, he defeats Sugar Ray Robinson but in the re-match a few weeks later, he loses the bout by decision from the judges.

Jake constantly worries about his new wife having an affair with other men and regularly has violent fights in and out of the ring with men he suspects have their eye on her. In particular, Jake suspects Salvy is trying to seduce Vickie, as well as attempting to tie him to the Mafia. At a subsequent match, Joey tells Jake that in order to win a championship he will have to deliberately lose a fight. After he is found out for doing so, Jake is suspended by the boxing board; however, he is eventually reinstated and goes on to win the middleweight championship.

Jake's jealousy leads to him asking Joey if he has had an affair with Vickie. Joey refuses to answer him. Jake then questions his wife and she sarcastically tells him she has slept with the whole neighbourhood,

82 Mirror Mirror

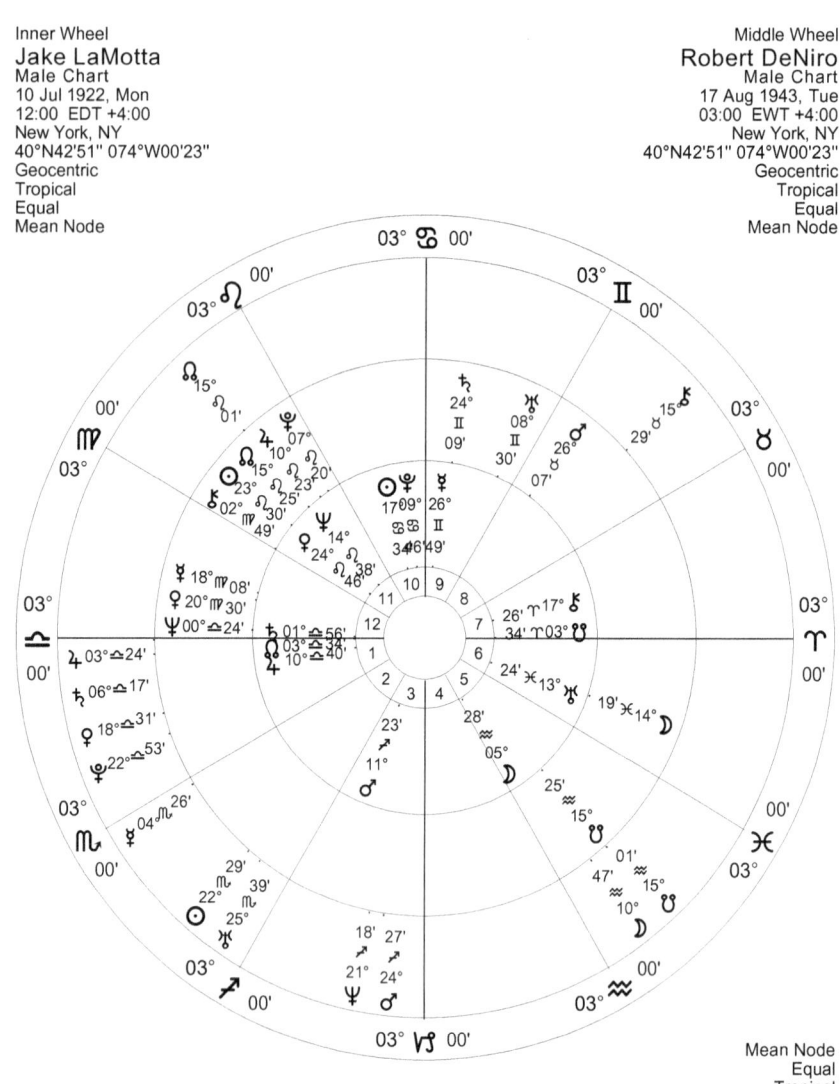

including his brother and several associates. Jake goes to his brother's house and beats him up in front of his wife and children then returns home and knocks his wife unconscious.

After winning a gruelling fifteen-round bout a few years later, Jake tries to make amends with his brother by telephone. However, he wrongly assumes the person on the other end of the telephone is Salvy rather than his own brother; Jake hurls insults down the line at the person he thinks is Salvy until eventually Joey silently hangs up the phone. From there, Jake's career takes a downturn and he retires.

Jake and his family move away but on one occasion he stays out all night; Vickie asks for a divorce and leaves him, taking the children with her. Jake is arrested for bringing underage girls to a club and tries to use the jewels from his championship belt to bribe the police. He is sent to jail and upon release tracks down his brother, and again asks for forgiveness.

The movie ends with Jake reciting "I could have been a contender" from *On the Waterfront* then shadowboxing, saying "I am the boss".

Within a two-degree orb, LaMotta's Sun in Cancer is conjunct DeNiro's ascendant. Within one degree, DeNiro's Moon in Pisces is conjunct the boxer's Uranus and his Neptune in Libra is conjunct LaMotta's Saturn. Additionally, the actor's North Node in Leo is conjunct the boxer's Neptune, which strengthens the karmic connection between the actor and the role he played.

Natally, LaMotta had a Saturn, North Node and Jupiter conjunction in Libra. When the film was released both Jupiter and Saturn in Libra had transited this conjunction. It was hoped, as the title mentions a bull, that the charts involved would show plenty of action in the sign of Taurus. Chiron, the Wounded Healer, was in Taurus and was in a square aspect to DeNiro's Nodes and LaMotta's Neptune in Leo. This is a film about an aging boxer remembering all the pain he suffered in his career.

DeNiro has Mars in Taurus conjunct the fixed star Algol (which rages very well on its own) and Uranus was in opposition in Scorpio when the film was released. DeNiro's Sun was conjunct LaMotta's Venus in Leo, both in a square aspect to the Mars/Algol conjunction. This was a disturbingly violent film befitting of its connections to the most malefic star in the heavens.

Despite its violence, the film was nominated for Best Picture at the Academy Awards and Robert DeNiro won Best Actor.

VENUS

In mythology, Venus was the goddess of love and beauty. Astrologically, it can tell us much about our relationships, as we see with Iris Murdoch (Kate Winslet/Judi Dench) and her husband John Bayley (Hugh Bonneville/Jim Broadbent) in *Iris*. Winslet, who played Iris as a young woman, had her Venus within six degrees of the author's own Venus in Virgo. Oscar Wilde and Stephen Fry have not only a Moon conjunction in Leo but also a Venus conjunction in Libra, the sign the planet rules.

The films in this section also feature beautiful women such as Michelle Williams as Marilyn Monroe in *My Week With Marilyn*. Monroe's Venus in Aries is sextile Williams' Jupiter/ascendant in Aquarius, showing a strong connection. Natalie Portman as Jacqueline Kennedy Onassis in *Jackie* has Sun/Venus conjunction in Gemini. Our values are also reflected in Venus as we see in *Diamond Jim*, with the actor and real-life person having their Venus in opposition within just a few degrees of orb. A Venus opposition also shows in *Lady Sings the Blues* with Billie Holiday and Diana Ross. In *Stand and Deliver*, a love of learning shows with the actor's (Edward James Olmos) Venus in a tight conjunction with the teacher's (Jaime Escalante) Mercury. The Dolly Sisters were twins but they were portrayed by different actresses. June Haver (who played Rosie), had Venus in Taurus conjunct the North Node of the twins, while Betty Grable (who played the tragic Jenny) had her MC on the fixed star Algol.

DIAMOND JIM

"Diamond Jim" Brady: 12 August 1856, 22:00, New York. A: RR
Edward Arnold: 18 February 1890, no time, New York City.
Source: Wikipedia
Release date: 2 September 1935

Jim Brady was born into poverty and orphaned at a young age. Around the time of his Saturn Return he is working as a baggage handler for a railroad company, but one day on a whim he rents a suit and some flashy jewellery from a pawn shop. He then leaves his job to become a

Venus 85

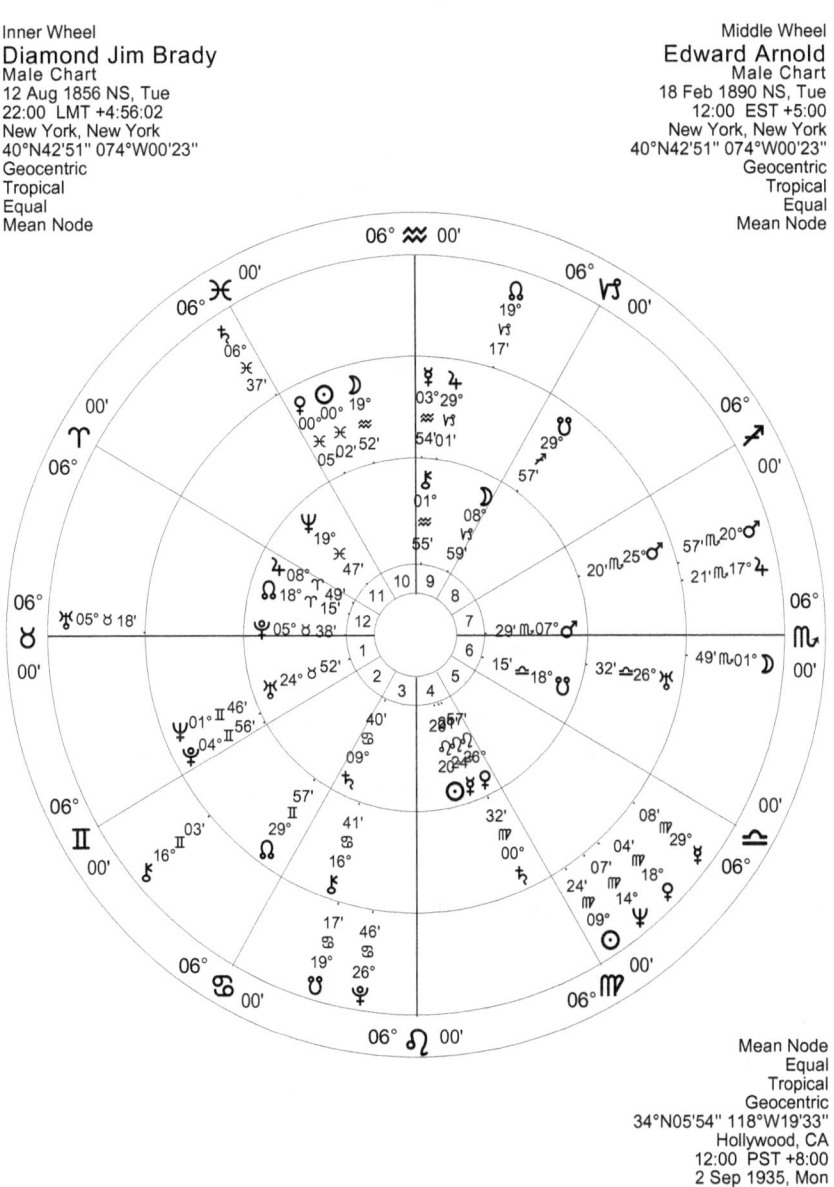

salesman for another company, where he proves to be highly successful. The time of the Saturn Return is often when a person gets the idea they need to change their lives. For Brady, it is the start of a life full of drama, gambling and chasing beautiful women.

While on a business trip, Brady encounters a con artist who is trying to take advantage of a colleague. Brady manages to save his friend from the fraud but they both have to jump from the train to escape. Brady discovers his friend is selling 'undertrucks' to railroad companies and, seeing an opportunity, he takes on the product to sell. It's a highly successful venture and Brady intends to invest his fortune by marrying his sweetheart. Unfortunately, he discovers she is already engaged. Heartbroken, he devotes himself to his business for distraction. Brady continues to find success and he begins to have diamond jewellery made for him, which leads to his nickname, Diamond Jim. Diamond Jim wants for nothing. He spends money, loses money through gambling and bad investments, chases women – and eats.

Eventually Brady meets a singer called Lillian Russell and he begins promoting her, to great success. He also falls in love with Jane, a woman who looks very like his former girlfriend and he proposes to her. However he is suspicious of her relationship with a banker. Drunk and raging with jealousy, he calls off the marriage the night before their wedding. The couple repair their friendship but she refuses his subsequent proposals. She has fallen in love with Jerry, a mutual friend, but neither can bear to hurt Diamond Jim's feelings with the news.

When the stock market crashes, Diamond Jim loses his fortune, but he is a clever enough businessman that he is able to re-build his life and fortune, despite a near fatal accident that leaves him hospitalised for a full year. He plans a trip to Europe for himself, Jane, Lillian and Jerry fully believing Jane will marry him. Instead, Jane and Jerry tell him they are in love. Heartbroken, Diamond Jim asks Lillian to marry him but she too refuses him. Diamond Jim is devastated and depressed, and returns home to eat himself to death, but before he dies he destroys all the IOUs in his possession.

Brady had Taurus, a sign known for its love of the finer things in life, as his ascendant. Pluto was conjunct his ascendant with Mars in opposition in Scorpio. Jupiter in Aries was the apex of the T-square with the Moon in Capricorn in opposition to Saturn in Cancer indicating he made up for the misery of his childhood with all the indulgences he could afford to buy. These astrological configurations would seem to at least partially account for his fluctuating fortunes – and expansive waistline. Brady also had Uranus conjunct the fixed star Algol which may explain his tumultuous love life with women who were out of his reach. A stellium in the last ten degrees of Leo could help explain Brady's ostentatious displays of wealth as he worked to amass it.

Edward Arnold's natal Mars in Scorpio was opposite to Brady's Uranus in Taurus. The actor's Venus/Sun conjunction was exactly opposite Saturn in Virgo which in turn was conjunct Brady's Venus in Leo within three degrees.

Edward Arnold was a huge man and he had often said that the heavier he became, the more roles he was offered. His signature role was the rotund rich man which he reprised for the film *Lillian Russell* in 1940. Uranus was transiting Brady's Pluto and ascendant when the film was released. Interestingly, 2021 marks the Uranus return of the film which may bring about a renewed interest in it.

IRIS

Iris Murdoch: 15 July 1919, 08:00, Dublin, Ireland. A: RR
Kate Winslet (young Iris): 5 October 1975, no time, Reading, England. DD: Craft
Judi Dench: 9 December 1934, no time, York, England. Source: Wikipedia
John Bayley: 27 March 1925, no time, Lahore, Punjab, India. Source: Wikipedia
Hugh Bonneville (young John): 10 November 1963, no time, London. Source: Wikipedia
Jim Broadbent: 24 May 1949, no time, Holton cum Beckering, England. Source: Wikipedia
Release date: 14 December 2001

Young Iris and John meet at Somerville College, Oxford; he is in awe of and occasionally repulsed by her free-spiritedness and refusal to conform. However, it is obvious she is talented and she is a good foil to his timid and repressed nature. Eventually they get married and she becomes

88 Mirror Mirror

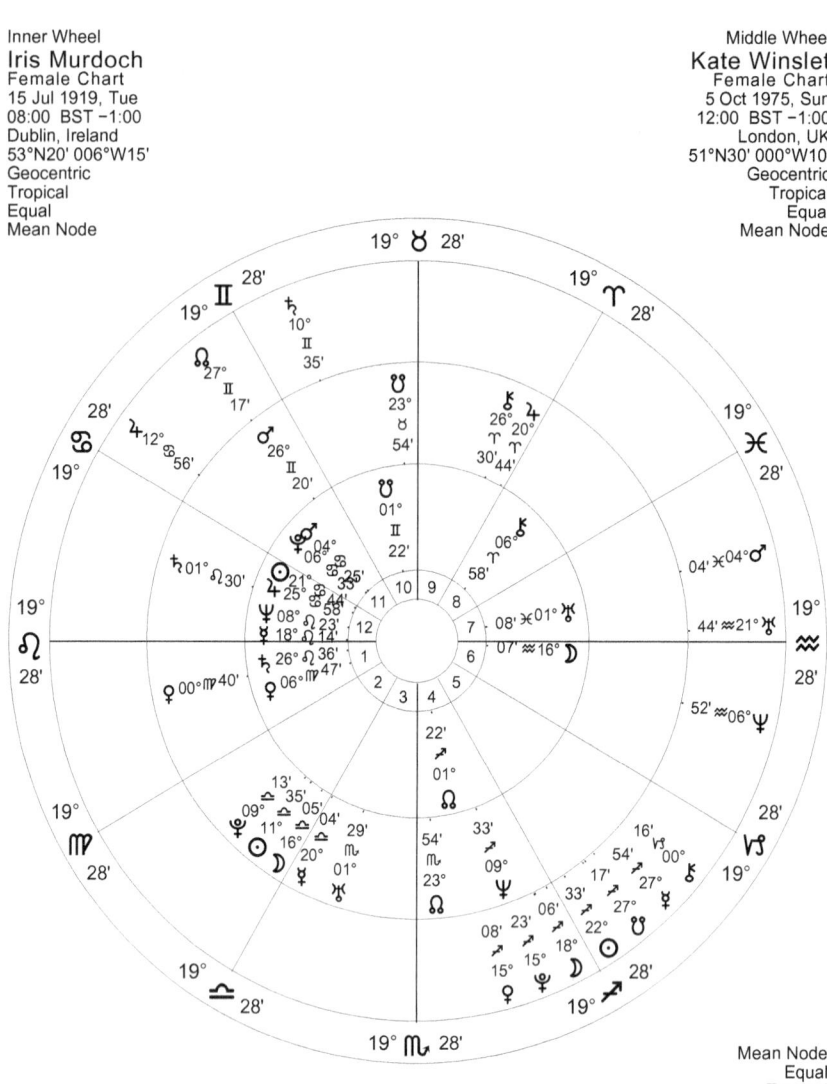

Venus 89

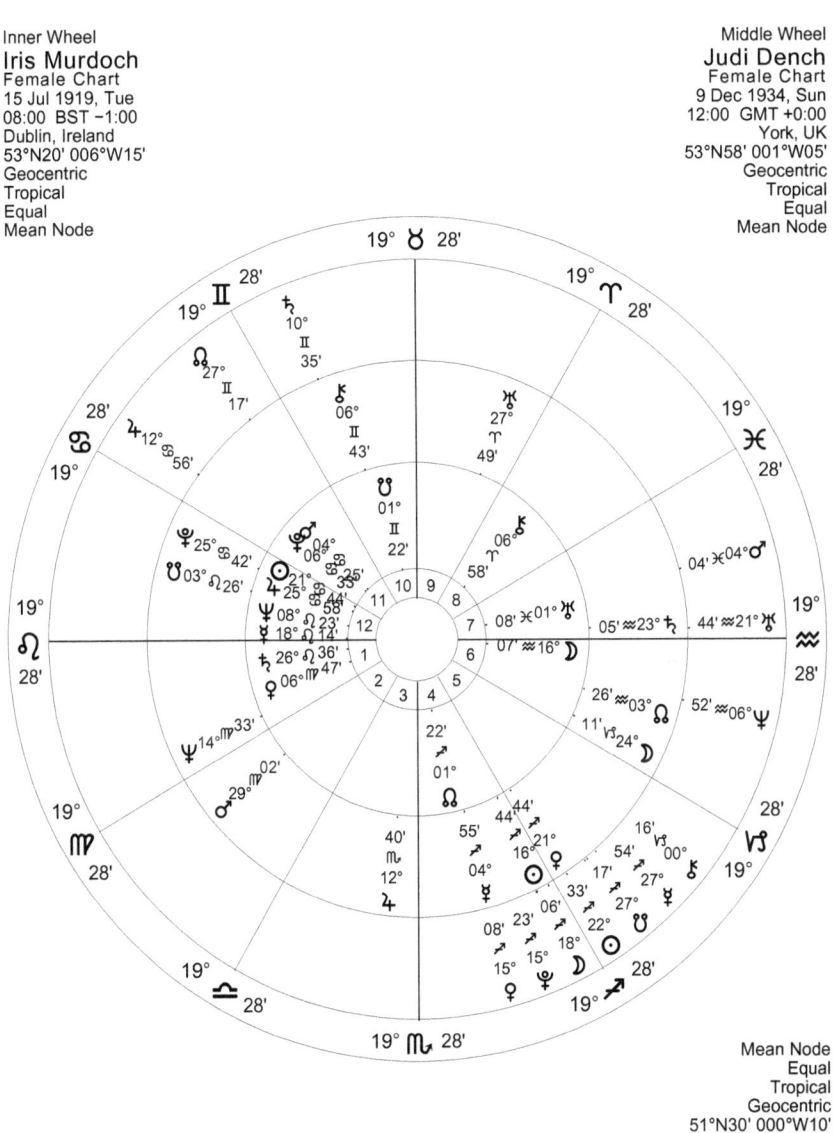

90 Mirror Mirror

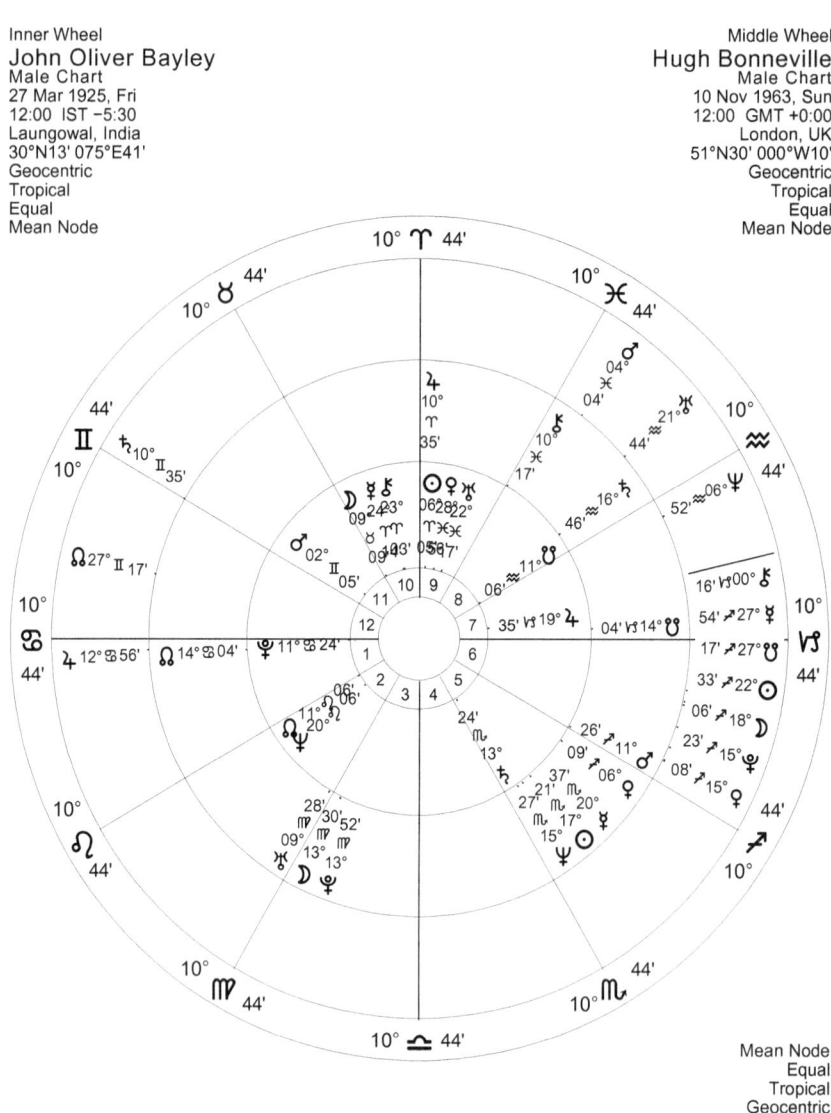

Venus 91

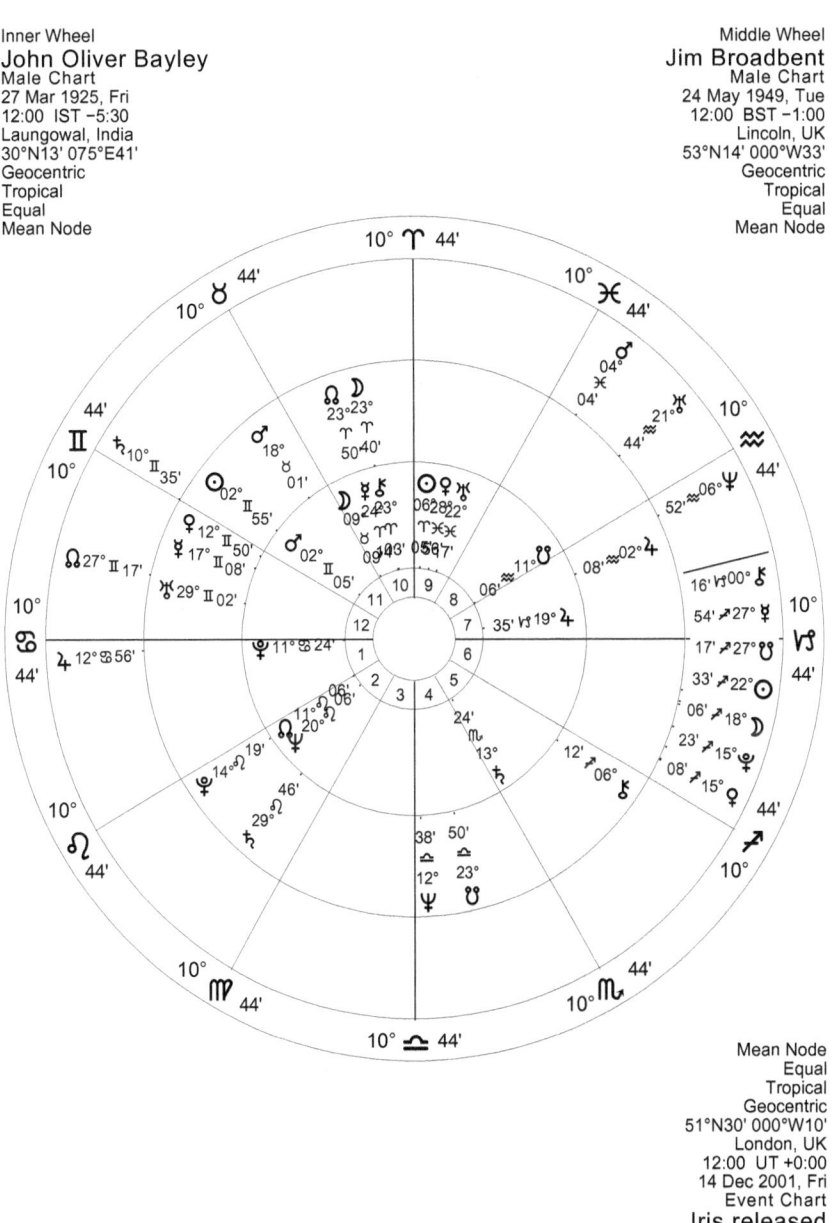

famous as an author. Many years later, the early stages of dementia begin to set in, and Iris becomes increasingly dependent on John as her carer.

Kate Winslet's Venus in Virgo was opposite Murdoch's Uranus within an orb of one degree. Winslet portrayed the rebellious part of Murdoch's life – skinny dipping, engaging in controversial behaviour and always arguing for the things she felt were right even if it went against how society thought a young woman should behave. On the film's release, transiting Neptune in Aquarius was opposite Murdoch's Neptune in Leo.

By contrast, Judi Dench plays the Murdoch who has been transformed by the ravages of Alzheimer's. The actress' Pluto in Cancer is exactly conjunct the author's Jupiter. Dench is portraying a woman for whom the learning process no longer functions normally. When the film was released, transiting Uranus in Aquarius was conjunct the actress' Saturn as well as the writer's descendant.

With an orb of nearly four degrees, Hugh Bonneville, who plays John Bayley as a young man, has Saturn in Aquarius opposite Bayley's Neptune, perhaps representing the passing of time in this role. Bonneville's natal North Node in Cancer is conjunct Bayley's natal Pluto, and Jupiter transited these points when the film was released.

Jim Broadbent's North Node in Aries is conjunct Bayley's Mercury/Chiron conjunction and the actor's Sun in Gemini is exactly conjunct Bayley's Mars. When the film was released, transiting Venus/Pluto in Sagittarius was opposite Broadbent's Venus/Mercury in Gemini. Transiting Uranus in Aquarius was opposite Bayley's Neptune.

Dench and Winslet were nominated for Best Actress and Best Supporting Actress respectively. Jim Broadbent won the Oscar for Best Supporting Actor.

JACKIE

Jacqueline Kennedy-Onassis: 28 July 1929, 14:30, Southampton, New York. A: McEvoy
Natalie Portman: 9 June 1981, no time, Jerusalem, Israel.
X: Treindl
Release date: 7 September 2016 (Venice)

Shortly after her husband's assassination, Jacqueline Kennedy is visited by a reporter to be interviewed about her husband's legacy. She reflects

Venus 93

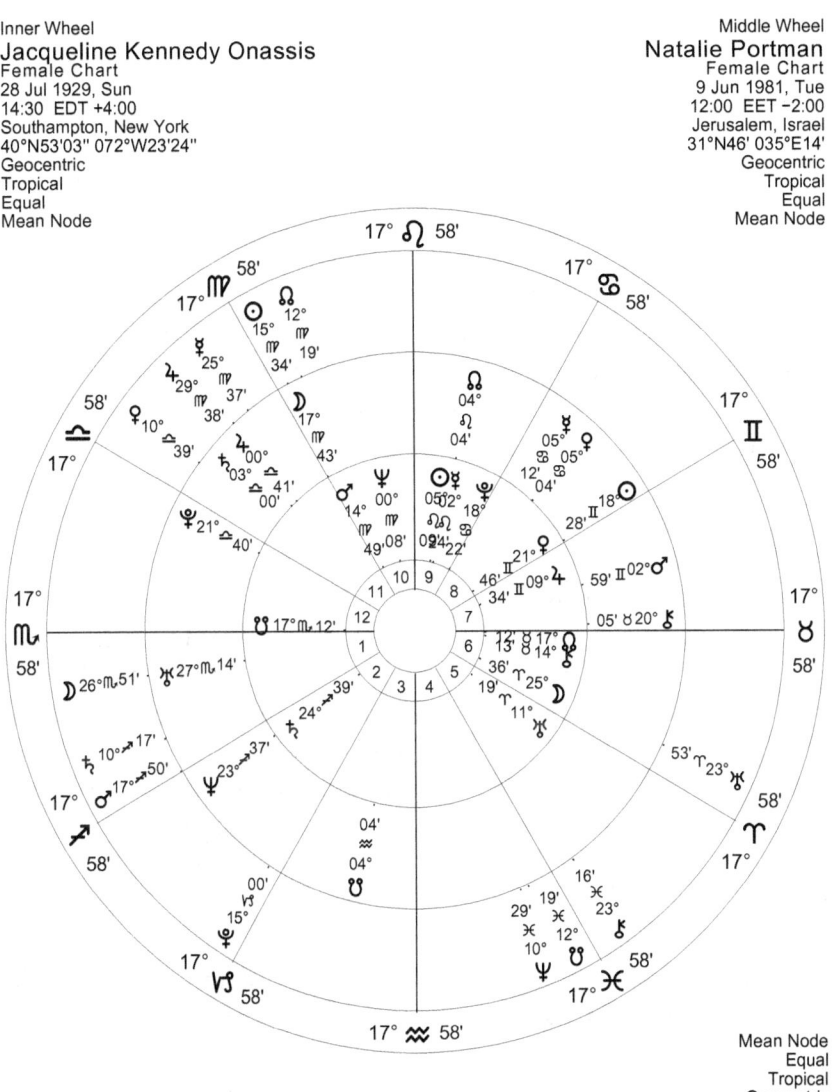

on the televised White House tour and the reporter asks about the assassination. Describing her shock and horror, she speaks about the events prior to the assassination. We see Jacqueline being comforted by members of the White House; her brother-in-law Robert comes to escort her back to Washington, and she expresses her concern for her children.

Robert has to deal with his own grief as he helps Jacqueline plan the funeral and look after the family. She relies heavily on alcohol and pills to help her sleep and seeks spiritual counsel from a priest. Robert and the newly sworn-in president and his wife see the murder of Lee Harvey Oswald on live television. Knowing how fragile Jacqueline is, Robert insists that he must be the person to tell her the news. However, she finds out on her own and is angry at him for withholding the news from her.

Jacqueline tells her priest that she has contemplated suicide and that she feels unbearable guilt for not protecting her husband.

At the end of the interview, Jacqueline tells the reporter that she has the right to control what parts of the interview are published in the press.

The film ends with Jacqueline re-interring the coffins of her miscarried and stillborn children next to her husband.

Portman's Sun in Gemini is conjunct Onassis' Venus which seems appropriate for these beautiful, eloquent women. Portman's North Node in Leo is conjunct Onassis' Mercury and Sun, and her Pluto in Libra is in opposition to Onassis' Moon in Aries. This is a perfect expression of Portman's acting skills and her ability to communicate Onassis' grief over the loss of her husband. Portman's Neptune in Sagittarius is conjunct Onassis' Saturn and so the glamour of Hollywood seems to obscure the banality of real life.

The movie was released as Uranus transited Onassis' Moon in Aries, giving us a unique insight into the marriage of this power couple. Transiting Pluto was within just a few degrees of opposition to her natal Pluto.

Transiting Mars in Sagittarius was in opposition to Portman's Sun in Gemini, perhaps giving her a little shot of confidence to help her portray one of America's most beautiful and beloved First Ladies.

Portman was nominated for an Oscar for best actress for her performance.

LADY SINGS THE BLUES
Billie Holiday: 7 April 1915, 02:30, Philadelphia. AA: RR
Diana Ross: 26 March 1944, 23:46, Detroit, Michigan. AA: CAH
Release date: 12 October 1972

Billie Holiday is perhaps best known for her musical talents, and sadly also for the drug addiction which eventually killed her. She has a natal stellium of planets in Pisces with Diana Ross' Venus in Pisces in the middle of these planets. However, make no mistake, both of these divas were Aries women who could fight their own corners. Ross' Mercury is in fact conjunct Holiday's Sun within an orb of one degree and thus she becomes the voice for Holiday.

As a young teenager, Holiday works as a cleaner in a brothel until she is raped by a man who follows her home. Her mother places her in another brothel, but Holiday realises she can make more money by becoming a prostitute instead. Growing tired of that life too, she later quits and auditions to sing in a night club. Eventually her beautiful singing voice is recognised and her career is launched. However, her experiences on tour lead to her taking drugs and eventually she becomes addicted. After the death of her mother, she checks herself into a rehabilitation centre. Unfortunately, she is arrested on a narcotics charge and removed from the clinic. She endures severe withdrawal symptoms in hospital then finishes her prison sentence. After returning home, she marries and tells her friends she doesn't want to perform again.

However, after a quiet period, the lure of performing becomes too strong; she wants to arrange a comeback tour, but her membership to sing at clubs in New York has been withdrawn due to her drugs charges. Her husband arranges a cross-country tour to restore public confidence in her, but while he's away trying to sort out a performance at Carnegie Hall, Holiday falls back into her old addictions.

Frail and traumatised by a bad drug deal, Holiday performs for a huge crowd at Carnegie Hall. However, her membership is never renewed and further appeals are denied. She is re-arrested on drugs charges and eventually dies at the age of forty-four.

Lady Sings the Blues was released during Ross' and Holiday's Saturn returns. Venus was transiting Ross' MC in Virgo which opposed her own

Mirror Mirror

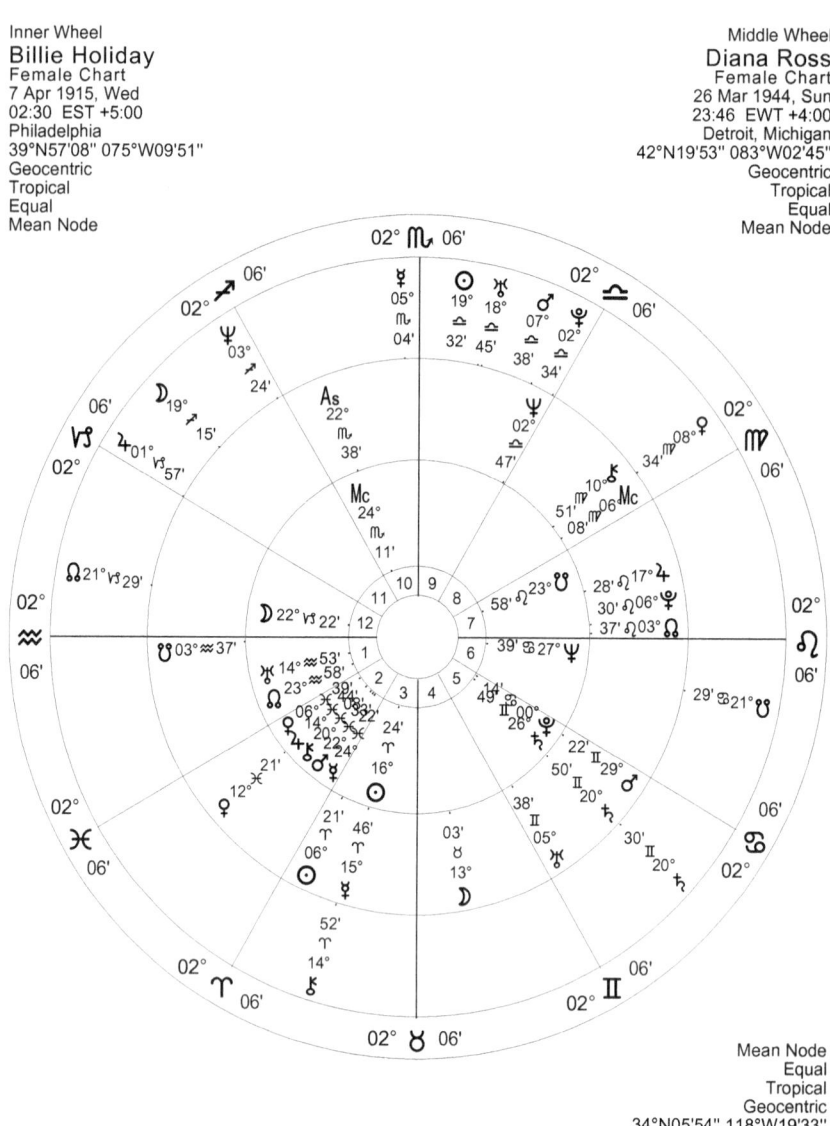

Venus and Holiday's stellium in Pisces. Chiron was transiting Holiday's Sun and Ross' Mercury in Aries.

Ross was nominated for an Academy Award for Best Actress and *God Bless the Child* is on the AFI's list of 100 years...100 songs.

MY WEEK WITH MARILYN
Marilyn Monroe: 1 June 1926, 09:30, Los Angeles, California.
AA: RR
Michelle Williams: 9 September 1980, 18:15, Kalispell, Montana.
AA: Viktor
Release date: 9 October 2011

Aspiring filmmaker Colin Clark travels to London in the hope of working with Laurence Olivier on his next production. Although he is told that there are no jobs available, Clark decides to wait and see Olivier himself to ask him in person. Olivier's wife Vivien Leigh takes pity on the young man and tells her husband to give him a job on his next film, *The Prince and the Showgirl*, starring Marilyn Monroe. Clark's job involves finding a home for Marilyn (and her playwright husband Arthur Miller) while they are in London for filming. The press discover the home but Clark has cleverly secured a second one for them which impresses his employer.

From the moment Marilyn lands at Heathrow, it is clear she is going to be mobbed by the press. Although she is uncomfortable with so many photographers, she does manage to relax at the press conference. Her lack of professionalism on the film set is frustrating to Olivier but everyone else is in awe of her. Clark asks Lucy, Marilyn's wardrobe assistant, out on a date. Marilyn becomes more difficult for Olivier to manage and he causes her to leave the set after insulting her. The other actors defend Marilyn and even Clark asks him to be more sympathetic towards her.

After Marilyn walks out, Clark goes to her house to check on her and finds the actress in tears over an argument she's had with her husband. Miller has written a play that seems to mock his wife and he returns to the United States shortly afterwards. Meanwhile, Vivien Leigh argues with her husband and even breaks down as she tells him that Marilyn lights up the screen with her mere presence.

98 Mirror Mirror

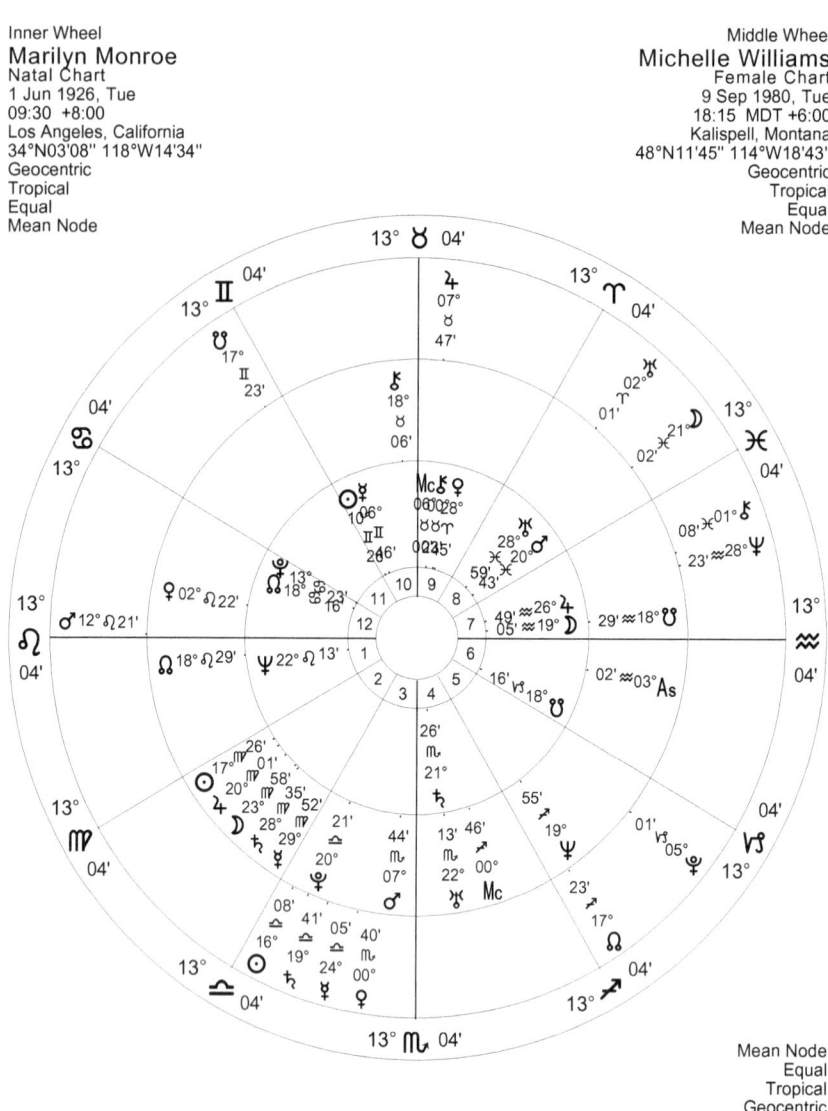

Marilyn fails to show up for filming after her husband's departure, but she asks Clark to come and speak with her in private. Once back on set, Marilyn performs a dance that captures everyone's attention and Clark is warned that she will break his heart. Lucy also notices he is captivated by Marilyn and she dumps him.

Clark and Marilyn visit various famous London sights together and they go skinny dipping in the Thames. Marilyn kisses Clark, at which point they are discovered by her bodyguard.

One evening, Marilyn locks herself in her room again and Clark is called to speak to her. He finds her in bed and she invites him to lie down next to her. In the morning, she wakes up in pain and explains she is having a miscarriage. After a doctor has been to see her, Marilyn tells Clark that her husband is coming back and that they should forget anything has happened between them.

When Marilyn finishes filming, Olivier reveals that she has killed any desire he had for directing. Marilyn comes to a local pub to personally thank Clark for his help. She kisses him goodbye and returns to the United States.

Williams' Saturn/Mercury conjunction in Virgo is opposite Monroe's Uranus in Pisces, a stabilising influence on her erratic behaviour as depicted in the film. Williams' South Node in Aquarius is also conjunct Monroe's Moon. Aquarius is the sign associated with doing things one's own way and with Jupiter expanding this tendency we can understand Olivier's growing exasperation with Monroe. Monroe is known for her enduring beauty so it is appropriate that Jupiter in Taurus was conjunct her MC when the film was released. To add a bit of sex appeal, Williams' Uranus in Scorpio is within one degree of Monroe's Saturn. Transiting Mars in Leo was within one degree of Monroe's ascendant when the film was released and transiting Saturn was conjunct Williams' Pluto in Libra. The transiting North Node was conjunct Williams' Neptune by two degrees.

Michelle Williams won a Golden Globe and was nominated for an Academy Award for Best Actress.

STAND AND DELIVER

**Jaime Escalante: 31 December 1930, no time, La Paz, Bolivia.
Source: Wikipedia
Edward James Olmos: 24 February 1947, 01:05, Los Angeles, California. AA: RR
Release date: 13 February 1988**

Based on a true story, Maths teacher Jaime Escalante leaves a higher paid job to work at a school with a mainly Hispanic population coming from a working class background. The students function far below national academic standards, and worse, are completely disinterested in learning. Escalante wants to change school expectations to help the students excel academically. Realising his Maths pupils have untapped potential, he sets them the goal of taking the Advance Placement Calculus exam by the end of their senior year. Embracing the philosophy of *ganas* (motivation), he works towards changing their mind-set.

Escalante sets up summer school classes and despite the cynicism and concerns over raising unattainable expectations, every pupil passes the AP Calculus exam, a first for the school. However, because similar mistakes are made amongst the students, the Educational Testing Service suggests that the pupils cheated. Escalante defends his students and believes the allegations were based on demographics and prejudice – he offers to have the students re-take the exam. After several months and with only a day's notice, all the pupils pass the exam again, ending all suspicion of cheating.

Escalante's Venus in Scorpio is conjunct Olmos' Jupiter within an orb of one degree and his Mercury in Capricorn is on the actor's Venus, showing an understanding of motivation as well as the sheer hard work it would take to meet the challenge Escalante has set.

Neptune passed over Escalante's Sun in Capricorn when the movie was released, highlighting his inspirational work with underprivileged students.

Olmos was nominated for an Academy Award for Best Actor.

Venus 101

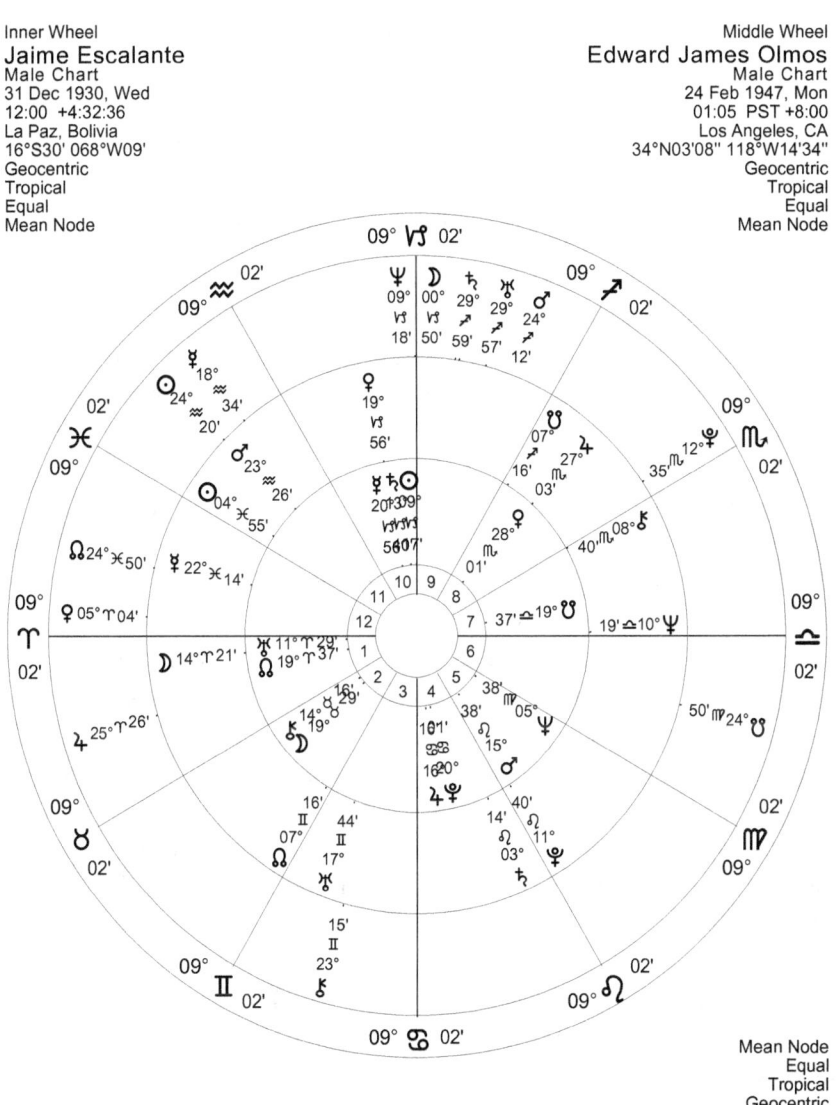

THE DOLLY SISTERS

Jenny and Rosie Dolly: 24 October 1892, no time, Balassagyarmat, Hungary. Source: Wikipedia
Betty Grable, (Jenny Dolly): 18 December 1916, 21:40, Saint Louis, Missouri. AA: RR
June Haver (Rosie Dolly): 10 June 1926, 21:12, Rock Island, Illinois. AA: Steinbrecher
Release date: 14 November 1945

The Dolly Sisters were identical twins from Hungary who made it big as young singing and dancing Vaudeville stars in the early twentieth century. Although they had fairly similar lives and interests, they died almost exactly a Saturn Return apart. They were noted for their extravagances and their high profile affairs with wealthy men. The sisters were also known to deliberately schedule individual performances at the same time in order to create the illusion of sibling rivalry. This seemed to work as they were highly successful and wildly popular.

Identical twin studies are interesting because no matter how identical they may look, each twin will find a part of their shared astrology chart to play. In *The Dolly Sisters*, each twin was played by a different actress, which seems appropriate as the sisters had very different lives. Rosie was married three times and Jenny was married twice. Although Jenny was a fairly successful gambler, hers was the tragic life cut short by first a serious car accident and then suicide in 1941.

June Haver played Rosie and with Venus in Taurus conjunct Rosie's North Node opposing Rosie's Mercury in Scorpio, it would seem the actress was able to understand the excesses and intense love life of this twin.

Although ten years older than Haver, Betty Grable played Jenny. The Wounded Healer Chiron in this twin's chart is conjunct Betty's ascendant. Jenny's car accident essentially bankrupted her and after falling into depression, she hanged herself. *The Dolly Sisters* was released in 1945, a few years after Jenny's death and as Venus in Scorpio transited the Sun of the sisters. It was a musical and the script did not cover her tragic end. The film was nominated for AFI's list of Greatest Movie Musicals of All Time.

Venus 103

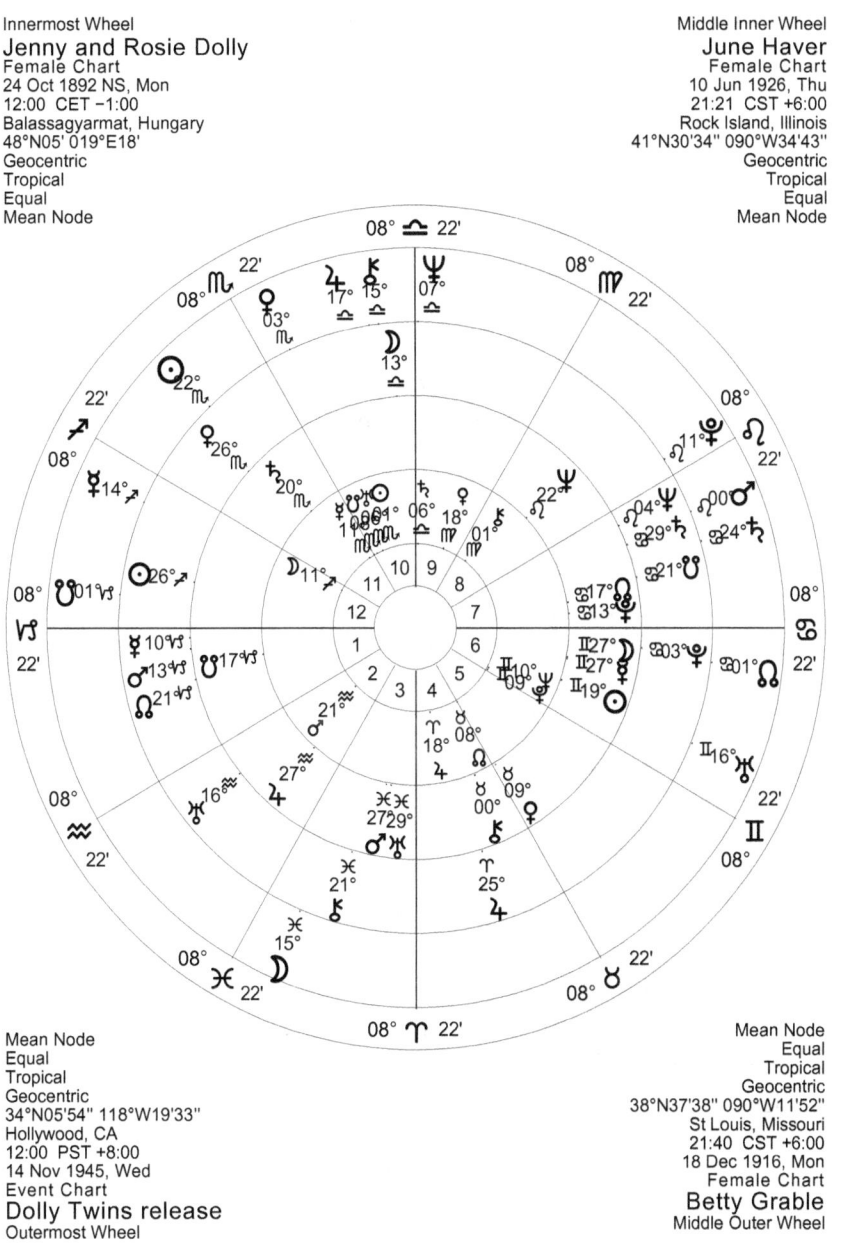

WILDE

Oscar Wilde: 16 October 1854, 03:00, Dublin, Ireland. C: RR
Stephen Fry: 24 August 1957, 06:00, London. B: Scholfield
Lord Alfred Douglas: 22 October 1870, 19:42, Worcester, England.
A: RR
Jude Law: 29 December 1972, 06:00, Lewisham, England.
C: deJabrum
Release date: 15 October 1997

The film begins with Wilde's lecture tour of the United States, during which he successfully entertains local silver miners with stories about a legendary Renaissance silversmith called Benvenuto Cellini. Wilde returns to London, marries Constance Lloyd and the couple have two sons in close succession. Throughout the film, parts of the children's story, *The Selfish Giant*, is part of the narrative with Wilde recounting it to his children.

Wilde is seduced by a young male guest who has been staying with them. On the opening night of his play, *Lady Windermere's Fan*, Wilde is re-acquainted with an aristocratic young poet, Lord Alfred Douglas, and they fall in love. Douglas often hires rent boys for sex, while Wilde watches on in secret.

The poet's father publically objects to his son's relationship with Wilde and denounces him at the theatre opening of *The Importance of Being Earnest*. Wilde sues for criminal libel but, with his homosexuality exposed, he is tried and convicted of gross indecency. Sentenced to two years' hard labour, he is visited by his wife who tells him she is taking her children to Germany and that he is welcome to visit, provided he never sees Douglas again. When Wilde is released, he goes into exile in Europe, where despite warnings and objections, he continues to see Douglas.

The film ends with Wilde narrating the end of *The Selfish Giant*.

Remarkably, Wilde and Fry both have Venus in rulership in Libra only two degrees apart. Their Leo Moons are within three degrees and square Wilde's Mercury (in Scorpio) opposition to Uranus, also conjunct Fry's nodal axis. It has been called the role that Fry was born to perform.

Law's Pluto in Libra is conjunct Douglas' Moon.

When the film was released, transiting Pluto was conjunct Law's natal Neptune and transiting Neptune opposed Douglas' natal Uranus in Cancer. Fry won a Golden Globe for Best Actor.

Venus 105

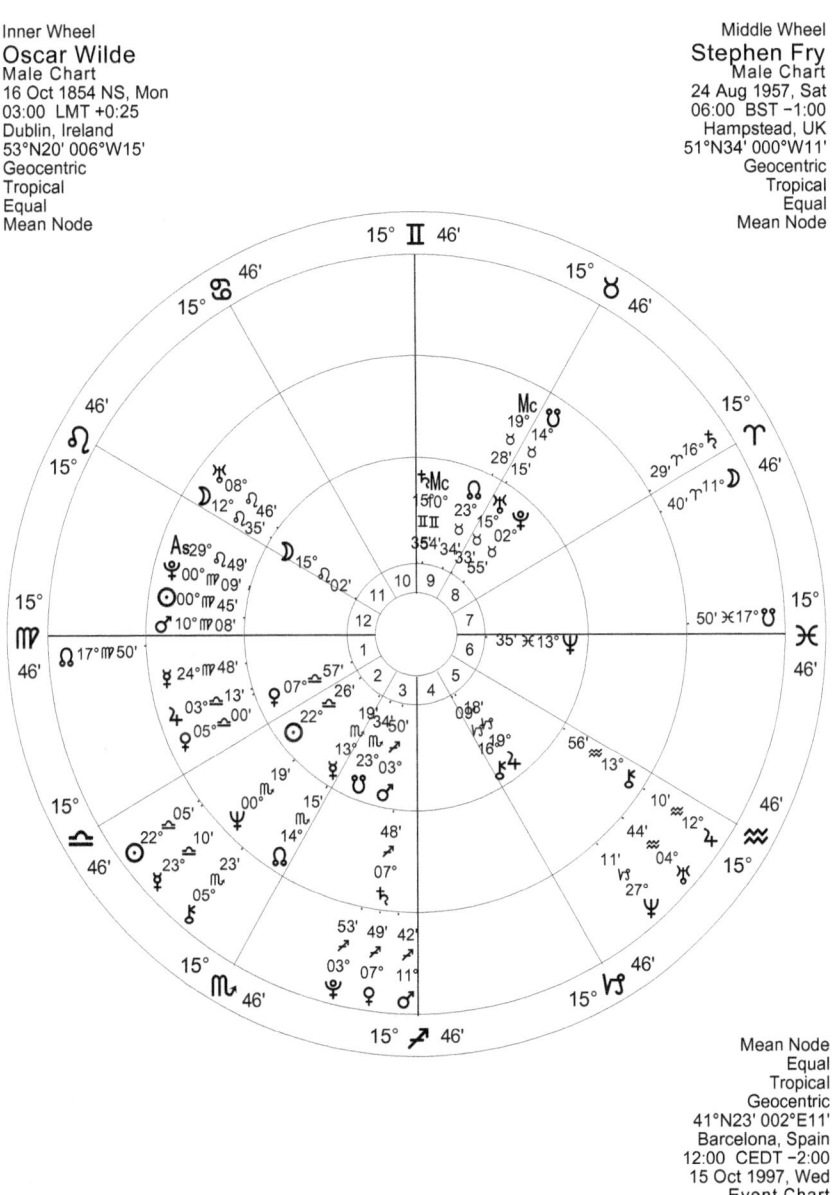

106 Mirror Mirror

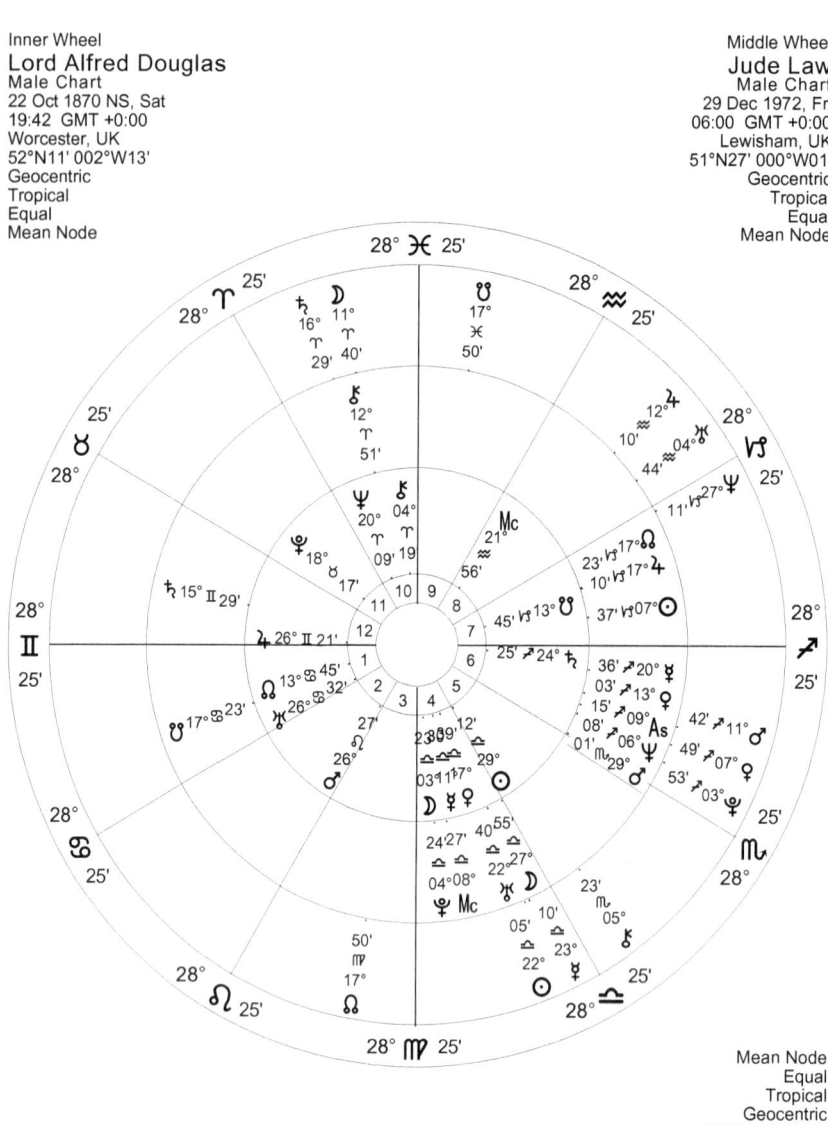

MERCURY

Mercury was the god of communication whose complicated messages were often known to drive humans to either elation or confusion. Films with themes of double messages seem to fit the idiom 'don't shoot the messenger' and these find their home under the winged feet of the messenger of the gods.

Bohemian Rhapsody (Rami Malek) which features the voice and music of Freddie Mercury, whose vocal talents helped create one of the biggest live concerts in history, is a suitable fit in this section. The actor and singer not only have a Sun/Moon conjunction but incredibly Freddie has an exalted Mercury on his descendant with Malek's equally exalted Mercury on the singer's MC. No wonder Malek won an Oscar! In *Frances*, writer and rebel Frances Farmer (Jessica Lange) had Saturn in Gemini (ruled by Mercury) in opposition to the actress' Venus/Mercury conjunction in Sagittarius. The refined Princess Grace in *Grace of Monaco* (Nicole Kidman) had to find her own voice in an unfamiliar culture, and she had a powerful connection to the actress' Mercury. Musician Bix Beiderbeck (Kirk Douglas in *Young Man With a Horn*) had his Uranus exactly conjunct the Mercury of the actor who portrayed him. The spy *Mata Hari* (Greta Garbo) had a natal Mercury/Mars conjunction in Leo and the actress' Venus was within one degree. No wonder this pair received so much attention!

BOHEMIAN RHAPSODY
Farrokh Bulsara (Freddie Mercury): 5 September 1946, 05:50, Zanzibar, Tunisia. A: Scholfield
Rami Malek: 12 May 1981, 08:41 Torrance, California. AA: Viktor
Release date: 23 October 2018, Wembley Stadium

Bohemian Rhapsody chronicles the life of Queen's lead singer, Freddie Mercury, as he rises to stardom – culminating in his unforgettable live performance at Live Aid on 13 July 1985 at Wembley Arena.

The film begins with Farrokh's early days as a baggage handler at Heathrow Airport and meeting Mary Austin, Brian May and Roger Taylor at a club. Farrokh demonstrates his vocals, and May and Taylor are so impressed that Farrokh becomes part of their band. With Mary's advice Farrokh begins experimenting with his stage costumes, eventually developing a signature style, and they begin to date.

Without any money, the band sell their van to buy space at a recording studio and they cut their first record. They change the band's name to Queen and Farrokh legally changes his name to Freddie Mercury. The band eventually hire Elton John's manager, John Reid, and have a hit record after appearing on *Top of the Pops*. Freddy and Mary become engaged and the band start touring. After their fourth successful album, the band want to experiment with opera but the music executive of their studio doesn't like *Bohemian Rhapsody* because it's too long. Freddie finds a DJ to play it and although the song receives mixed reviews, it eventually becomes a smash hit. Freddie begins an affair with Paul, the band's day-to-day manager, during their world tour and breaks up with Mary, though they promise to remain good friends.

As their fame continues to rise, Freddie becomes more dependent on drugs and alcohol, and his desire to break out into other genres of music causes tensions within the band. During an extravagant party, Freddie meets a man named Jim who tells Freddie to come back once he's learned to like himself. Freddie also fires Reid when he suggests Freddie record as a solo artist like Michael Jackson. Further difficulties arise when their video *I Want to Break Free* is banned from MTV. Following this, Freddie announces to the band that he is going solo after all, and the band break up.

Mary grows concerned for Freddie's deteriorating health and urges him to return to the band to perform at *Live Aid*. When Freddie discovers that Paul has deliberately kept news about *Live Aid* from him, he decides to sever all ties with him. Paul retaliates by going to the press with details about Freddie's sexuality and debauched behaviour. After some thinking time, Freddie finds Jim again and they became close.

When the band re-unite, Freddie tells them that he has been diagnosed with HIV and that they should keep the news to themselves so the media frenzy doesn't overshadow their music.

The film ends with their performance at *Live Aid*. Title cards inform the audience that Freddie had remained close to Mary and Jim and that the Mercury Phoenix Trust was founded in his honour.

Rami Malek portrayed Mercury and the connections to the planet Mercury couldn't be more spectacular. Freddie's natal Mercury, in its rulership, is conjunct his own ascendant in Virgo. Malek's Mercury, in its rulership, is conjunct Freddie's MC in Gemini. They have a Sun/Moon conjunction in Virgo – ruled by Mercury. No wonder audiences forgot they were watching an actor when they saw the movie! Can it get any better? Well yes – transiting Venus was conjunct Freddie's MC (in Gemini) on the day of his *Live Aid* performance.

However, acting is more than simple mimicry. It takes stamina to stay in character and fortunately for Malek, his North Node is conjunct Freddie's Saturn. Malek was pretty much channelling Mercury's work as a performer. The sheer hard work and determination to sing with the vocal range of a superstar like Freddie Mercury is remarkable. That Sun/Moon conjunction would have been a huge help too.

Bohemian Rhapsody also details Freddie's descent into drugs and alcohol. His Moon in Sagittarius is within a four degree orb of Malek's Neptune. The modern interpretation of Neptune is associated with music, imagination and escapism. It is an etheric, soulful connection that assisted in bringing out the playfulness of Freddie's extravagant image and performances. Malek is not a singer by trade (although this may change!), so it would take a very confident actor to pull off such a performance.

Neptune was also on Malek's side when he won the Best Actor Academy Award on 24 February 2019: Neptune was transiting his MC by conjunction and was within a four degree orb of opposition to singer and actor's Sun/Moon conjunction.

110 Mirror Mirror

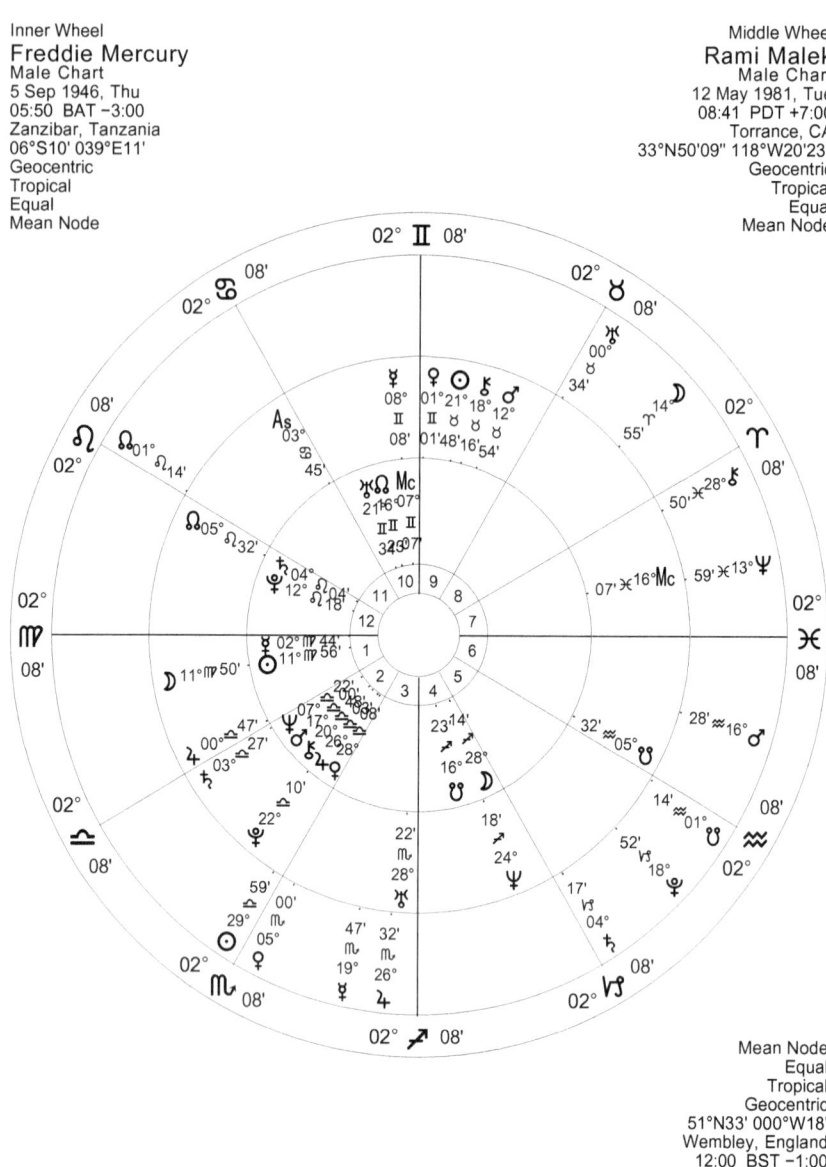

Important events in a person's life can often show up in a person's chart before they were born or even after the day. In Malek's case, *Live Aid* took place four years before he was born. However, the timed chart of Queen's performance (13 July 1985, 18:41, Wembley Arena) had Venus transiting Malek's (pre-natal) Mercury. Mercury, who had died twenty-seven years before the 91st Academy Awards, had transiting posthumous Uranus opposing his Venus in Libra when Malek won the Oscar for Best Actor. The movie has addressed Mercury's homosexuality in a way that couldn't be done when he was alive. Transiting Jupiter was at the midpoint of his South Node and natal Moon during the Academy Awards as well, bringing a sense of destined greatness to the event.

In addition to an Oscar, Malek won a Golden Globe, a Screen Actors Guild and a BAFTA for his performance. The film was nominated for an Oscar for Best Picture and won the same award at the Golden Globes as well as a BAFTA.

FRANCES

Frances Farmer: 19 September 1913, 04:45, Seattle, Washington.
AA: Wilsons
Jessica Lange: 20 April 1949, 11:00, Cloquet, Minnesota.
AA: Steinbrecher
Release date: 3 December 1982

Frances Farmer is a rebel as demonstrated by her award-winning high school essay *God Dies*. She wins an all-expenses paid trip to Moscow to visit the city's Art Theatre and decides to become an actress. However, she wants to conquer Hollywood on her own terms. Broadway playwright Clifford Odets, with whom she begins an affair, persuades her to join a theatre in New York. Farmer learns the world of the theatre and uses her notoriety to attract more ticket sales, but Odets replaces her with an actress from a wealthy family because the group needs more financial backing. When Odets' wife returns from Europe, he also ends their affair.

Farmer accepts uninspiring parts in a few low budget movies and begins to abuse alcohol and amphetamines. The continual pressure to cope with legal problems and her mother's constant criticism after she

112 Mirror Mirror

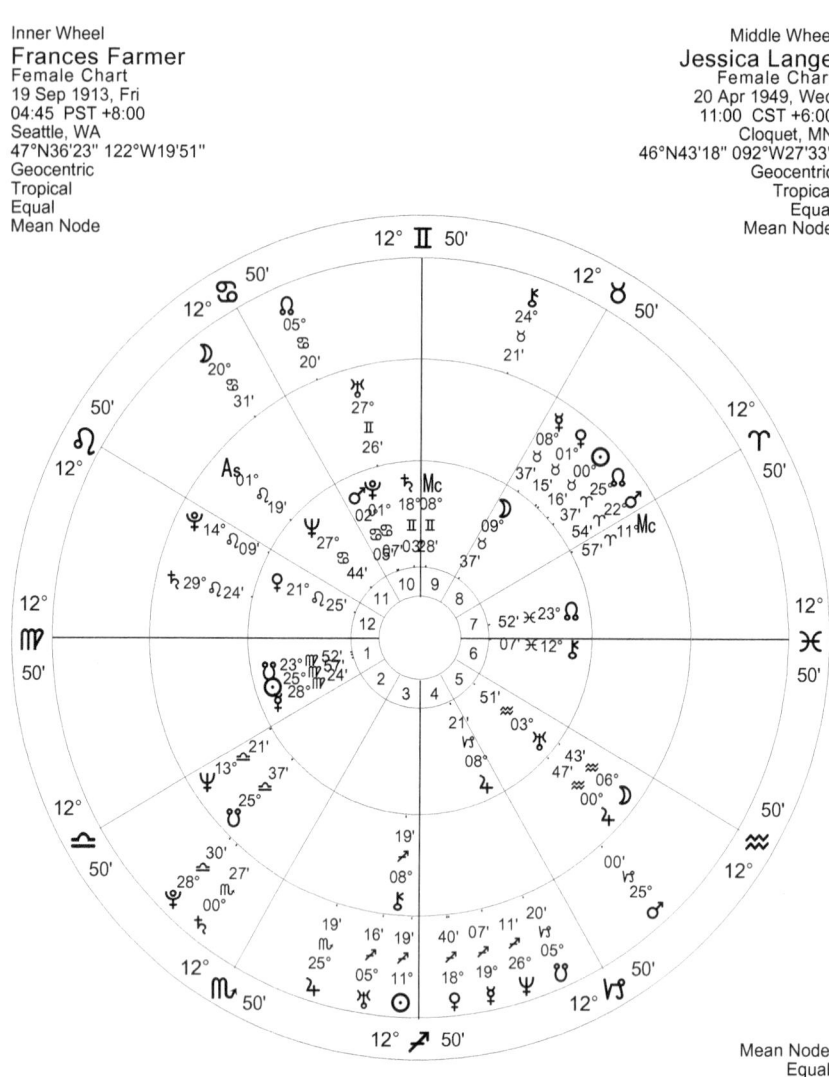

becomes her legal guardian leads to a complete nervous breakdown and an admission to a sanatorium, where she is forced to undergo various shock treatments. When her mother tries to force her to return to Hollywood, Farmer assaults her mother and is admitted to another hospital where she has more shock therapy, is beaten and raped by orderlies and visitors and then involuntarily lobotomised before being released.

Years later, she was the subject on *This is Your Life* and when asked about the past problems, she denied all of them, saying, "If you're treated like a patient, you'll act like one." The film ends with her being honoured at a Hollywood party and the end credits said she had hosted a local Indiana television programme and died at the age of 56.

Jessica Lange's Mercury in Taurus is conjunct Farmer's Moon, so who better to tell her story? Lange's Moon and Jupiter in Aquarius is also conjunct Farmer's Uranus, perhaps making the actress suitable for highlighting the rebelliousness. Lange's Chiron in Sagittarius was exactly on Farmer's IC, allowing Lange to tell of Farmer's painful relationship with her mother. Transiting Uranus was within three degrees of conjunction to this conjunction when the film was released. It is worth pointing out that Chiron was conjunct Algol at the time and Jupiter was in opposition in Scorpio. The film is intense, uncomfortable viewing, with extreme demonstrations of the control used to restrain Farmer.

Lange's performance was widely praised and it is generally cited as being her best performance.

Lange was nominated for an Academy Award for Best Actress.

GRACE OF MONACO

Grace Kelly: 12 November 1929, 05:31 Philadelphia, Pennsylvania.
AA: Steinbrecher
Nicole Kidman: 20 June 1967, 15:15, Honolulu, Hawaii.
A: Scholfield
Prince Rainier: 31 May 1923, 06.00, Monte Carlo, Monaco. A: RR
Tim Roth: 14 May 1961, no time, Dulwich, England.
Source: Wikipedia
Release date: 14 May 2014

Before she became a princess, Grace Kelly was a movie star. However, her life as a princess is limited in scope and she is mostly doing charity work for hospitals and other humanitarian organisations, so when film director Alfred Hitchcock comes to Monaco to offer her a comeback role in his film *Marnie* for one million dollars, she is tempted. Her husband Prince Rainier seems open to letting her go ahead, if that's what she really wants.

Politically, tensions are rising between Monaco and France. France has given Monaco trade favours and is clearly hoping the Prince will give up his sovereignty in Monaco. The Prince declines and France takes steps towards a trade embargo and pressures the Prince's sister and her husband to persuade the Prince to give in. The political tension also causes friction in the marriage of the Prince and Princess and he even says he wishes to take back his offer of allowing her to accept the film opportunity. The Princess' reaction is to take a step back and re-evaluate her responsibilities.

After careful consideration, the Princess decides to show her continued concern for the improvement of local hospitals and, as she had been a movie star, she manages to get ample press support and begins organising a charity ball to raise the prestige of Monaco.

Unexpectedly, she receives photographic evidence that the Prince's sister and husband are collaborating with France. The Princess reports this to her husband and he quickly denounces them. He then makes preparations to lawfully exile them from Monaco.

The charity ball organized by the Princess is a huge success and generates much interest and capital, allowing the couple to preserve the sovereignty of Monaco.

Mercury 115

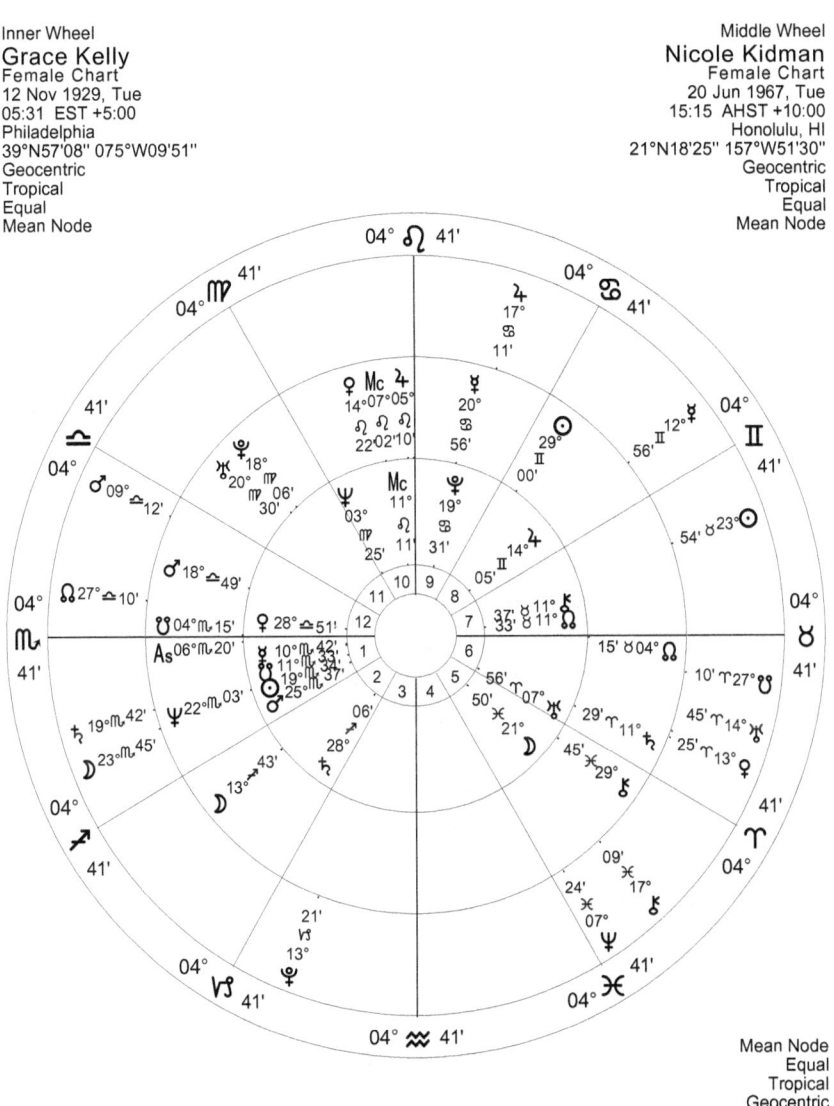

Princess Grace's Pluto in Cancer was conjunct Nicole Kidman's Mercury, which seems rather apt for a film about a power struggle within the family. They also had all four of their angles in the same sign: ascendant in Scorpio, descendant in Taurus, IC in Aquarius and MC in Leo. Kelly's stellium in Scorpio was conjunct Kidman's Neptune so the glamour aspect of the role was emphasised. The Princess' diplomacy skills were incredible for someone who had not been born into royalty; her Jupiter in Gemini opposite Kidman's Moon in Sagittarius shows the confidence it would take for the actress to play such a part. Kidman's Sun in Gemini in opposition to Kelly's Saturn in Sagittarius shows how the actress conveyed the difficult decision between choosing the limelight of a major film or devotion to royal duties.

Prince Rainier's Sun in Gemini conjunct Tim Roth's Mercury seems appropriate for a man who had excellent communication skills. The Prince's Jupiter in Scorpio conjunct Roth's Neptune echoes the glamour factor of the women's roles and also the exceptional business that preserved his sovereignty. (Chart not shown.)

The film was released as Saturn in Scorpio transited Kelly's Sun, which highlights a closely guarded secret. It is doubtful that audiences were aware of the power struggles faced in Monaco in the 1960s and this is also echoed with transiting Pluto in Capricorn opposing Kelly's natal Pluto in Cancer. Transiting Jupiter in Cancer was also conjunct Kelly's natal Pluto, highlighting the power struggles which Kidman was able to convey with her natal Mercury in the same place.

Chiron was transiting the Prince's South Node and Uranus conjunction in Pisces. Monaco is a peaceful country and an internal rift involving the exile of a family member must have been stressful (to say the least).

Neptune in Pisces transiting the Chiron and South Node of Roth, as well as the transiting Uranus/Venus conjunction in Aries transiting his Venus, shows a change in the type of roles he is normally seen in. For once, he gets to play a king with a beautiful wife rather than the violent thug as seen in *Reservoir Dogs* and *Pulp Fiction*.

The Grimaldi family criticised the film for its historical inaccuracies and over-emphasis on glamour.

MATA HARI

Mata Hari : 7 August 1876, 13:00, Leeuwarden, Netherlands.
A: Steinbrecher
Greta Garbo: 18 September 1905, 19:30, Stockholm Sweden.
AA: RR
Release date 26 December 1931

Mata Hari may not have been 100% historically accurate but that didn't prevent the film from becoming MGM's biggest money spinner of 1931. It was also the most successful role for Greta Garbo who is remembered to this day for her portrayal of the exotic dancer who moonlighted as a spy. *Mata Hari* was filmed before censorship guidelines were enforced in films and Garbo's famous dance to Shiva – as well as other controversial scenes – were chopped and are now lost.

The film opens with a harrowing scene of a firing squad shooting bound traitors during World War I. One man who has seen two men before him shot is interrogated by DuBois, the head of the French Spy Bureau. Already suspecting Mata Hari of treason, DuBois offers to set the man free if he will only reveal the name of the spy he is protecting. The man refuses and DuBois orders him to be shot, commenting that Mata Hari bewitches men. DuBois is determined to see the celebrated dancer before the firing squad – but then says he is going to see her dance later that night.

In the meantime, Alexis Rosanonff, a Russian officer carrying important messages, lands in Paris and is commended for his bravery for flying over Germany by his commanding officer, General Shubin. Rosanoff declines Shubin's invitation to dinner claiming he is too tired. However, he perks up when he learns Mata Hari will be dancing.

After her performance, a young woman who has been in the audience whispers in Mata Hari's ear, telling her that a man called Andriani wants to see her at a local casino. It can be seen that the young woman is also a spy when she drops a concealed message and it is swapped with another when picked up by an observer.

Shubin and Mata Hari have a conversation after her performance and it is revealed he has passed on secret information to her. He is in love with her and knows this has put his life in jeopardy. After playfully spurning his advances, Mata Hari goes to the casino to see Andriani.

Andriani, a spymaster, tells Mata Hari that he wants her to intercept Russian messages from Rosanoff. To obtain the messages, Mata Hari sleeps with Rosanoff then gives him the cold shoulder the following morning.

Later, DuBois tells Shubin that he suspects Mata Hari is a spy. The Russian laughs at the accusation but DuBois tells him that she has also slept with Rosanoff, inciting the older man's jealousy. When Mata Hari comes to visit him, Shubin confronts her about Rosanoff and although she tells him she is just doing her job, Shubin calls DuBois to tell him it's true that Mata Hari is a spy. She shoots Shubin and goes on the run.

Andriani discovers Mata Hari has actually fallen in love with Rosanoff and tells her this will make her a useless spy. He tells her that Rosanoff has been severely injured in a plane crash on his way back to Russia. She resigns from her post and goes to visit the blinded and injured Rosanoff. She is arrested shortly afterwards.

At her trial, she confesses her crimes when it is suggested Rosanoff will be brought in to testify. She is given the death penalty but tells Rosanoff she can't see him as she has to go to a sanatorium to recover her health.

Just before her execution, Rosanoff is brought to her. All who attend to Mata Hari in her final hours keep her secret. In their final conversation, Rosanoff tells Mata Hari he expects to recover his sight and that he looks forward to a future spent with her.

Most appropriately for a spy, the real-life Mata Hari had a natal Scorpio ascendant with Jupiter rising. Mars, the traditional ruler of her chart was conjunct Mercury, Uranus and the Sun in Leo. What was she most famous for? Being an exotic dancer and a spy.

Like Mati Hari, Garbo also had Jupiter rising although in her case, it was in the sign of Gemini. Mercury was her ruling planet which was in opposition to Mati Hari's Saturn and Moon in Pisces, enabling the actress to convey the slipperiness of the spy. Within a five degree orb, Garbo's Moon was conjunct Mata Hari's Pluto which may have given her an insight into the motives behind her crime.

Greta Garbo's natal Venus was conjunct Mata Hari's Mercury/Uranus conjunction. This combination shows an interaction between the manner in which Mata Hari communicated but it may also over-dramatise the relationships. Indeed the film focused on Mati Hari's

Mercury 119

Inner Wheel
Mata Hari
Female Chart
7 Aug 1876 NS, Mon
13:00 LMT −0:23:04
Leeuwarden, Netherlands
53°N12' 005°E46'
Geocentric
Tropical
Equal
Mean Node

Middle Wheel
Greta Garbo
Female Chart
18 Sep 1905, Mon
19:30 CET −1:00
Stockholm, Sweden
59°N20' 018°E03'
Geocentric
Tropical
Equal
Mean Node

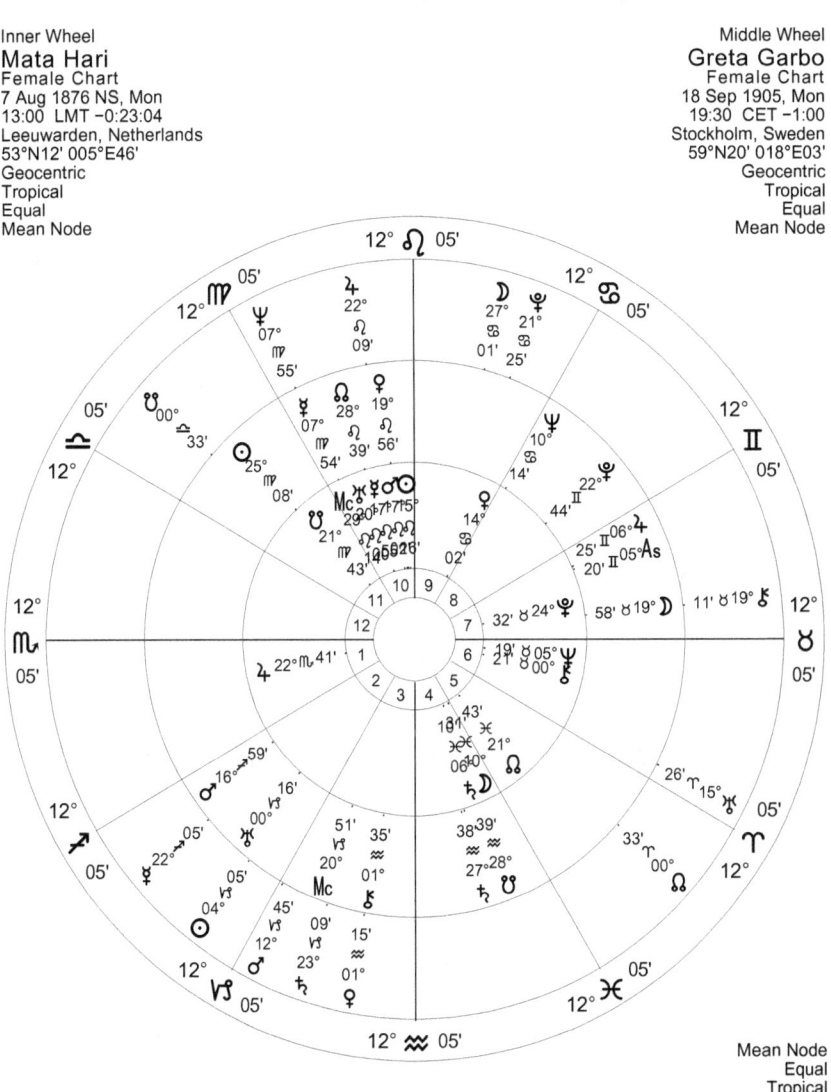

Mean Node
Equal
Tropical
Geocentric
34°N05'54" 118°W19'33"
Hollywood, california
12:00 PST +8:00
26 Dec 1931, Sat
Event Chart
Mata Hari release
Outer Wheel

relationships with Russian officers whilst under suspicion of the head of a French spy bureau. It was all rather complicated and difficult to follow as one might expect with a Mercury/Uranus conjunction.

The film was released as Jupiter transited their planets in Leo.

YOUNG MAN WITH A HORN
Bix Beiderbecke: 10 March 1903, 02:00, Davenport, Iowa. B: RR
Kirk Douglas: 9 December 1916, 10:15, Amsterdam, New York.
AA: Steinbrecher
Release date: 9 February 1950

Young Man with a Horn is an example of a true storyline that is too sad even for Hollywood.

Kirk Douglas plays the role of the famed cornet player Bix Beiderbecke, re-named Rick Martin for the film. The film focuses on the musician's love affairs and how his legendary alcoholism affects his wife's (played by Lauren Bacall) drinking habits. In the film he even goes so far as to blame her for his slide into addiction.

The film follows his musical success from an orphan yearning for a cornet that he sees in the window of a pawn shop, to his popularity as an outstanding musician. He plays in a big band and is repeatedly told off for improvising, which eventually gets him fired. Jo, the female singer of the band (played by Doris Day) finds him a job in New York where he meets the complicated Amy who is studying to be a psychiatrist. Although warned about Amy, he marries her anyway. Amy doesn't like his music or show any interest in his career. Instead, she returns to school to become a doctor and the couple begin to have serious disagreements. Realising that Amy never loved him and that she's in need of help with her problems, he leaves her. However, he also succumbs to alcoholism, is fired from his orchestra and ends up destroying his horn. One night he collapses in the street and is taken to a sanatorium. His friend Jo rushes to his side and as he recovers they fall in love and he eventually returns to his musical career.

Sadly, although this last sentence constituted the ending of the film, it never happened that way in the tragic life of Bix Beiderbecke. Pneumonia was cited as the official cause of his death at the age of 28 on 6 August

Mercury 121

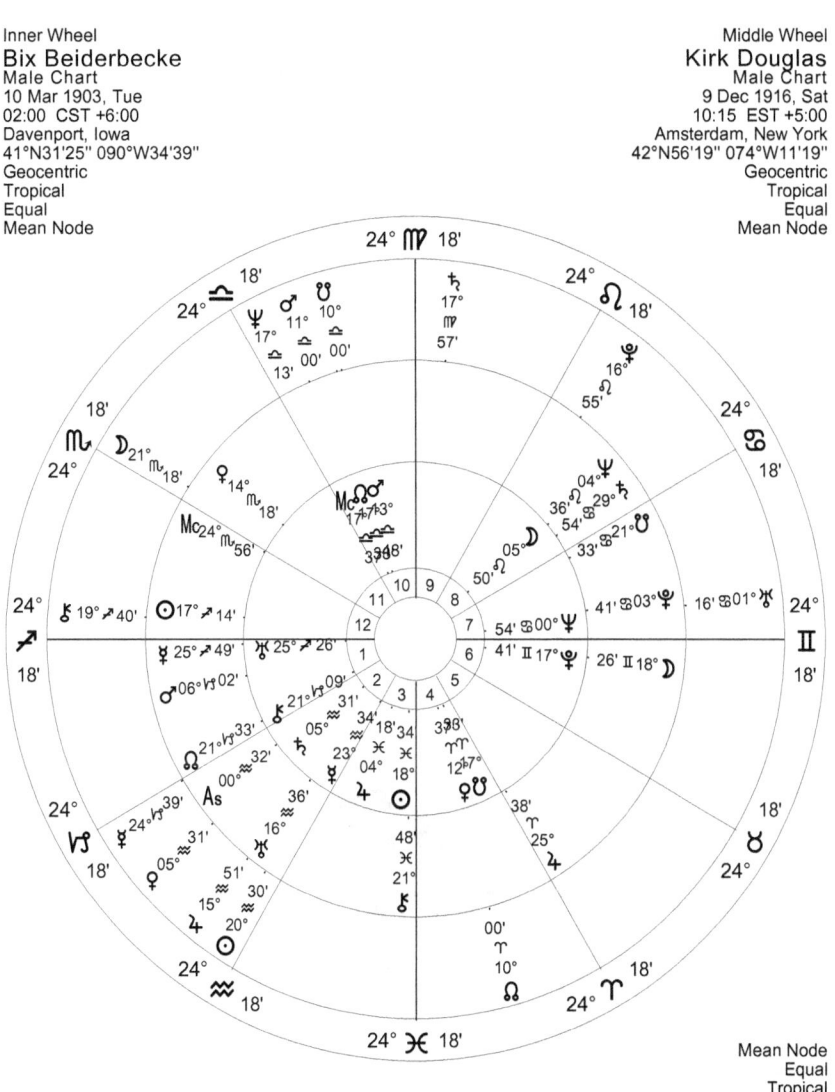

1931, but the effects of long term alcoholism were contributory factors. According to conspiracy theories, his bootleg liquor was poisoned.

Douglas' natal Mercury was conjunct Beiderbecke's ascendant and Uranus conjunction, so the actor was tuned into Beiderbecke's instability. With Douglas' Gemini Moon conjunct the musician's Pluto, the actor was able to plunge to the depths to understand and communicate his role. Also the actor's North Node was exactly conjunct Beiderbecke's Chiron so this may have been a role that was painful for him to portray. Douglas' natal Neptune was conjunct the musician's Moon in Leo, and interestingly, Beiderbeck died when a Venus/Jupiter conjunction took place within one degree of his Moon.

Transiting Neptune was exactly conjunct Beiderbecke's North Node and MC in Libra when the film was released. Transiting Chiron on that night also touched the actor's Sun and opposed the musician's Pluto.

Although the script was criticised, the performances of the actors were praised – but it was the soundtrack that was the real star of the show.

THE MOON

The Moon in astrology is about our connections to the past, especially to the mother or mother-figure in our lives. These connections are built on emotional reactions to events in our lives and the memories we hold of them.

To understand a character, an actor must be able to empathise with how the real-life person feels about their circumstances. From the heartbreak and tragedy of war in *The Pianist*, to the triumph over adversity in *My Left Foot*, seeing an actor successfully portray how a person feels can leave us heartbroken, or cheering for their victories.

The Moon can also help us to understand how or why a person cares so much about the person they love or care for. *The Queen* depicts the impact of the death of Diana, Princess of Wales on the British Royal Family and Her Majesty's struggle to understand the grief of her country as well as manage her own personal struggle to honour a woman who challenged the stability of the monarchy. Of course, feelings are not just limited to people. In *Gorillas in the Mist*, we see the passion behind Dian Fossey's efforts to protect the mountain gorillas in Rwanda that she had come to love as if they were human.

Walt Before Mickey chronicles Walt Disney's early struggles as a young animator and his later reflections on how far he had come; he became phenomenally successful as the hero of the millions of children who came to love his creations. *Chaplin too* is a reflection of a man who grew up in challenging circumstances, but eventually found success even amongst the scandals and twists and turns in his life.

The films in this chapter have a profound impact on us, and the actors' skills in getting in touch with the real-life person's emotional state increases our ability to empathise with them. It is interesting indeed that these feelings stayed with the actors too and apparently changed their outlook on life long after the cameras stopped rolling.

CHAPLIN

Charlie Chaplin: 16 April 1889, 20:00, London. XX: RR
Robert Downey Jr: 4 April 1965, 13:10, Manhattan, New York.
A: March
Release date: 18 December 1992

The film begins with an elderly Chaplin being interviewed by a fictional journalist who is editing Chaplin's autobiography.

Chaplin grew up in gruelling poverty in London. His only escape was to sneak into music halls to watch his mother perform. One night, when he was about four years old, she suffered an extreme panic attack and Chaplin took her place on stage. Sadly, his mother's condition descends into full blown psychosis and she is committed to an asylum. Chaplin and his brother continue to perform and eventually he becomes a hit with a comedy drunk act. He falls in love and begs his girlfriend to come to America with him but she declines.

In America, Chaplin creates his famous Tramp routine and begins to direct his own movies, with the goal of one day owning his own studio. A few years later, he begins a relationship with a questionably young child actress and eventually marries her. He also has an argument with J. Edgar Hoover which would extend to a forty-year attempt to ruin Chaplin's reputation.

After the early death of their only child and Chaplin's continued devotion to filmmaking, he and his wife divorce and her lawyers try to seize the movie *The Kid* as part of their shared assets. Chaplin and his brother flee to another city to finish editing it and then release it to resounding success.

The brothers arrange to have their mother freed from the asylum to join them in America. However, although they are initially happy to see her, they have to admit they can't cope with her worsening psychosis. For a break, Chaplin returns to the UK but realises he doesn't fit in any more.

After returning to America, Chaplin comes under suspicion of being a member of the Communist Party, a remnant of his argument with J. Edgar Hoover. He is also forced to consider the effect the "talkies" will have on his filmmaking.

The Moon 125

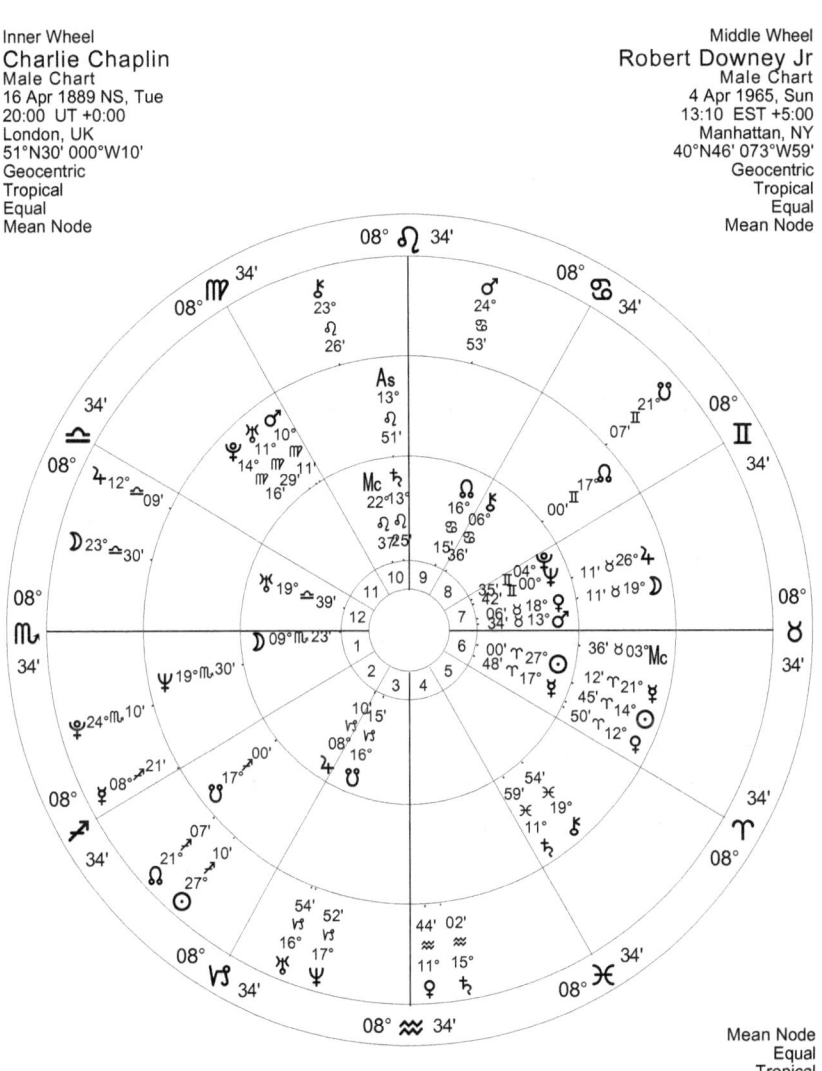

He re-marries, and despite having two children he divorces the mother and marries another actress. Unfortunately, his devotion to finishing his movie *Modern Times* takes its toll on his marriage and they end up divorcing.

At a party, Chaplin causes a scandal by refusing to shake hands with a member of the Nazi Party. Another actor jokes that Chaplin looks like Hitler, inspiring him to create *The Great Dictator*. Hoover tries to infer the film is anti-American propaganda.

After marrying the daughter of playwright Eugene O'Neill, Chaplin is forced to pay child support to a former lover despite a blood test proving the child is not his. This severely affects his reputation and he stays out of the limelight for several years. During the McCarthy scandal, he and his wife return to the UK, but he discovers almost immediately that he is denied entry back into America.

The final scene shows Chaplin moved to tears as he is given an award for Lifetime Achievement at the Academy Awards ceremony. After watching clips from his famous films, he receives a long standing ovation.

Chaplin's Venus in Taurus is conjunct Downey's Moon within an orb of one degree and Chaplin's Mercury is conjunct Downey's stellium in Aries. Chaplin's Saturn in Leo is exactly conjunct Downey's ascendant.

The film was released as transiting Venus and Saturn in Aquarius straddled Downey's descendant (opposing Chaplin's natal Saturn) and was widely regarded as one of Downey's greatest acting achievements. Transiting Uranus in Capricorn was exactly conjunct Chaplin's South Node when the film was released. The film gives us a unique perspective into Chaplin's life and his contribution to the early film industry.

Robert Downey Jr. was nominated for an Academy Award and a Golden Globe for Best Actor. He won a BAFTA in the same category.

GORILLAS IN THE MIST
Dian Fossey: 16 January 1932, 11:17, San Francisco, California.
AA: Viktor
Sigourney Weaver: 8 October 1949, 18:15, Manhattan,
New York, AA: RR
Release date: 23 September 1988

Dian Fossey's efforts have prevented the extinction of mountain gorillas. The film shows how, inspired by anthropologist Louis Leakey, Dian Fossey writes several letters to him asking for a job studying rare mountain gorillas in Africa. She attends one of Leakey's lectures in Kentucky and manages to prove her devotion to the project.

They travel to the Congo together and Leakey arranges for her to make contact with the gorillas and meet local trackers. The Congo Crisis disrupts their research and they are forced to leave their research site. Fossey's expression of concern for the gorillas leads to her being accused of spying and causing trouble.

With a new host's encouragement, Fossey manages to establish a new research site in Rwanda where she discovers several traps set by poachers who have bribed law enforcers to turn a blind eye to their activities. In spite of this, she and her team carry out ground-breaking research which impresses Leakey. Eventually they attract the attention of National Geographic, who send photographer Bob Campbell to record their progress; they also agree to fund her project.

Fossey falls in love with the married photographer and eventually he offers to divorce his wife to marry her. Unable to bear the thought of spending time away from the gorillas, Fossey declines the proposal and ends their relationship. Devoting herself to her work, she forms strong bonds with Digit, one of the gorillas, and works towards stopping traders from exporting the animals.

Increasingly disturbed by the poaching of gorillas for their hides, hands and heads, Fossey eventually complains directly to the Rwandan government and although she is dismissed, a government official agrees to assemble an anti-poaching squad. However, Digit is found beheaded, and a devastated Fossey begins leading her own anti-poaching campaigns, burning down poaching camps and staging a mock execution of one of the offenders. Her determination to stop poaching alienates her from

128 Mirror Mirror

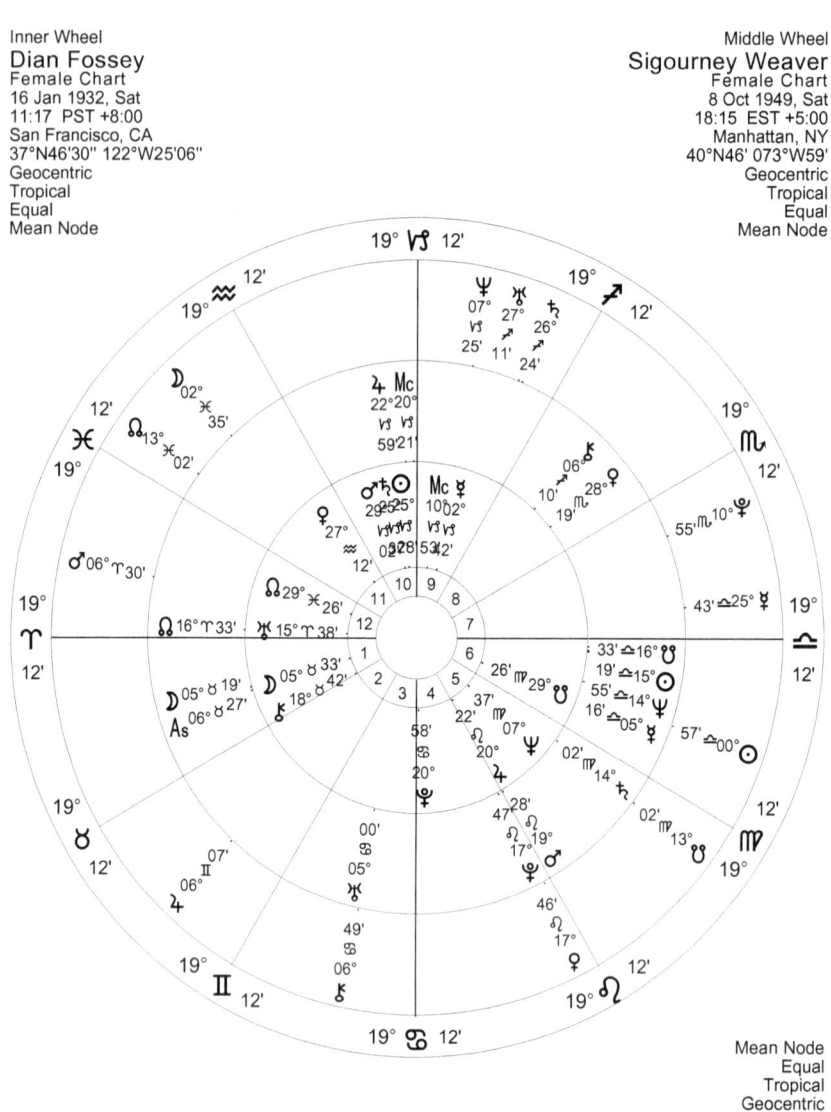

her research assistants and threatens the burgeoning industry of gorilla tourism.

On December 27, 1985, Dian Fossey was murdered in her home and her assailant was never caught. She was buried in the same cemetery as Digit and other gorillas. The graves of Fossey and Digit were linked by stones, a symbol that they rest in peace together.

Incredibly, Fossey and Weaver both have their Moon at five degrees of Taurus, conjunct Weaver's ascendant. If that wasn't enough, Fossey's three-planet stellium in Capricorn is conjunct Weaver's MC and Fossey's Jupiter in Leo is on Weaver's Pluto/Mars conjunction. Transiting Venus was on this conjunction and Pluto opposed their Moons within a four-degree orb when the movie was released, indicating their united passion. Weaver continues to support the Dian Fossey Foundation to this day.

Weaver was nominated for an Academy Award for Best Actress and won a Golden Globe. The film was nominated for a Golden Globe for Best Film.

MY LEFT FOOT
Christy Brown: 5 June 1932, no time, Crumlin, Dublin, Ireland.
Source: Wikipedia.
Daniel Day-Lewis: 29 April 1957, no time, London.
Source: Wikipedia
Release date: 24 February 1989

Christy Brown was one of fifteen children born to his mother in 1930s Dublin. Although he was unable to walk or talk due to severe cerebral palsy, he was loved and supported by his family, particularly his mother. When she fell down the stairs whilst in labour, Christy discovered he could control the use of his left foot and he managed to summon help from the neighbours by kicking the wall.

One day, Christy writes the word "mother" in chalk with his left foot which leads to learning how to paint with his one controllable limb. The neighbouring children are charmed by Christy and include him in their activities. When their father loses his job and the family face extreme poverty, Christy comes up with a plan to get his brothers to steal coal. With some careful saving, the family are eventually able to buy Christy a wheelchair.

130 Mirror Mirror

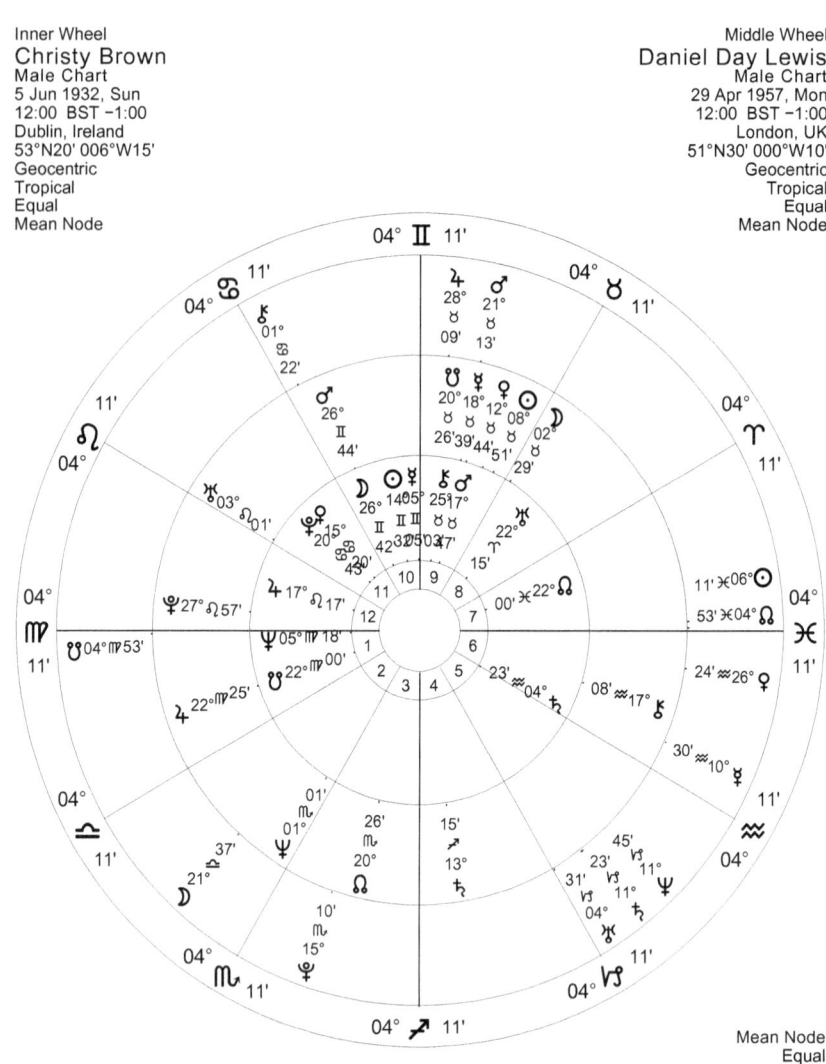

Christy is introduced to Eileen Cole who enrols him in her school for cerebral palsy patients and arranges for him to hold an exhibition of his paintings. Over a short period of time, Christy falls in love with her but over dinner one evening, she announces she is engaged to be married. Depressed, Christy considers suicide but his mother helps him to focus on the future by helping him to build his own studio. However, his father dies of a stroke and during the wake following the funeral, Christy starts an argument that turns into a full punch-up.

Christy begins writing his autobiography, My Left Foot and makes amends with Eileen. Eventually he becomes close to one of his nurses who is reading his biography and she encourages him to continue writing.

The physicality of a healthy actor portraying the severe disabilities of a cerebral palsy sufferer would be a challenge for anyone. Daniel Day-Lewis, a method actor, insisted on using a wheelchair for the entirety of filming. The actor's Mars in Gemini is exactly conjunct Brown's Moon, giving him an insight into the emotional state of Brown as well as the strong connection to Brown's mother. Day Lewis was so convincing he won his first Academy Award for the role, no doubt helped by the sense of destiny created with his Jupiter in Virgo conjunct Brown's South Node.

Transiting Pluto in Scorpio opposed Day-Lewis' Venus/Mercury conjunction as well as Brown's natal Mars when the film was released.

Day-Lewis won a BAFTA and an Academy Award for Best Actor. Brenda Fricker, who portrayed Christy's mother, won an Academy Award for Best Supporting Actress.

THE PIANIST

Wladyslaw Szpilman: 5 September 1911, no time, Sosnoweic, Poland. Source: Wikipedia
Adrian Brody: 14 April 1973, 15:30, Woodhaven, New York.
A: Ackerman
Wilm Hosenfeld: 2 May 1895, 15:00, Hunfeld, Germany.
A: Starkman
Thomas Kretschman: 8 September 1962, no time, Dessau, Germany
Release date: 24 May 2002 (Cannes)

Wladyslaw Szpilman's Mercury in Virgo is exactly conjunct the ascendant and within a few degrees of the Moon of Adrian Brody, the man who portrayed him in the Oscar-winning movie, *The Pianist*.

With the Moon rising in his timed natal chart, Adrian Brody is able to reflect the emotions of the people he encounters. However, it is his interactions with his film family and his separation from them that is absolutely heart-breaking. The Szpilman family is a close-knit unit and it is from their point of view that we see the horrors of World War II as they unfold. The scene when the Germans throw a wheelchair-bound neighbour from a window is particularly shocking. The scene marks the turning of the film from a vague threat of war into something far more terrifying and menacing than expected.

The Szpilmans are transported to Treblinka on 16 August 1942. Neptune had transited Wladyslaw's natal Venus during this time and this in turn is conjunct Brody's Moon within a four degree orb. Wladyslaw's family is sent to an extermination camp but he is able to escape. The sight of the distraught man as he stumbles through the remains of his home and without his family is painfully difficult to watch.

Wladyslaw finds shelter with friends who are able to hide him. Sadly, he is eventually reported by a neighbour and has to flee. Starving, he finds a can of pickles but is unable to open it. A German officer finds him and eventually discovers that this is the great Polish pianist Wladyslaw Szpilman. Impressed by Szpilman's talents, the soldier, Wilhelm Hosenfeld, gives the pianist his greatcoat. The compassion shown by Hosenfeld to Szpilman is very nicely reflected astrologically by the real life Hosenfeld's South Node in Virgo exactly conjunct Brody's Mercury in Virgo and his Saturn exactly conjunct Szpilman's South Node.

The Moon 133

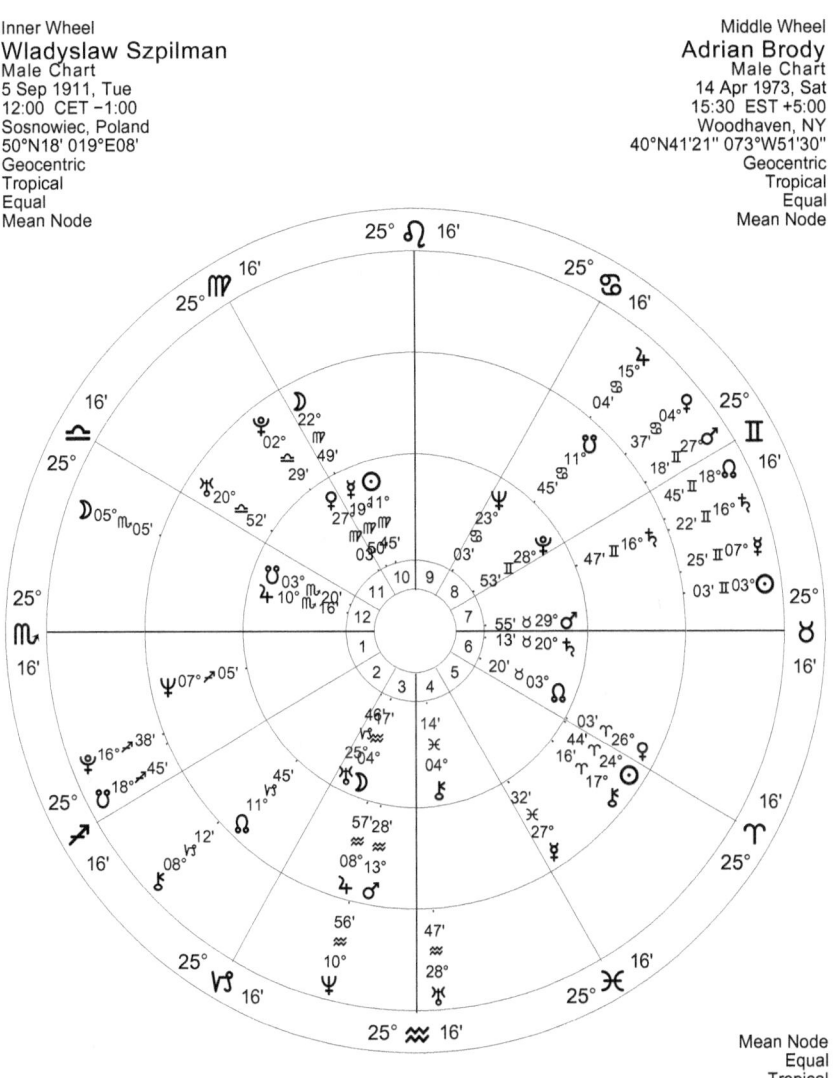

134 Mirror Mirror

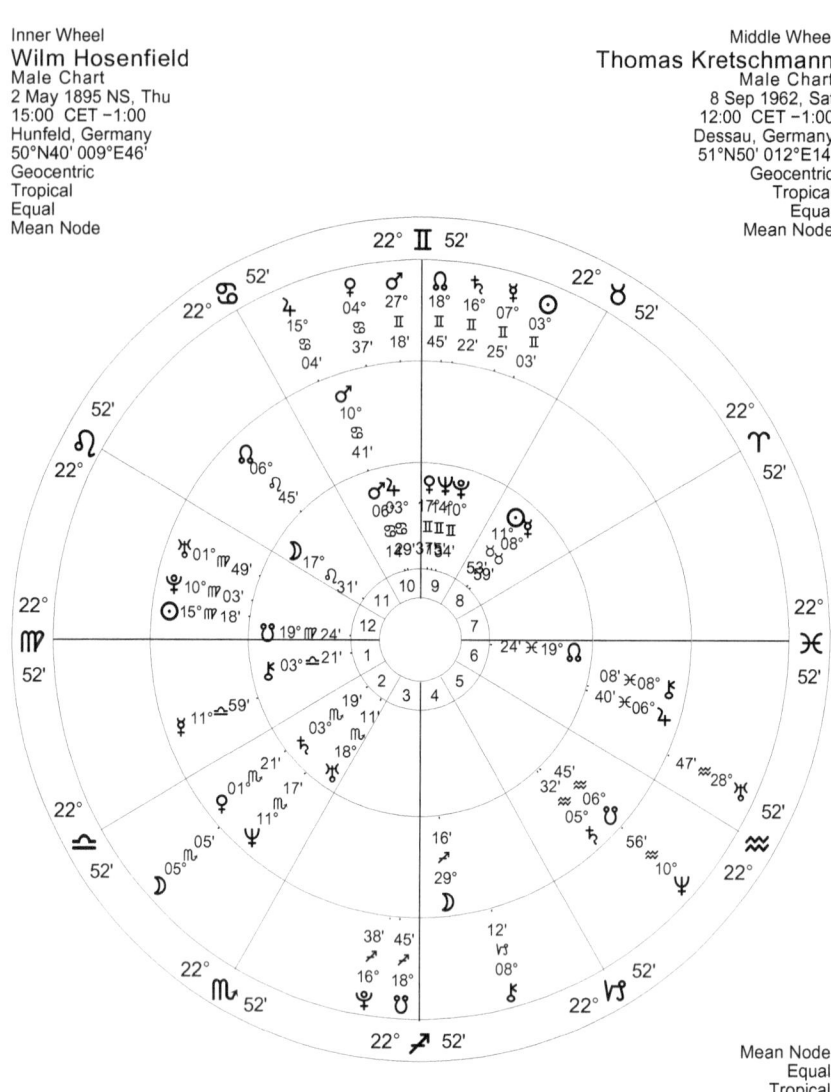

Neptune was transiting Brody's Jupiter when *The Pianist* was released on 24 May 2002. Transiting Mars was conjunct Szpilman's Pluto, ensuring that this incredible tale of survival during the Holocaust would be heard by huge audiences. Almost a year later on 23 March 2003, as Neptune transited Brody's Mars and Jupiter in Aquarius, *The Pianist* won Oscars for best director (Roman Polansky), Best Adapted Screenplay and Best Actor for Brody. It was also nominated for best picture and is listed in BBC's Greatest Films of the 21st Century. Transiting Saturn in Gemini was conjunct Brody's natal Saturn, making it a Saturn return for him. The incredibly moving story of triumph over extreme adversity would become one that would never be forgotten.

Adrian Brody was nominated for Screen Actors Guild for Best Actor and won the Oscar, Golden Globe BAFTA.

The Pianist was nominated for best picture at the Academy Awards and won the BAFTA.

THE QUEEN

Queen Elizabeth II: 21 April 1926, 02:40, London, England.
AA: RR
Helen Mirren: 26 July 1945, 02:00, London, England.
B: Scholfield
Tony Blair: 6 May 1953, 06:10, Edinburgh, Scotland. AA: Gerard
Michael Sheen: 5 February 1969, no time, Newport, Wales.
Source: Wikipedia
Release date: 2 September 2006

The year is 1997, and party leader Tony Blair has just won the election for the Labour Party; as British Prime Minister he delivers a manifesto outlining his plans to reform and modernise the UK. Shortly afterwards, Diana, Princess of Wales dies in a car accident in Paris with her lover.

Her death, aside from the shock and grief it generates, presents major problems for the Royal Family. The Princess was the mother of a future King yet she was no longer a member of the Royal Family, and the Spencer family call for her funeral to be private.

The general public's massive outpouring of grief for Diana, as evidenced by the floral tributes and her being dubbed as "The People's Princess" by Blair, is unprecedented. They begin to turn on the Royal Family; the Queen's popularity plummets while Blair's immediate response to Diana's death means that his popularity rises. All of this means that the Royal Family have no choice but to formally acknowledge Diana's influence and return to London, rather than remain on holiday at Balmoral Castle.

The Queen is reluctant to be guided by Blair, who sees the public display of feeling as mass hysteria. Both her own and the private secretaries of Prince Charles quietly encourage Blair to change her mind. As the Queen reflects on how the world has changed since she was first on the throne, Blair understands how Diana symbolises the change the Queen is now resisting.

After ending discussion about the controversy, the Royal Family walk amongst the floral tributes and the Queen pays a moving tribute to Diana's contributions to humanity on live television. The funeral, which is made public, is attended by the Royal Family at Westminster Abbey.

Although the turnaround is a victory for Blair's ideas of modernising the Royal Family, the Queen warns him that public opinion could mean they turn against him in the future.

In real life, Blair's Chiron in Capricorn is conjunct the Queen's ascendant and South Node so it is very likely he understood her difficulties with modernisation. His Mercury in Aries is conjunct her Chiron so it is not difficult to imagine his new ideas were irritating to her.

Mirren's Pluto in Leo is a few degrees away from the Queen's Moon so she understood the power behind the throne and was able to reflect it to the audience as her Moon in Aquarius is in opposition to the Queen's. Filming took place as Saturn transited these points. Neptune was transiting Mirren's Moon and MC, also bringing in a transit to the Queen's Mars when the film was released.

Within an orb of five degrees, Blair and Sheen have a Sun/Moon conjunction is Aquarius which is an indication the actor had an understanding of the innovation and change Blair was hoping to achieve. Transiting Neptune was conjunct this configuration, along with a transiting opposition from Saturn when the film was released. Sheen's Neptune in Scorpio in opposition to Blair's Jupiter in Taurus is an indication of the behind the scenes negotiations he had to portray.

The Moon 137

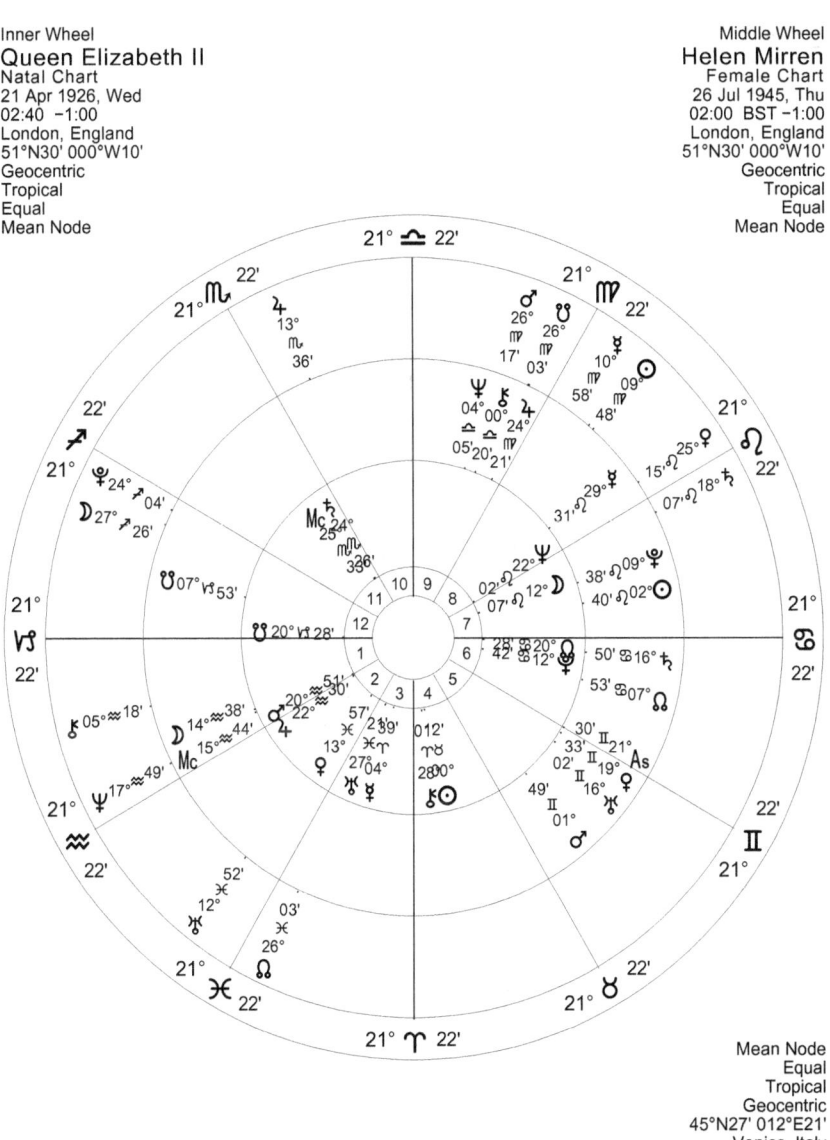

138 Mirror Mirror

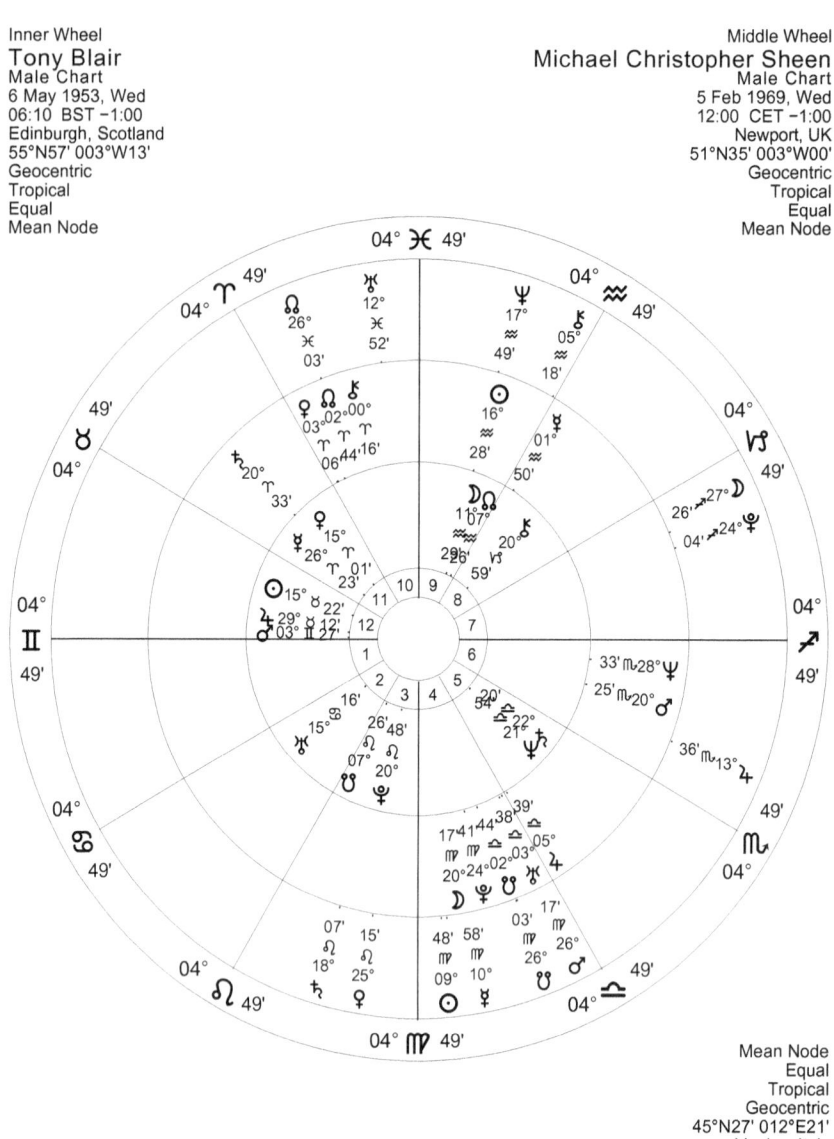

Mirren won an Academy Award, a Golden Globe, a Screen Actors Guild Award and a BAFTA for Best Actress for her portrayal of the Queen. The film won a BAFTA for Best Picture.

WALT BEFORE MICKEY

Walt Disney: 5 December 1901, 00:35, Chicago, Illinois. A: RR
Thomas Ian Nicholas: 10 July, 1980, no time, Las Vegas, Nevada.
Source: Wikipedia
Release date: 14 August 2015

Walt Disney has been fascinated with animation since he was a teenager. In his late teens, he is hired as an artist and when that business closes down, he sets up his own business creating "Laugh-O-Grams" for cinemas and eventually founds a studio. However, the studio struggles and eventually goes bankrupt. Disney has become fascinated with a mouse that occupies the studio and just before the bankruptcy he is able to pitch an idea for a live action animated series.

Walt moves to Los Angeles to live with his brother for financial support and finishes his animation series. With the success of the series, he is again able to open his own studio and hire other artists. Unfortunately, Walt does not have control over the rights of his creations.

A competitor persuades Walt's artists to join his studio for better pay and only one animator chooses to stay with Walt. Walt and his remaining animator create the character that becomes known as Mickey Mouse – which he does own the full rights to.

The film ends with Walt reflecting on how far he has come since his "Laugh-O-Gram" days.

By a wide orb, Disney's Uranus is conjunct his IC in Sagittarius and his Pluto is conjunct his MC in Gemini. His early instability in the business world forced him to make decisions that would give him power in his career through his communication with people. Of course he did this with cartoons. And there was no other animator as powerful as Walt Disney in his heyday. However, he would have had to learn to use that power wisely.

140   Mirror Mirror

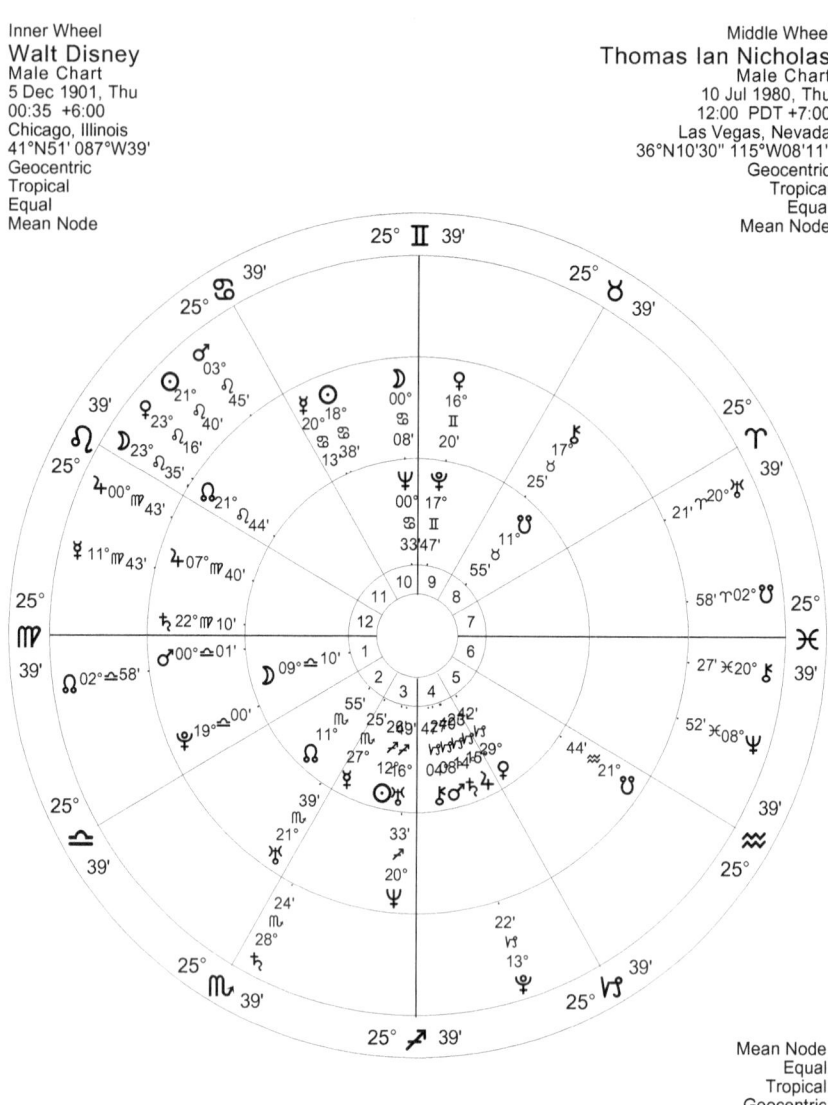

Thomas Ian Nicholas had Venus conjunct Disney's Pluto and this helps make Disney's display of power a little more attractive and easy to accept. Nicholas also had Neptune conjunct Disney's Uranus in Sagittarius so this would be a further cushion for the reputation of the subject of this film, like a gloss over the bad patches. Nicholas' Moon was exactly conjunct Disney's Neptune so he was able to tap into and completely understand his creativity.

Transiting Pluto in Capricorn was conjunct Disney's Jupiter/Saturn and transiting Saturn in Scorpio was conjunct his Mercury. What we see in this film is the early work of this much beloved cartoonist who created some of the best known films for children in the twentieth century. Venus in Leo was transiting Nicholas' North Node, bringing attention to this lesser-known actor.

The film received no major awards.

THE SUN

The Sun is the centre of our universe and all of life revolves around it, so it's not surprising that the films in this section feature characters important for their impact on culture as well as the issues they raised. It follows that the actors, in turn, needed to have a deep connection with the real-life person in order to portray that strength.

Boys Town with the saintly Father Flanagan (Spencer Tracy) was a true father figure for many delinquent boys so it is fitting that the actor's Saturn is conjunct Flanagan's Sun. It is the same connection between actor and activist in *Cry Freedom* (Steve Biko/Denzel Washington and Donald Woods/Kevin Kline) with the added bonus that Uranus was transiting Biko's Sun when the film was released. In *Hotel Rwanda* (Paul Rusesabagina/Don Cheadle), the actor's North Node in Gemini was exactly conjunct the hotelier's Sun, showing a true understanding of life purpose. In *La Bamba*, Ritchie Valens had Mars in Aquarius which was exactly conjunct Lou Diamond Phillips' Sun: the film made an instant sex symbol of the actor. In *The Elephant Man* (Joseph 'John' Merrick/John Hurt), Merrick's Sun in Leo was exactly conjunct the actor's ascendant, demonstrating a strong connection between the actor and the real-life person.

BOYS TOWN

Father Edward Flanagan: 13 July 1886, no time, Leabeg, Roscommon, Ireland. Source: Wikipedia.
Spencer Tracy: 5 April 1900, 01:57, Milwaukee, Wisconsin. C: RR
Release date: 9 September 1938

When Father Flanagan is called to counsel a young man about to be executed, he realises that troubled boys come from impoverished backgrounds. With his motto, "there's no such thing as a bad boy", Flanagan sets up Boys Town, a community where boys are looked after with love and attention.

Whitey Marsh is a boy who sorely tests Flanagan's philosophy. Scrappy and with a criminal older brother, Joe, who is the run, Whitey is a

The Sun   143

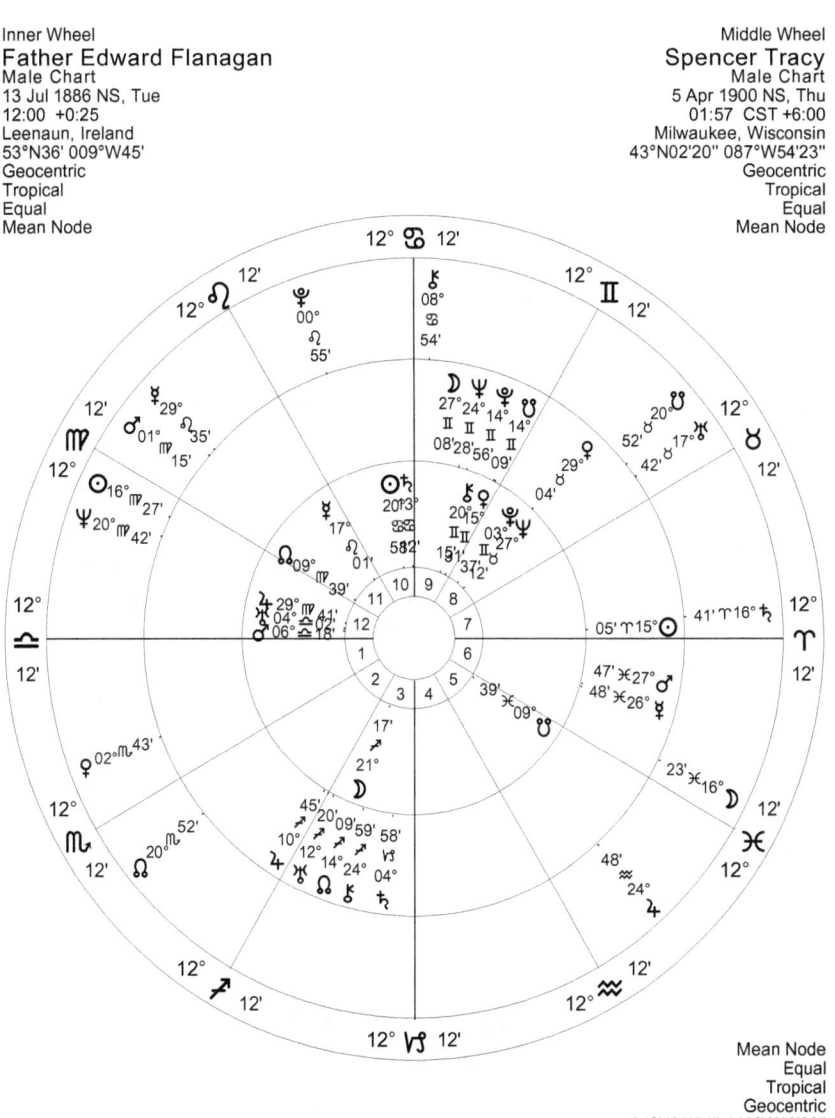

tough-talking kid who wants to run for Mayor of Boys Town with the slogan "Don't be a sucker". The rest of the boys have different ideas however and they vote for a boy with physical limitations as their mayor. Furious at not being elected, Whitey decides to leave Boys Town and as he stomps off down the road, a smaller boy chases after him, begging him to stay. Whitey tells the boy to leave him alone and as the boy turns away in tears he is hit by a car.

Feeling guilty, Whitey continues to run and eventually finds his brother, who is in the middle of carrying out a bank robbery. Whitey is accidentally shot in the leg; Joe and his gang bring him to safety in a church before going into hiding again, but call Father Flanagan to come and take Whitey back to Boys Town. When the police arrive, Father Flanagan saves Whitey from being arrested by promising to take full responsibility for him. Whitey refuses to tell anyone where his brother and his gang are hiding because he promised Joe he wouldn't say anything. When Boys Town is threatened with closure for harbouring criminals, Whitey's brother realises how important the community is and he gives himself up. Boys Town is flooded with donations from grateful citizens and Whitey is elected as mayor of Boys Town.

Spencer Tracy's Pluto and South Node in Gemini are within one degree of Flanagan's Venus, and Spencer's descendant in Cancer is exactly conjunct Flanagan's Sun. Tracy's portrayal of Flanagan was noted for its sensitivity and the role helped promote the real Boys Town in Nebraska.

Transiting Saturn in Aries was conjunct Tracy's Sun when the film was released.

CRY FREEDOM

Bantu Stephen Biko: 18 December 1946, no time, Tarkastad,
Eastern Cape, South Africa. Source: Wikipedia
Denzel Washington: 28 December 1954 00:09, Mount Vernon,
New York. AA: Steinbrecher
Donald James Woods: 15 December 1933, no time, Hobeni,
Transkei, South Africa. Source: Wikipedia
Kevin Kline: 24 October 1947 09:11, St. Louis, Missouri. AA: RR
Release date: 6 November 1987

When a white liberal South African journalist, Donald Woods, hears of the demolition of a slum, he travels the area to meet Stephen Biko, one of the most respected freedom fighters in the country. Biko is forbidden by law from leaving a defined area of the district and he invites Woods to visit the black township to witness the poverty and the effects of the apartheid system for himself. Although Woods had been initially critical of Biko's views, a friendship grows between them. As a result of their discussions Woods begins to agree with Biko's desire for equality between the different groups in South Africa.

The police are tipped off by an informer, and Biko is arrested for being outside of his banishment zone and speaking to a group of gatherers. His subsequent court testimony eloquently advocates non-violence but later the church he regularly attended is vandalised by the security officers who interrogated him. In an attempt to find support for Biko, Woods appeals directly to Jimmy Kruger, the South African Minister of Justice. Although Kruger appears to listen, Woods and his family are harassed by security forces who imply they have been sent by the Minister himself.

After being released, Biko travels to Cape Town to address a student meeting. He is arrested and beaten severely, resulting in a serious head injury. Rather than treat him in Cape Town where it's feared he could escape, Biko is thrown into the back of a police van and transported 700 miles along a bumpy road to Pretoria. The journey further aggravates his injuries and he dies en route, although police reports and other sources indicate Biko died as the result of a hunger strike.

Woods attempts to prove that Biko has not died as a result of a hunger strike, but as a result of police brutality, by exposing recently taken photographs of a healthy-looking Biko at the student protest. As

146 Mirror Mirror

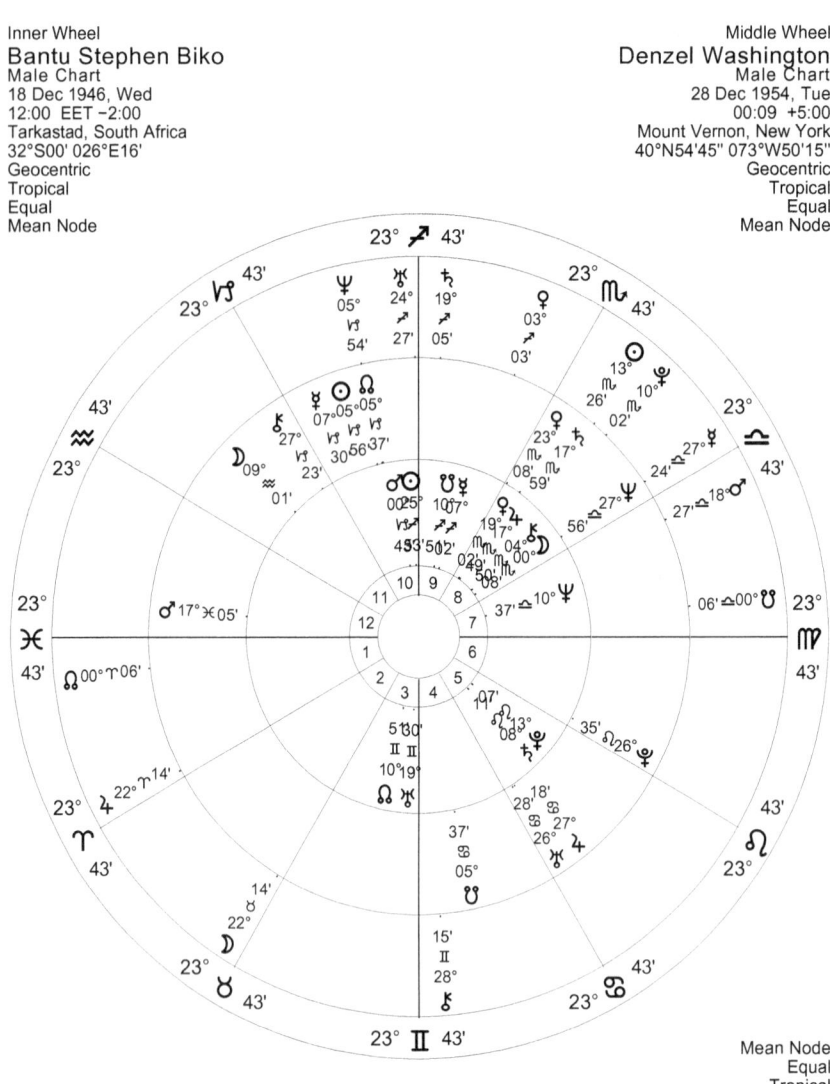

The Sun   147

Inner Wheel
Donald Woods
Male Chart
15 Dec 1933, Fri
12:00 UT +0:00
Hobeni, South Africa
51°N30' 000°W10'
Geocentric
Tropical
Equal
Mean Node

Middle Wheel
Kevin Kline
Male Chart
24 Oct 1947, Fri
09:11 +6:00
Saint Louis, Missouri
38°N37'38" 090°W11'52"
Geocentric
Tropical
Equal
Mean Node

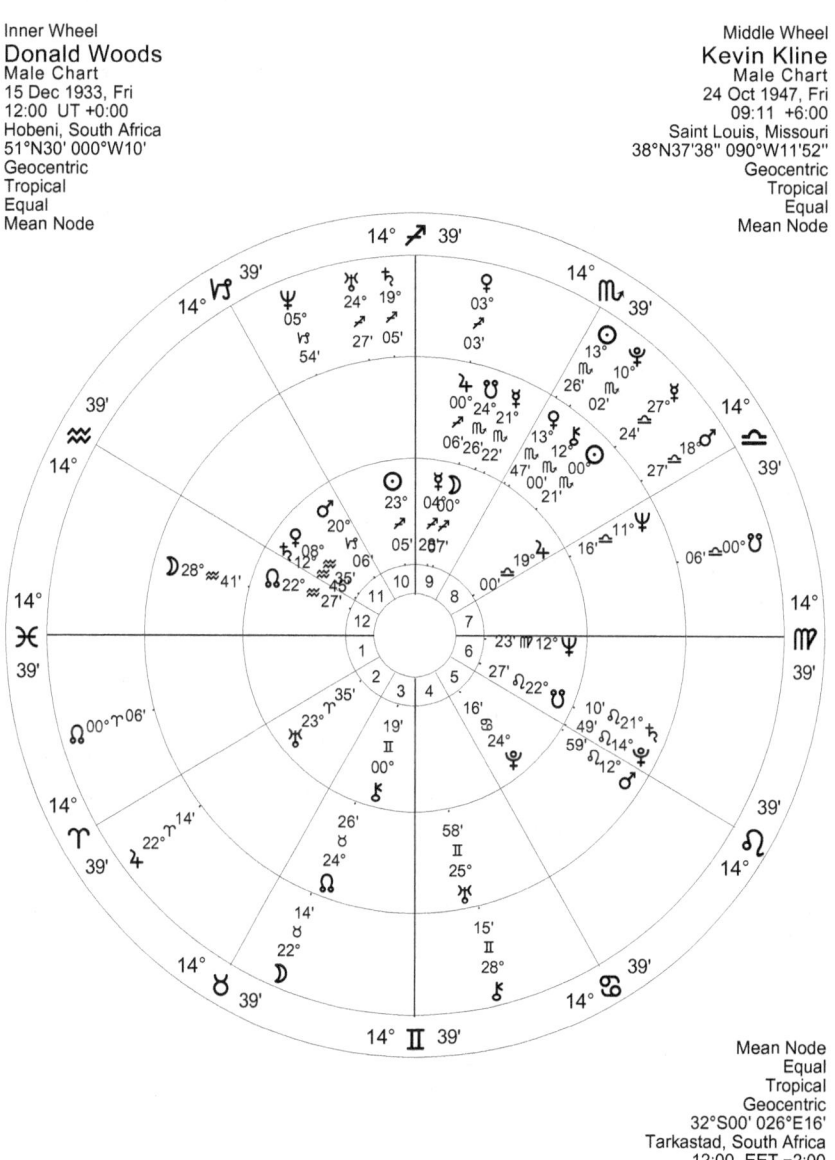

Mean Node
Equal
Tropical
Geocentric
32°S00' 026°E16'
Tarkastad, South Africa
12:00 EET −2:00
6 Nov 1987, Fri
Event Chart
Cry Freedom release
Outer Wheel

Woods tries to leave the country, he is informed that he is not allowed to leave South Africa. He and his family are repeatedly harassed by security police and he decides to seek asylum in England. Disguised as a priest, he makes the long journey to a neighbouring state and is later joined by the rest of his family. Eventually the family is granted political asylum and are flown to London under United Nations passports.

The film ends with a highly disturbing list of anti-apartheid activists who died under suspicious circumstances while imprisoned by the South African government.

Natally, the Suns of Biko and Woods were just a few degrees apart in Sagittarius. Although a shared Sun sign is not the only indication of common ground in astrology, being in Sagittarius is a pretty good place for two political activists to have theirs. Transiting Uranus in Sagittarius was within a degree of both Suns when the film was released in 1987. Transiting Chiron in Gemini would have transited their Suns by opposition during filming as well. *Cry Freedom* helped bring the horrors of the apartheid regime to the attention of the northern hemisphere and the risks that both Biko and Woods took to wake the world up should not be underestimated.

Donald Woods' South Node in Leo was within one degree of Kevin Kline's Saturn and his Mercury in Sagittarius was conjunct the actor's ascendant. Venus transited their ascendant/Mercury conjunction when the film was released. The transiting Sun was also exactly conjunct the actor's natal Venus in Scorpio.

Biko had a Venus/Jupiter conjunction in Scorpio that was conjunct Washington's Saturn/Venus conjunction. Transiting Neptune was exactly conjunct the actor's North Node as well and only two degrees away from his natal Mercury. Washington would become known for his portrayals of other real-life figures such as Malcolm X, Rubin "Hurricane" Carter, Herman Boone, Melvin B. Tolson and Frank Lucas.

Cry Freedom was nominated for Academy Awards, BAFTAs and Golden Globes for Best Picture and Best Supporting Actor (Denzel Washington and John Thaw)

HOTEL RWANDA
**Paul Rusesabagina: 15 June 1954, no time, Murama,
Ruanda-Urundi. Source: Wikipedia
Don Cheadle : 29 November, 1964, no time, Kansas City, Missouri.
Source: Wikipedia
Release date: 11 September 2004**

Paul Rusesabagina, a Hutu, is the manager of the Hôtel des Mille Collines in Rwanda along with his wife Tatiana, a Tutsi. Tensions between the Hutus and Tutsis arise and their marriage becomes a source of friction in the Hutu area where they live.

The political situation in the country deteriorates following the death of the President and after seeing neighbours killed, Paul begins to bribe people of influence with money and alcohol, hoping to keep his family safe. After some very tense moments, Paul manages to procure their safety and bring them back to his hotel.

As the genocide continues, more and more Tutsi refugees arrive at the hotel seeking safety as Tatiana desperately searches for members of her family amongst the violence. To keep everyone safe, Paul has to pretend the hotel is functioning as usual. He enlists the help of the Hutu military to keep supplies coming in and is informed that all the Tutsis will be murdered. As Paul and his assistant return to the hotel via an unfamiliar road, they discover that the road is full of bodies and Paul realises that things are far worse than he had guessed.

Back at the hotel, Paul discovers that foreign peacekeepers are forbidden to intervene in the conflict. Foreign nationals are evacuated but Rwandans are left behind to sort out their own conflict. Paul begs the head of the Tutsi Army for help and when his bribe doesn't work, he tells the general he will be tried as a war criminal. Eventually, Paul's family and the rest of the refugees are allowed to leave the hotel in a UN convoy and are reunited with their families.

Cheadle's North Node in Gemini is exactly conjunct Rusesabagina's Sun, making him a great choice for a man who has to reconcile two sides in a war. Cheadle has a stellium of planets in Virgo, the sign of service, and Mars would have transited these as filming took place. Rusesabagina has a stellium of planets in the sign of Cancer, a sign noted for its caring nature. Saturn would have transited these planets during filming.

150 Mirror Mirror

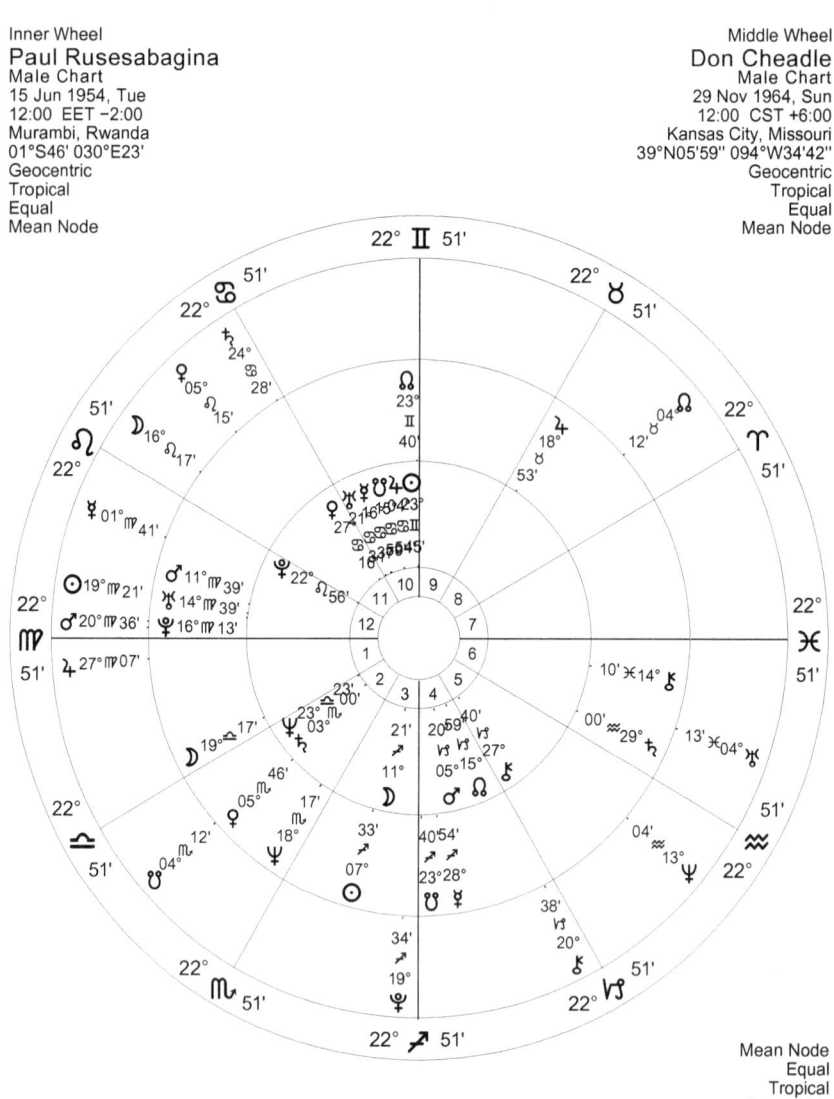

The film was nominated for numerous awards including for Cheadle who was nominated for Best Actor at the Academy Awards. Most importantly the film was noted by critics as being a sobering tale about the massacre in Rwanda that took place as the rest of the world looked away.

LA BAMBA
Ritchie Valens: 13 May 1941, 00:56, Los Angeles, California.
AA: RR
Lou Diamond Phillips: 17 February 1962, 17:17, Olongapo, Phillipines. AA: Scholfield
Plane Collision: 31 January 1957, 11:18, Los Angeles, California.
Source: Wikipedia
Plane Crash: 3 February 1959, 1:05, Clear Lake, Iowa.
Source: Wikipedia
Release date: 24 July 1987

On 3 February 1959, everyone was waking up to the news that Buddy Holly, The Big Bopper and Ritchie Valens had been killed in a plane crash. A young paper boy named Don McLean would grow up to immortalize the event in his epic song, *American Pie*.

Ritchie Valens was the youngest victim of the disaster. At seventeen years of age, he was just starting to become known and was persuaded to join *The Winter Dance Tour*, which would criss-cross the snowy Mid West, not knowing the beat-up old bus they would be travelling in didn't have heating. Although he was afraid of flying, he had become ill and accepted a seat on the plane on that fated wintry night.

Valens had five planets in Taurus, with Uranus conjunct Jupiter smack on Algol. Venus was just out of orb at 28 degrees Taurus and the Sun at 22 degrees and Saturn at 18 degrees Taurus.

Lou Diamond Phillips played the lead role of Ritchie Valens, although he mimed the singing. He was a relatively unknown actor but he was so good, so impossibly handsome, that no one would forget him.

Phillips had five planets in Aquarius, all clustered around Valens' ascendant. Most notably, Phillips' Sun was conjunct Valens' Mars and Phillips' MC was exactly conjunct Valen's Saturn. These connections bode well for an actor to be able to understand the role he is playing.

Although the film depicts Valens' upbringing in a poor Mexican family and the conflicts with his half-brother, there is a sense of

152 Mirror Mirror

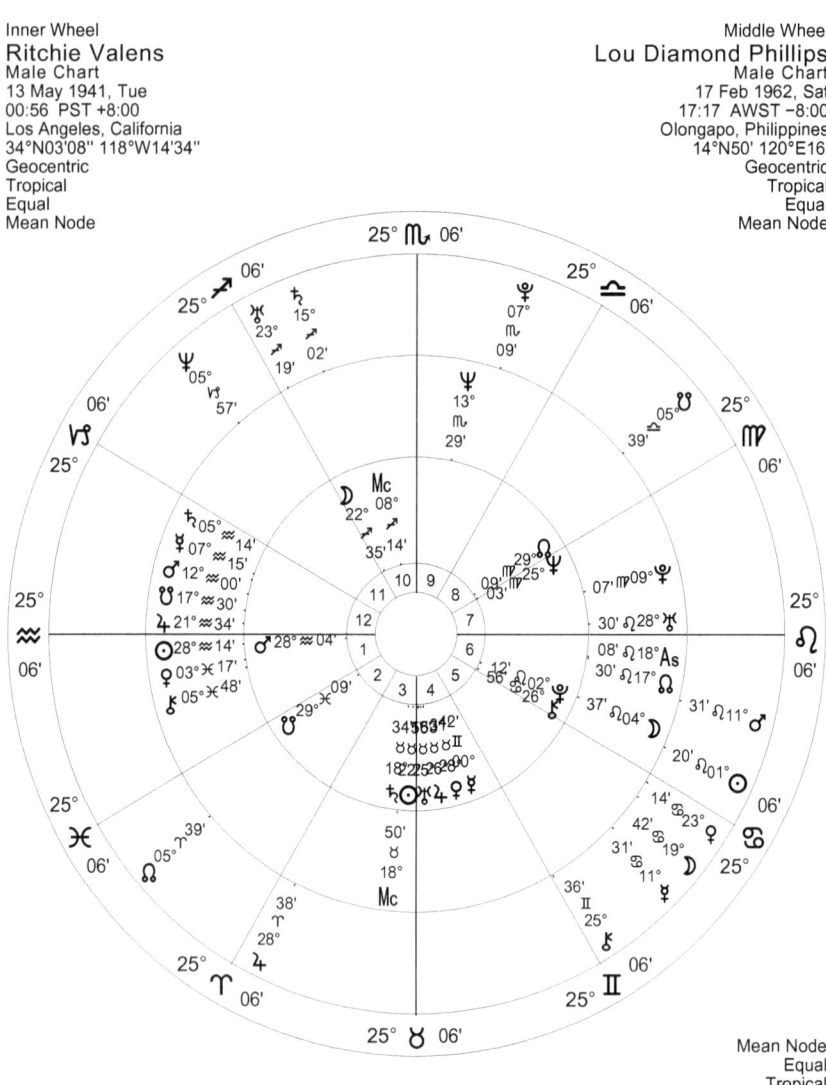

impending doom. The audience know how this movie is going to end before it even starts.

One scene that keeps repeating as a flashback to create the sense of tragic foreboding is a plane collision. At 11:18 on 31 January 1957, two planes collided over a Los Angeles suburb. The debris from the collision fell into the playground of Ritchie's school, killing his best friend and wounding many others. Had Ritchie been in school that day, he would have been with his friend and would have suffered a similar fate. A chart for this collision (not shown in this book) shows the South Node exactly on Algol – and Valens' natal Jupiter/Uranus conjunction. He had had a lucky escape.

However a couple of years later, on the 3 February 1959, sadly Valens' luck ran out. As the musicians of *The Winter Dance Tour* were flying to their next destination, transiting Mars was on Algol. All on board suffered massive trauma to the head.

The film was nominated for a Golden Globe for Best Picture.

THE ELEPHANT MAN
John Merrick, 5 August 1862, no time, Leicester, England.
Source: Wikipedia
John Hurt, 22 January 1940, 17:30 GMT, Shirebrook, England.
A: Fisher
Frederick Treves, 15 February 1853, no time, Dorchester, England.
Source: Wikipedia
Anthony Hopkins, 31 December 1937, 09:15 GMT, Port Talbot, Wales. A: RR
Release date: 3 October 1980 (New York)

Like *Mask* and to a certain extent *Monster*, *The Elephant Man* uses heavy prosthetics to transform how the actor looks. John Hurt, who won an Academy Award, is completely unrecognisable in his role and spent hours in the makeup artist's chair to become the Elephant Man.

Dr. Frederick Treves, a surgeon, finds a hideously misshapen man called Joseph "John" Merrick at a Victorian freak show in London's East End. The man's "owner" is cruel and sadistic and keeps the "freak's" head covered with a hood. Dr. Treves pays the owner so he can bring this barely recognisable human to his hospital for medical assessment. It's discovered that Merrick is unable to sleep lying down because the

154   Mirror Mirror

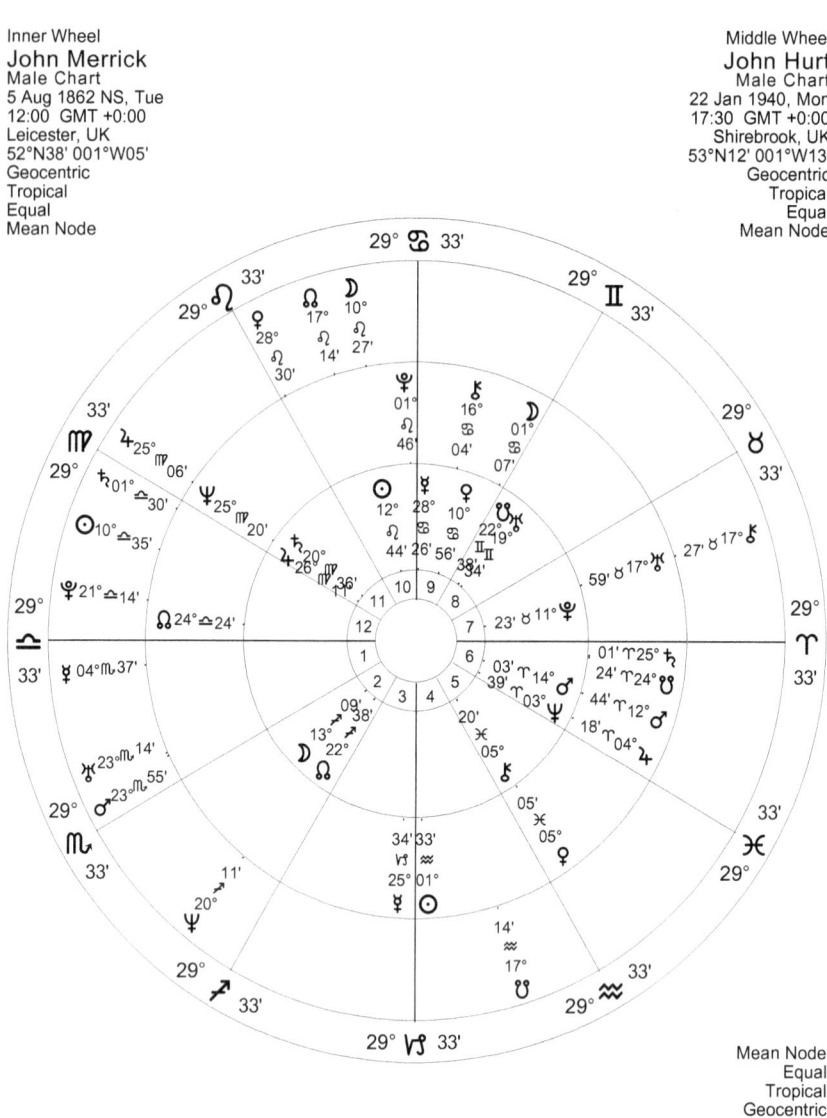

The Sun 155

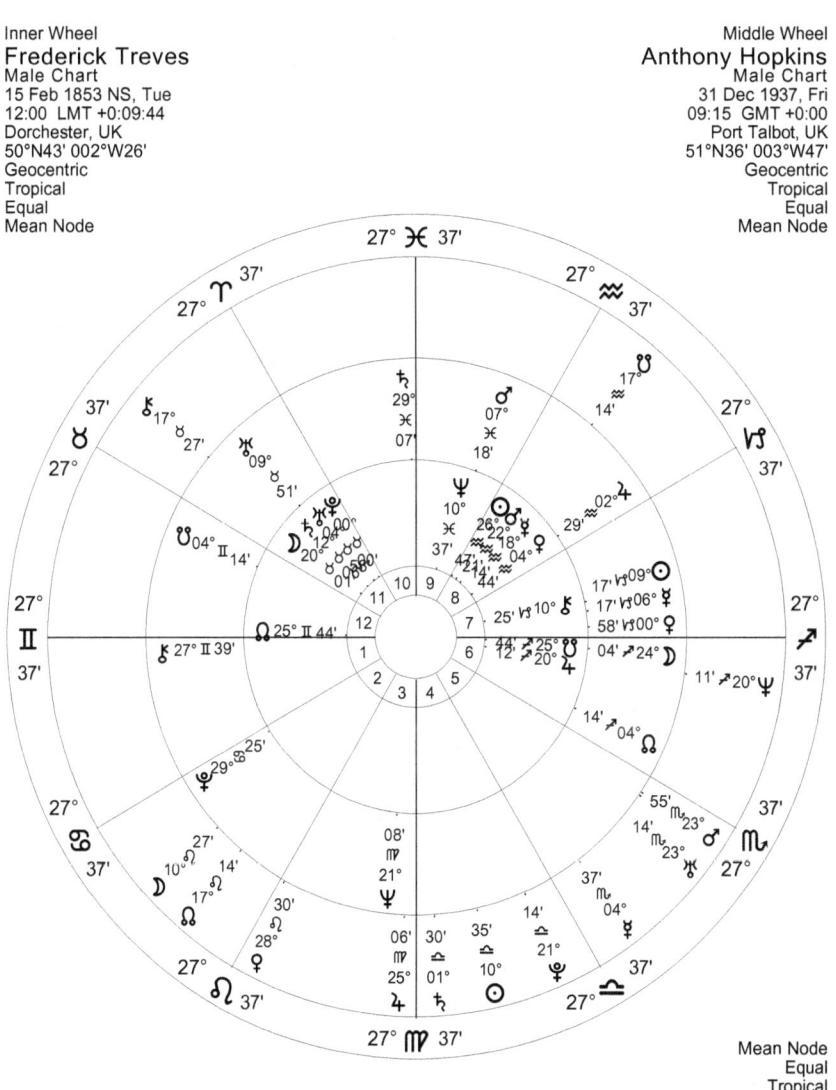

weight of his skull prevents him from breathing. Once Dr. Treves finishes his assessment, Merrick is returned to his owner. However one night the owner beats Merrick so badly that Treves has to be called to treat him. The owner realises that if Merrick dies, he will lose his livelihood.

Taken to hospital, Merrick is cared for by a no-nonsense matron, the only nurse who isn't afraid of him. Hospital administrators protest at Merrick's admission as he is considered incurable and simply taking up bed space for someone who could be helped. To prove that Merrick can be helped, Dr. Treves teaches him to speak a few common phrases. The administrators aren't fooled and as it has been assumed Merrick is also severally mentally disadvantaged, they are astounded when he recites the 23rd Psalm. It was something Treves had not taught him.

It emerges that Merrick can also read and has memorised the Psalm because it is his favourite. He's permitted to stay in the hospital and spends his time practising his language skills and building a model of a cathedral he can see from his window.

Eventually, it's shown that Merrick's character is sweet and gentle in contrast to his monstrous appearance. Dr. Treves brings his wife to meet Merrick for tea in his room. Overwhelmed by their kindness, Merrick shows them a photograph of his mother, who was completely normal. Merrick says that his mother would have been disappointed in him but that she would be proud to see him with his lovely friends.

Over time, Merrick begins to welcome guests to his room, including a well-known actress who introduces him to the works of Shakespeare. Soon, Merrick becomes an object of curiosity to the upper class and the matron expresses concern that he has become a freak show again. This leads Dr. Treves to question whether he has done the right thing. Problems escalate when a night porter starts selling tickets so people can come and stare at "The Elephant Man".

When hospital administrators again try to have Merrick released from the hospital, Princess Alexandra intervenes on behalf of the hospital's royal patron, her mother, Queen Victoria, and Merrick is granted permanent residency.

One night Merrick is kidnapped by his "owner" and taken to Belgium to be a circus attraction again. Weak and dying, Merrick is locked in a cage, but the other freak show attractions help Merrick escape back to England. However, he's harassed by a crowd and is unmasked. In the confusion, Merrick accidentally knocks down a young girl and an angry mob corners him. Before he collapses, Merrick cries out: "I am not an elephant! I am not an animal! I am a human being! I ... am ... a ... man!"

Merrick is returned to the hospital and recovers some of his health but Treves knows that Merrick is dying. Together with the hospital matron, he is taken to watch his actress friend perform at the theatre. She dedicates her performance to him and Merrick receives a standing ovation.

Upon their return to the hospital, Merrick thanks Dr. Treves for all he has done. Merrick goes to bed, determined to lay down like everyone else. After one final sleep he passes away, soothed by a vision of his mother reciting Lord Tennyson's poem *Nothing Will Die*.

John Merrick was born with the Sun in Leo and even with an untimed birth, his Moon was in Sagittarius. This fiery energy brings a terrible sadness: had he been "normal" he probably would have been a wonderful actor rather a sideshow freak. The indignities he suffered at the hands of his audience show with Uranus conjunct his South Node in Gemini within a three-degree orb. His sensitivity of manner and communication shows with Mercury and Venus in Cancer.

John Merrick's Sun in Leo was conjunct John Hurt's ascendant. They also both have Mars in Aries within a couple degrees of orb and Jupiter and Neptune in conjunction either way in their charts. When the film was released, transiting Jupiter was conjunct Hurt's Neptune and Merrick's Jupiter. Also transiting Saturn in Libra opposed Merrick's Neptune and Hurt's Jupiter in Aries.

Dr. Treves had Jupiter conjunct his South Node in Sagittarius which was directly opposite Merrick's South Node and Uranus in Gemini, demonstrating his role as a benefactor in this poor man's life. Anthony Hopkins (Dr. Treves) had his Chiron in Gemini opposing this common point in their charts. *The Elephant Man* was released as Neptune in Gemini transited this point too.

Hopkins' Mercury and Sun in Capricorn were also on Treves' Chiron: he became the healing voice of the doctor in this film. The two men also had a Mars/Neptune conjunction in Pisces, the sign of healing.

The film was nominated for Academy Awards for Best Picture and Best Actor and was nominated in several categories at the BAFTAs. It won Golden Globe Awards in the same categories. The line "I am not an animal. . ." was nominated for entry in AFI's list, 100 Years. . .100 Quotes.

THE NODES

Some actors bring a certain quality of 'fatedness' to their roles, making us believe they were born to play the part. In *Coco Before Chanel*, the fashion designer and the actress who portrayed her (Audrey Tautou) had their nodes within two degrees of conjunction. Barbra Streisand as Fanny Brice in *Funny Girl* had her nodal axis conjunct Brice's Jupiter in Pisces. Ben Kinsley as Mahandas Gandhi in *Gandhi* had his North Node and Pluto conjunction within a few degrees of Gandhi's North Node in Leo. Daniel Day Lewis as Abraham Lincoln in *Lincoln* had his Sun in Taurus on the politician's South Node. Further examples are Renee Zelleger as Beatrix Potter in *Miss Potter* who had her Chiron on the author's South Node in Aries. George C. Scott as George S. Patton in *Patton* had his North Node in Gemini conjunct the general's ascendant. Jamie Foxx as Ray Charles in *Ray* had an exact match of the singer's nodal axis even though they were born decades apart. Selena Quintanilla-Perez and Jennifer Lopez have a Venus/North Node conjunction in Pisces. In *The Aviator* Leonardo DiCaprio played Howard Hughes and actor's North Node was exactly conjunct Hughes' adventurous Moon in Sagittarius. Finally, in *The Buddy Holly Story*, we see that the actor's North Node in Cancer was exactly conjunct the singer's Pluto, a powerful connection that reflects the changes brought to Busey's life when the film was released.

A CRY IN THE DARK
(Released as *Evil Angels* in Australia and New Zealand)

Lindy Chamberlain, 4 March 1948, no time, Whakatane, New Zealand. Source: Wikipedia

Meryl Streep, 22 June 1949, 8:05, Summit, New Jersey. RR:AA
Release date: 3 November 1988

Lindy Chamberlain and her family, including her 9-week-old daughter Azaria, were camping in the Australian Outback. Sadly, what was supposed to be a happy break from the city turned into an unthinkable tragedy. As the Chamberlains were enjoying a barbeque with other families, Azaria cried out from the tent where she had been sleeping. Alarmed, Lindy went to check on her daughter and as she did so saw a dingo with something in its mouth running back into the darkness of the outback. Azaria was gone. Everyone joined in the search for the missing baby but she was not found. It was taken as fact that a dingo had carried off the child and an inquest later confirmed it.

However, as time went on, the general public began circulating rumours that the couple had murdered their daughter in a bizarre religious ritual. It emerged that "Azaria" meant "a sacrifice in the wilderness" and this fuelled speculation that the couple had even decapitated their child with scissors. That the grieving Lindy was perceived as not showing enough emotion in the aftermath of the event did little to foster sympathy for her.

Another inquest was opened and with new witnesses and forensic evidence, the subsequent media furore was seen in papers around the world. Lindy, who was seven months pregnant at the time of the new trial, refused to follow her attorney's suggestion that she try to show more grief to gain sympathy from the jury. Coupled with a faltering witness statement from her husband, the jury had no difficulty in finding Lindy guilty. She was sentenced to life in prison with hard labour while her husband received an 18-month suspended sentence.

Over three years after the trial, police searching for a missing tourist in the same area Azaria had gone missing found the coat the baby had been wearing when she was carried away. Lindy was released from prison and the case was reopened with all convictions against the

160 Mirror Mirror

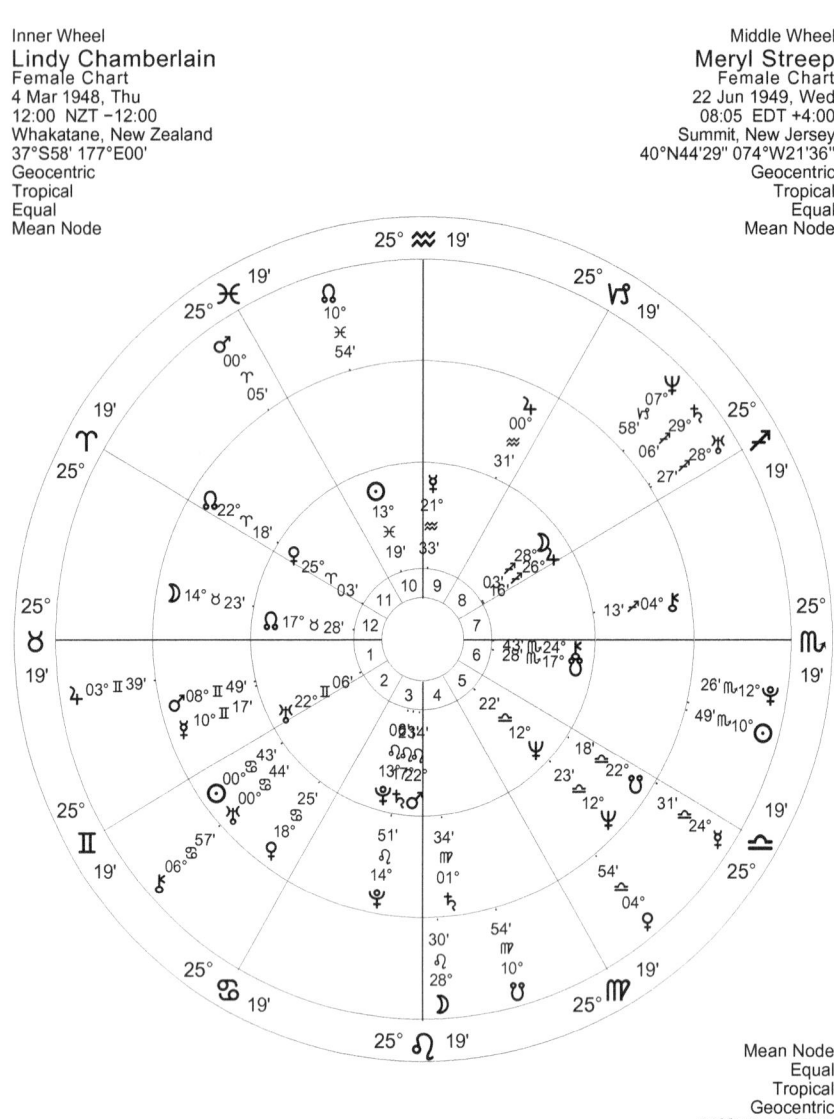

Chamberlains overturned. The film ended with Lindy's husband saying it was an ongoing battle to clear the family's name.

Streep and Chamberlain were born only a year apart and so they have similar outer planets. Within four degrees, Chamberlain's Jupiter in Sagittarius formed a dissociative opposition to Streep's Sun/Uranus conjunction and Uranus transited this when the film was released. Sagittarius is noted for being a sign of adventure while Uranus is a planet often marking sudden changes. There really is nothing more implausible than a wild dog carrying off a human child.

Chamberlain's inability to play the part of grieving mother can perhaps be seen in her natal Venus in Aries. Venus in Aries often does not have the patience to dwell on complicated emotion such as grief. Viewed this way, it can be seen why Chamberlain was perceived as not caring enough about the fate of her daughter. Streep's North Node in Aries is within a couple of degrees of Chamberlain's natal Venus. Additionally, Streep's Moon in Taurus is conjunct Chamberlain's North Node so we can see the actress had a clear sense of the mother's instinct. It is worth noting that transiting Mercury was transiting the actress's South Node and opposing Chamberlain's Venus. This transit shows the gossip that surrounded a mother's relationship to her daughter. Streep also had the opportunity to demonstrate mastery of yet another accent to great acclaim.

Streep was nominated for an Academy Award for Best Actress and won a Golden Globe in the same category for her performance.

COCO BEFORE CHANEL
Coco Chanel: 19 August 1883, 16:00, Saumur, France.
AA: Holliday
Audrey Tautou: 9 August 1976, 09:55, Beaumont, France.
AA: DeJabrun
Release date: 22 April 2009

After being abandoned by her father, Gabrielle Chanel leaves the orphanage she grew up in and works at a local bar. To make ends meet, she sews costumes for performers and also sings in the cabaret with her sister, earning the nickname 'Coco' from patrons. During an affair with a French aristocrat, she has the opportunity to develop her talents making

162 Mirror Mirror

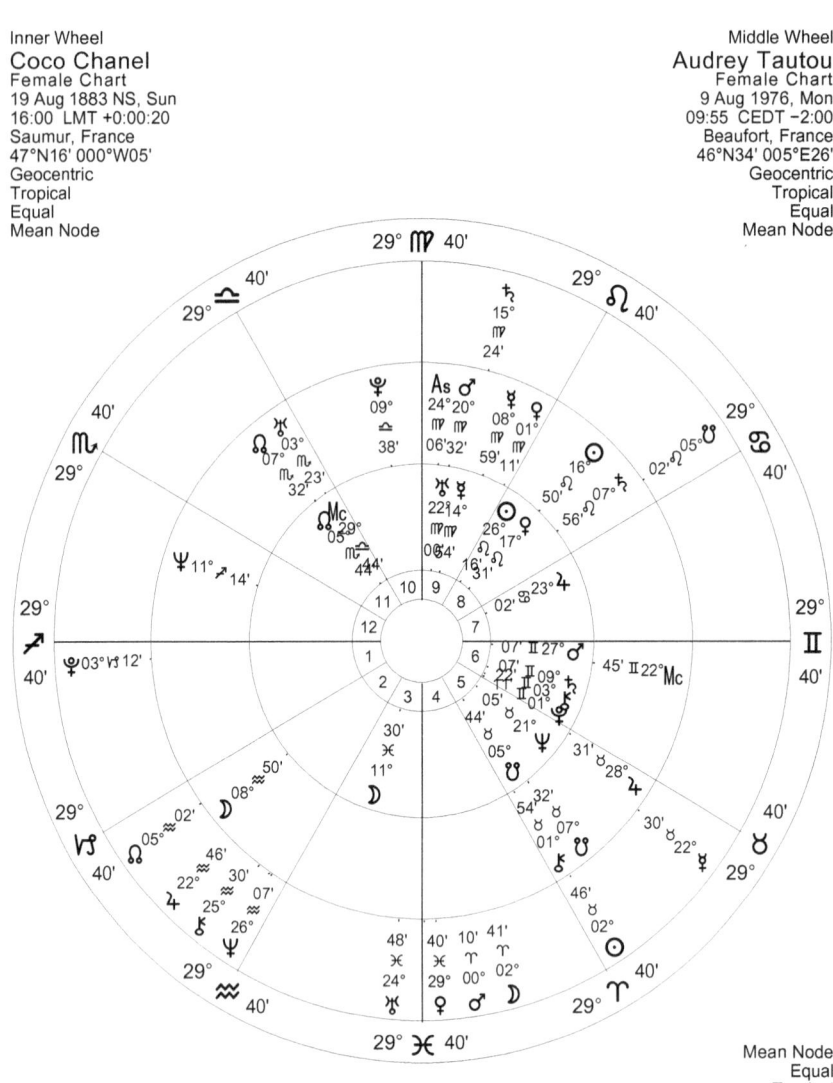

cleverly designed hats that were popular amongst French high society at the time.

Coco then falls in love with an English businessman who believes in her unique work and admires her tenacity to develop her own style. Coco's fashion business goes from strength to strength and when her lover dies in an accident, she realizes she can carry on with the business as a way of keeping his memory alive.

Tautau and Chanel have their North Nodes in Scorpio conjunct within a two degree orb, indicating the actress is able to understand designer's sense of business as well as her motivation to use her talents to make money. Tautou's Sun and Chanel's Venus are in conjunction in Leo. Here we can see how the actress understands the designer's sense of fashion and the need to be seen as well as respected.

Additionally, Tautou has Mars in Virgo conjunct Chanel's Uranus within a two degree orb showing the actress understood the designer's unique contributions to the fashion industry. However, Virgo is a sign noted for its sense of precision: Chanel's designs were not known for their bizarre design, but for how well-made the accessories were. Even today, Chanel's brand remains highly desirable and is a significator of high couture. Tautou's natal Neptune in Sagittarius was in opposition to Chanel's Saturn in Gemini showing the actress had the ability to take the hard edge from the designer's work and make it appear far more glamorous than it would have been in real life.

The movie was released as transiting Saturn in Virgo was conjunct Chanel's Mercury. The term "mad as a hatter" comes from the effects of working with Mercury that hat makers exhibited in the industrial age. The glyph (symbol) for Mercury in astrology also has a "hat" so it seems very appropriate this planet in Chanel's chart was transited by Saturn in a Mercury-ruled sign. Transiting Mercury in Taurus was conjunct the designer's natal Neptune. The film tells the tale of how a designer made her dreams come true by using her imagination.

Transiting Uranus in Pisces was exactly conjunct Tautou's descendant. Following her success in the film, Tautou became Chanel's new spokesperson, an unexpected perk gained through understanding the work ethic of the person she was playing.

The film was nominated for several awards but sadly didn't win any. However it grossed over $43 million on a production budget of $23 million.

FUNNY GIRL

**Fanny Brice: 29 October 1891, 00:03 (unverified), New York.
DD: RR
Barbra Streisand: 24 April 1942, 05:08, Brooklyn,
New York. AA: Steinbrecher
Release date: 18 September 1968**

For a movie called *Funny Girl* this film opens on a rather sad note: a woman waiting for her husband to get out of prison. The story of comedian and variety show performer Fanny Brice is told through an extended flashback.

When Fanny is young, she gets her first job in Vaudeville and meets the very handsome Nicky Arnstein during her first performance. They continue to meet and as she becomes more famous, they fall more and more in love. She is eventually seduced by Nicky and she decides to leave stardom to be with him.

While they are travelling around together on a ship, he wins a fortune playing poker and, being wealthy through his own efforts, he and Fanny get married. They move into a beautiful home, have a child together and Fanny returns to showbiz.

However, Nicky becomes involved in dodgy business deals and loses all his money. He refuses financial support from his wife and is eventually sent to prison for embezzling money. Once released, he and Fanny agree to separate.

The role of Fanny Brice was played to great acclaim by Barbra Streisand. Her Neptune is conjunct Brice's Saturn in Virgo and her Saturn/Uranus conjunction in Taurus is on Brice's North Node, allowing her an imaginative access to the hardships of the Variety performer's life. Also Streisand's South Node is conjunct Brice's Jupiter.

Transiting Jupiter was in opposition to Streisand's Venus when the film was released, forcing an expansion of her artistic skills. Although she was becoming known as a singer, her acting talents had not been recognised at the time. During production and filming, transiting Neptune would have been conjunct Brice's South Node.

Streisand won an Academy Award for Best Actress and the film is on several AFI lists, most notably number sixteen in Greatest Movie Musicals.

The Nodes 165

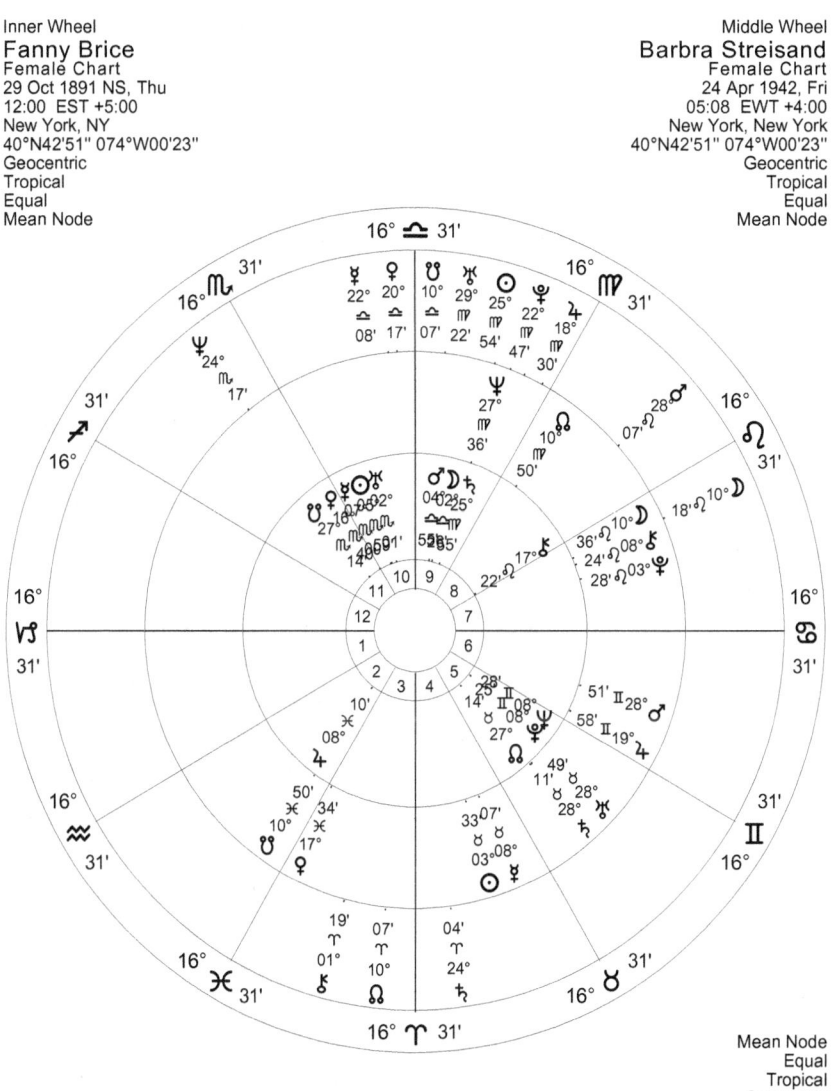

GANDHI

Mohandas Gandhi: 2 October 1869, 07:08, Porbandar,
Kathiawar Agency, W. India. AA:C
Ben Kingsley: 31 December 1943, no time, Scarborough, England.
X: Starkman
Release date: 30 November 1982

After evening prayers, a very old Gandhi is assisted as he greets a large number of visitors. From out of the crowd, a man shoots him in the chest. Gandhi cries out "Oh God," then falls down.

The film then goes back to Gandhi's early life as a young man on a South African train. He is thrown off for sitting in first class even though he has a first class ticket. He decides to start nonviolent protests to bring attention to the fact that the laws of South Africa are biased against Indians. After several arrests and international attention, the South African government begins to recognise the rights of Indians and Gandhi returns to India as a hero. He is urged to take up the fight for India's independence from the British Empire and he coordinates millions of Indians to take part in a nonviolent campaign.

Despite setbacks and the Jallianwala Bagh massacre, the protests put Britain under intense pressure. Gandhi organises the Salt March to highlight British taxes on salt and he visits London to discuss Britain's departure from India. It isn't until after World War II that Britain finally grants independence to India. The problems are far from over though, as the country is divided by religion; a new country, Pakistan, is created to encourage Muslims to live separately. Although Gandhi is very much against this idea, the partition of India is carried through. Hindus and Muslims continue to fight and Gandhi declares a hunger strike in an effort to make it stop.

Gandhi spends his last days attempting to bring peace to both sides of the controversy. The film ends with an earlier voiceover from Gandhi, as his ashes are scattered in the holy Ganges.

Both Ben Kingsley and Gandhi had their North Node in Leo within a four-degree orb. Ben Kingley's Pluto in Leo was also exactly conjunct his North Node. As filming took place, Chiron in Taurus transited Gandhi's Jupiter/Pluto conjunction. Cows, a symbol of Taurus, are sacred in India so it seems to be a striking representation of healing a country

The Nodes 167

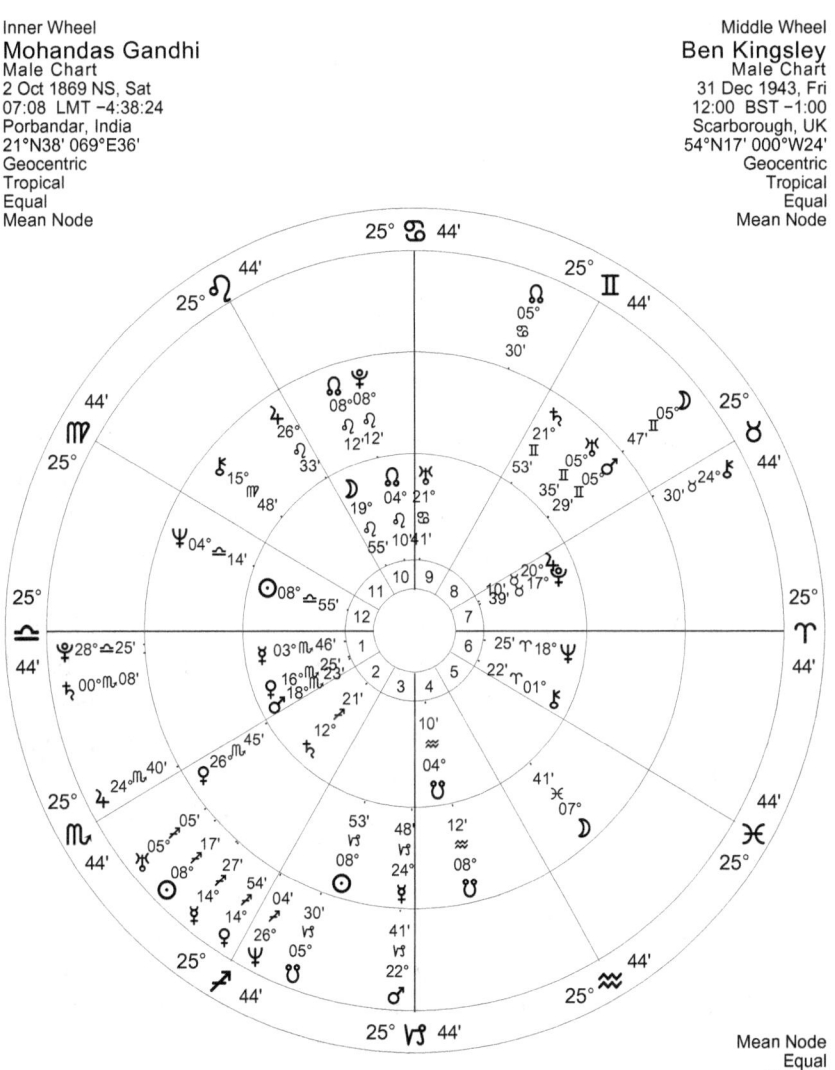

in turmoil. When the film was released, Jupiter transited Kingsley's Venus in Scorpio. To have both benefics activated in the sign of war and destruction seems very much like a nonviolent protest.

The film won Academy Awards, Golden Globes and BAFTAs for Best Picture and Best Actor.

LINCOLN
Abraham Lincoln: 12 February 1809, 06:54, Hodgenville, Kentucky. B: RR
Daniel Day Lewis: 29 April 1957, no time, Kensington, London. AX: Scholfield
Release date: 8 October 2012

Abraham Lincoln was a well-known and much-loved nineteenth century American president. It is not too much of an exaggeration to say he is an American hero as well as a character steeped in the mythology of the United States. *Lincoln*, directed by Steven Spielberg, covers the final four months of Lincoln's life and focuses on his work in getting the Thirteenth Amendment to the American Constitution passed by the US House of Representatives. The Thirteenth Amendment abolished slavery and involuntary servitude (except as a punishment for crime) and was also the first of three Reconstruction Amendments that were made in the wake of the American Civil War.

By the beginning of January 1865, where the film begins, the Civil War has been raging for some four years. This war was particularly tragic as it divided a nation (and the scars of the war and preceding events have never been resolved). Uncannily, Day-Lewis makes a most remarkable Abraham Lincoln, a figure no living person has seen alive and with only limited photographs (and no film footage) to guide the actor. Watching this legend walk and talk sends shivers down the spine.

Natally Lincoln has Uranus conjunct his North Node in Scorpio. Considering his revolutionary ideas, his insistence on freedom and equality that transformed the history of all the people of the United States, it makes perfect astrological sense to have the planet so associated with liberty in this position. Lincoln also has Saturn conjunct Neptune in Sagittarius which symbolically disintegrates rigid political policies. It seems apt that Lincoln, as well as anyone similar in age to him, would

The Nodes

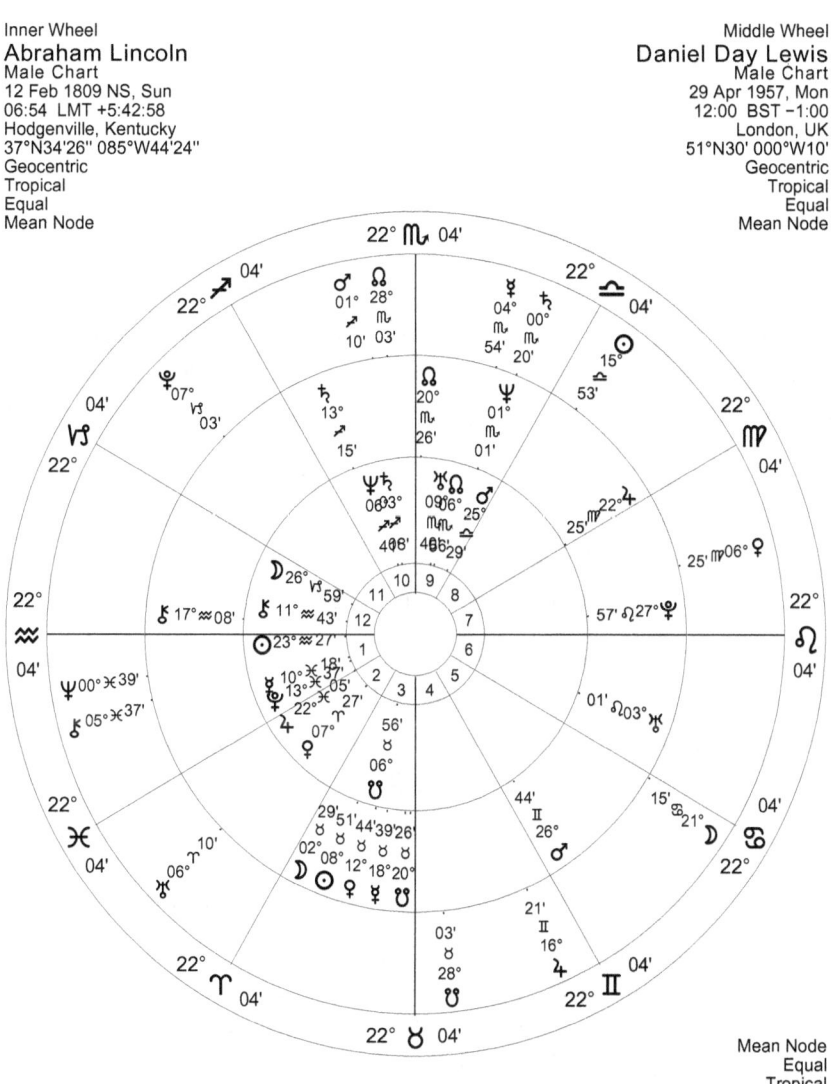

have this in their charts. The discovery of both Uranus (1791) and Neptune (1846) are fascinating stories in themselves and they coincided with the rapid expansion of the world, improved means of travel as well as trade and a whole heap of brand new issues to contend with.

Day-Lewis' Sun is conjunct Lincoln's South Node which opposes Lincoln's Uranus/North Node. Fate seems to be at work here. Although technically out of orb to be in conjunction, Day-Lewis' Saturn is also in Sagittarius and even more amazing is that both men have the same aspect of Chiron-Saturn at similar degrees apart in the same signs. Perhaps most remarkable is that both men have opposing Jupiter to the exact degree: Lincoln's in the deeply spiritual sign of Pisces and Day-Lewis' in the more methodical sign of Virgo. The actor was able to hone in on Lincoln's faith and philosophical thought: this is most likely why, with this portrayal, Day-Lewis was able to secure his third win for Best Actor for this role, more than any other actor in Academy Awards history.

Lincoln received significant praise and Day-Lewis' acting won him a Golden Globe as well as an Academy Award for Best Actor. The film was also a commercial success and grossed over $275 million at the box office.

PATTON

George Patton: 11 November 1885, 18:38, San Marino, California.
AA: RR
George C. Scott: 18 October 1927, 23:30, Wise, Virginia.
A: Shaw
Release date: 4 February 1970 (New York City)

In the opening scene, General George S. Patton speaks directly to the cinema audience on the topic of the importance of winning, as if he is addressing American troops in need of a morale boost.

The scene then shifts to the defeat of the US troops and Patton's manner of discipline amongst them in North Africa. In a meeting, Patton reports that the reason the Americans were defeated in battle was because there had not been adequate air cover. After being promised there would be no further German air strikes, the sky was full of German planes. Patton successfully defeats the German attack but is bitterly disappointed that one of his enemies had been on medical leave and has thus survived.

The Nodes 171

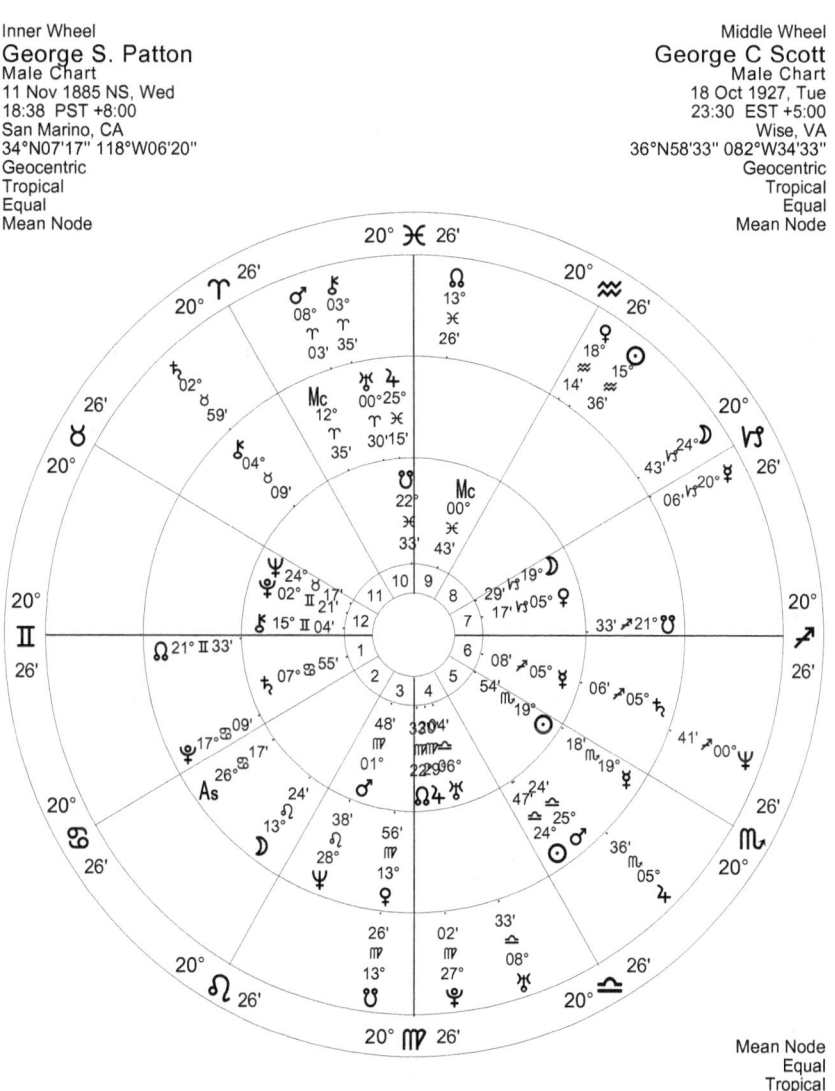

Patton and the British officer, Bernard Montgomery, then formulate competing plans to attack Italy. Patton's plan is to trap both the Germans and Italians, but President Eisenhower favours Montgomery's more cautious plan. Although the plan is partially successful, Patton has been forced to defy orders but still manages to achieve his objective better than Montgomery. Later Patton insists that it was Montgomery's ambition to monopolise success in the war that caused friction between the two.

While visiting a field hospital, Patton comes across a crying shell-shocked soldier. Patton slaps him and calls him a coward, demanding that the soldier be returned to the front line. As a punishment, Eisenhower relieves Patton of his command and orders that he not only apologise to the soldier but to the witnesses of the altercation and the entire command. He also has to serve as a decoy during the D-Day landings of 1944.

Patton begs to be returned to command before the end of the war, and Eisenhower agrees, placing Patton under a subordinate's command. Patton performs extremely well until his tanks run out of fuel. He is outraged to learn that supplies have been allocated to Montgomery's operation. Despite this, Patton leads another victory as his troops are able to successfully invade Germany.

At a war drive in England, Patton's outspoken remarks lead to him losing his command again and he is assigned to oversee the rebuilding of Germany.

The final scene shows Patton walking his dog as he tells the story about a slave warning a returning hero of ancient Rome that all glory is fleeting.

George C. Scott's North Node in Gemini was within one degree of Patton's ascendant, making it seem as if the actor was born to play this role. Within three degrees, the actor's Jupiter in Pisces was conjunct the general's South Node. Most strikingly, Scott's Mercury in Scorpio was exactly conjunct Patton's Sun and the actor's Saturn in Sagittarius was exactly conjunct Patton's Mercury within an orb of 10 minutes. Make no doubt about it: that voice of command the audience heard from Scott was Patton himself.

The movie was filmed during Patton's Uranus Return in Virgo and released when transiting Pluto was conjunct Patton's Jupiter in Virgo and opposing Scott's Jupiter in Pisces.

The film won Academy Awards for Best Picture and Best Actor. Film critic Roger Ebert said of Scott's performance: "It is one of those sublime performances in which the personalities of the actor and the character are fulfilled in one another".

MISS POTTER

Beatrix Potter: 28 July 1866, no time, London. X: Scholfield
Renée Zellweger: 25 April 1969, 14:41, Baytown, Texas. AA: Przy
Norman Warne: 6 July 1868, no time, London. Source: Wikipedia
Ewan McGregor: 21 March 1971, 20:10, Perth, Scotland. AA: RR
Release date: 3 December 2006

The film opens with Beatrix Potter telling us that she lives in London and is a spinster. As she packs up her notebooks and sketches, she reveals that her ambition is to become a children's author and that everyone disapproves of the idea. She and her travelling companion visit a publishing house called Harold and Fruing Warne, who confirm they will publish her book, *The Tale of Peter Rabbit*. Beatrix is very happy and takes a celebratory drive through the countryside. However, it is revealed that the Warne brothers think the book is silly, will never sell, and they only agreed to publish it to give their younger brother Norman something to do.

Norman visits Beatrix at her home and they make decisions about the design of the book. Norman is as excited as Beatrix and he tells her he has never done anything like this before. Beatrix realises what his brothers have done and she and Norman resolve to prove them wrong. They go to print and copies of her books start to sell.

Beatrix meets Norman's family and becomes fast friends with his sister Millie, who is overly excited that Beatrix is a spinster, as she thinks men are so boring. The family enjoy Beatrix's visit and it is clear she has been accepted into their fold. Her own family, particularly her mother, disapprove of her spending time with tradesmen and they argue over Beatrix's decision not to marry. Her mother says her book will not be successful.

However, the book proves to be very successful and copies make it into shop windows. Norman encourages Beatrix to continue writing and she submits more material for publication. Although her family are not especially supportive, her father buys one of her books after hearing all his friends talking about them.

For Christmas, Beatrix invites Norman and Millie to her home for a party. Norman spikes Beatrix's chaperone's coffee with brandy and she falls asleep. Beatrix reveals she is writing a story especially for Norman and shows him her studio where she writes and draws. Norman then proposes marriage but before Beatrix can answer him, her mother comes into the room to ask them to join the other guests in the drawing room. Beatrix whispers to Millie about the proposal and to her surprise, Millie encourages her to accept. The guests are entertained by Beatrix's stories but her mother doesn't see why adults would find such things so amusing.

Just before Norman leaves, Beatrix accepts his proposal, but this soon turns to disappointment as her father dismisses him when he asks for consent; the family have an argument over her insistence that she will marry Norman, saying that he is beneath them as he comes from a family of tradesmen. Beatrix reminds her parents that her grandfathers were also tradesmen and that her brother married the daughter of a tradesman. Their response is that they will cut her off financially. Beatrix tells them she can make a living from her books and when her father tries to reason with her, she says she wants to marry for love and not just to be taken care of.

Beatrix wants to buy a house in the country and visits her bank to ask if she has enough money. She is stunned to discover she has amassed enough in book royalties to buy several estates if she so desires. Armed with this knowledge, she is able to accept a deal with her parents: she will not announce her engagement to Norman yet, but will accompany them to their holiday home for the summer. At the end of the summer, if she still wants to marry him, they will not object. Beatrix warns them to prepare for an October wedding.

Norman and Beatrix kiss at the railway station, knowing they will soon marry. They keep in contact through romantic letters, but after not hearing from Norman for a while a letter arrives from Millie informing her that Norman is sick. When Beatrix hurriedly travels back to London, she is told Norman has already died. Grief-stricken, Beatrix tries to find comfort in her drawings but the pictures she draws are shown fading off the page.

The Nodes 175

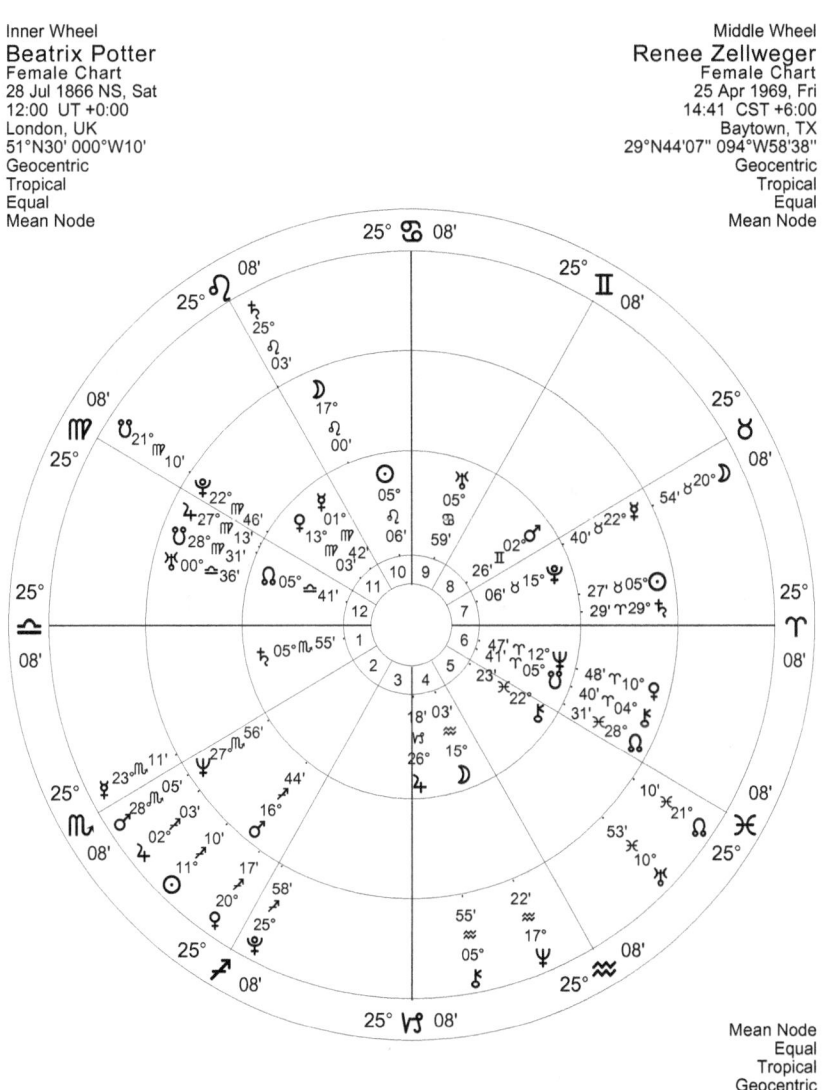

Millie comes to offer support, and Beatrix tells her she needs to move out of the family home. She subsequently buys a house in the north of England and continues to write. A solicitor helps her to buy auctioned farms and land to preserve the beauty of nature in the face of encroaching industry. Eight years later, with her mother's disapproval, she marries the solicitor and the land she purchased eventually becomes part of the Lake District National Park.

Beatrix Potter and Renée Zellweger have their Suns exactly square so it was difficult to see Zellweger beyond her other roles, particularly *Bridget Jones*. Potter's South Node in Aries is conjunct Zellweger's Chiron so that helped the audience understand the restrictions a young woman of that era would have faced. Potter's Neptune in Aries is conjunct the actress' Venus, which no doubt contributed to the fluffy bunny imagery. When the movie was released, the North Node was transiting Potter's Chiron.

Norman Warne's Jupiter in Aries is conjunct Ewan McGregor's Sun. (Chart not shown.) Transiting Saturn in Leo was within three degrees of Warne's North Node and transiting Mars in Scorpio was conjunct his natal Saturn when the film was released. Transiting Jupiter in Sagittarius was exactly conjunct McGregor's Neptune when the film was released.

There were no major awards for the film though the animation techniques were praised.

RAY

Ray Charles: 23 September 1930, no time, Albany, Georgia. X: RR
Jamie Foxx: 13 December 1967, no time, Terrell, Texas.
X: Taglilatelo
Release date: 29 October 2004

The film begins in 1948 as a young Ray Charles boards a bus and lies about how he lost his sight during the war in order to get a free ride on public transportation. He travels to Seattle and due to his extraordinary piano playing gets a job with the resident band. Things soon go sour as he realises he's being exploited by the club's owner.

 Charles leaves Seattle and in 1950 joins a country band whose members make him hide his damaged eyes with dark glasses during performances. As they travel around on tour, his childhood is revealed through flashbacks. When he was five years old, his younger brother drowned in front of him, and shortly afterwards, Charles began to lose his sight. By the age of seven, he had completely lost his vision but his mother taught him to be as independent as possible.

On the tour, Charles demands to be paid in one-dollar bills so he can feel the thickness of the money, having been conned in the past. His popularity increases and eventually he is invited to record an album and has his first hit single. He marries a preacher's daughter, Della Bea, but she isn't happy about him mixing gospel and soul together. He goes off on tour and teams up with a singer, Marie Anne Fisher. On one of his trips home Della discovers his drug kit in his wash bag; by this point she is pregnant and she demands he give up heroin. He refuses and walks out on her.

Ray's fame continues to rise and he has further affairs and his love life becomes increasingly complicated. In Atlanta, he joins the civil rights protest by refusing to play if the black concertgoers have to sit in the balcony. Consequently he is barred from performing in the state of Georgia. A few years later, he writes his hit *Georgia on my Mind*.

At one point Charles is arrested for possession of drugs but is released on a technicality because the police don't have a search warrant. However, a few years later, he's deported from Canada and has to cancel his concert there. He learns his former lover and singing partner has died of an overdose but denies getting her addicted. Forced to go into treatment, he suffers from withdrawal symptoms and nightmares. In one flashback, his brother tells him that he wasn't to blame for his death.

Conquering his addiction was one of Charles' greatest achievements and that same year, the state of Georgia apologises to him and makes *Georgia on my Mind* their official state song.

The film is dedicated to Ray Charles who died the year before it was released.

Ray Charles was born so close to the cusp that it isn't possible to ascertain whether he had the Sun in Virgo or Libra. However, even with an untimed chart, he would have had the Moon in Libra ruled by Venus in Scorpio which may partially account for his complicated relationships. Another factor that may have contributed was his Uranus in Aries square his natal Mars in Cancer which was also conjunct Jupiter and Pluto.

178 Mirror Mirror

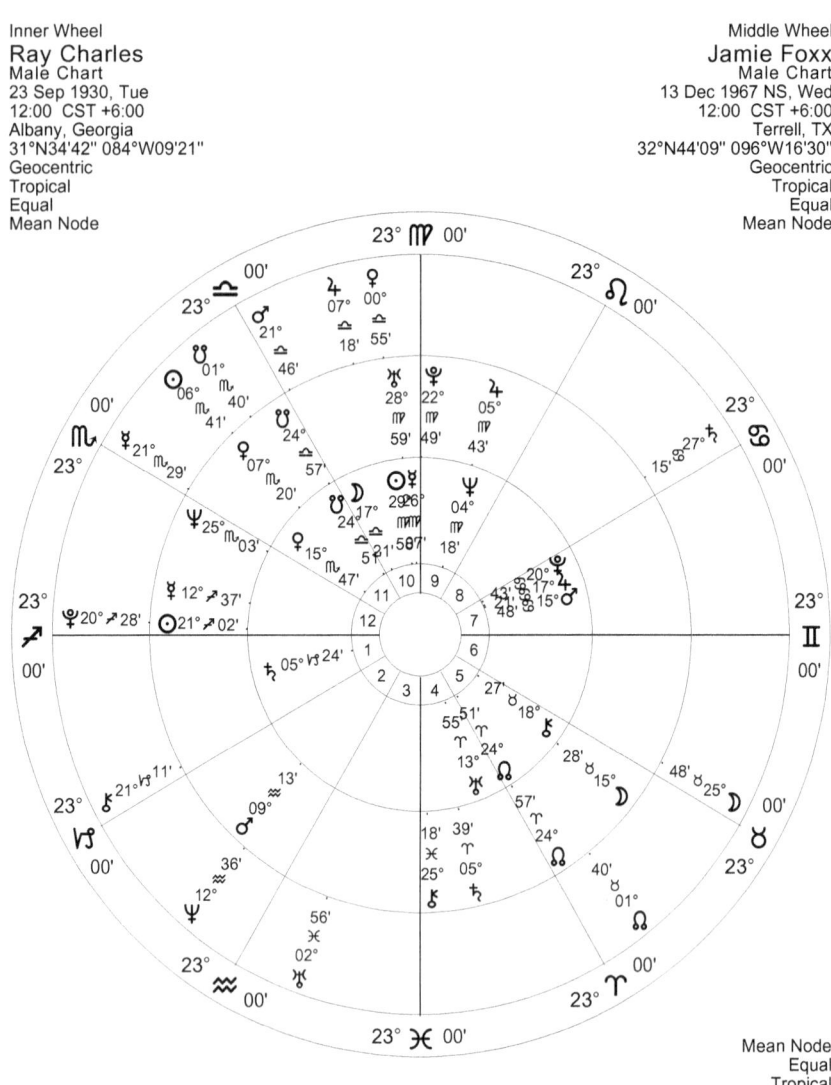

Incredibly both men have the North Node at 24° Aries which shows a true connection to destiny. Additionally, Foxx's Jupiter in Virgo is just one degree from Charles' Neptune, allowing the actor the opportunity to dig into the singer's musicality as well as his addictions. The actor's Uranus is conjunct Charles' Sun/Mercury conjunction too.

Transiting Venus had just entered Libra when the film was released and so was conjunct Charles' Sun and Mercury and Foxx's Uranus, and Foxx's Sun in Sagittarius was transited by Pluto.

Foxx was awarded an Academy Award, a BAFTA, a Golden Globe and a Screen Actors Guild as well as many other accolades for Best Actor. The film was nominated for Best Picture at the Academy Awards.

SELENA

Selena Quintanilla-Pérez: 16 April 1971, no time, Freeport, Texas.
Source: Wikipedia
Jennifer Lopez: 24 July 1969, no time, Bronx, New York.
Source: Wikipedia
Release date: 21 March 1997

In the early 1960s, a young Latino band called The Dinos fail an audition due to the "Whites Only" policy of the Texan restaurant they were to perform in. Later, when they perform for a Mexican audience, they cause a riot through not performing Hispanic music.

By 1981 Abraham, the leader of the band, has fallen in love with and married Marcella Samora, and in time encourages their children to form their own band, Selena y Los Dinos, with the youngest, Selena, as lead singer. Abraham insists that the children learn Spanish so that they appeal to Mexican audiences at the family-owned restaurant. Sadly, the restaurant fails and the family move to a different part of Texas where the children also begin incorporating dancing in their act.

As the band grow in popularity, a guitarist called Chris Perez helps them to write music, and he and Selena fall in love. Even though her father has expressed disapproval, the young couple elope. Unfortunately, they are popular enough that Abraham hears about the marriage on the radio and fearing the worst, Selena goes back to speak to him. She is surprised when he says he only wants the best for her, and her husband is welcomed into the family.

180 Mirror Mirror

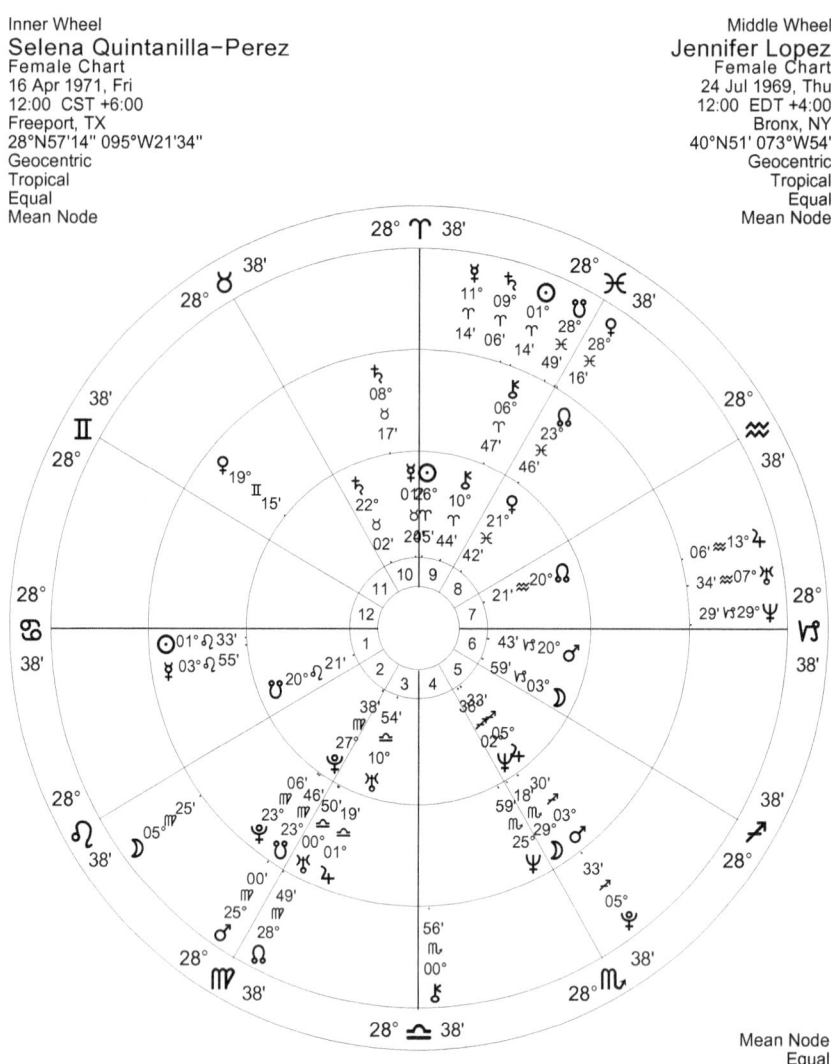

During a live performance, Abraham is offered an English language record deal, and on the back of this success Selena opens a boutique called Selena Etc. which is managed by her fan-club president, Yolanda Saldivar. The album *Selena Live* wins a Grammy but Yolanda is suspected of embezzling funds from Selena's accounts. When confronted over the missing accounts, Yolanda shoots Selena and following a stand-off with the police she's arrested for murder.

The final scenes of the film show clips of Selena performing.

Lopez's natal South Node and Pluto in Virgo are exactly conjunct, and are within a two degree orb of opposition to Perez's Venus in Pisces. Perez's Venus was on Lopez's North Node allowing success for the actress not only as a singer but in identifying with this particular singer. Additionally, Lopez's Mars in Sagittarius is conjunct Perez's Jupiter/Neptune conjunction. She could reactivate the dreams of the singer. The film was released when Mars in Virgo was transiting Lopez's South Node and Pluto, and Pluto in Sagittarius was transiting the conjunctions in Sagittarius.

Lopez was nominated for a Golden Globe for Best Actress.

THE AVIATOR
Howard Hughes: 24 December, 1905, no time, Humble, Texas.
Source: Wikipedia
Leonardo DiCaprio: 11 November 1974, 02:47, Los Angeles.
AA: RR
Katherine Hepburn: 12 May 1907, 17:47, Hartford, Connecticut.
AA: RR
Cate Blanchett: 14 May 1969, 06:40, Melbourne, Australia.
C: Scholfield
Ava Gardner: 24 December 1922, 19:10, Boon Hill,
North Carolina. AA: RR
Kate Beckinsale: 26 July 1973, no time, Chiswick, England.
Source: Wikipedia
Release date: 14 December 2004

As a young child, Howard Hughes' preoccupation with germs is apparent and this becomes increasingly problematic as he grows older.

As a young man, he is interested in making films, particularly in the new field of "talkies". He uses his business skills to make – and borrow – impossible sums of money. His success attracts famous and beautiful actresses such as Katherine Hepburn, even though his OCD traits are becoming more obvious to her.

Hughes' interests move to aviation and he breaks several flying records, often bringing Hepburn on less dangerous flights so she can fly too. On a solo test flight, he crash lands a plane in a beet field but escapes serious injury. His eye for perfection leads him to designing faster airplanes and even brokering huge deals for the purchase of airline companies. However, his OCD eventually becomes impossible for Hepburn to tolerate and she leaves him for Spencer Tracy. It doesn't take long for Hughes to find another young love interest in Faith Domergue, but that doesn't stop him from bribing the newspapers to keep Hepburn and Tracy out of the media.

Hughes then falls in love with Ava Gardner which angers his young girlfriend to the point she deliberately smashes her car into his, to the delight of the waiting paparazzi.

After a horrific plane crash which nearly kills him, Hughes' OCD becomes more out of control and he begins tapping Gardner's phone lines – which infuriates her. During an investigation into a suspected illegal business deal, FBI agents track mud into his home; aghast, Hughes locks himself in a germ-free room and doesn't emerge for months. Assuming he would not be well enough to attend a hearing, Hughes is offered a deal to have the charges against him dropped if he will sell his airline. He declines, and Gardner helps him prepare for the hearing by getting him cleaned up and presentable. He successfully negotiates a deal in court, though his mental health continues to decline. The film ends with him repeating "the way of the future" over and over as flashbacks of his life are played.

Hughes has a stellium in Sagittarius, the sign associated with speculation and long distance travel, conjunct DiCaprio's North Node/Neptune conjunction. The film depicts Hughes' complicated romantic life involving legendary actresses, so it is interesting indeed that Pluto in Sagittarius would have transited his Venus during filming.

Katherine Hepburn's natal Moon is conjunct the fixed star Algol which signifies intensive, passionate romances. Hepburn and Cate Blanchett have their Suns in Taurus only a couple of degrees apart. Hepburn's Saturn in Pisces is conjunct Cate's North Node within just a couple of degrees.

The Nodes 183

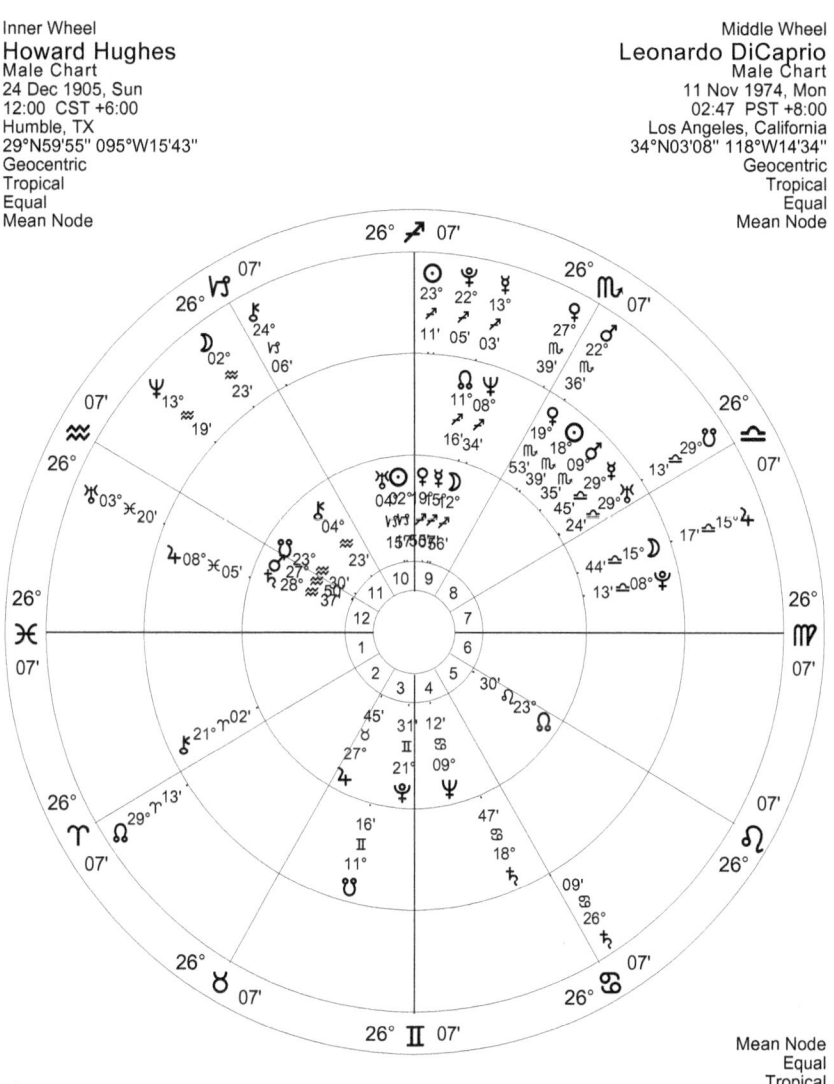

184   Mirror Mirror

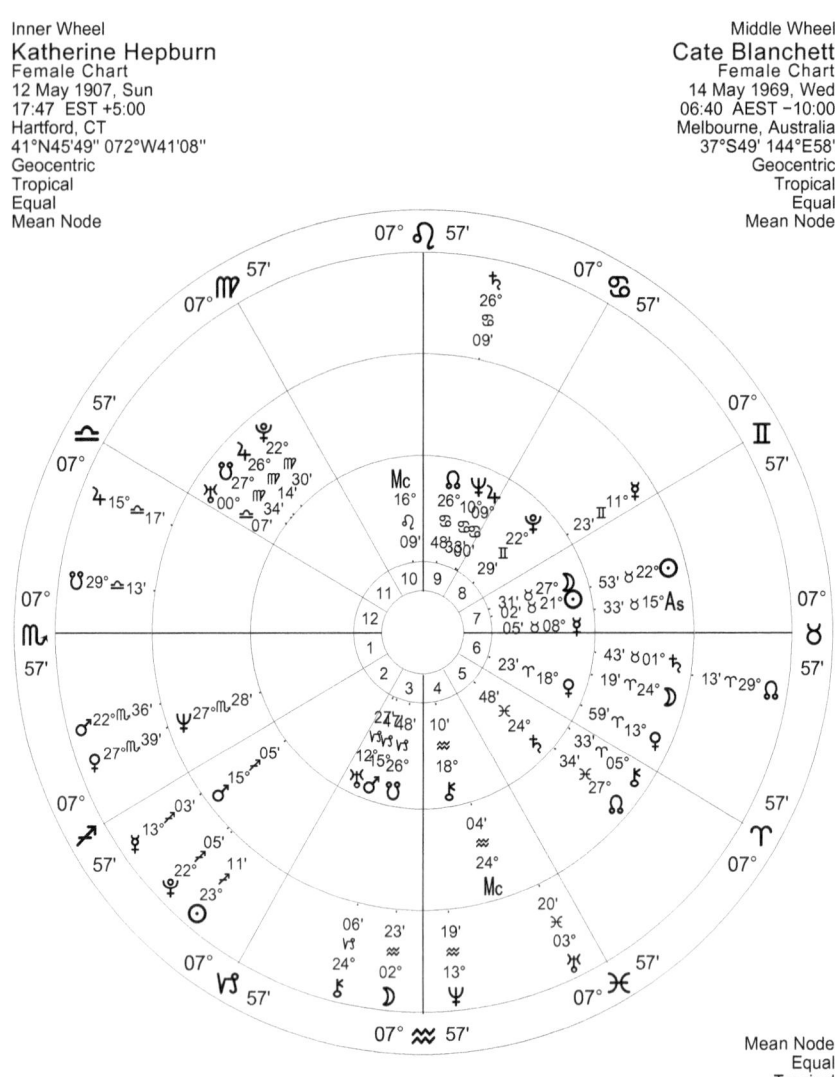

The Nodes 185

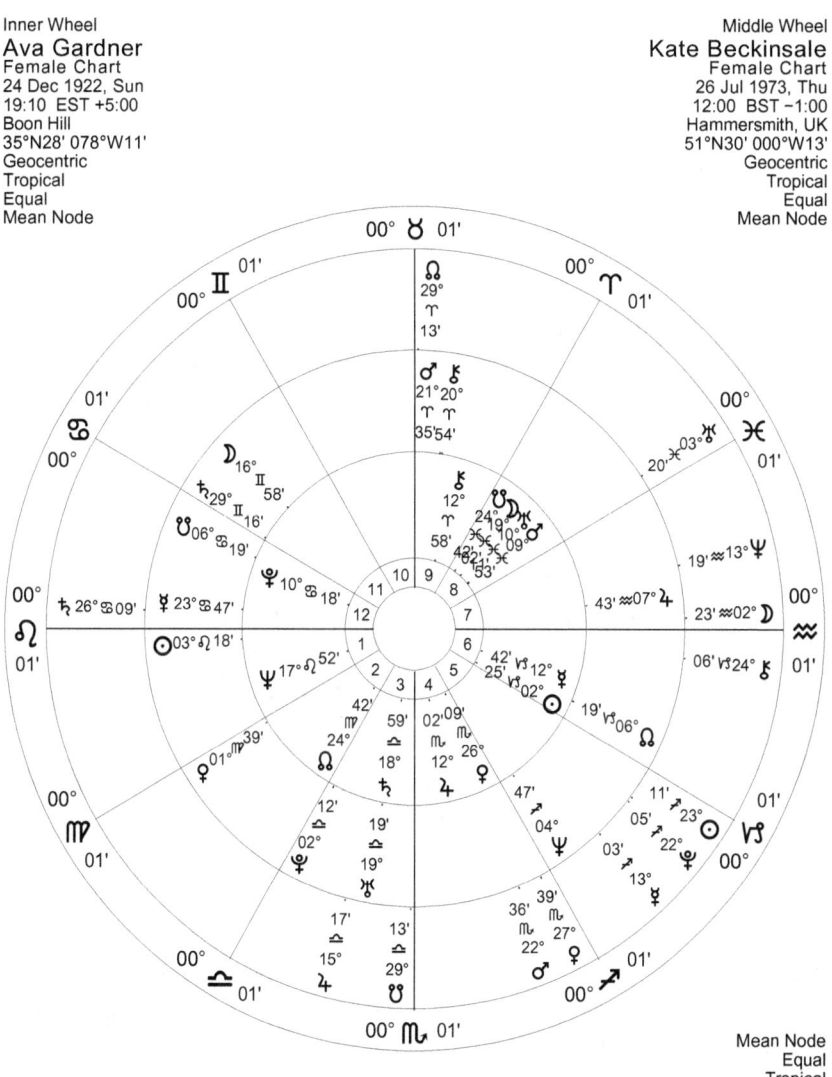

Transiting Saturn in Cancer was conjunct Katherine's North Node and transiting Chiron was in opposition to both when the film was released. Transiting Venus in Scorpio was exactly conjunct Cate's Neptune and transiting Jupiter in Libra was in orb of opposition to both actresses' Venus when the movie was released.

Kate Beckinsale's Sun in Leo is conjunct Ava Gardner's ascendant within a three degree orb and her Chiron in Aries is conjunct Garner's MC. Additionally, Beckinsale's Uranus in Libra is conjunct Gardner's Saturn, and Jupiter was transiting this conjunction when the film was released.

The film was nominated for eleven Academy Awards and Blanchett won for Best Supporting Actress. It was nominated for fourteen BAFTAs and won Best Film and Best Supporting Actress. It was nominated for six Golden Globes and won Best Film and Best Actor as well as a Screen Actors Guild Award for Best Supporting Actress for Blanchett.

THE BUDDY HOLLY STORY

Buddy Holly: 7 September 1936, 15:30, Lubbock, Texas. A: Keely
Gary Busey: 29 June 1944, 11:50, Baytown, Texas. A: RR
Plane Crash: 3 February 1959, 01:00, near Clear Lake, Iowa.
Release date: 18 May 1978

It is difficult to watch a movie if you already know the ending. And everyone knows that the 3rd of February 1959 was the worst day in rock and roll history. *The Buddy Holly Story* was released as transiting Neptune was conjunct the Moon of the plane crash that killed Buddy Holly and transiting Uranus was conjunct the ascendant of the disaster. Gary Busey was praised for his performance of the adorable singer.

Holly's Sun/Neptune conjunction is on Busey's ascendant and Holly's Moon is conjunct the actor's Uranus. Buddy Holly got his start through his insistence on playing the band's music the way they wanted to.

The film traces Holly's humble beginnings as an unknown star who falls in love with his producer's secretary and eventually marries her. His backing band, The Crickets, also feature in the film. At one point they decide to leave but want to return to re-form the band during the disastrous *Winter Dance Tour*. Many of Busey's natal planets fall on

The Nodes   187

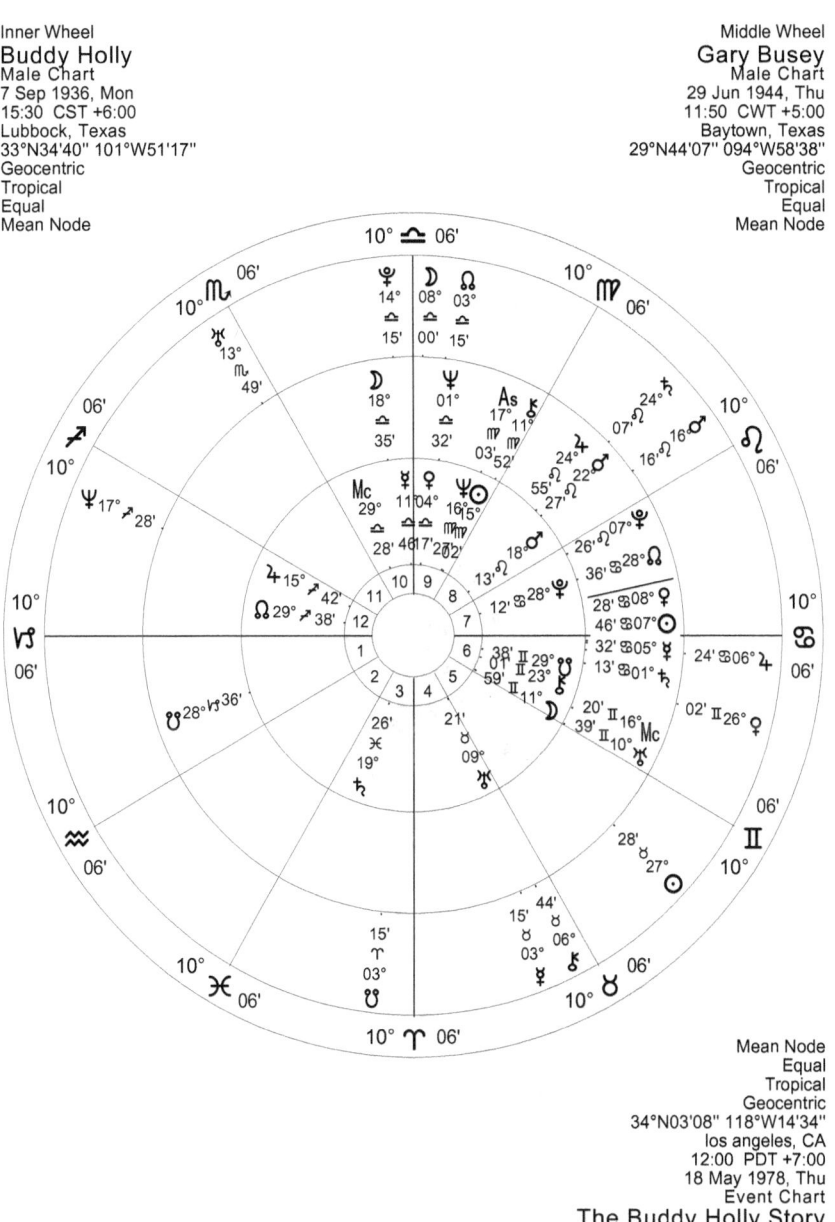

Inner Wheel
Buddy Holly
Male Chart
7 Sep 1936, Mon
15:30 CST +6:00
Lubbock, Texas
33°N34'40" 101°W51'17"
Geocentric
Tropical
Equal
Mean Node

Middle Wheel
Gary Busey
Male Chart
29 Jun 1944, Thu
11:50 CWT +5:00
Baytown, Texas
29°N44'07" 094°W58'38"
Geocentric
Tropical
Equal
Mean Node

Mean Node
Equal
Tropical
Geocentric
34°N03'08" 118°W14'34"
los angeles, CA
12:00 PDT +7:00
18 May 1978, Thu
Event Chart
The Buddy Holly Story
Outer Wheel

Holly's descendant. If the events of the film are to be believed, The Crickets turn up on Holly's pregnant wife's doorstep to say they want to re-unite. Early the next morning, Buddy Holly and several members of the Winter Dance tour die in a plane crash.

Busey's portrayal of Holly changed his life as demonstrated by the actor's North Node conjunct the singer's Pluto. Aside from a stint on the UK's *Celebrity Big Brother* television programme, Busey's subsequent acting roles have been rather thin, following a motorcycle accident that nearly killed him in 1988.

Busey was nominated for an Academy Award for Best Actor.

CHIRON

Mythologically, Chiron was the Wounded Healer who, in trying to find the cure for his own ailments, accidentally found cures for many others.

In this section, we see examples of this theme with the connections in the complicated lives of wounded people. It's as if the actors truly understand the suffering of their subjects. Ruth Ellis, played by Miranda Richardson in *Dance With a Stranger* had her Jupiter in Aquarius within two degrees of the actress' Chiron. In *Factory Girl*, Edie Sedgwick had her Mercury in Taurus conjunct Sienna Miller's Chiron. Judy Garland, portrayed by Renee Zellweger in *Judy*, had her South Node conjunct the actress' Chiron in Aries. Meryl Streep as Karen Silkwood had her South Node conjunct the activist's Chiron in Libra. Although a television production, *The Karen Carpenter Story* with Cynthia Gibb in the eponymous role, had her Chiron in Pisces conjunct the singer's Sun.

DANCE WITH A STRANGER
Ruth Ellis: 9 October 1926, 18:41, Rhyl, Wales. C: RR
Miranda Richardson: 3 March 1958, no time, Southport, England.
Source: Wikipedia
Release date: 1 March 1985

Ruth Ellis had worked as a nude model and prostitute before becoming the manager of a drinking club in London whose clientele were mainly race car drivers. She lives in the flat above the club with her illegitimate son. Ellis has lost custody of another child who now lives with her ex-husband's family.

One night at the club, she meets an attractive race car driver from a wealthy family and falls for him. Unfortunately, he drinks much of his money away which also impedes his success as a professional driver. Unable to find suitable work, he refuses to marry Ruth. With two children from two different men and a chequered past, there is no way Ruth would be accepted by his family. The couple have an argument at the club and he makes a scene, which leads to her being fired and evicted from her flat.

190   Mirror Mirror

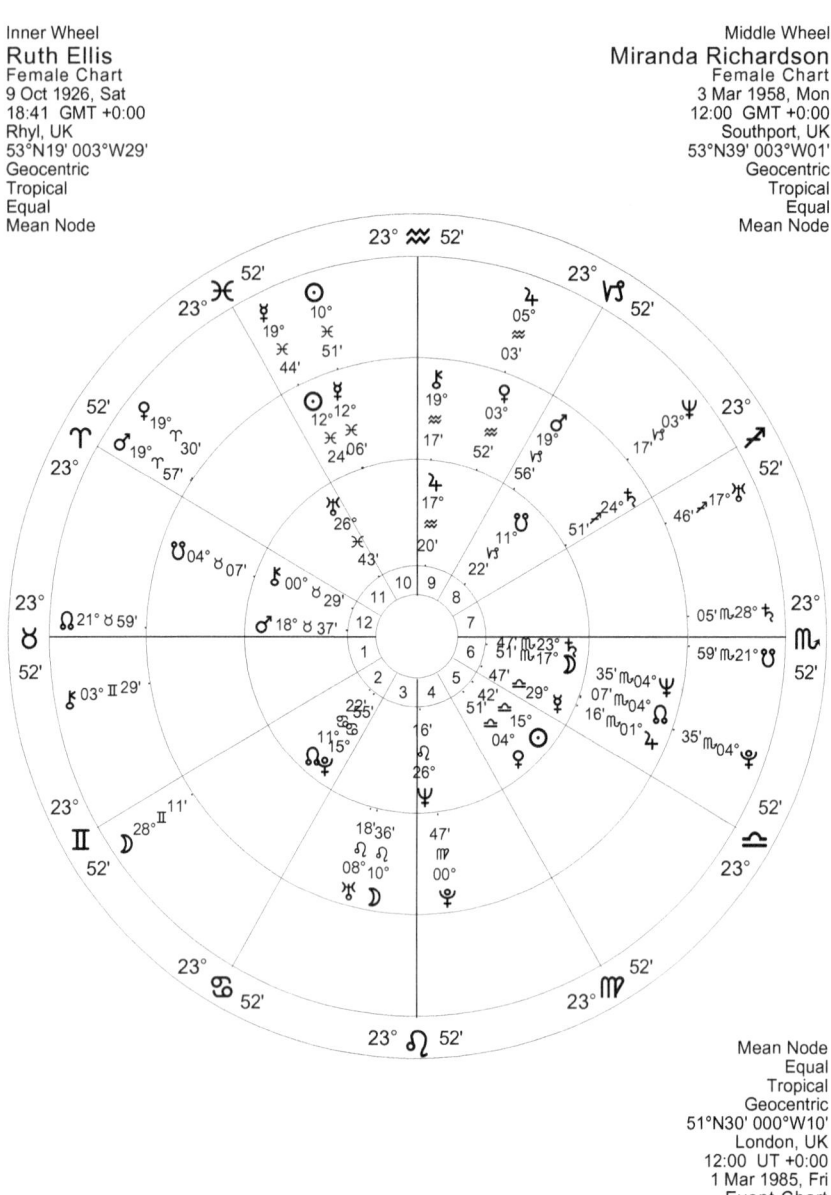

A wealthy admirer helps her secure another home and eventually she continues seeing the racing car driver. When she tells him she is pregnant, he still refuses to marry her and the hurt of the rejection leads to Ruth having a miscarriage. Devastated, she goes to look for him and sees him take another woman to a pub. When he comes out, she shoots him four times; she is arrested and eventually tried and hanged.

Ellis had Saturn in Scorpio exactly conjunct her descendant which says much about the type of men who were drawn to her: the type that would want to dominate and control her. With her Jupiter in Aquarius, it would not have been easy for her to give up her freedom. Perhaps, had she lived in a time when unmarried mothers had more choices, the outcome of her life would have been very different. It took Miranda Richardson, who had her Chiron conjunct Ellis' Jupiter, to live this freedom out for her in the film.

During filming, transiting Saturn would have crossed over Ellis' descendant, and transiting Pluto was exactly conjunct Richardson's North Node in Scorpio when the film was released. *Dance With a Stranger* was reported to have made a comfortable profit and Richardson won a minor award for her portrayal of the tragic Ruth Ellis.

FACTORY GIRL

Edie Sedgwick: 20 April 1943, 09:47, Santa Barbara, California.
AA: RR
Sienna Miller: 28 December 1981, no time, New York City.
Source: Wikipedia
Andy Warhol: 6 August 1928, 06:30, Pittsburgh, Pennsylvania.
B: RR
Guy Pearce: 5 October 1967, 16:15, Ely, England. A: Clifford
Release date: 29 December 2006

Sedgwick's story is told in flashback as she was in hospital many years after her split from the artist Andy Warhol.

The story begins with Edie's move to New York City where she plans to study art, and it's here she is introduced to Andy Warhol. Edie is a troubled – but very beautiful – young heiress, and Warhol asks her to be a part of one of his experimental films. She eventually becomes a major

192 Mirror Mirror

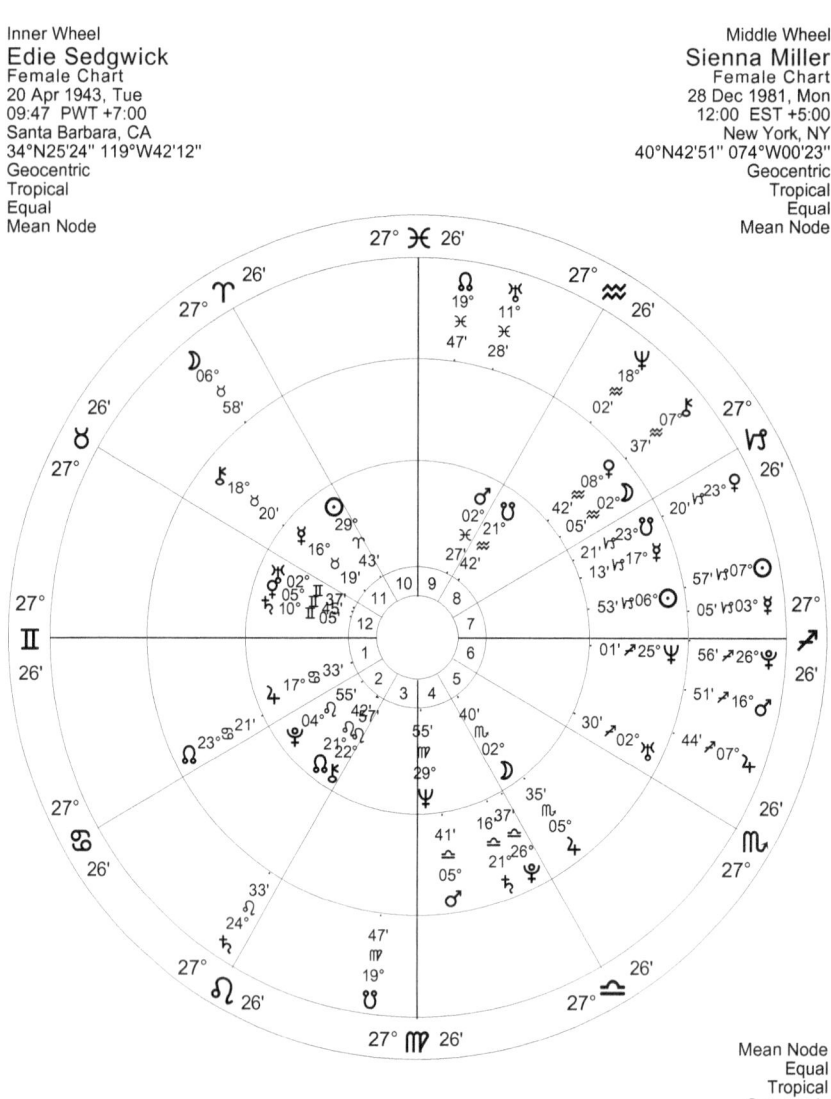

Chiron 193

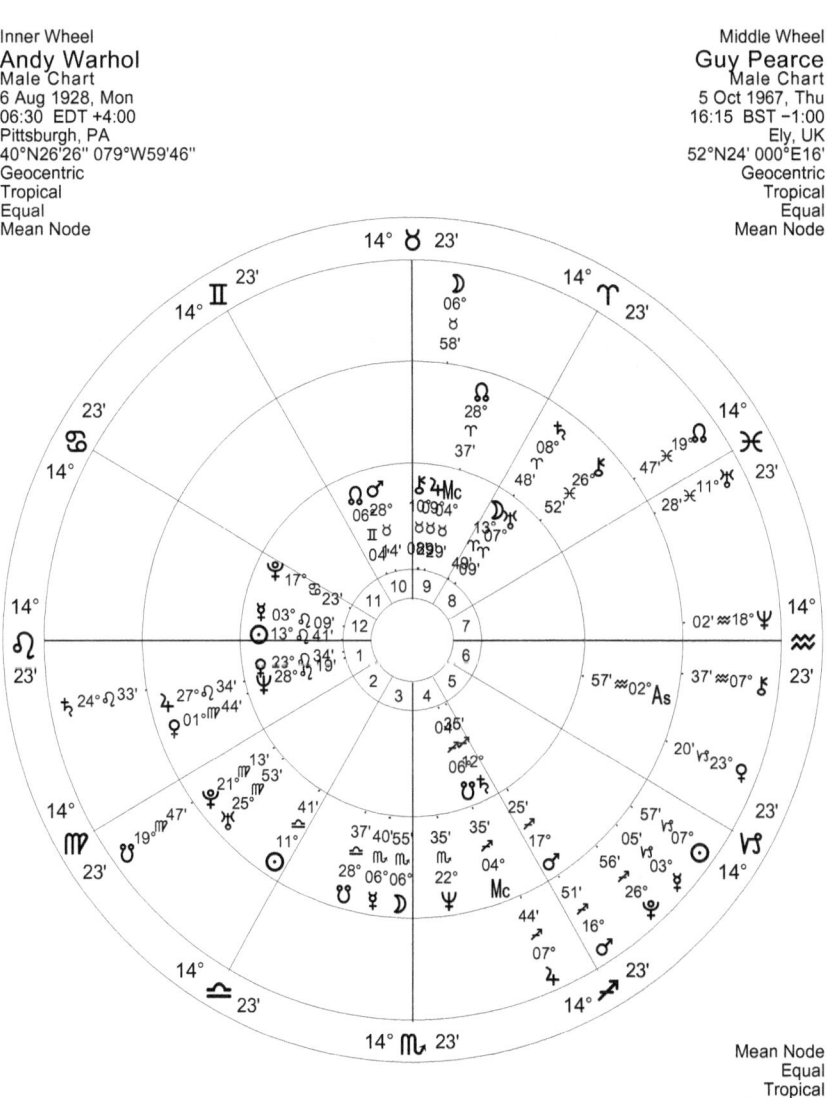

inspiration for him and his connections help to launch her international career.

However, she has several unresolved issues that manifest in poor financial management and drug addiction. It's revealed that she has been sexually abused by her father and is grieving over the death of her brother, to whom she was very close.

Edie eventually meets a folk singer and they begin a relationship, which causes Andy to become jealous. To smooth things over, Edie arranges for her boyfriend to do some filming at Andy's now famous Factory. However, the boyfriend and his friends are very rude and dismissive of Andy and his work and he even tells her that Andy is a bloodsucker and that her continued friendship with him will lead to her death. She defends Andy and her boyfriend leaves her.

This doesn't stop Edie and Andy's friendship from disintegrating. Although Edie has everything from money to international fame with high fashion magazines, she can't control her drug addiction and it alienates her from Andy's Factory crowd. After she nearly dies in a house fire that she caused by falling asleep with a burning cigarette whilst high, fashion magazines also withdraw their support.

At her lowest point, she is visited by a friend as she is being filmed naked by strangers. After throwing out the strangers, the friend shows Edie a photo of herself when she was clean. Devastated by the state of her life, she runs out into the street hysterically crying.

The film returns to the hospital interview a few years after the incident and Edie says she is living in California where she's pursing an art degree again.

The audience is told Edie that died at the age of twenty-eight and that the day after she died, Andy Warhol nervously said he barely knew her at all.

Warhol had Mars in Taurus conjunct the fixed star Algol with an exact square from Neptune. He had a reputation for becoming obsessed then disinterested with his muses. Sedgwick's natal Neptune in Virgo was trine to Algol so it can be seen how their attraction to each other would have been intense with elements of jealousy and obsession. This is magnified by his Pluto being conjunct her Jupiter in Cancer and her Pluto in Leo conjunct his Mercury. His Venus was also conjunct her

Chiron and North Node in Leo so it is possible he brought out the anguish of her childhood and sense of loss.

Guy Pearce's noticeably subtle performance of Warhol (after all, this was a film about Sedgwick) can perhaps be seen in his Saturn in Aries conjunct Warhol's Moon/Uranus conjunction. The film was released as Jupiter transited Warhol's natal South Node and Saturn in Sagittarius and Saturn was transiting his Venus in Leo. This portrayal was hardly a flattering one. For Pearce, the film was released during his Mars return in Sagittarius.

Within a two-degree orb, Sienna Miller's Neptune was conjunct Sedgwick's descendant so the actress was very able to understand the difficulties of the subject's addiction. Transiting Pluto was conjunct this point when the film was released. Miller's Jupiter in Scorpio is just a few degrees away from Sedgwick's Moon and so the overt sexuality of the character could be made prominent. Sedgwick had Mercury in Taurus and Miller's Chiron was only two degrees away, meaning she was easily able to convey Sedgwick's rampant materialism.

During filming, Uranus in Pisces was transiting Sedgwick's MC and Saturn in Leo was transiting her North Node and Chiron: the film was about the disintegration of a life that should have been successful. Transiting Pluto in Sagittarius was conjunct Miller's Neptune and Venus in Capricorn was conjunct her South Node. This was one of Sienna Miller's more successful films and she received high praise for her performance.

JUDY
Judy Garland: 10 June 1922, 06:00, Grand Rapids, Minnesota.
AA: Steinbrecher
Renée Zellweger: 25 April 1969, 14:41, Baytown, Texas. AA: Przy
Release date: 30 August 2019 (Telluride)

The film opens with a young teenaged Judy being told she has a gift no one else has and that she could surpass the success of Shirley Temple. Judy is then shown performing with her two children and later being turned away from their hotel room for non-payment of a previous bill. Judy is forced to return to her ex-husband.

196 Mirror Mirror

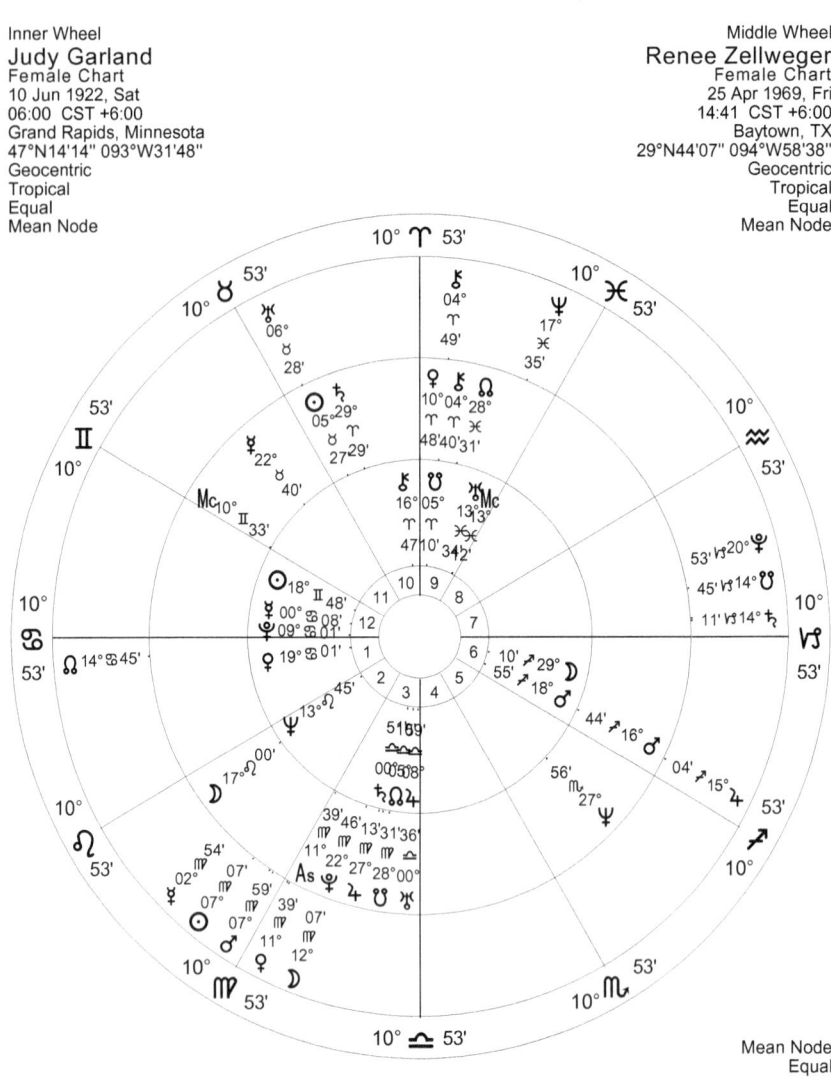

There is another flashback to Judy's teenage years on a date with Mickey Rooney. Her studio minder interrupts the date to give her amphetamines to control her appetite. The film then returns to her later years where she is being told she has gained a reputation for being unreliable and moody in the US. She moves to the UK, leaving her children with her ex, which is very difficult for her.

Her substance abuse problems prevent her from performing reliably on stage and she is late for her own London premiere. Assistants are called in to check on her and fix her make-up, and she goes on to perform beautifully. Another flashback to her teenage years show her complaining about being given pills to help her manage her schedule.

Back in London, she finishes another performance and is met by fans at the stage door. She joins in their commiserations and they bond over their problems. A friend (later her fifth husband) joins her in London as a surprise visit and cheers her up. However, Judy still has problems with performing and another flashback shows her being bullied and intimidated into keeping an impossible schedule.

In London, she has a medical examination that shows she is suffering from physical and mental exhaustion and that she needs to rest. She misses her children but is told they are happily attending school in California. Money worries mean she has to stay in London to make ends meet, and one night she passes out on stage and is heckled by the audience. On her last night on stage, she breaks down as she sings "Over the Rainbow" but is supported and encouraged by the audience who assure her that they will always remember her.

Judy died six months later at the age of 47.

Judy's unreliability can be seen astrologically with her Uranus in Pisces conjunct her MC. Her addiction to stimulants and depressants (as well as alcohol) is also apparent with this configuration: any of those addictions would account for her erratic stage behaviour. Judy's South Node was conjunct Renée Zellweger's Chiron and so the actress would have been aware of the Judy's pain and suffering. They both have Mars in Sagittarius within two degrees so share an enthusiastic spirit for adventure. Judy's Jupiter in Libra is in opposition to Zellweger's Venus in Aries so there is also a mutual understanding of the need for relationships under their own terms.

The film was released on Zellweger's Chiron return and as Jupiter was transiting both her and Judy's Mars in Sagittarius. During production, Neptune was transiting Judy's Uranus and MC in Pisces.

To date, Zellweger's performance is a critical and commercial success and has grossed $38 million at the time of writing. She has won a Golden Globe, the Critics Choice Movie Award for Best Actress and has been nominated for the Screen Actors Guild Award, a BAFTA and an Oscar.

SILKWOOD
Karen Silkwood: 19 February 1946, 21:50, Longview, Texas.
AA: RR
Meryl Streep: 22 June 1949, 08:05, Summit, New Jersey.
AA: Steinbrecher
Release date: 14 December 1983

Karen Silkwood makes MOX fuel rods for nuclear reactors and lives under the constant threat of contamination. She shares a rundown house with her boyfriend and her lesbian friend who also works at the plant.

After witnessing incidents of co-workers being "cooked" by radiation, she begins to suspect that the corporate practices of the plant are adversely affecting the health of its workers. After the plant falls behind on a contract, workers are obligated to work beyond the hours considered safe. Silkwood becomes convinced that the management are falsifying safety reports and making financial decisions that compromise workers' rights to work without fear of contamination from radioactive materials. She becomes active in the union and starts lobbying for safeguards. However, union officials seem more interested in the publicity she is generating for them to drive up their membership subscriptions than in the welfare of her and her co-workers.

Shortly afterwards she is "cooked" and then accused of deliberately contaminating herself by breaching safety standards. After she discovers records of inadequate safety measures, she begins her own investigation. When she thinks she has enough evidence, she contacts a reporter from the New York Times and arranges a night time meeting. Carrying the evidence from a union meeting, she makes her way to meet the journalist.

Chiron 199

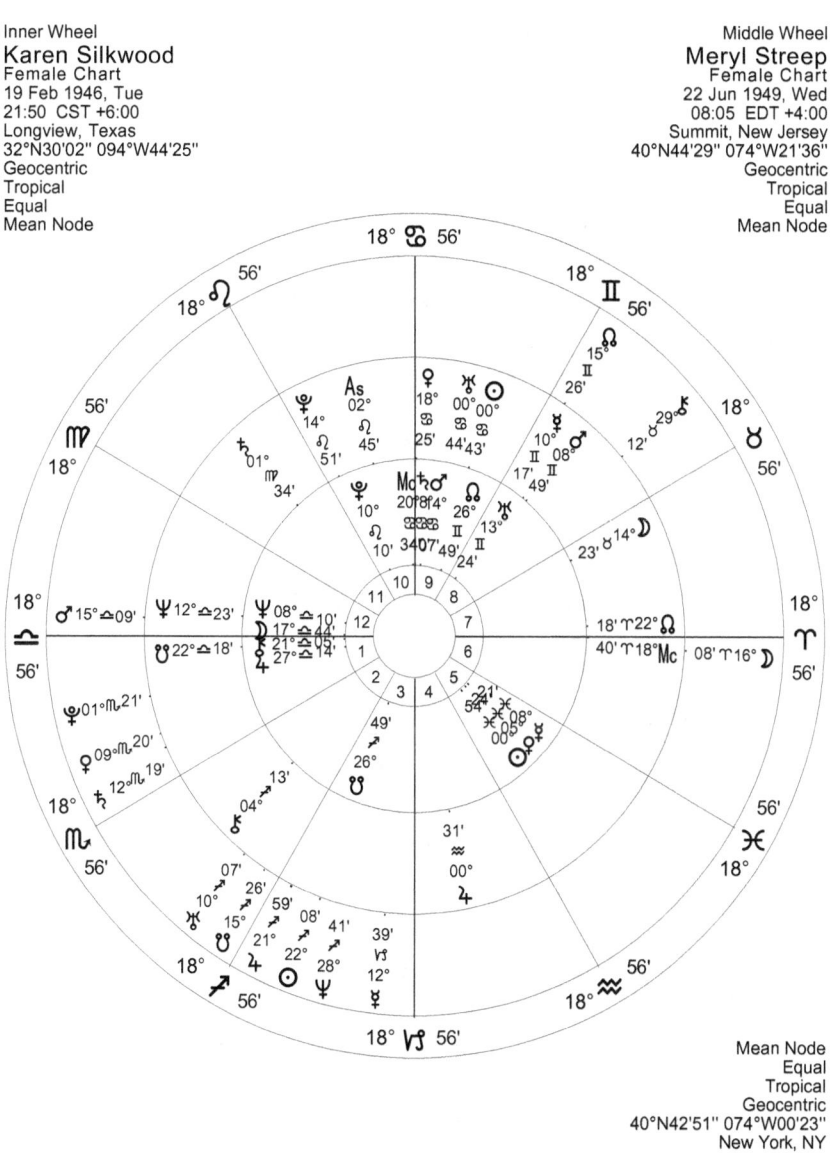

The final scene shows her in her car being blinded by headlights from behind and then crashing. According to the investigation of the fatal one-car crash, no documents were ever found in the car.

Silkwood had a cluster of planets near her ascendant in Libra with the Moon and Chiron in conjunction. Streep's South Node was within one degree of Silkwood's Chiron, showing a great amount of sympathy for the character. The Mars of the movie's release was within a three degree orb of Silkwood's ascendant and Streep's natal Neptune. Streep's Venus in Cancer was exactly conjunct Silkwood's Saturn, perhaps showing an admiration for the character's work. Streep's MC was exactly conjunct Silkwood's descendant so it should be no surprise that the role won the actress a great deal of acclaim.

The film was nominated for Academy Awards, Golden Globes and BAFTAs for Best Picture and Best Actress. Cher won a Golden Globe for Best Supporting Actress.

THE KAREN CARPENTER STORY

Karen Carpenter: 2 March 1950, 11:45, New Haven, Connecticut.
AA: Steinbrecher
Cynthia Gibb: 14 December 1963, 09:34, Bennington, Vermont.
AA: Craft
Release date: 1 January 1989

Karen's story is told in reverse order with her collapse and subsequent death being the opening scene. Flashbacks show her as a teenager roller-skating on the day her family moved to Connecticut. The music of The Carpenters plays in the key scenes. According to the actress who played Karen, Richard (Karen's brother) insisted she wear Karen's clothes and that he made a nuisance of himself on set by insisting on being present for every scene, which creeped some people out. Cynthia Gibb said she felt she had become the singer by the end of filming.

The film gives some explanation for Karen's descent into anorexia and the pressures of being on stage. Karen and Richard were notoriously close and the fact that Richard had been on set gives rise to some speculation that some of the sequences of events were manipulated to keep surviving family members mollified. In particular, the mother's

Chiron 201

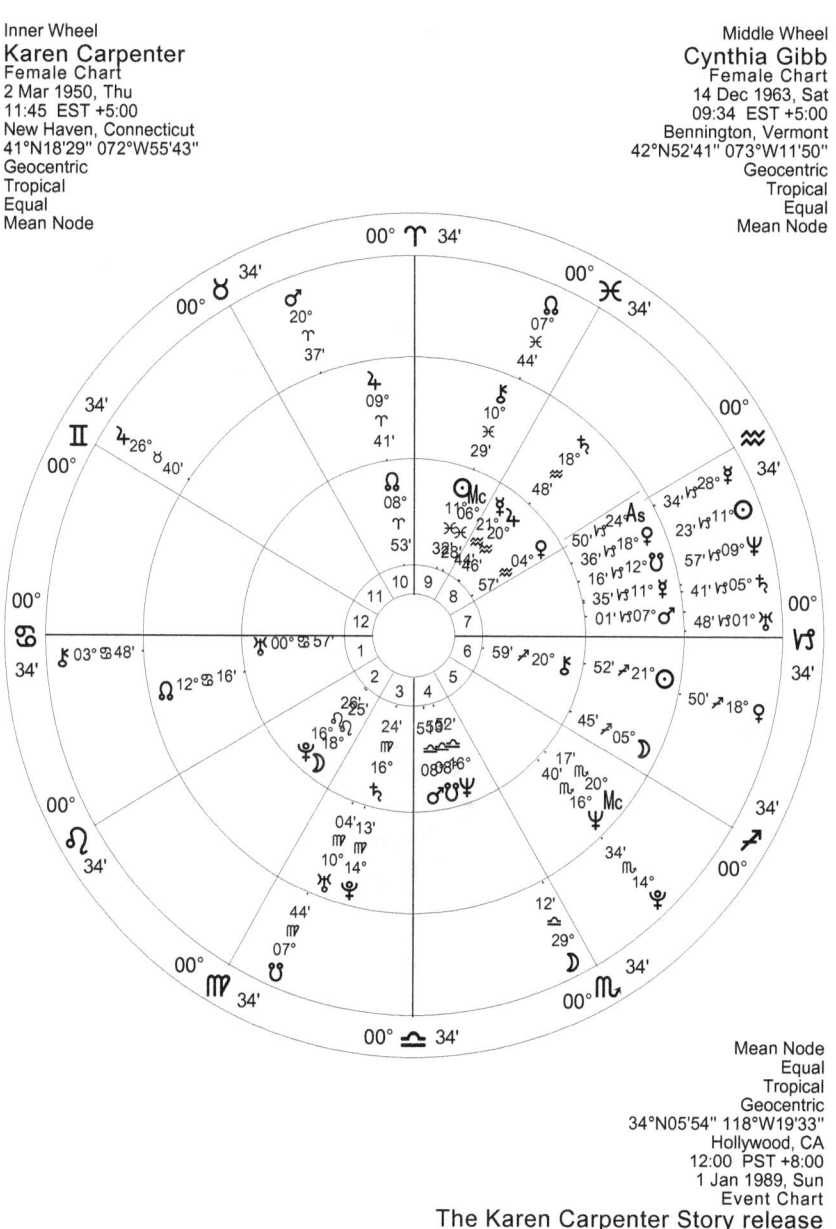

declaration of love for her daughter seemed a little too convenient and well placed.

What is clear is that a great talent was lost due to the pressures of showbiz and lack of support in the music industry as young people ascend the ladder of success.

Karen's ruling planet, the Moon in Leo, was conjunct Pluto so it is apt she had intense relationships with members of her family – even posthumously. The singer and the actress had a Sun/Chiron conjunction both ways and Cynthia Gibb's Jupiter was conjunct Karen Carpenter's North Node. This can account for the actress feeling she had become the musician.

The movie was released as transiting Uranus was on Karen's descendant in Aquarius and Venus was transiting Gibb's Sun and Carpenter's Chiron.

The made-for-television film received high ratings.

MULTIPLE VERSIONS

Sometimes a real-life character has such a profound impact on culture that more than one film is required, such as Ted Bundy in *The Deliberate Stranger* (Mark Harmon), *Ted Bundy* (Michael Reilly Burke), *The Stranger Beside Me* (Billy Campbell) and *Extremely Wicked, Shockingly Evil and Vile* (Zac Efron). At other times, the length of a person's life means one actor is required as the younger version and a different actor is needed for the older version, as in Thomas Edison in *Young Edison* (Mickey Rooney) and *Edison, the Man* (Spencer Tracy) and Elizabeth I in *Fire over England* (Flora Robson) and *Shakespeare in Love* (Judi Dench). Harry Houdini gets the special treatment too in *Houdini* (Tony Curtis) and the made-for-TV film *Houdini* (Adrian Brody). One of my favourite actresses, Judi Dench, had the opportunity to play Queen Victoria in two different periods of her life in *Mrs Brown* and *Victoria and Abdul* while two different takes on Stephen Hawking's life were portrayed in *Hawking* (Benedict Cumberbatch) and *The Theory of Everything* (Eddie Redmayne). Also featured in this section are the tragic portrayals of Dorothy Stratten in *Death of a Centerfold: The Dorothy Stratten Story* (Jamie Lee Curtis) and *Star 80* (Mariel Hemingway). And how can we forget *Richard III*, a part coveted by every budding actor? Laurence Olivier, Ian McKellen and Al Pacino all give the evil king their best interpretation.

TED BUNDY

There have been at least eight biopics made about the serial killer Ted Bundy. It would seem we are fascinated with how someone who was so good looking and had such charisma could choose to inflict extreme violence on another human being.

Before going any further, it is important to emphasise that whilst serial killers may share astrological significators, there are approximately 250 people across the world who were born the same minute as Ted Bundy and would therefore have exactly the same chart as him. For this reason, one cannot look at a chart and proclaim it belongs to a serial killer. There are environmental as well as many other factors that can alter the course of a person's life. Thankfully there are few avenues (or so it seems, given how few serial killers there are in the world) one can go down in order to reach such unimaginable depths.

We can be thankful there was only one Ted Bundy and one would have thought a single biopic about this despicable man was enough. It is not the intention here to glorify his crimes but rather to see how someone could step into the monster's shoes from an astrological perspective.

The gorgeous actor Mark Harmon was one of the first to take on Bundy in *The Deliberate Stranger*, receiving critical acclaim for his portrayal. Michael Reilly Burke's portrayal was less noted for its factual accuracy but the actor tapped into the opportunism of the killer's crimes. *The Stranger Beside Me* was based on Ann Rule's book on her friendship with Bundy and how she did not suspect that someone she was close to could commit such ghastly deeds. Zac Efron also took on the role of Bundy in *Extremely Wicked, Shockingly Evil and Vile* just over a full Saturn cycle after Bundy's execution.

These are uncomfortable films to watch, but they serve as continual reminders that you really can be deceived in the most horrific ways by someone you thought you could trust.

The Deliberate Stranger
Ted Bundy: 24 November 1946, 22:35, Burlington, Vermont.
AA: RR
Mark Harmon: 2 May 1951, 10:40, Burbank, California.
AA: Wilsons
Released: 4 May 1986

Fascination with Ted Bundy can most likely be attributed to the need to understand why someone would kill another human being. Three years before Bundy's execution, the actor Mark Harmon stepped into the monster's shoes to provide some insight into the soul of man who, like anyone else, was once an adored baby (or was he?). Harmon's portrayal was praised for its accuracy but what is most interesting is that this role transformed Harmon from just another pretty face in a soap opera or beer commercial to an acclaimed actor.

Bundy and Harmon were only born a few years apart so the outer planets are in similar positions. As both charts have "AA" ratings, the angles and Moon can be examined.

Bundy was born with a Saturn/Pluto conjunction and Harmon's Mars is within one degree of Bundy's Saturn and four degrees of his Pluto. These three planets would be expected by a lot of astrologers to be important connections: Saturn for its link to endings (death), Pluto for obsession, particularly of a sexual kind and Mars for violence, blood and aggression (particularly of a sexual kind). From this simplified definition, it can be surmised that Harmon's sense of aggression was charged by Bundy's obsession with death. We are all capable of violence and all that is needed for the explosion is the lighting of the fuse. It is also important to note that Bundy's four-planet stellium (Chiron, Venus, Jupiter and Mercury) in Scorpio was traditionally ruled by Mars which was in the sign of Sagittarius. Viewed this way, it can be seen that Harmon was able to channel this potentially negative tendency into the role he played. Still on death row at the time when the movie was released, Bundy declined the opportunity to watch this film about his life. At the film's release, transiting Chiron was on his North Node, opposing his natal Moon and Mars in Sagittarius.

Harmon was nominated for a Golden Globe.

206 Mirror Mirror

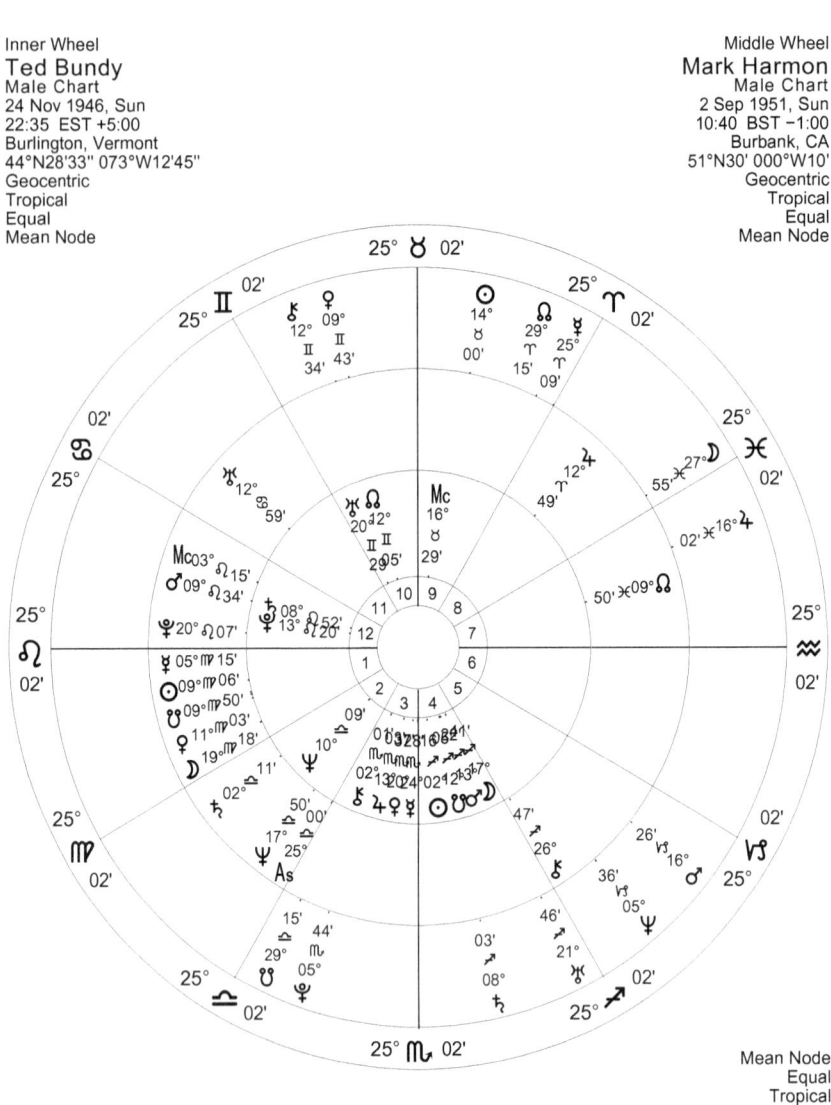

Ted Bundy

Ted Bundy: 24 November 1946, 22:35, Burlington, Vermont.
AA: RR
Michael Reilly Burke: 27 June 1964, no time, Los Angeles, California. Source: Wikipedia
Released: 22 November 2002

Ted Bundy is not noted for its factual accuracy. In this film, Michael Reilly Burke plays Bundy and there is far more emphasis on the opportunistic nature of his dreadful crimes: like feigning injury to lure women in to his car or disguising himself as a policeman. The film makes Bundy appear lucky to be in the right place at the right time with the right disguise or manner to be convincing. In mythology, Jupiter had the ability to shape shift. In one story, he disguised himself as a cold bird who appeared to the goddess Hera (who later became his wife); he appeared as a shower of gold to Danae and as a swan to Leda (as well as many other disguises to seduce the objects of his affections). Burke's natal Jupiter is within one degree of Bundy's natal MC and his natal Neptune hovers over the killer's stellium in Scorpio.

Michael Reilly Burke's Neptune in Scorpio was conjunct Bundy's Venus and Jupiter, and his Venus was conjunct Bundy's Uranus. This earlier film left out the significance of Bundy's apparently normal relationship with Liz Kloepfer. The film was released two days before Bundy's birthday and with transiting Pluto conjunct his Moon in Sagittarius.

Incredibly, transiting Pluto was conjunct by seventeen minutes to the natal Neptune of Burke when Bundy's execution was carried out at 07:16, 24 January 1989 at Florida State Prison. Transiting Jupiter had opposed Bundy's natal Mercury too.

208 Mirror Mirror

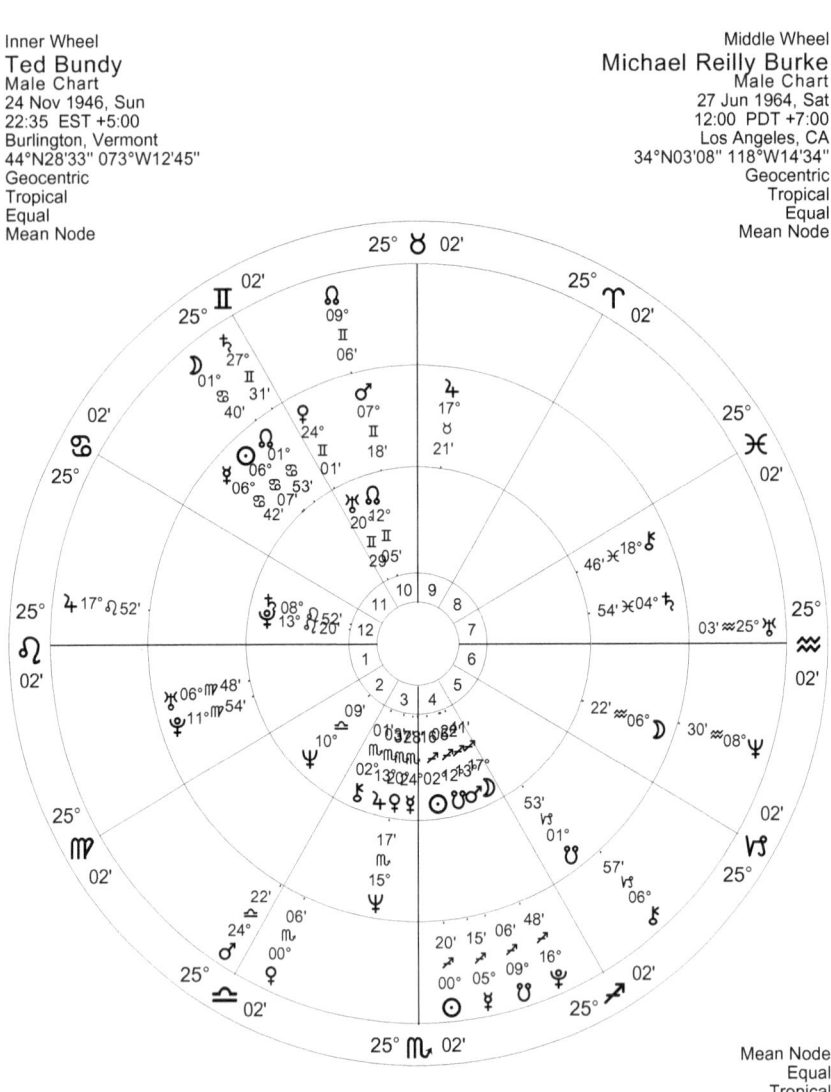

The Stranger Beside Me
Ted Bundy: 24 November 1946, 22:35, Burlington, Vermont.
AA: RR
Billy Campbell: 7 July 1959, no time, Charlottesville, Virginia.
Source: Wikipedia
Ann Rule: 22 October 1931, no time, Lowell, Michigan.
Source: Wikipedia
Barbara Hershey: 5 February 1948, 10:01, Los Angeles, California.
AA: RR
Release date: 21 March 2003

Unlike the previous films, *The Stranger Beside Me* provides insight into Bundy's odd childhood, written from the perspective of one of his friends, a crime reporter who had been hired to cover a string of grisly murders. Originally a book written by Anne Rule, a friend of Bundy's, this film shows more of Bundy's famed likeable charm. Played by Billy Campbell, Bundy is far less menacing and far more charismatic than he is in the other films.

Campbell's Uranus/Mercury was in conjunction with Bundy's Saturn/Pluto in Leo. This combination would appear to have unexpectedly softened the edges of Bundy's concealed brutality. Campbell's Jupiter conjunct Bundy's Mercury in Scorpio again brings a terrifying shape-shifting theme to mind and explains why a future crime writer completely missed the signals that she was friends with one of the most notorious serial killers of the twentieth century.

However, *The Stranger Beside Me* is more about the relationship between Bundy and Rule. Natally Rule's Sun/Jupiter conjunction is trine Bundy's Sun. Here we have two people who bring out the natural creativity and buoyancy in each other. Her Mercury was very close to his ascendant so they probably had a lot to talk about as well and with her Chiron opposite his Mercury, it isn't surprising that they met and worked together at a crisis centre.

In the film, Ann Rule was played by Barbara Hershey, a well-known actress. Rule's Saturn in Capricorn was within a few degrees of Hershey's MC. This placement of Saturn emphasizes Hershey's status as an actress: playing Rule may have placed a strong need to get the part right, and the actress may have felt an overwhelming responsibility to Rule to

210 Mirror Mirror

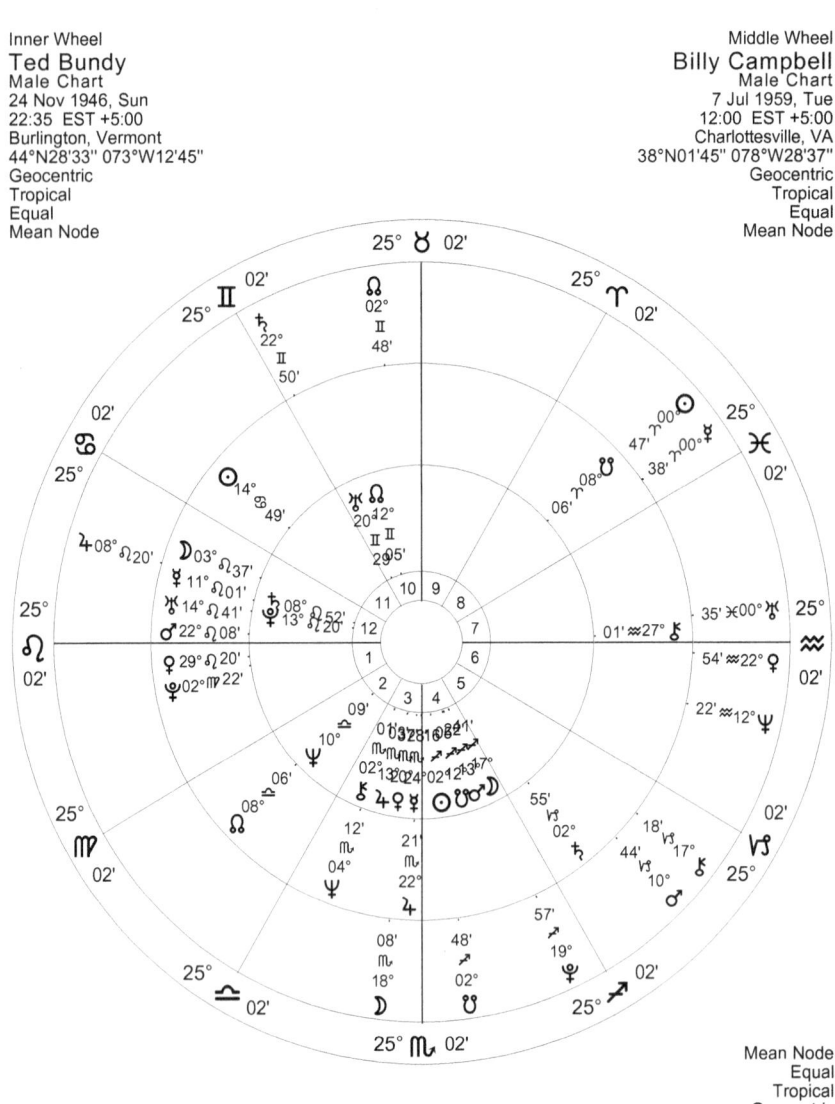

Multiple Versions 211

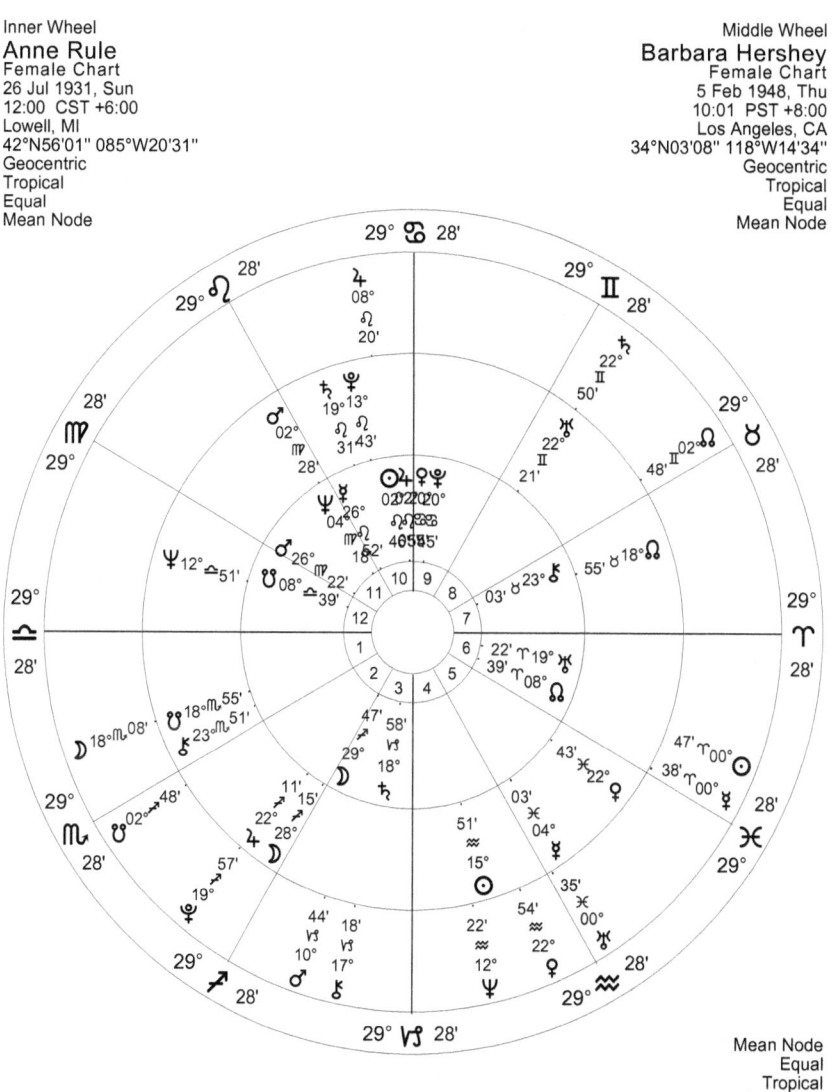

portray her in an accurate manner. The other significant contact is Rule's Neptune in Virgo within two degrees of Hershey's Mars. This is a challenging aspect for someone in a position of authority because the ability to take the lead is weakened. Did Hershey come across as compromised in some way or was she able to transcend this and deliver something far more authoritative? This question pales next to the more pertinent cautionary tale of being careful who you invite to be your closest friend.

Extremely Wicked, Shockingly Evil and Vile
Ted Bundy: 24 November 1946, 22:35, Burlington, Vermont.
AA: RR
Zac Efron: 18 October 1987, 13:22, San Luis Obispo, California.
AA: Taglilatelo
Release date: 26 January 2019

Both *Extremely Wicked, Shockingly Evil and Vile* and *Bundy* follow the horrific crimes of the serial killer Ted Bundy. *Extremely Wicked, Shockingly Evil and Vile* differs from *Bundy* as it focuses on the relationship between Ted Bundy and Liz Kloepfer (she wrote under the pseudonym Kendall), a secretary and single mother. Liz had a seemingly normal relationship with Bundy and believed in his innocence until she paid him one last visit just before his execution.

Bundy had a stellium of planets in Scorpio and a stellium of planets in Sagittarius opposing Uranus. Efron also had a stellium of planets in Scorpio, most notably an exact conjunction of Venus and Pluto and his Mercury in Scorpio was conjunct Bundy's Jupiter. Efron had a couple of planets in Sagittarius, where his Saturn was exactly conjunct Bundy's Moon. The actor's MC was conjunct the killer's Chiron as well so it is possible there may have been a degree of sympathy for the suffering he caused. During the film release, transiting Jupiter and Venus were conjunct their planets in Sagittarius and Saturn was transiting Efron's ascendant. So much for his sweet boy-next-door appearance!

Multiple Versions 213

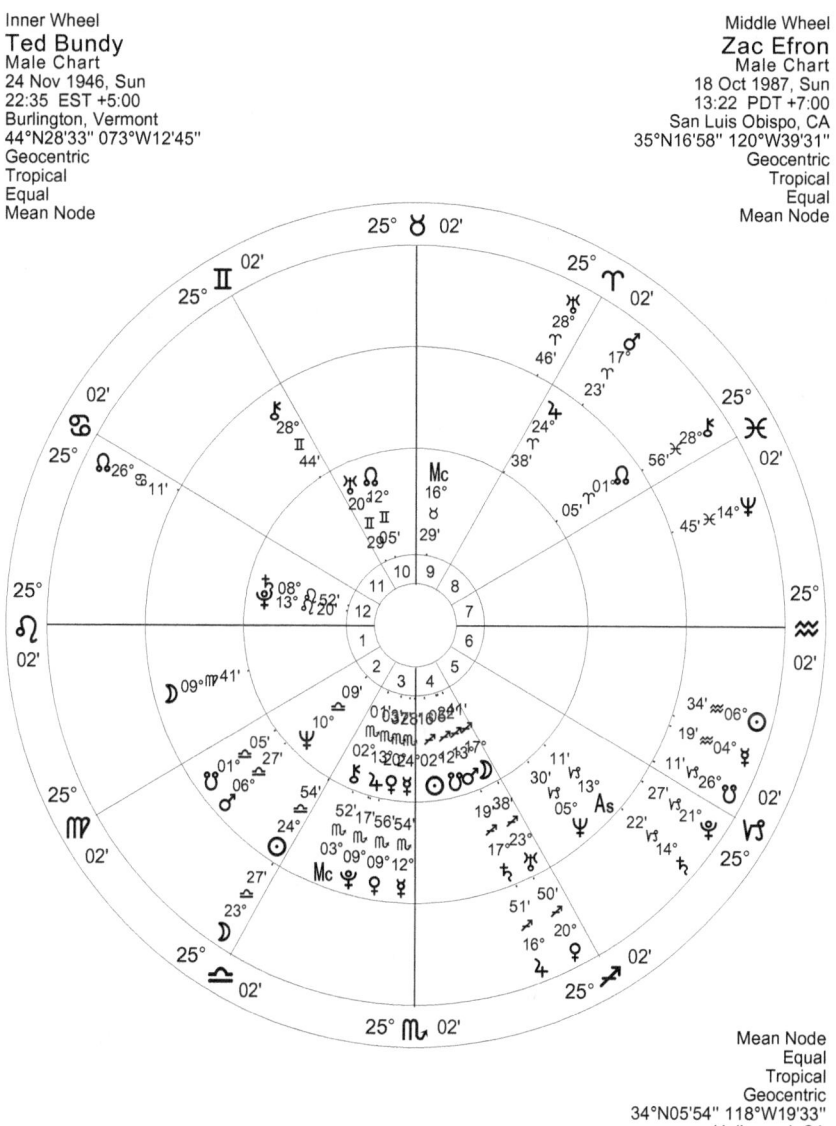

THOMAS EDISON
Young Thomas Edison
Thomas Edison: 11 February 1847, no time, Milan, Ohio.
Source: Wikipedia
Mickey Rooney: 23 September 1920, 11:55, Brooklyn, New York.
B: RR
Release date: 15 March 1940

As the title implies, this film covers Edison's early life as a young man. Tom is a precocious boy who is often in trouble for tinkering with chemicals; his younger sister, Tannie, is often caught up in his mischief-making. They are a close-knit family but there are tensions due to Tom's curiosity and his habit of conducting experiments. His mother recognises her son is different from other boys and often defends him when his father complains about him. Tom starts a business selling sweets on trains and he begins writing and selling a daily newspaper. Generally, he is regarded by the local townspeople as being a pest.

Tom teaches his sister Morse code and they often communicate with each other in this way. One day, in his single room schoolhouse, his sister is asked a question she doesn't understand. Tom taps out the answer for her with his ruler but he is struck by his teacher for being disruptive during the lesson. Tannie defends her brother by blurting out that he is using Morse code to help her. Both are sent to the cloakroom for cheating. As they leave the class, a bully trips up Tom and yanks Tannie's hair hard enough to make her cry out.

Tom works out how to create a smoke bomb by combining two chemicals, and he demonstrates his findings at school, making everyone think the schoolhouse is burning down. This is the final straw for his teacher and Tom is expelled, much to the disapproval of his father.

When Tom's mother falls ill, he devises a way to focus light by shining it into a mirror so the doctor can see well enough to operate and save her.

While on the train one day, Tom learns that an approaching bridge has been washed away, endangering the lives of all on board an oncoming train. Tom alerts the train engineer in Morse code, averting a major disaster and elevating his reputation from pest to hero.

The real-life Edison had Jupiter in Gemini, the hallmark of a

Multiple Versions 215

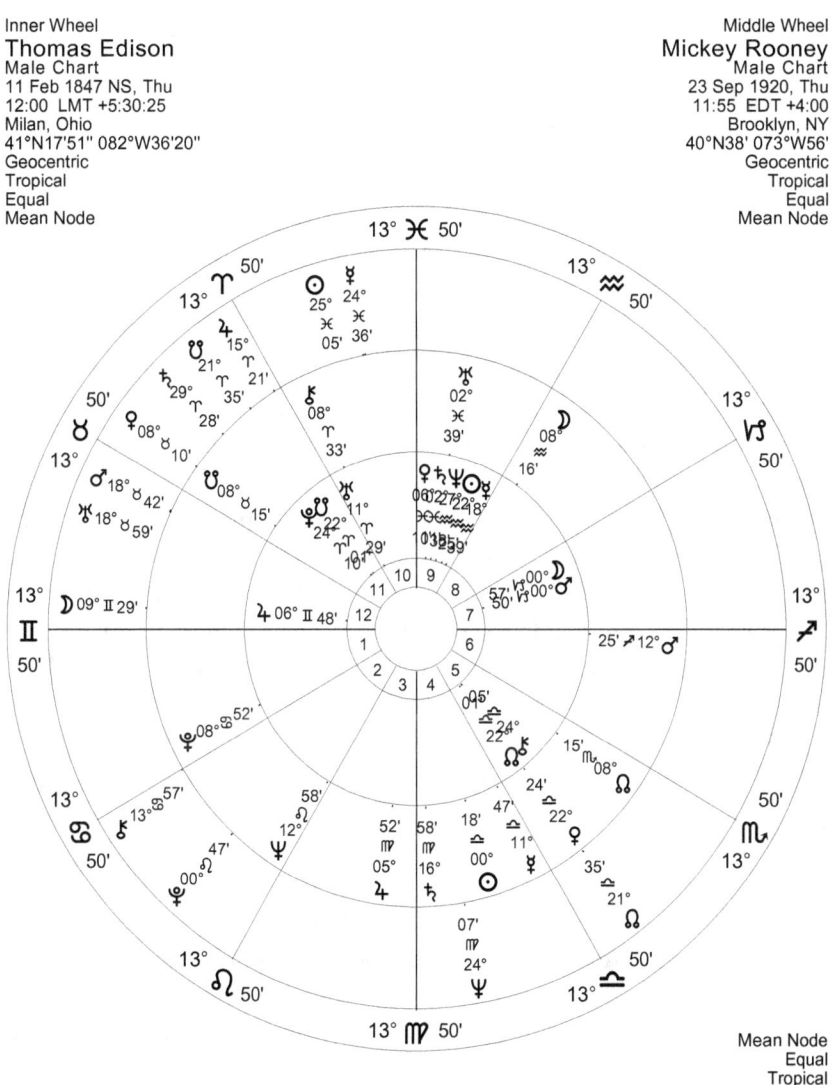

classroom learner who has a wide variety of interests and a tendency to become easily distracted when bored. As I point out in *Growing Pains* teachers tend to become lulled by their ability to mimic what they hear or see and think these students are ready for more complicated lessons. Faced with information that is over their heads, they begin chatting (or in Tom's case using Morse code) as a way to alleviate the boredom. Mercury, Jupiter in Gemini's ruling planet, is in the sign of Aquarius, the sign associated with experimentation and innovation. Put together, it's really not surprising that he would become one of the world's greatest inventors.

Rooney was a well-known child star by the time this film was released. Within an orb of one degree, his Jupiter in Virgo was square Edison's Jupiter and both are ruled by Mercury. The actor's Uranus in Pisces was also conjunct Edison's Saturn in Pisces which brings an understanding of the need to improve on existing inventions. Rooney's Venus in Libra was conjunct Edison's North Node which could account for the importance of Edison's mother and sister in the film. When the film was released, the transiting North Node in Libra was conjunct Edison's own North Node bringing a sense of destiny to the mix. Transiting Venus in Taurus was exactly conjunct Rooney's South Node and the transiting North Node in Libra was conjunct his natal Venus

The film received high praise for Rooney's performance and it was noted that the film was a departure from his usual performances as a child actor.

Edison, The Man
Thomas Edison: 11 February 1847, no time, Milan, Ohio.
Source: Wikipedia
Spencer Tracy: 5 April 1900, 01:57, Milwaukee, Wisconsin. C: RR
Release date: 10 May 1940

The inventor, Thomas Edison, had a stellium in Aquarius: Mercury, the Sun and Neptune. In the film, Edison exclaims: "I'm an inventor. I can't be told what to do. I've got to do the things I want to do. I work with ideas, visionary things. Nobody – not even I – knows how useful they're going to be or how profitable until I have a chance to work them out in

Multiple Versions 217

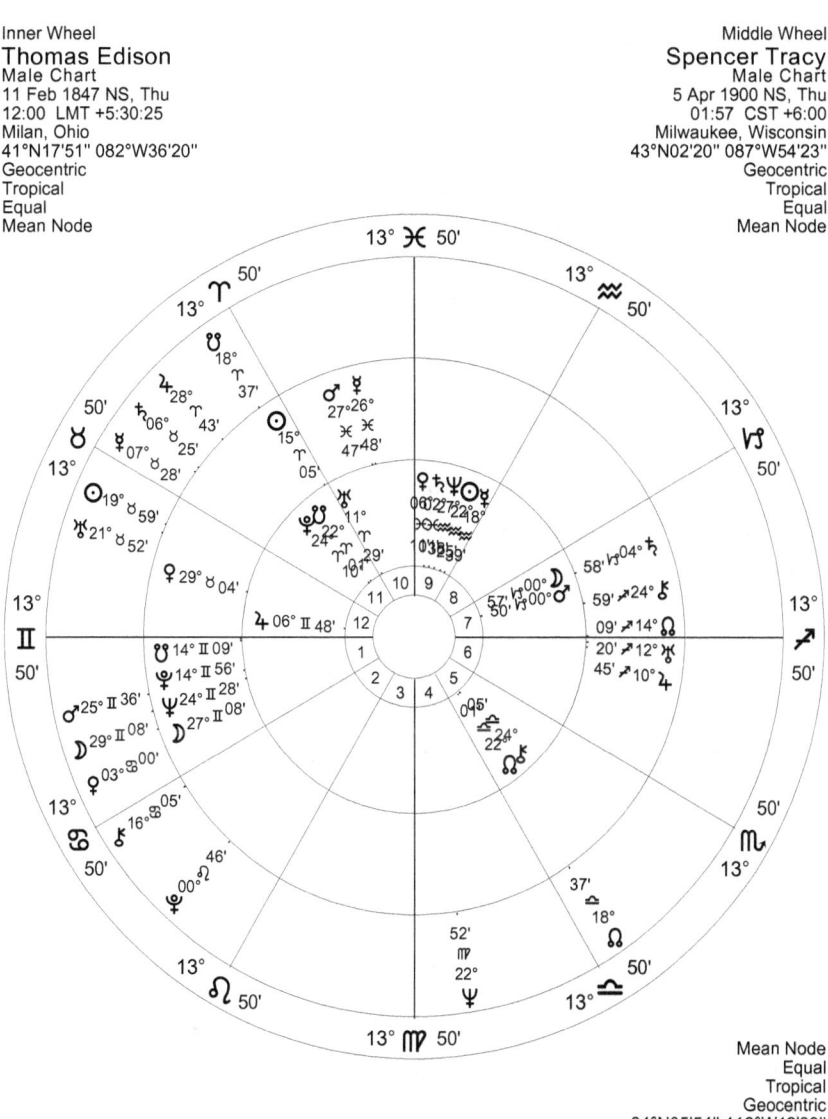

my own way." This quote is very fitting for someone who had so many planets in Aquarius.

Natally, Edison also had hard-working Mars in Capricorn which was in turn conjunct Spencer Tracy's Saturn in the sign of its dignity. Spencer Tracy would have known much about hard work and determination. Edison was noted for his stamina and for being able to function on surprisingly little sleep. In this film he was working under an extremely tight deadline and had just six months to fulfil his promise to produce an invention that would change the world: the light bulb. Tracy's Moon/Neptune conjunction in Gemini was trine Edison's Sun/Neptune conjunction in Aquarius. As both Gemini and Aquarius are Air signs, it can be seen that both men were driven by mental energy. *Edison, The Man* was released as Venus in Cancer opposed their planets in Capricorn.

The film was noted for exaggerating the events in Edison's life. It was also nominated for a place in the American Film Institute's list 100 Years...100 Cheers category.

ELIZABETH I
Fire Over England
Queen Elizabeth I of England: 7 September 1533 OS, 14:54, Greenwich, England. AA: RR
Flora Robson: 28 March 1902, no time, South Shields, County Durham, England. Source: Wikipedia
Release date: 5 March 1937

The year is 1588, and with Spanish merchantmen regularly being caught bringing gold in from the New World, Queen Elizabeth is growing concerned over the strength of the Spanish Armada. With several chief advisors at her disposal, it seems relations between neighbouring countries and England are extremely fragile. Cynthia, the granddaughter of one of her advisors, is the Queen's Lady-in-Waiting and the aging Queen is jealous of the girl's beauty and charm. Cynthia (played by Vivien Leigh) is the sweetheart of Michael Ingolby (played by Laurence Olivier) who is captured in a failed sea battle with the Spanish.

Michael is allowed to escape and he swims to shore where his wounds are tended to by an enamoured young lady called Elena who seems to

Multiple Versions 219

Inner Wheel
Elizabeth I of England
Female Chart
7 Sep 1533 OS, Sun
14:54 LMT +0:00
Greenwich, England
51°N29' 000°W00'
Geocentric
Tropical
Equal
Mean Node

Middle Wheel
Flora Robson
Female Chart
28 Mar 1902, Fri
12:00 GMT +0:00
Durham, England
54°N47' 001°W34'
Geocentric
Tropical
Equal
Mean Node

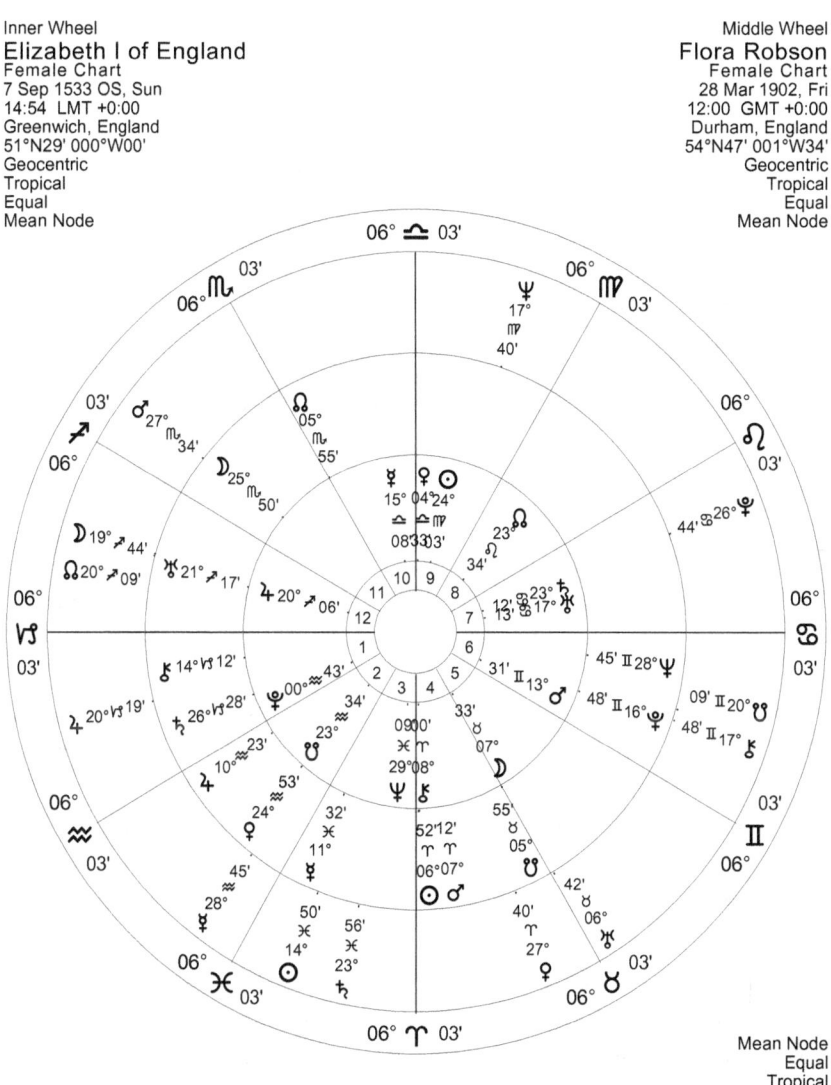

Mean Node
Equal
Tropical
Geocentric
34°N05'54" 118°W19'33"
Hollywood, CA
12:00 PST +8:00
5 Mar 1937, Fri
Event Chart
Fire Over England
Outer Wheel

forget she is engaged to be married when Michael is around. Michael eventually recovers and although he misses Cynthia, he is very attracted to Elena.

When Michael hears his father has been executed as a heretic, he flees to England where he urges the Queen to fight the Spanish in any way she can. Impressed with his devotion, the Queen orders Michael to dress as an English spy who has been executed by the Spanish.

Michael, in his disguise, goes to the Spanish court and intercepts letters ordering the assassination of Queen Elizabeth. Michael again meets Elena who is now married. Her father was killed by the English but she agrees to keep Michael's identity a secret long enough for him to escape.

The King of Spain recognises the disguised Michael and orders his arrest. However, as his wife has helped Michael escape, Elena's husband is obligated to help him so it will not become known his wife is a heretic. As Michael is about to leave, the Spanish fleet set sail to fight against England. As the Queen addresses her fleet at Tilbury before they sail off to battle, Michael reveals the names of the traitors. Michael is knighted, the English fleet win the battle and Elizabeth allows Michael and Cynthia to marry.

Although this film features a fictionalised romance, it is still notable for a few things. Firstly, it was the first British film to capture the attention of an American audience. Its success also caught the attention of David O. Selznick, producer of *Gone With the Wind*, who cast Vivien Leigh on the strength of her performance. Also, the synastry between Flora Robson and Queen Elizabeth is rather remarkable.

Robson's Uranus in Sagittarius was conjunct the Queen's Jupiter. This role portrays a Queen ahead of her time by insisting on credit for her intelligence. Robson's South Node in Taurus is conjunct the Queen's Moon which would have been transited by Uranus when the film was released and her Sun/Mars conjunction in Aries is conjunct the Queen's Chiron. Robson's Chiron in Capricorn is exactly conjunct the Queen's ascendant and Jupiter would have transited during filming and editing. Robson managed to come across as a Queen who deserved the respect of her court.

Multiple Versions 221

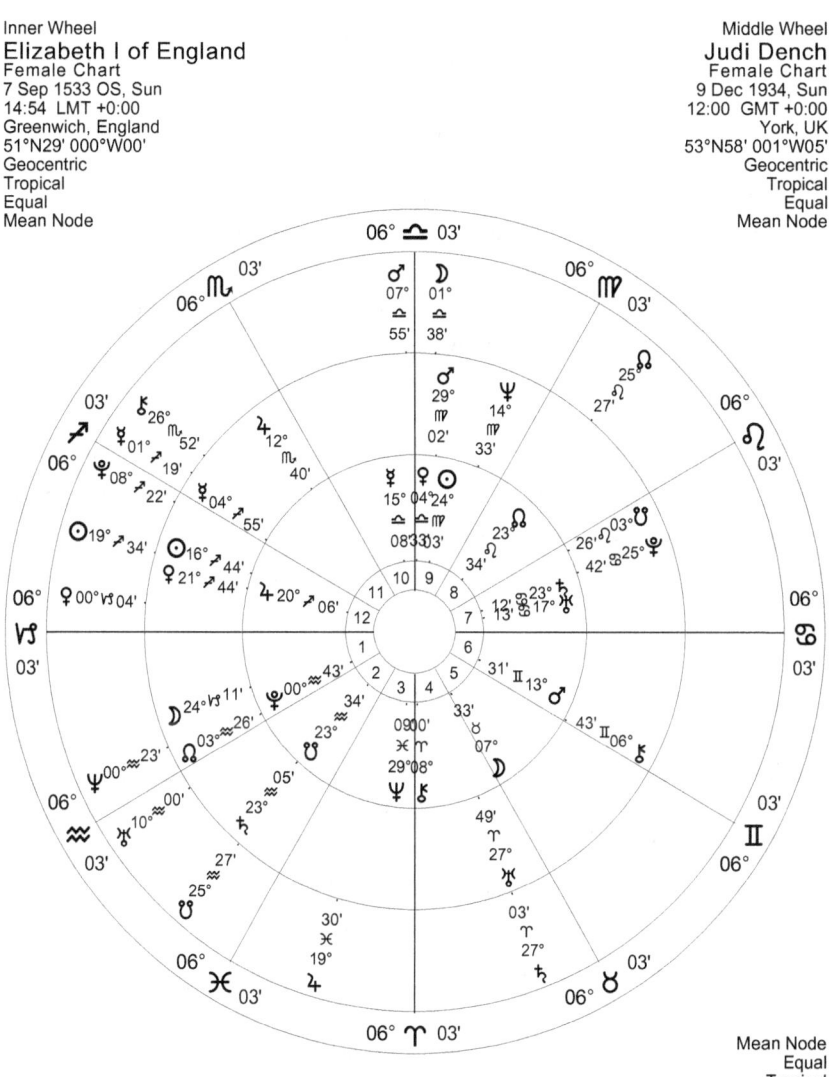

Shakespeare in Love
Queen Elizabeth I: 7 September 1533, 14.54, Greenwich, England
AA: Harvey
Judi Dench: 9 December 1934, no time, York, England.
Source: Wikipedia
Release date: 11 December 1998

This film is a highly fictionalised account of Shakespeare's life as a playwright. As there is dispute over who the real Shakespeare could be, the Bard can't be used as a case study. However, Dench's performance as Elizabeth I earned her an Academy Award for Best Supporting Actress which is remarkable given she was only on screen for a short period of time.

Dench's Saturn in Aquarius is exactly conjunct the Queen's South Node and they also have a Venus/Jupiter conjunction in Sagittarius. When the film was released, the Sun in Sagittarius was transiting that conjunction and transiting Saturn in Aries was conjunct the actress' Uranus and the transiting Nodes in Leo were aligned with the Queen's own Nodes.

STEPHEN HAWKING

Hawking
Stephen Hawking: 8 January 1942, no time, Oxford, England.
Source: Wikipedia
Benedict Cumberbatch: 19 July 1976, 12:00, Hammersmith, London. B: Scholfield
Release date: 13 April 2004

At his 21st birthday party, Stephen Hawking manages to impress a new female friend, Jane Wilde, with a conversation about the cosmos. However, he has increasing difficulties with coordination, and when he's unable to stand up unaided he is admitted to hospital, where he is diagnosed with motor neurone disease. Given just two years to live, Stephen finds it difficult to be enthusiastic about life at Cambridge University and falls into a deep depression, cheered up only by visits from Jane.

The most popular theory about cosmology at that time was the 'Steady State' which essentially means the universe has no beginning or end and

Multiple Versions   223

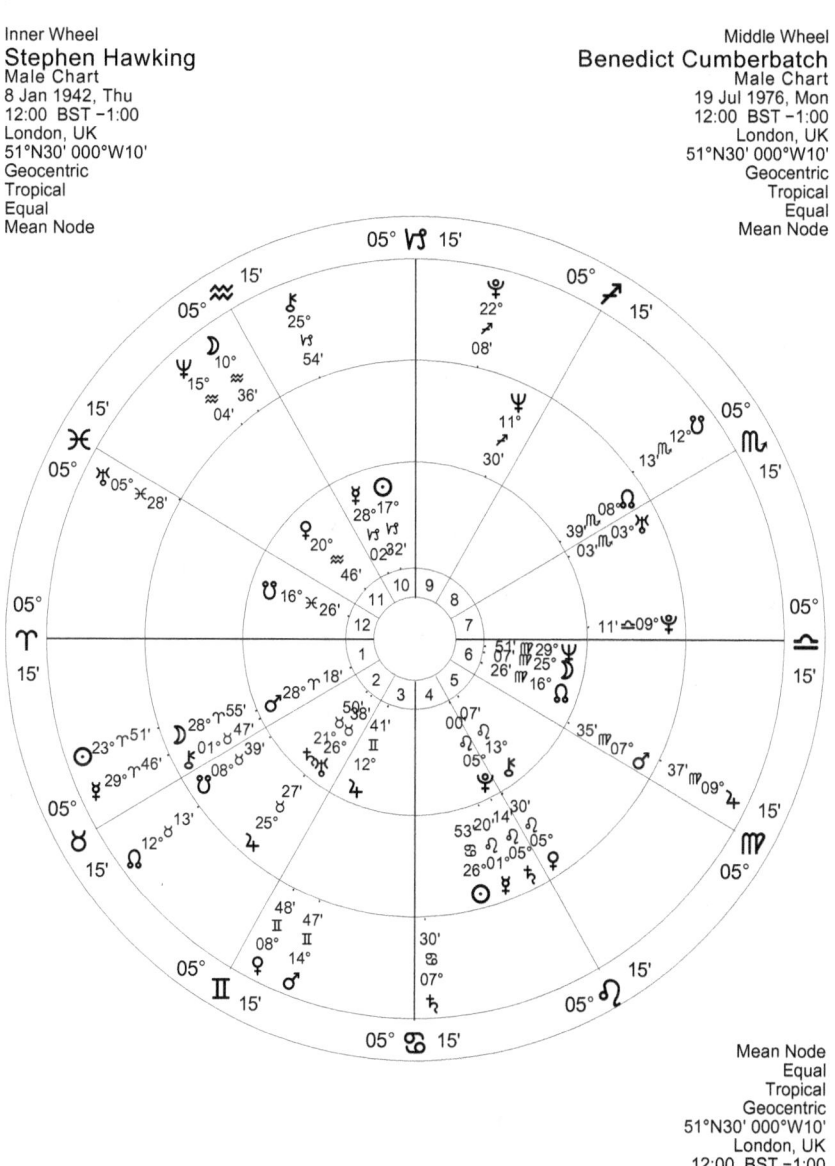

has always existed. It was a theory supported by the popular TV scientist, Fred Hoyle. However, Stephen finds a mistake in one of the calculations Hoyle is preparing for a public lecture and publicly confronts him. The ensuing argument gives Stephen the impetus to begin his own research. He is particularly interested in dying stars and how they collapse in on themselves, forming a black hole. It is this topic that forms the basis for Stephen's PhD.

Stephen's condition continues to decline but with a new focus, he declares his love to Jane and asks her to marry him. He produces a PhD thesis with far-reaching implications and academic brilliance. He not only survives the terms of his initial medical prognosis but he also proves that the 'Big Bang' was something that could have actually happened.

Other scientists worked to locate the source of the leftover heat of the explosion that created the universe. Their research would prove Hawking's theory and provide physical proof of the first 'Big Bang'.

Benedict Cumberbatch's natal Saturn/Venus conjunction in Leo is conjunct Hawking's Pluto, perhaps highlighting the hard work required of the scientist. The actor's Jupiter in Taurus is conjunct Hawking's Uranus and both are on Algol which is an indication of the obsessive nature of the research.

The movie was released as Mercury in Aries transited Hawking's Mars. This was a film about how a man's intellect overcame the physical limitations of his body. Transiting Mars in Gemini was conjunct Hawking's Jupiter, a perfect indication of all those big ideas. Jupiter in Virgo transited Cumberbatch's Mars: here we have a perfectly healthy young man portraying a very sick one.

Cumberbatch won a BAFTA for Best TV Actor.

The Theory of Everything
Stephen Hawking: 8 January 1942, no time, Oxford, England.
Source: Wikipedia
Eddie Redmayne: 6 January 1982, 20:00, Westminster, London.
C: Schofield
Jane Hawking: 29 March 1944, no time, St Albans, England.
Source: Wikipedia
Felicity Jones: 17 October 1983, no time, Birmingham, England.
Source: Wikipedia
Release date: 7 September 2014

Having Suns within a one degree orb is a fairly good indication that there is mutual understanding between two people. But there is more to this than bringing to life the story of a man with a brilliant mind being trapped in a damaged body.

Most of us will recognize Hawking as the man in a wheelchair who used a computer to talk. We may have even attempted to understand *A Brief History of Time* to impress our future spouses when the book came out in 1988. By this time though, Hawking was already in a wheelchair and it might be fair to say that this is probably all that popular culture knew of him. Hawking even appeared this way in an episode of *The Simpsons*. His robotic computer voice was instantly recognizable by this time. However, the young Stephen Hawking, before motor neuron disease took over, was able to talk and walk like the rest of us. And this is the tragedy of the story – and the brilliance in the performance of Eddie Redmayne.

Watching Hawking's physical decline was profoundly moving. The man who helped us understand the universe we lived in was trapped in an infirm body and we are left to wonder what life would have been like had this disease not taken over.

Hawking's Saturn in Taurus is within a few degrees of Redmayne's Chiron. Mythologically, Chiron was the Wounded Healer whose desperation to find a cure for his own ailments led to the discovery of remedies to help others heal theirs. Like the myth, Hawking's suffering led to inventions that would allow many other sufferers to live more complete lives. It's also interesting that Redmayne achieved great fame playing a wounded man.

226 Mirror Mirror

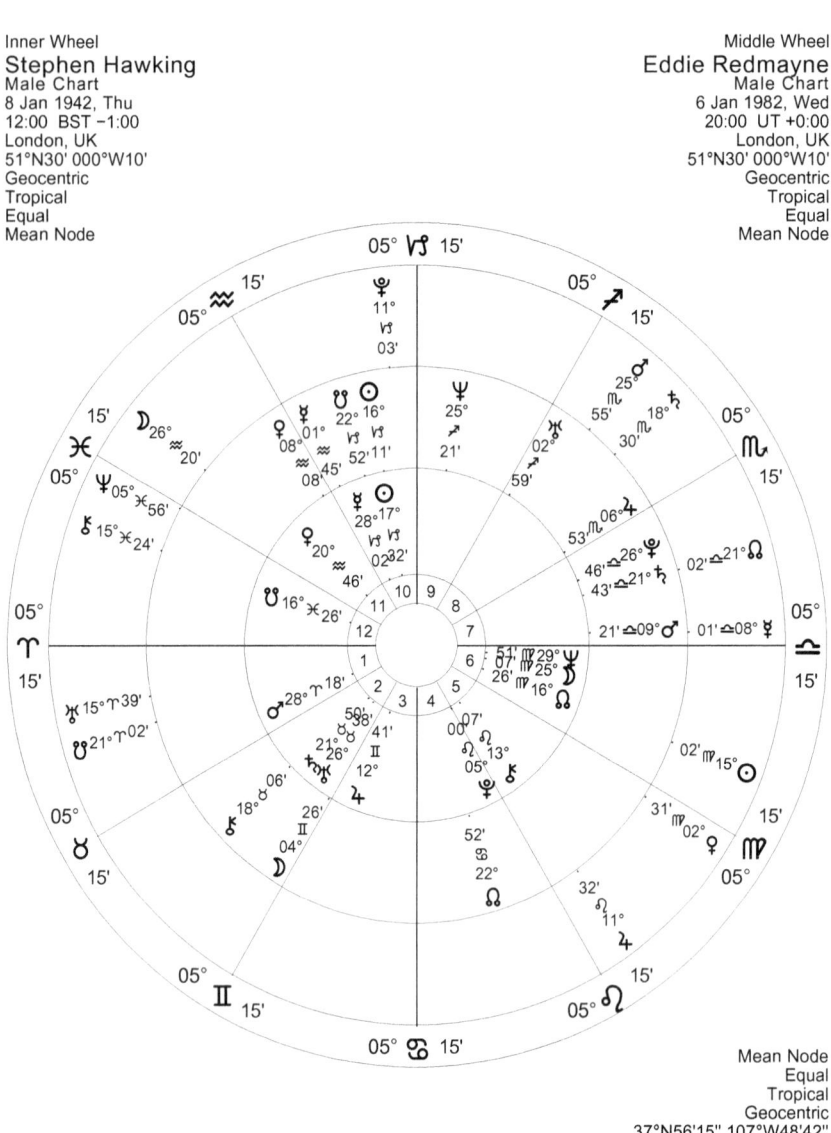

Multiple Versions   227

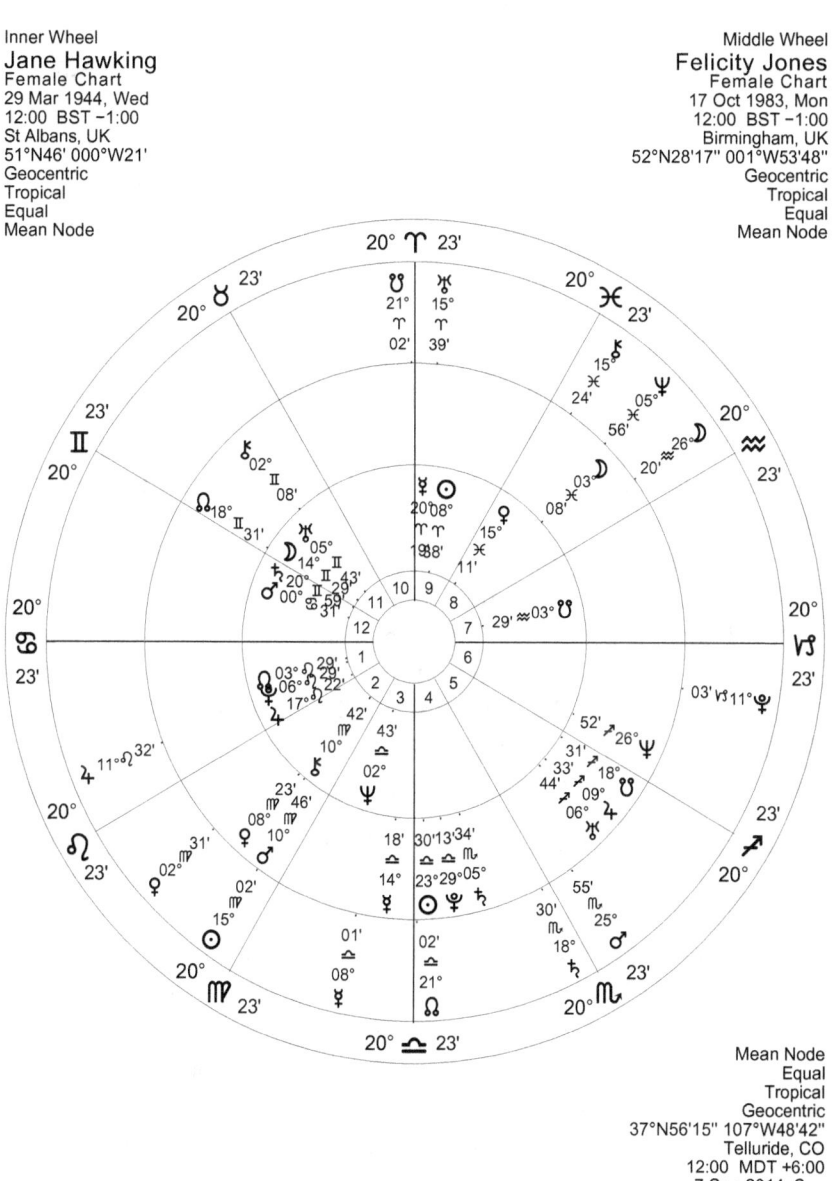

The actress Felicity Jones has her Mars in Virgo exactly conjunct Jane Hawking's Chiron and her North Node in Gemini on Jane's Saturn. Transiting Chiron in Pisces was conjunct Jane's natal Venus and transiting Neptune in Pisces was opposite Jones' natal Venus/Mars conjunction in Virgo when the film was released.

It is hard to imagine how much study was put into understanding Hawking's movements but Redmayne was so convincing that in 2015 he won an Oscar, a Golden Globe and a Screen Actors Guild Award. Transiting Saturn in Scorpio was in opposition to his Chiron when *The Theory of Everything* was released on 7 September 2014.

HARRY HOUDINI
Houdini
Harry Houdini: 24 March 1874, 04.00, Budapest, Hungary.
B: RR
Tony Curtis: 3 June 1925, no time, New York City.
Source: Wikipedia
Bess Houdini: 23 January 1876, no time, Brooklyn, New York.
Source: Wikipedia
Janet Leigh: 6 July 1927, 14:15, Mercer Falls, California.
C: Astrotheme
Release date: 2 July 1953

According to the film, the young Harry Houdini first sees Bess, his future wife, while he is performing with a Coney Island act. She intervenes when she thinks his "trainer" is beating him up for a misdemeanour. When he performs again later that day as a magician, he sees her in the audience and invites her to come on stage with him. Embarrassed, she runs away but then shows up to watch more of his performances. Eventually, she admits she is attracted to the showman and they not only get married but she becomes his assistant. However, she tires of the gruelling schedule and the low pay and convinces her husband to take on a job as a locksmith. It is while studying how locks work that Houdini gets the idea of how to escape from one of the large factory safes. Soon he is working on how to escape from straightjackets and performing his feats for fellow magicians. When he wins a cash prize, Bess persuades him to put a down-payment on a house.

Harry is still fascinated with escaping from safes, and one day at work he locks himself inside one to see if he can get out. Just before he is about to succeed, the foreman blows the safe open to rescue Harry and then fires him.

The lack of security causes arguments between husband and wife and Harry walks out when Bess insists he quit magic. However, Bess eventually persuades him to come to Europe with her and Harry makes the front pages of London newspapers for escaping from Scotland Yard's jail cells.

At their next stop in Berlin, Harry is arrested for fraud. To prove he is neither a fraud nor invoking supernatural forces, Harry locks himself in a courtroom safe and escapes from it in front of an astounded courtroom.

They return to New York and for publicity, Houdini hangs himself upside down from a skyscraper flag and escapes from a straightjacket. In Detroit, he prepares for a new trick by submerging himself in iced water in his bathtub. He then attempts the trick in the icy Hudson River but the current is so strong it sweeps him, and the box he is trying to escape from, under the ice. When he fails to re-emerge, it is assumed he has drowned. But to Bess's relief, he returns later to their hotel room and explains that his mother's voice had guided him to a gap in the ice so he was able to escape. At that moment, they receive word that Harry's mother had died at the exact time he heard her voice.

Following his mother's death, Harry refuses to perform. Instead he tries to contact her spirit in séances without success. After exposing a medium as a fake during a séance in which it it's claimed Harry's mother has been contacted, he begins preparing for an escape from a watery torture cell. Bess is so frightened that she threatens to leave him if he performs the trick and he agrees not to do it. But audiences demand the trick and Harry eventually relents, even though he had complained about a sore appendix before going ahead with it. Immersed upside down in a tank of water, he is too weak to escape and an assistant has to break the glass on the tank. As he dies, he tells Bess he will come back to her if it is possible.

If signs in the zodiac could be associated with being slippery (to aid in the goals of an escape artist) then this tendency might belong to the mutable signs. Houdini had Mercury in Pisces and the Moon in Gemini in an exact square aspect. Tony Curtis had his Venus on the

Mirror Mirror

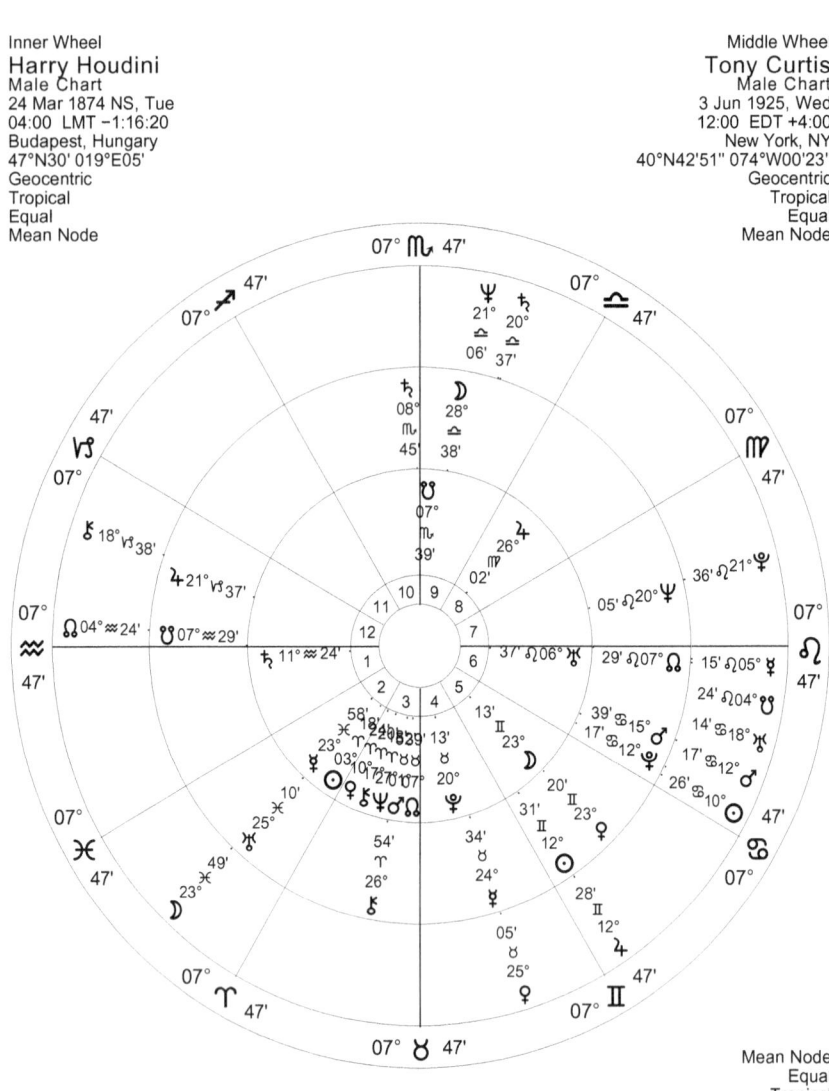

Multiple Versions 231

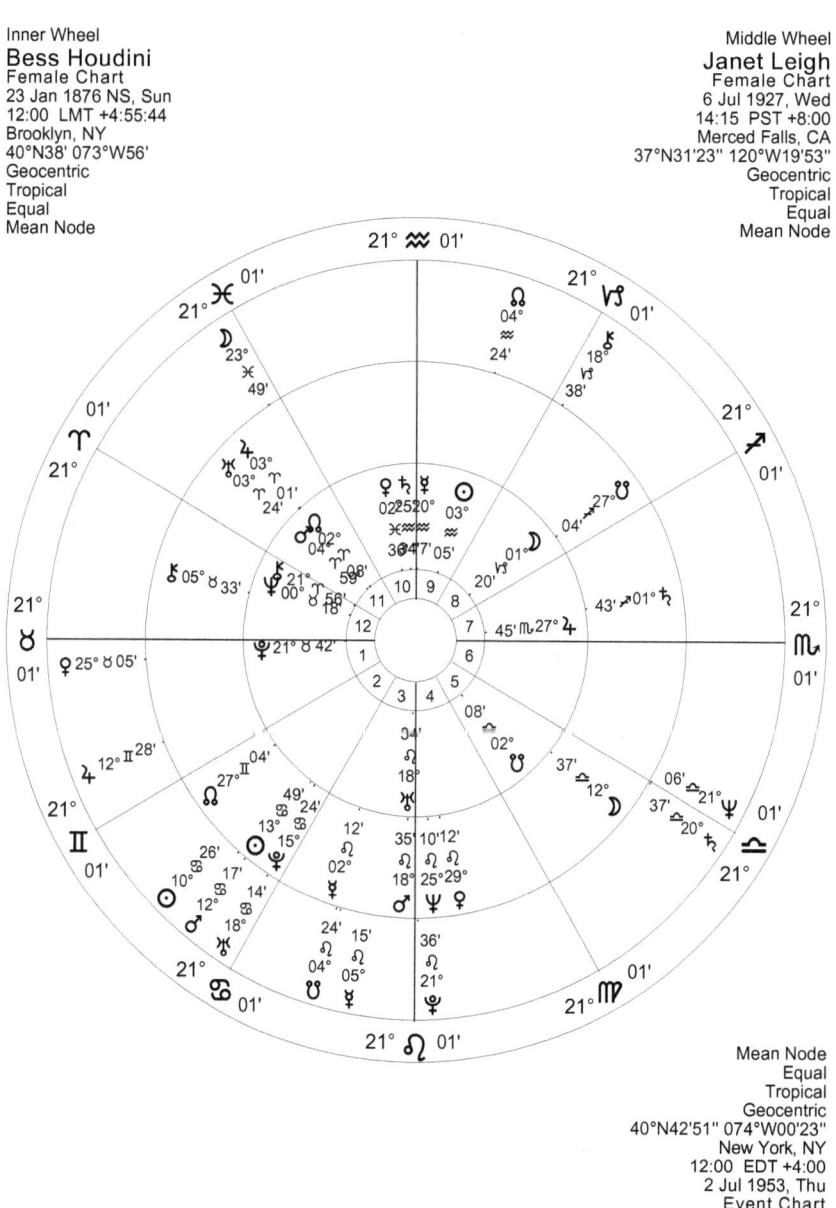

escapologist's Moon and his Uranus conjunct to his Mercury within a two degree orb. Additionally, Houdini had Saturn in Aquarius opposite Uranus in Leo on his ascendant/descendant axis, so he was able to use his skills in unconventional ways. Curtis' North Node was conjunct Houdini's Uranus within a two degree orb. On the night the film was released, Mercury was transiting this conjunction.

Bess Houdini's Uranus was conjunct Janet Leigh's Mars, and her North Node and Mars in Aries were conjunct the Jupiter and Uranus of the actress. The film is noted for being a heavily fictionalised version of Houdini's life. However, it was one of the top box office hits of 1953.

Houdini (TV Film)
Harry Houdini: 24 March 1874, 04.00, Budapest, Hungary.
Source: B: RR
Adrian Brody: 14 April 1973, 15:30, Woodhaven, New York.
Source: Wikipedia
Release Date: 1 September 2014

Harry Houdini is probably one of the most influential stage magicians and escapologists of the twentieth century. His stunts would draw huge crowds for their death-defying feats and breath-taking close calls.

Quite remarkably, Harry Houdini and the actor who portrayed him, Adrian Brody, were born exactly a Chiron cycle apart within an orb of four minutes. Perhaps there could be no other actor who could tap into the suffering of Houdini than Adrian Brody.

Brody's Venus/Sun conjunction in Aries is in turn conjunct Houdini's Neptune and Brody's Neptune is conjunct Houdini's MC. As we know, in stage magic, the ability to use deception and distraction is very important in getting tricks to work. Astrologically, Neptune is a very slippery customer indeed.

Mercury, the astrological Trickster, is very important in magic tricks too. Brody and Houdini have their Mercurys within a few degrees of orb in Pisces – which of course, using modern rulerships, is ruled by Neptune.

Mythologically, Jupiter (Zeus) was a shape shifter, appearing as a shower of gold, a shivering bird on the windowsill of his future long-

Multiple Versions   233

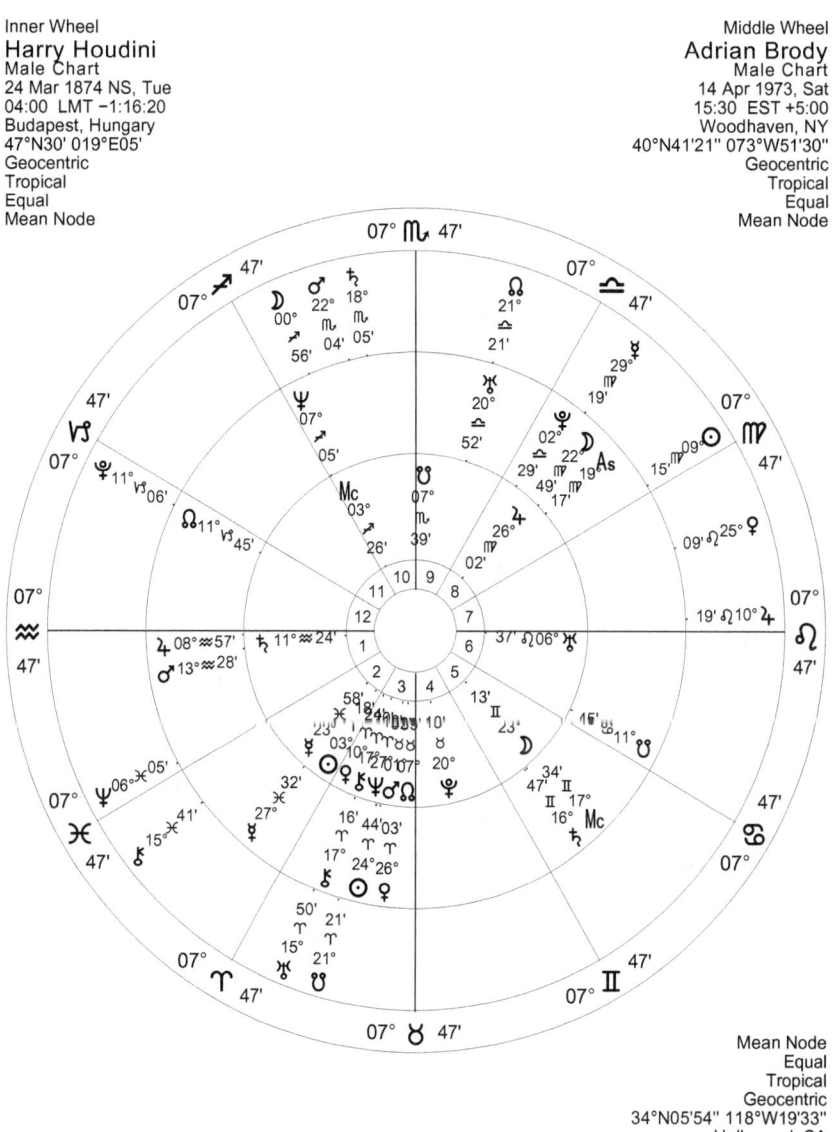

suffering wife Hera, as a swan and many other manifestations. Jupiter was known to seize opportunities to get what he wanted. So Brody's Moon conjunct Houdini's Jupiter helped Brody to understand the character he was portraying.

Houdini was known for his physical strength. He had Saturn conjunct his ascendant with Brody's Jupiter conjunct to it within a degree of orb. Uranus was transiting the Chiron conjunction when the made-for-television film was released.

RICHARD III
Richard III
Richard III: 2 October 1452 (OS), 09:02, York, England. C: RR
Laurence Olivier: 22 May 1907, 05:00, Dorking, England. AA: RR
Release date: 13 December 1955

William Shakespeare's *Richard III* is arguably literature's biggest baddy. Jealous of his brother King Edward, Richard plots and plans and murders his way to the throne of England. But only if you believe Shakespeare's version of events. Shakespeare's patron was none other than Elizabeth I who was a descendant of the man who took the throne from Richard III. The opening soliloquy delivered by Richard III outlines his physical deformities as well as revealing his plans to claim the throne.

The first thing Richard does is to frame his brother, the Duke of Clarence, for conspiring to kill the King. With his brother in the Tower of London, Richard then hires two thugs to kill the Duke before Edward's pardon can be delivered. Richard blames Edward for Clarence's death, and the shock of this hastens the King's death. But before the King dies, Richard persuades his brother to make him protector of his children, particularly, the young future king. Richard goes on to seduce Edward's widow, the Lady Anne, over her husband's coffin by telling her she will be out in the cold without a royal connection.

After causing general mayhem in the court, Richard places the young king in the Tower of London with his younger brother just to be extra sure that he (Richard) will be next in line for the throne. He then manages to make himself extremely popular with the common people.

However, once on the throne, Richard realises his popularity is dwindling and he puts together an army to defend his throne. During

Multiple Versions 235

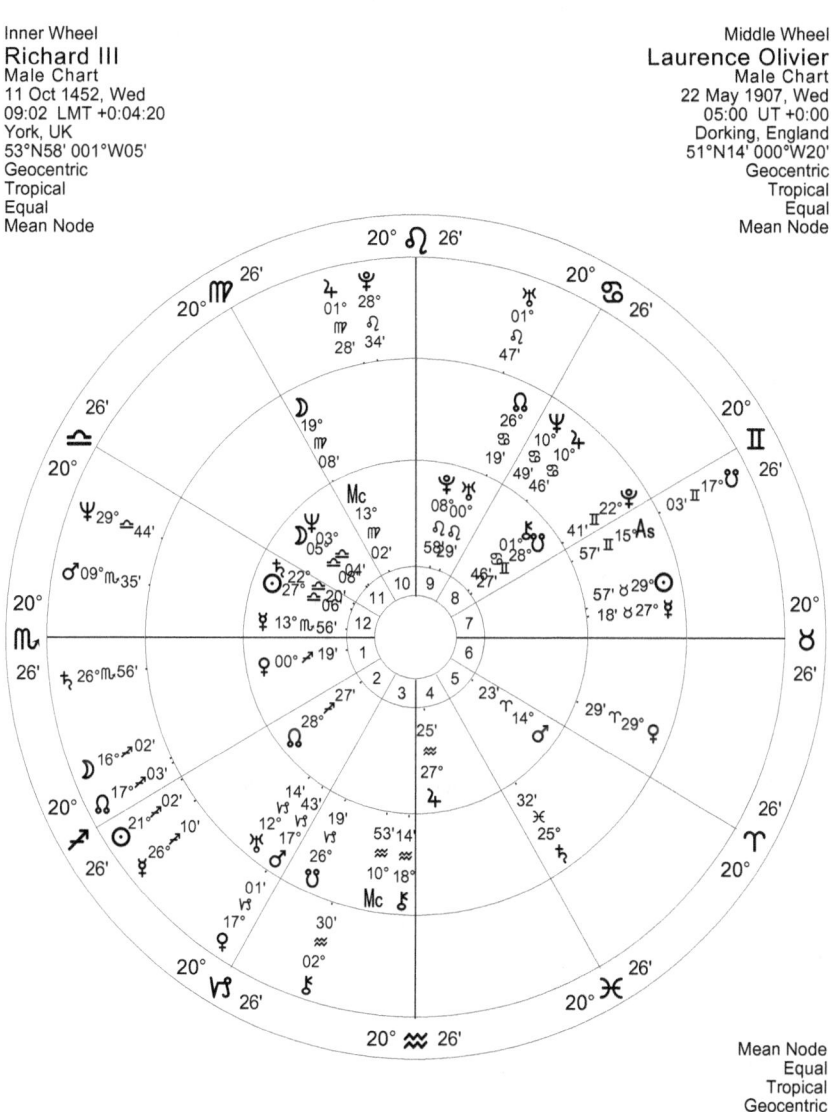

one battle, Richard is unseated and cries out "A horse! A horse! My kingdom for a horse!" Eventually Richard is killed, his crown recovered in a nearby bush and placed on the head of Queen Elizabeth's grandfather, Henry VII.

Richard III's Pluto is conjunct Laurence Olivier's IC in Leo which indicates an understanding of the emotional mindset of a power-crazed monarch. Additionally, the actor's North Node in Cancer is square to the King's Sun in Libra perhaps showing the role was meant to be performed by Olivier. The actor's Mercury in Taurus is within one degree of Algol and is square Richard's Jupiter in Aquarius, although as fixed stars move about one degree per century Algol would be out of orb to be square to Jupiter. However, the actor was able to use the energy of this evil star to portray Richard doing some truly cruel things to unsuspecting people. Actor and King also have squared Mars in cardinal signs and Venus in Capricorn was transiting Olivier's Mars when the film was released. Olivier stepped into history and seized the crown, securing his place as one of cinema's greatest Shakespearean actors. Olivier's version of *Richard III* was released just in time for the despot's fifth Uranus Return in Leo.

Laurence Olivier was nominated for Best Actor at the Academy Awards.

Looking for Richard
Al Pacino: 25 April 1940, 11:02, Manhattan, New York. AA: RR
Release date: 11 October 1996

This version of *Richard III* was more a documentary than a biopic. However, there are interesting connections as an American tries to explain to other Americans the significance of Richard III.

Pacino's Pluto in Leo is exactly conjunct Richard's Uranus and the actor's Uranus in Taurus is within one degree of the King's descendant. The King's Saturn in Libra is within three degrees of the actor's North Node. Selling Shakespeare to a largely American audience would be no easy task: other than as a brief introduction to the works of the Bard, few Americans would have a reason to study this great play. Pacino attempted to both explain as well as make Richard III appealing.

Transiting Chiron in Libra was conjunct Pacino's North Node and IC which also means it was conjunct Richard's Saturn. Pacino's efforts served as a bridge between classical actors and their modern contemporaries.

Multiple Versions 237

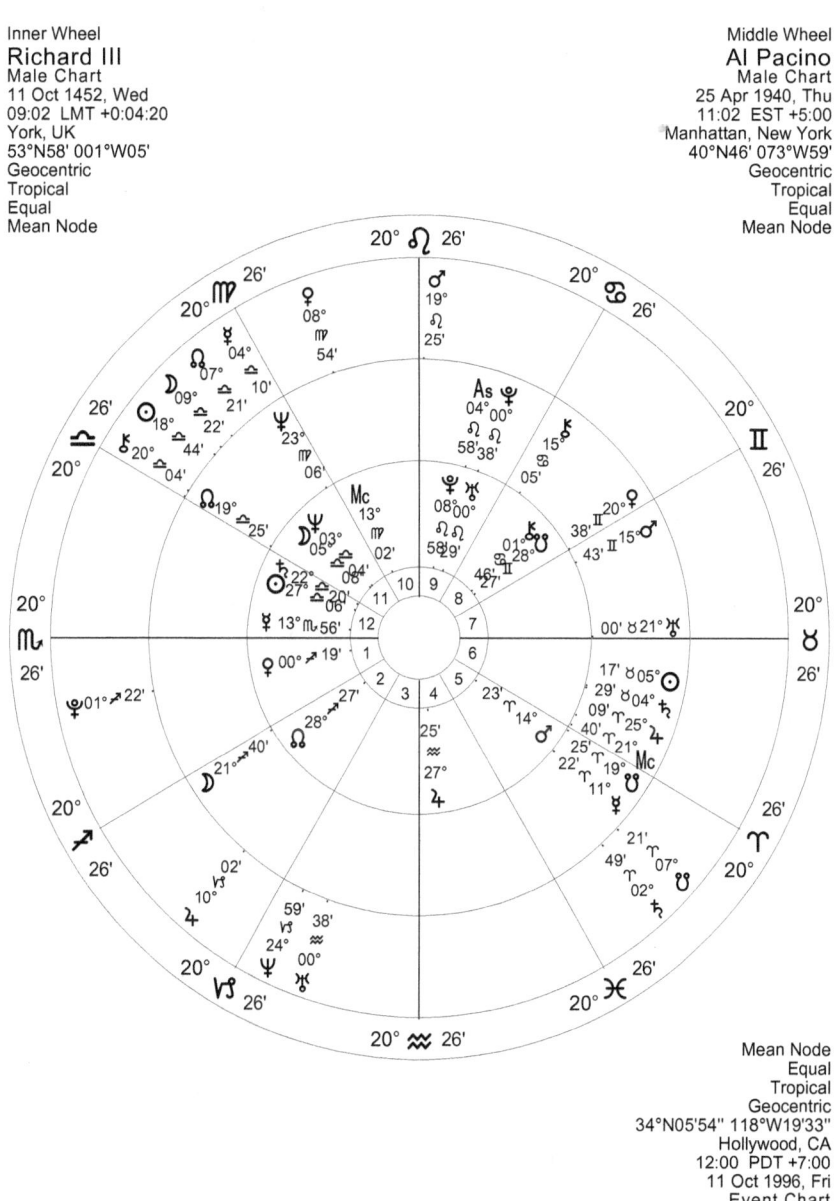

DOROTHY STRATTEN

Death of a Centerfold: The Dorothy Stratten Story
Dorothy Stratten; 28 February 1960, 22:58, Vancouver,
British Columbia, AA: Steinbrecher
Jamie Lee Curtis: 22 November 1958, 08:37, Los Angeles,
California. AA: RR
Paul Snider: 15 April 1951, no time, Vancouver, British Columbia.
Source: Wikipedia
Bruce Wietz: 27 May 1943, 03:17, Norwalk, Connecticut. C: RR
Release date: 1 November 1981

Dorothy Stratten is working at an ice cream shop when she meets Paul Snider, a pimp and con artist. With his charm and flattery, he's able to convince her to take him to her prom and then pose for nude photographs. Snider uses the photographs to persuade a professional photographer to assemble a portfolio for her so he can send it to *Playboy*. Eventually, *Playboy* invites Stratten to Los Angeles to meet Hugh Hefner and be made "Playmate of the Month". Hefner is so taken by Stratten that he even allows her be a bunny at his famous club.

Snider pressures Stratten into marrying him and she continues to find success in small film and television roles. She becomes 1980's "Playmate of the Year" and to celebrate, Snider buys vanity license plates for his new Mercedes that read "Star 80". However, after repeated business failures, Snider begins to feel jealous of his wife's success.

Stratten meets a film director at the Playboy mansion who encourages her to read for an upcoming role. Snider hires a detective to spy on Stratten and discovers she is having an affair with the film director. Stratten tells Snider she is leaving him, and he goes out to buy a shotgun. The film director pleads with Stratten not to see her husband again, but she agrees to meet with him to reach a financial settlement. Snider begs her not to leave him, then flies into a rage, rapes her and shoots her before also shooting himself.

Chillingly, Paul Snider's Pluto is exactly conjunct Stratten's MC in Leo and his Mars in Taurus is one degree away from her descendant. The fixed nature of these conjunctions as well as the obsession and violence are apparent. *Death of a Centerfold* was released when the Sun was

Multiple Versions 239

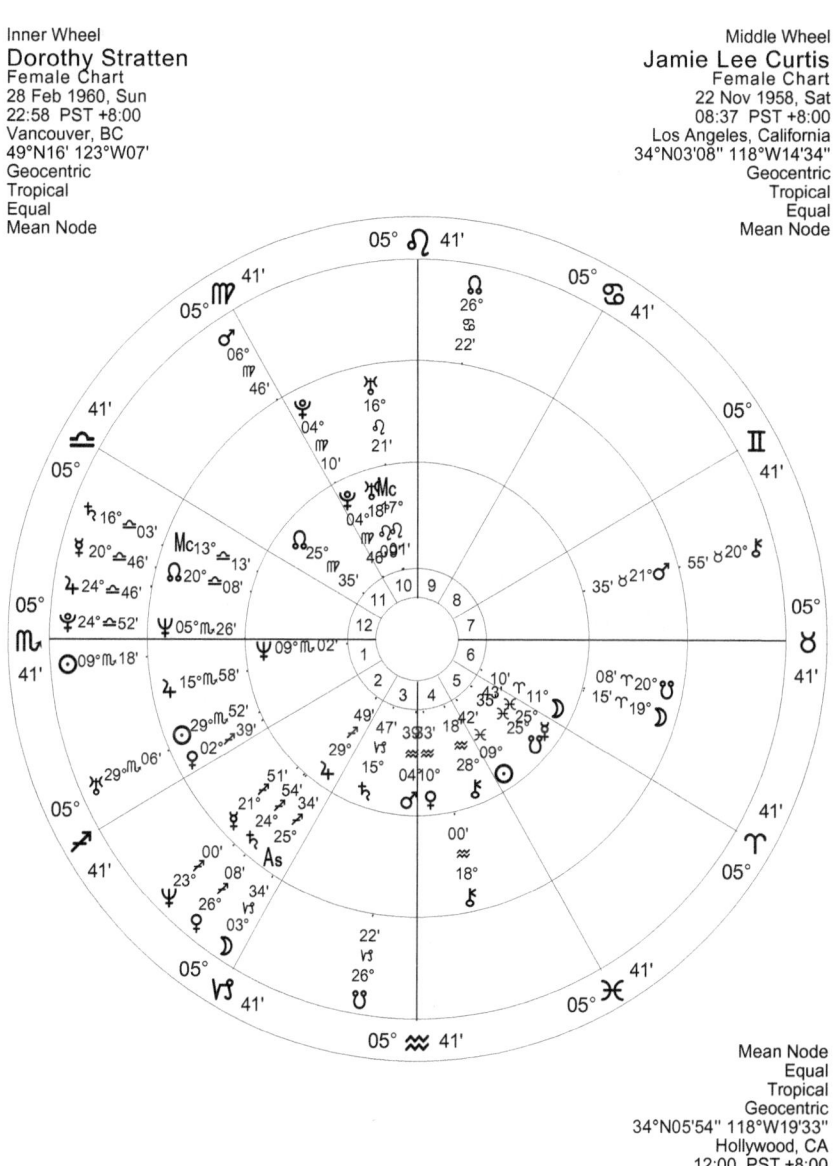

240 Mirror Mirror

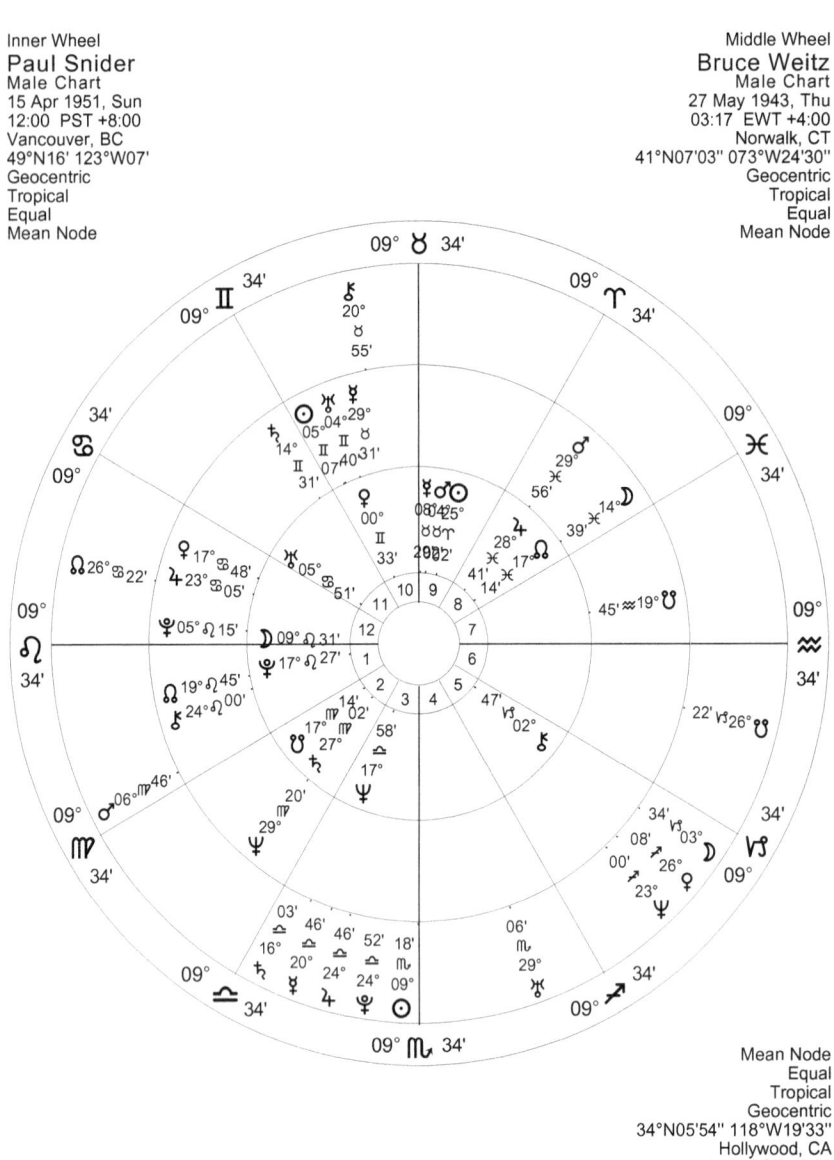

exactly conjunct Stratten's Neptune and transiting Saturn was conjunct Snider's Neptune.

As both actresses, Dorothy Stratten and Jamie Lee Curtis, were born within a couple of years of each other, they have Pluto on the same degree in Virgo. *Death of a Centerfold* was filmed as Mars transited Stratten's Uranus and MC and released when Mars was conjunct the natal Pluto of both women. Curtis' Uranus is conjunct Stratten's MC within an orb of one degree and Curtis' Neptune is exactly conjunct Stratten's ascendant. Transiting Uranus was exactly conjunct Curtis' Sun when the film was released.

Bruce Weitz, who played Paul Snider, has his North Node conjunct Snider's Pluto within two degrees. Weitz has Mars in Pisces opposite Neptune in Virgo which is conjunct Snider's Jupiter in Pisces opposite Saturn in Virgo.

Star 80
Mariel Hemingway: 22 November 1961, 05:20, San Rafael, California. AA: Angel
Eric Roberts: 18 April 1956, no time, Biloxi, Mississippi.
Source: Wikipedia
Release date: 10 November 1983

Star 80 also dramatised the murder of Dorothy Stratten so the plotlines of the two movies about the centerfold's life are very similar.

Dorothy Stratten and Mariel Hemingway had similar angles on their charts with Neptune very close to their ascendants. Stratten also had Uranus in Leo conjunct her MC with Hemingway's North Node near to this conjunction. Stratten had Mars in Aquarius and Hemingway had Jupiter in Aquarius two degrees from each other – Stratten had a natural streak of independence, which the actress Hemingway was able to magnify and bring out.

As Eric Roberts and Paul Snider were born a few days apart (in different years), they both have Sun in Aries and additionally, Roberts' Neptune was opposite his Sun. When *Star 80* was released, Pluto transited their Suns by opposition.

Star 80 was released when transiting Mars was exactly conjunct Stratten's North Node in Virgo and transiting Saturn was conjunct her natal Neptune in Scorpio shortly after crossing her ascendant.

242   Mirror Mirror

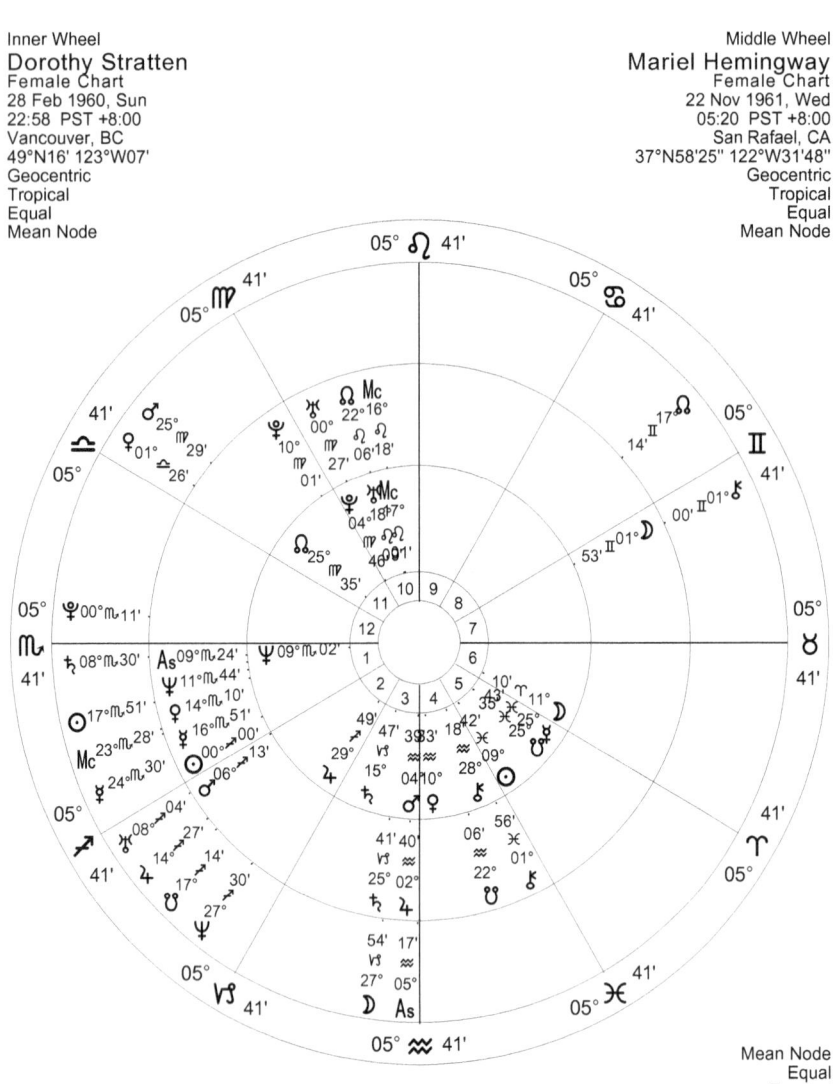

Multiple Versions 243

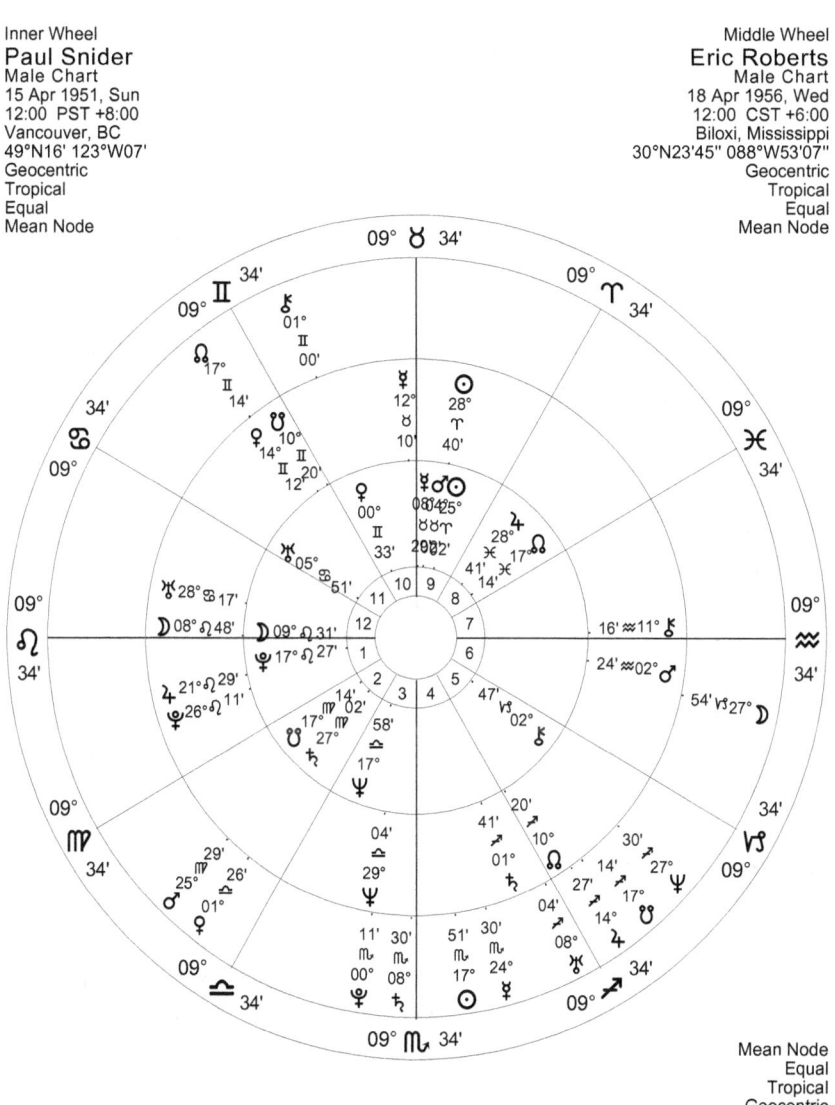

QUEEN VICTORIA
Mrs Brown
Queen Victoria: 24 May 1819, 04:15, London. AA: RR
Judi Dench: 9 December 1934, no time, York, England.
Source: Wikipedia
John Brown: 8 December 1826, no time, Crathie, Aberdeenshire, Scotland. Source: Wikipedia
Billy Connelly: 24 November 1942, 04:30, Glasgow, Scotland. AA: Clifford
Albert "Bertie" Prince of Wales (later Edward VII, King of England): 9 November 1841, 10:48, London. AA: RR
David Westhead: 1 June 1963, no time, London.
Source: Wikipedia
Release date: 18 July 1997

The film begins in the year 1863.

After the death of her husband, Queen Victoria goes into deep mourning and John Brown, her husband's faithful servant, is asked to coax the Queen back into public life. However, Brown's casual manner and control of the Queen's daily activities creates tension between himself and other members of the royal family and their servants. In particular, calling the Queen "woman" instead of her royal title causes outrage.

The Queen's continued seclusion results in her declining popularity and her friendship with Brown causes speculation. The British Prime Minister persuades Brown to convince the Queen to resume public duties, particularly making her speech at the opening of Parliament.

Fearing the Queen will feel betrayed by him, Brown nevertheless urges her to return to London, and they argue. When Brown next refers to her as "woman", she snaps at him and withdraws his status as favoured servant.

Eventually, the Queen does return to her royal duties but it is in her own time. This turns public opinion to her favour. Brown serves the Queen for the rest of his life but he is reduced to leading her security team, who have grown tired of his controlling ways and mock his concerns as paranoia. However, during a public event, a potential assassin jumps out

Multiple Versions 245

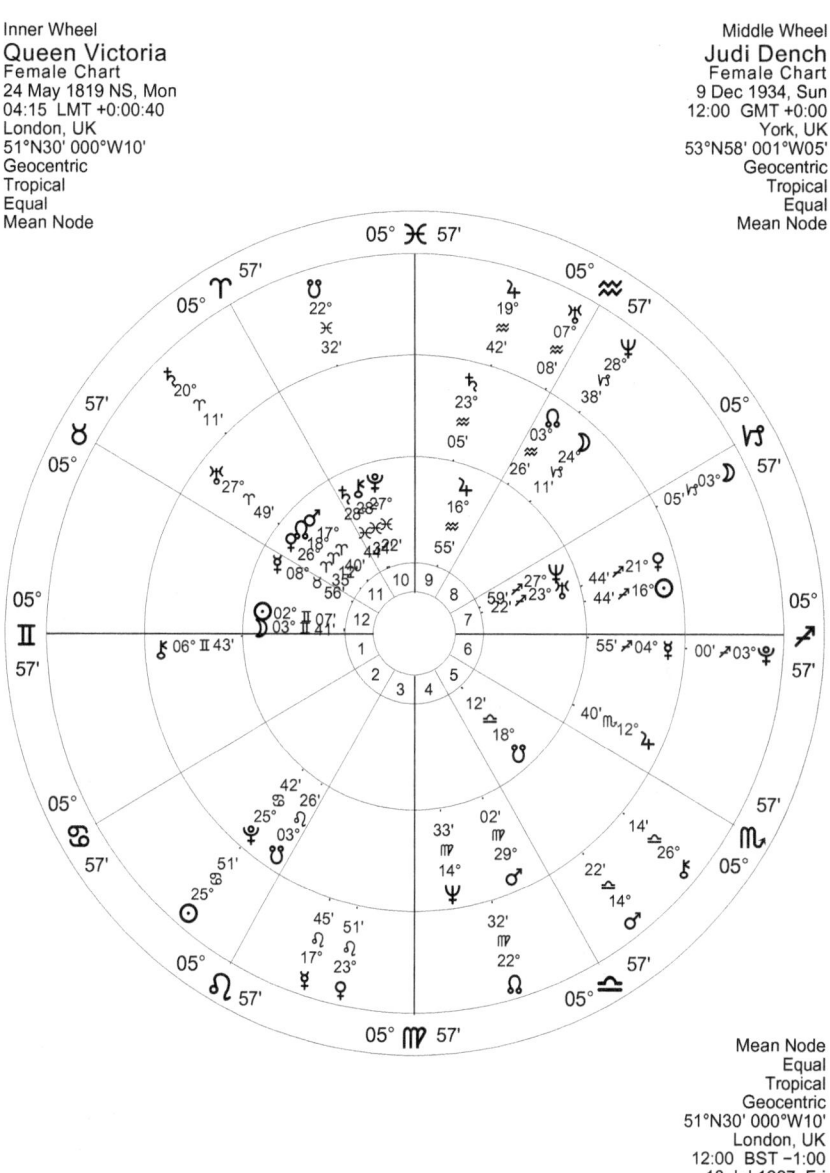

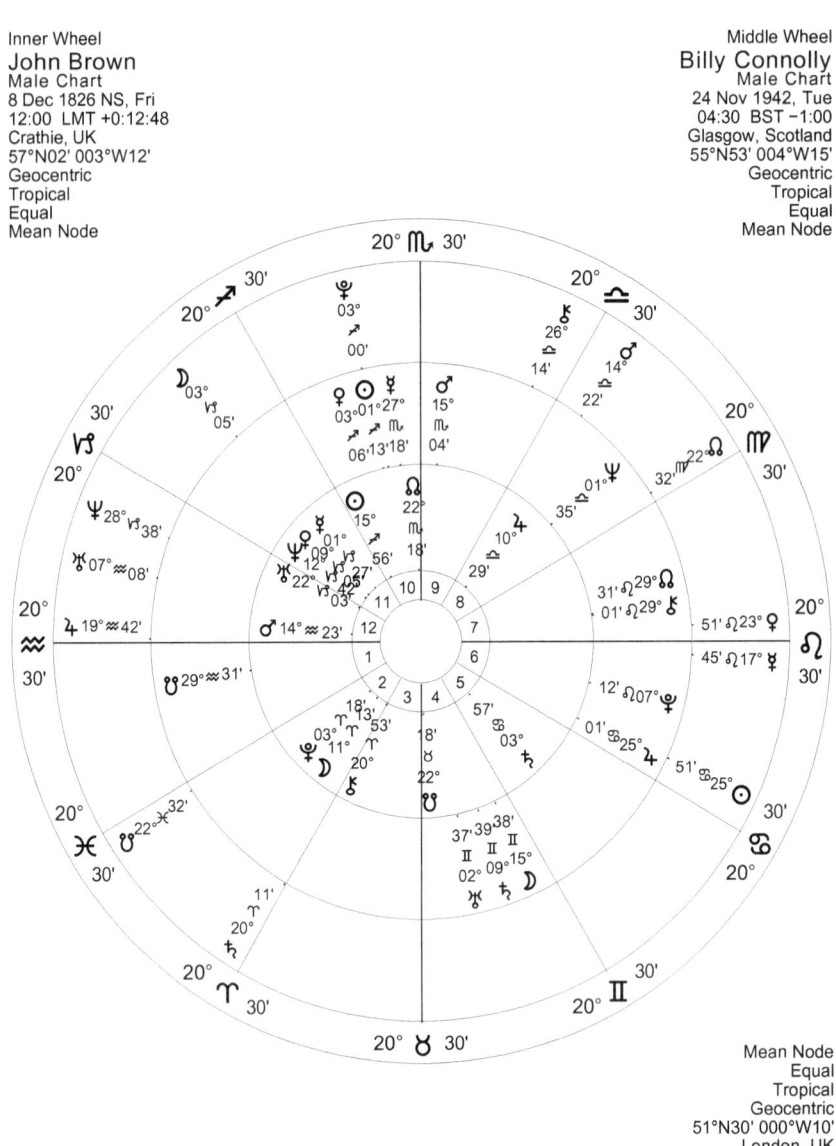

of the crowd but Brown, who takes his role as her security guard very seriously, manages to thwart the attempt to assassinate the Queen.

At dinner the next night, Victoria's son Bertie boasts to dinner guests that he had tipped off Brown that an assassin was in the crowd. Knowing that he is lying, the Queen announces that Brown will be given a special medal for bravery.

After contracting pneumonia from looking for potential palace intruders in wintry woods, Brown is on his death bed and the Queen visits him for the last time. She tells him that she should have been a better friend to him. After his death, his diary is discovered and it is agreed by the Queen's advisors that it must never be found. One of the advisors reveals that the Queen's son had thrown Brown's bust over the palace wall.

Judi Dench's Chiron/Mercury opposition falls within one degree of the Queen's ascendant in Gemini and her North Node in Aquarius is on the Queen's MC, an indication that the monarch's desire for companionship was understood by the actress. And it's a good job too as Dench played Queen Victoria twice! Dench's Uranus in Aries is conjunct the Queen's Venus so she is very capable of understanding her need for independence. Pluto in Sagittarius was transiting the Queen's descendant and Dench's Mercury when the film was released.

John Brown's Jupiter in Libra is within three degrees of Billy Connelly's ascendant so the actor can appreciate Brown's diplomacy. Brown's Uranus in Capricorn is conjunct Connelly's IC and in opposition to his Jupiter which shows an understanding of the devotion required to serve the Queen as well as an enjoyment of the privilege. Pluto in Sagittarius was transiting Connelly's Mercury and Bertie's Venus/Sun conjunction when the film was released.

David Westhead's Neptune/Venus opposition (chart not shown) is within three degrees of Bertie's Sun in Scorpio which perhaps shows the treachery displayed by the future king. The film was released as Saturn was conjunct Bertie's Pluto in Aries in opposition to his Venus in Libra. *Mrs Brown* was released on the Queen's Jupiter return in Aquarius, as Pluto transited her descendant in Sagittarius and Saturn was on her South Node and Mars in Aries.

Judi Dench was nominated for an Academy Award and a Screen Actors Guild Award and won a BAFTA and a Golden Globe for Best Actress. Connelly was nominated for a BAFTA and a Screen Actors Guild Award for Best Supporting Actor. The film was nominated by BAFTA for Best Film.

Victoria and Abdul
Queen Victoria: 24 May 1819, 04:15, London. AA: RR
Judi Dench: 9 December 1934, no time, York, England.
Source: Wikipedia
Albert, 'Bertie', Prince of Wales: 9 November 1841, 10:48, London. AA: RR
Eddie Izzard: 7 February 1962, 19:30, Aden, Yemen. C: Scholfield
Release date: 3 September 2017

In 1887 Abdul Karim, a young prison clerk from British India, is selected to travel to England for Queen Victoria's Golden Jubilee and present Her Majesty with a *mohur*, a specially minted gold coin. While Abdul is looking forward to the adventure, Muhammad, his companion, bitterly resents having to go to a cold country where the people eat pigs' blood. Abdul and Muhammad are puzzled by the pomp and ceremony of life in the castle but Abdul manages to make an impression on the Queen when he kisses her feet as a mark of respect.

Soon Abdul is invited to visit the Queen in her office and she urges him to teach her Urdu and the Quran. She affectionately calls him "The Munshi" which means "Teacher" in Urdu. The other members of the household, most notably her son Bertie the Prince of Wales, become resentful over the Munshi's influence. In the meantime, the Queen continues to bestow special gifts and privileges on Abdul, even taking him to where she used to spend time with John Brown. When she finds out the Munshi is married, she implores him to bring his wife to England to meet her.

The Munshi's wife – and mother-in-law – arrive in full burkas and with a young servant boy. While other members of the royal household look on with thinly-veiled disgust, the Queen is fascinated and asks Abdul if she can see his wife without the burka. He tells her that as they are both women, there is no problem. With her mother's help, Abdul's wife removes her veil in front of the Queen.

The Queen's interest in India continues to flourish and inspires her to build a Durbar Room at Osborne House for state functions. It is decorated with intricate Indian carvings, carpets, a replica of the Peacock Throne – and a very flattering portrait of Abdul as well as other prominent Indians on the wall.

Jealous that his mother treats the Munshi better than him, Bertie and other members of the household plot together to find a way to wreck their relationship. When Victoria erroneously relays a one-sided story of the Indian Mutiny told to her by the Munshi, they seize the opportunity to tell her she is wrong. Embarrassed, she confronts the Munshi and tells him it is time he left. However, she changes her mind before he leaves.

Next, the Prime Minister presents a dossier to the Queen proving that the Munshi is from a more ordinary family background than she had thought. The Queen insists that her doctor examine the Munshi's wife to determine why she has not yet fallen pregnant. To the doctor's shocked delight, the Munshi has a severe case of gonorrhoea; he gleefully tells the queen and expects her to dismiss the Munshi. Unabashed, she tells him that as he is a doctor, it is his duty to treat him. She then reveals she intends to give the Munshi a knighthood.

The royal household eventually decide they will all resign and have Victoria certified as insane if she does not break ties with the Munshi. The Queen summons everyone to the Durbar Room and asks them directly who wants to resign. No one steps forward. She announces she will include the Munshi on her next honours list.

Victoria falls ill and begs the Munshi to return to India so she can protect him, because when she dies, the court will take their revenge on him. The Munshi tells her he will stay with her and he comforts her as she dies. After her death in 1901, Bertie (now the King), throws the Munshi out of his home, burns all the gifts the Queen had given him and sends the family back to India.

The end of the film shows Abdul kneeling at a monument of the Queen near the Taj Mahal. As he kisses the feet of the statue, it is revealed he lived in India until his death in 1909.

Eddie Izzard's four-planet stellium (plus the South Node) are conjunct Bertie's Neptune and the actor's Mars and Saturn in Aquarius are

250 Mirror Mirror

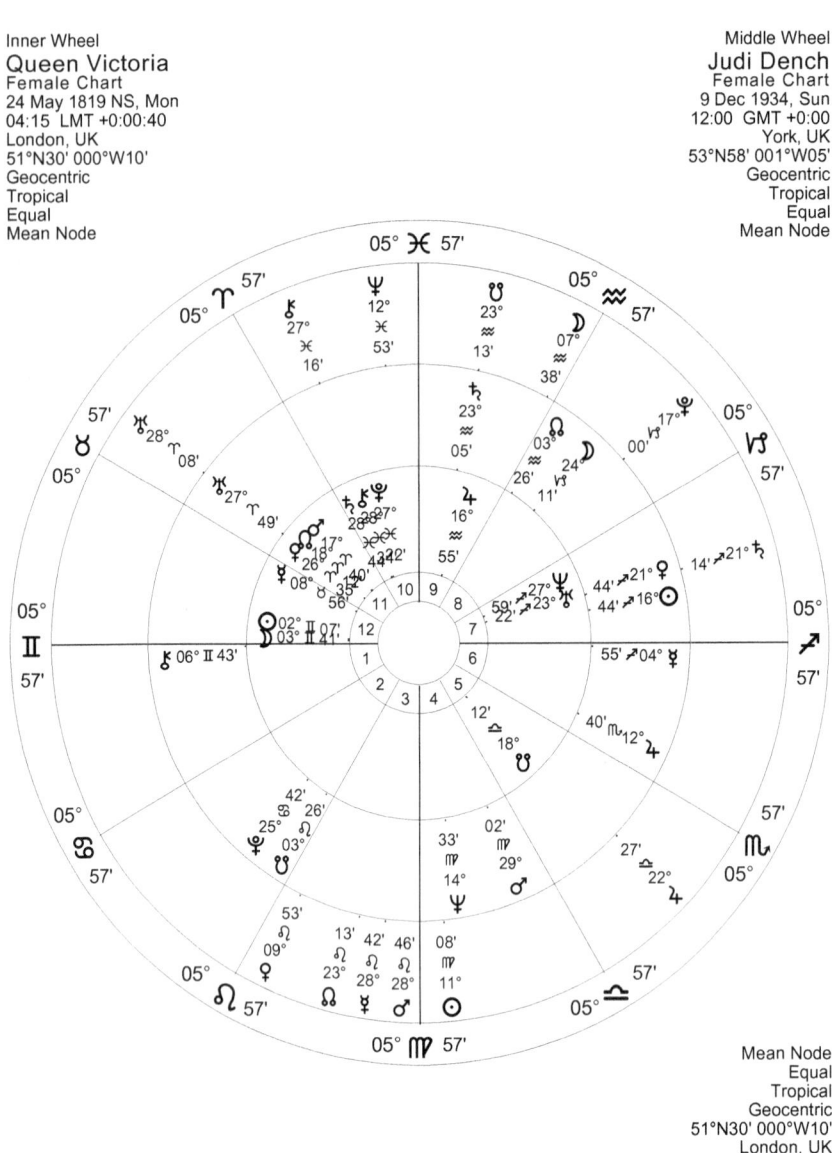

Multiple Versions 251

Inner Wheel
King, Edward VII
Male Chart
9 Nov 1841 NS, Tue
10:48 LMT +0:00:40
London, UK
51°N30' 000°W10'
Geocentric
Tropical
Equal
Mean Node

Middle Wheel
Eddie Izzard
Male Chart
7 Feb 1962, Wed
19:30 BAT −3:00
Aden, Yemen
12°N45' 045°E12'
Geocentric
Tropical
Equal
Mean Node

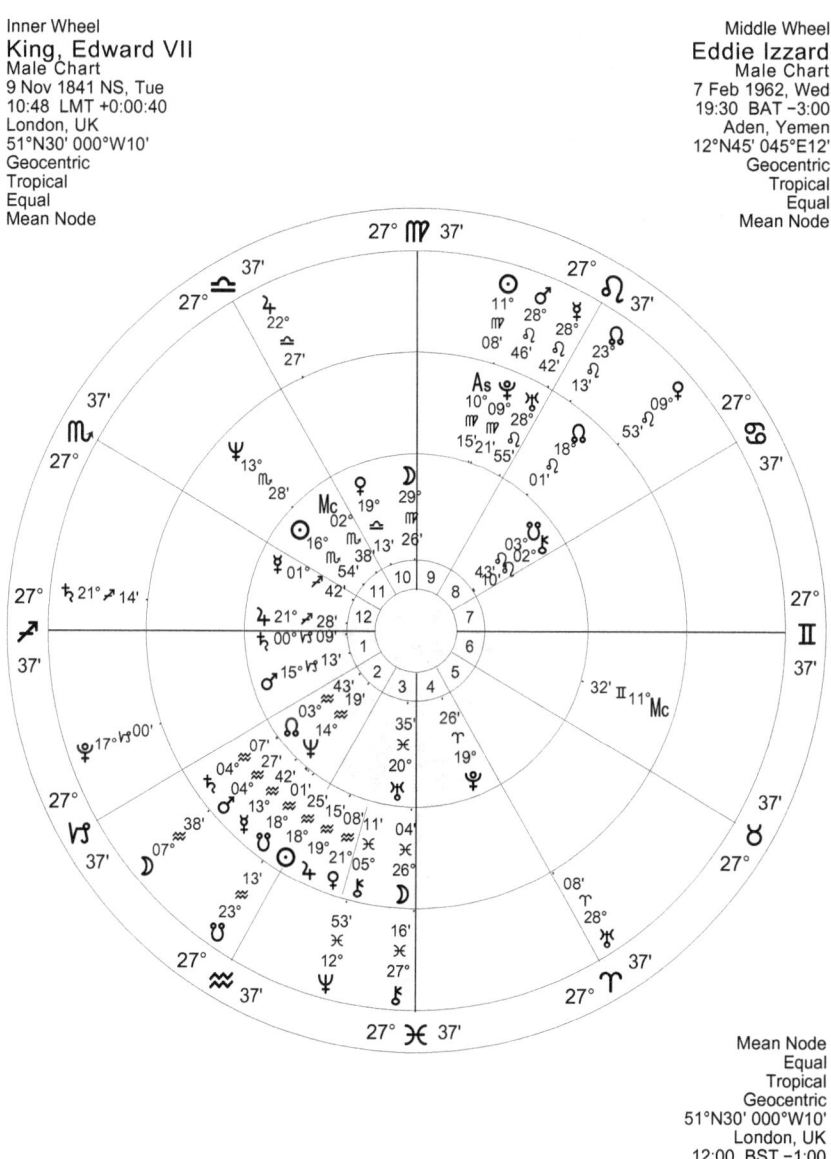

Mean Node
Equal
Tropical
Geocentric
51°N30' 000°W10'
London, UK
12:00 BST −1:00
3 Sep 2017, Sun
Event Chart
Victoria and Abdul release
Outer Wheel

conjunct the monarch's North Node. This role was a radical departure from the type of character Izzard usually played.

The movie was released as Saturn in Sagittarius was exactly conjunct Bertie's Jupiter, and Pluto in Capricorn was conjunct his Mars. Transiting Neptune in Pisces was conjunct Izzard's descendant within an orb of two degrees and the Mars/Mercury conjunction in Leo was exactly conjunct his Uranus.

Judi Dench was nominated for Best actress at the Academy Awards.

FAVOURITES

How to choose a favourite biopic? I was so enthralled with the performances that I had forgotten the actors weren't the real people. At first, I thought this fascination was just down to acting talent. But then I realised something else was going on: the real life people had astrological connections to my own astrology chart. For example, Jim Morrison's Sun in Sagittarius is exactly opposite my Jupiter. Alan Turing (*The Imitation Game*) and Julia Child (*Julie and Julia*) have the same ascendant as me at six degrees Gemini – and Elton John's North Node is also on the same degree and Johnny Cash's Mercury/Sun conjunction in Pisces is square. You get the picture. Try comparing your own chart to your favourite celebrity.

I also loved it when actors learned new skills as in the singing Val Kilmer's portrayal of Jim Morrison in *The Doors*, as well as Joaquim Phoenix and Reese Weatherspoon as Johnny and June Cash in *Walk the Line*, or Dennis Quaid's piano playing as Jerry Lee Lewis in *Great Balls of Fire* or Margot Robbie ice skating as Tonya Harding in *I, Tonya*. How on earth did Colin Firth master Bertie's stutter in *The King's Speech* so convincingly? It takes great devotion to learn new skills well enough to convince a critical audience that they are as good as the real person.

Then there were actors who physically changed to get into their roles. Charlize Theron was unrecognisable as serial killer Aileen Wournos in *Monster* and Eric Stoltz was practically buried under prosthetics to play Rocky Dennis in *Mask*.

How about when an actor pulls off the impossible? When I first heard of *Behind the Candelabra* about the great Liberace who, like Julia Child, I adored as a kid, I didn't hold out much hope for Michael Douglas. How wrong I was! Speaking of not a lot of hope, how is a heartthrob going to get into the role of a Vietnam vet? Only the astrology can explain the magic of Tom Cruise playing Ron Kovic in *Born on the Fourth of July*. Sean Penn had his work cut out for him as Harvey Milk (*Milk*) but a tough guy like him conveyed the challenges of the homosexual politician with ease.

I love women with balls, so of course *Erin Brockovich* (Julia Roberts) and Edith Piaf *La Vie en Rose* (Marion Cottiliard) made it to this section.

Truman Capote is one of my favourite writers and I've always admired Philip Seymour Hoffman's work so *Capote* also made the cut. Although I'm not a fan of scary movies, the skills and continued influence of Alfred Hitchcock in *Hitchcock* (Anthony Hopkins) was enthralling.

Some scenes are simply unforgettable and make the film worth watching again. The sight of *Lawrence of Arabia* (the gorgeous Peter O'Toole) trying on his new robes is something I could watch on a loop. However, I saved the very best for last! I loved Elton John well before I saw *Rocketman* but his music was so wonderfully – and convincingly – delivered by the adorable Taron Egerton. If you pass through East London and happen to hear a very poor rendition of *Goodbye Yellow Brick Road*, you'll know it's me.

BEHIND THE CANDELABRA

Wladzia Valentino Liberace: 16 May 1919, 23:15, West Allis, Wisconsin. AA: Steinbrecher

Michael Douglas: 25 September 1944, 10:30, New Brunswick, New Jersey. AA: Steinbrecher

Scott Thorson: 23 January 1959, no time, La Crosse, Wisconsin. Source: Wikipedia

Matt Damon: 8 October 1970, 15:22, Boston, Massachusetts. AA: RR

Release date: 21 May 2013

Behind the Candelabra is a light-hearted glance at the life-long work of a man who used his Saturn in Leo to disguise his true self (very much like Elton John). Saturn in Leo may seem odd for a man who became known for his stage persona – but he guarded his "real" character very carefully indeed. This was a man who clearly understood his strengths and weaknesses and knew exactly which side to face to the cameras.

The film tells the story from the point of view of Liberace's young male lover Scott Thorson. Thorson becomes entangled in Liberace's extravagant life when he uses his veterinary skills to treat the performer's dog. Eventually, Thorson realises that Liberace is attempting to control him more and more. A palimony suit ends their formal partnership but Liberace denies they had any sort of sexual relationship. Just before his death, Liberace calls Thorson to say goodbye. The last scene is at

Favourites 255

Inner Wheel
Liberace
Male Chart
16 May 1919, Fri
23:15 CWT +5:00
West Allis, Wisconsin
43°N01' 088°W00'25"
Geocentric
Tropical
Equal
Mean Node

Middle Wheel
Michael Douglas
Male Chart
25 Sep 1944, Mon
10:30 EWT +4:00
New Brunswick
40°N29'10" 074°W27'08"
Geocentric
Tropical
Equal
Mean Node

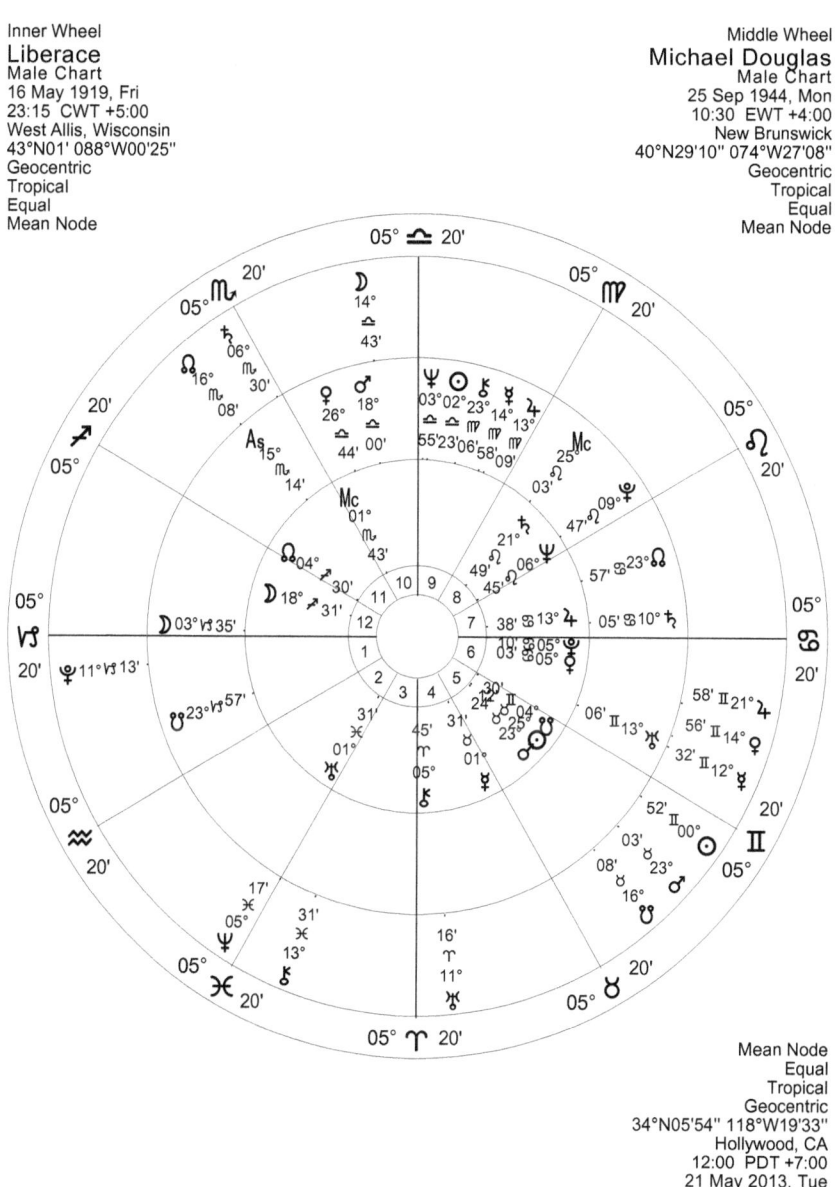

Mean Node
Equal
Tropical
Geocentric
34°N05'54" 118°W19'33"
Hollywood, CA
12:00 PDT +7:00
21 May 2013, Tue
Event Chart
Behind the Candelabra
Outer Wheel

256 Mirror Mirror

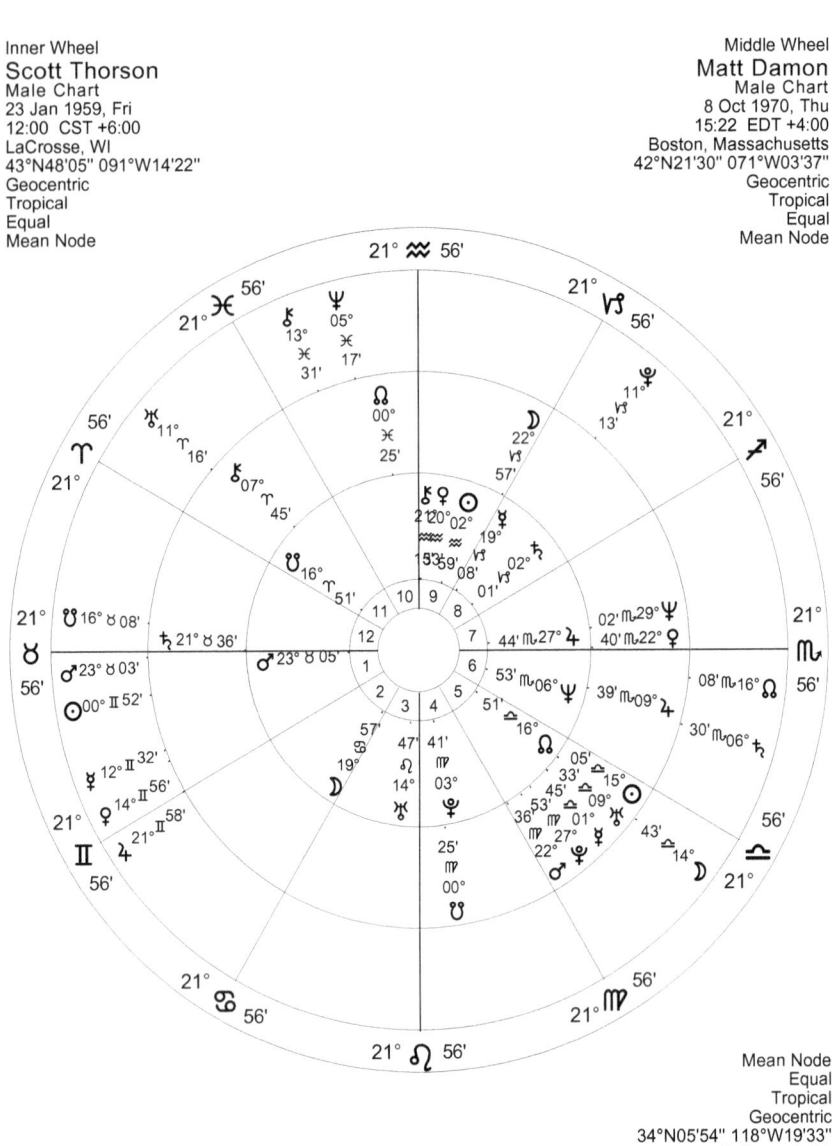

Liberace's funeral where Thorson imagines the performer ascending into heaven with his usual flamboyance.

Natally, Liberace had a Venus/Pluto conjunction exactly on his descendant. The descendant tends to be the first signals the native puts "out there" to others and can in turn be the type of people they draw to them. Venus/Pluto is magnetic indeed; some people might even say hypnotic. Viewed this way it isn't surprising Thorson was both attracted to and then repelled by Liberace's attempts to control him, even to the extent of making him have plastic surgery to look like him or adopting him as his son.

Liberace also had a Sun/Mars conjunction on the dreaded fixed star Algol: intense entertainment indeed! It's a further example of the power he had over his fans and lovers. As we have two AA timed birth charts, we can use the angles. Douglas' MC in Leo is within four degrees of Liberace's Saturn, which enabled the actor to understand the pianist's need to develop an onstage persona. Further, Douglas' Moon in Capricorn is within two degrees of Liberace's ascendant and this makes for a powerful emotional connection, particularly when it comes to business and success (Liberace always took great pride in being from a humble background).

As a straight man, playing a flamboyant gay man was a total role reversal for Michael Douglas. Transiting Venus and Mercury in Gemini were conjunct the actor's Uranus when the film was released.

Matt Damon's MC is conjunct Thorson's Jupiter in Scorpio by an orb of just one degree. The film focuses on the sexuality of the characters as well as the presence of manipulation in their relationship. Damon's Sun in Libra is just one degree from an exact conjunction to Thorson's North Node. Transiting Mars was conjunct Thorson's Mars and opposed Damon's Venus when the film was released.

Pluto had crossed over Liberace's ascendant, Neptune had transited his natal Uranus and transiting Uranus passed over his natal Chiron as filming took place. Perhaps most tellingly, transiting Saturn had passed over his natal MC when the film was released bringing out another truth to his public image. If that wasn't enough, transiting Mars was exactly conjunct Liberace's natal Mars, pulling in the natal Sun's connection to Algol.

The made-for-television film received critical acclaim from critics for both the film itself as well as the performances of the actors.

BORN ON THE FOURTH OF JULY
Oliver Stone: 15 September 1946, 09:58, Manhattan, New York.
AA: Wilsons
Ron Kovic: 4 July 1946, 22:14, Ladysmith, Wisconsin. AA: RR
Tom Cruise: 3 July 1962, no time, Syracuse, New York X: RR
Release date: 20 December 1989

Few topics can provoke more intense emotions in America than the Vietnam War. Fifty years on and the country is still coming to grips with this awful chapter of its history.

The director of the film, Oliver Stone, is a veteran of the war, and after reading Ron Kovic's bestselling autobiography *Born on the Fourth of July* he bought the film rights. Stone and Kovic worked collaboratively on the script, discussing their experiences in Vietnam as they wrote. Born within months of each other, they share similar placement of outer planets. Kovic's Mercury and Pluto are conjunct in Leo, bringing passion and intensity to his writing. Stone's Saturn and MC are on Kovic's conjunction. Their material was heavy with the emotions of regret, loss and the search for redemption, mixed with the very human need to be accepted in society. One of the best examples of this is Kovic's sorrow at losing the ability to have intimate relationships with the opposite sex due to his paralysis. The film also features Kovic's physical recovery in a hopelessly ill-equipped veteran's hospital and the lack of a warm welcome when he finally returns to his family home.

Astrologically, Tom Cruise and Ron Kovic share very revealing connections. They both have Venus at 19° Leo so the audience is in no doubt of the heartbreak Kovic suffered when he was emasculated by the war. Kovic's Uranus/North Node conjunction is on the same degree as Cruise's Mercury: here is an actor communicating Kovic's vital message of finding compassion for the men who fought in the unpopular war. Perhaps most revealing is Kovic's Mars on Cruise's Pluto and Cruise's North Node conjunct Kovic's Pluto: from gung-ho soldier to paralysed and rejected veteran, Cruise's portrayal of Kovic is heartbreakingly realistic and haunting. One might even say it was a fated connection.

Released on 20 December 1989, transiting Chiron is within two degrees of Cruise's and Kovic's Sun.

The Vietnam War started on 1 November 1955 and that Kovic

Favourites 259

Inner Wheel
Oliver Stone
Male Chart
15 Sep 1946, Sun
09:58 EDT +4:00
Manhattan, New York
40°N46' 073°W59'
Geocentric
Tropical
Equal
Mean Node

Outer Wheel
Ron Kovic
Male Chart
4 Jul 1946, Thu
22:14 CST +6:00
Ladysmith, WI
45°N27'47" 091°W06'14"
Geocentric
Tropical
Equal
Mean Node

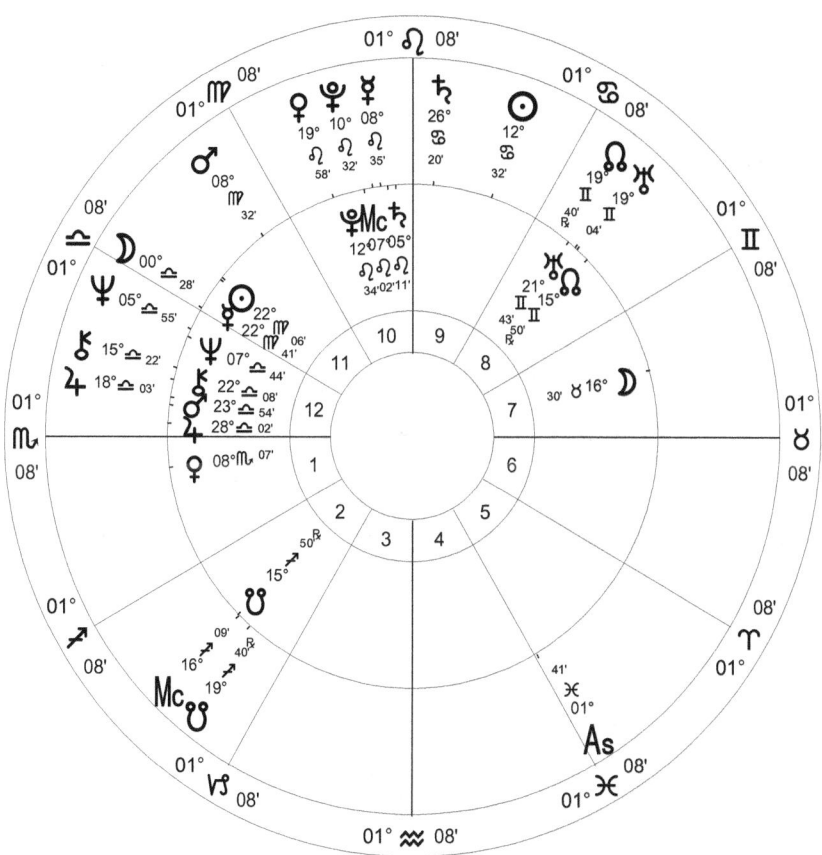

260 Mirror Mirror

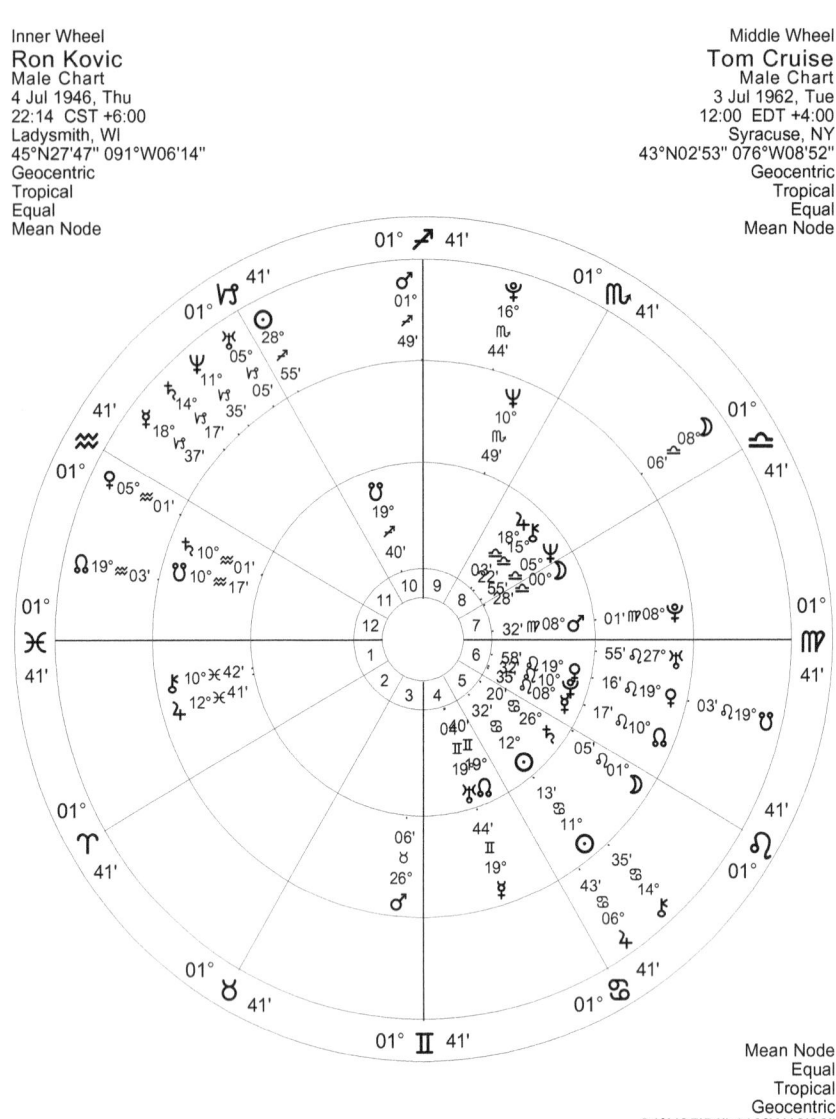

Favourites   261

Inner Wheel
Oliver Stone
Male Chart
15 Sep 1946, Sun
09:58 EDT +4:00
Manhattan, New York
40°N46' 073°W59'
Geocentric
Tropical
Equal
Mean Node

Outer Wheel
Vietnam War
Event Chart
1 Nov 1955, Tue
12:00 USZ6 −7:00
Saigon, Vietnam
10°N45' 106°E40'
Geocentric
Tropical
Equal
Mean Node

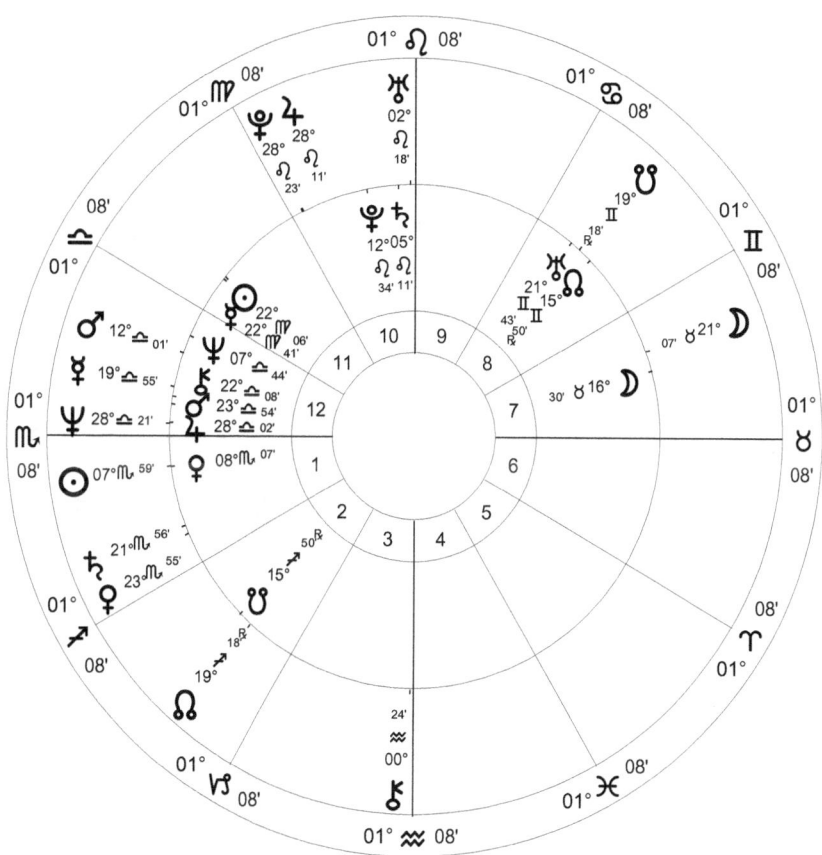

262   Mirror Mirror

Inner Wheel
Ron Kovic
Male Chart
4 Jul 1946, Thu
22:14 CST +6:00
Ladysmith, WI
45°N27'47" 091°W06'14"
Geocentric
Tropical
Equal
Mean Node

Outer Wheel
Vietnam War
Event Chart
1 Nov 1955, Tue
12:00 USZ6 −7:00
Saigon, Vietnam
10°N45' 106°E40'
Geocentric
Tropical
Equal
Mean Node

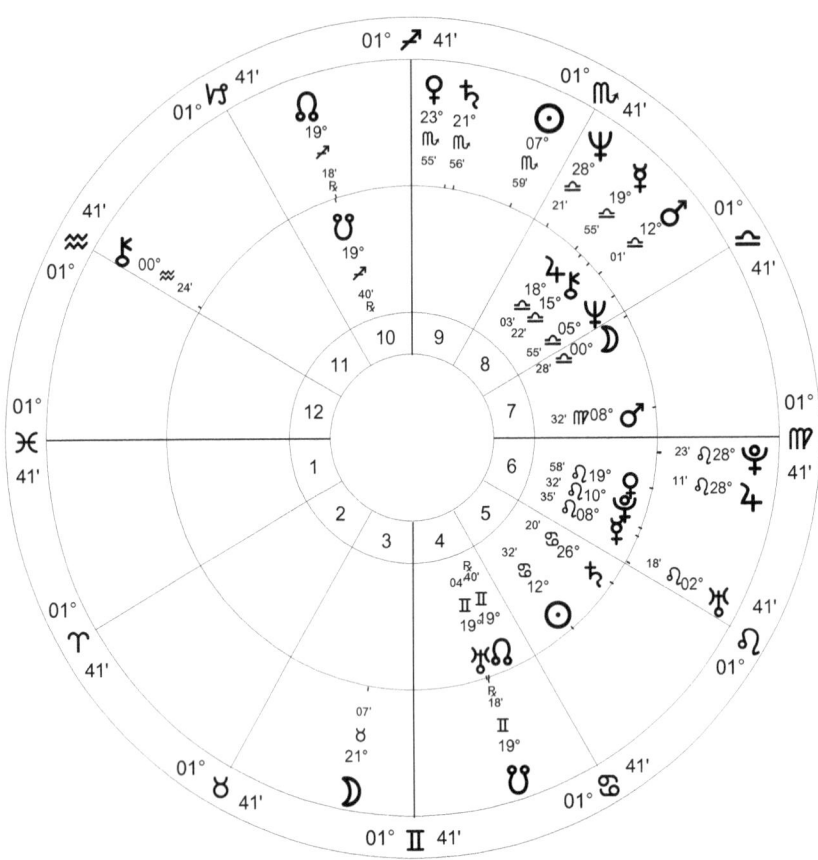

Favourites 263

Inner Wheel
Tom Cruise
Male Chart
3 Jul 1962, Tue
12:00 EDT +4:00
Syracuse, NY
43°N02'53" 076°W08'52"
Geocentric
Tropical
Equal
Mean Node

Outer Wheel
Vietnam War
Event Chart
1 Nov 1955, Tue
12:00 USZ6 −7:00
Saigon, Vietnam
10°N45' 106°E40'
Geocentric
Tropical
Equal
Mean Node

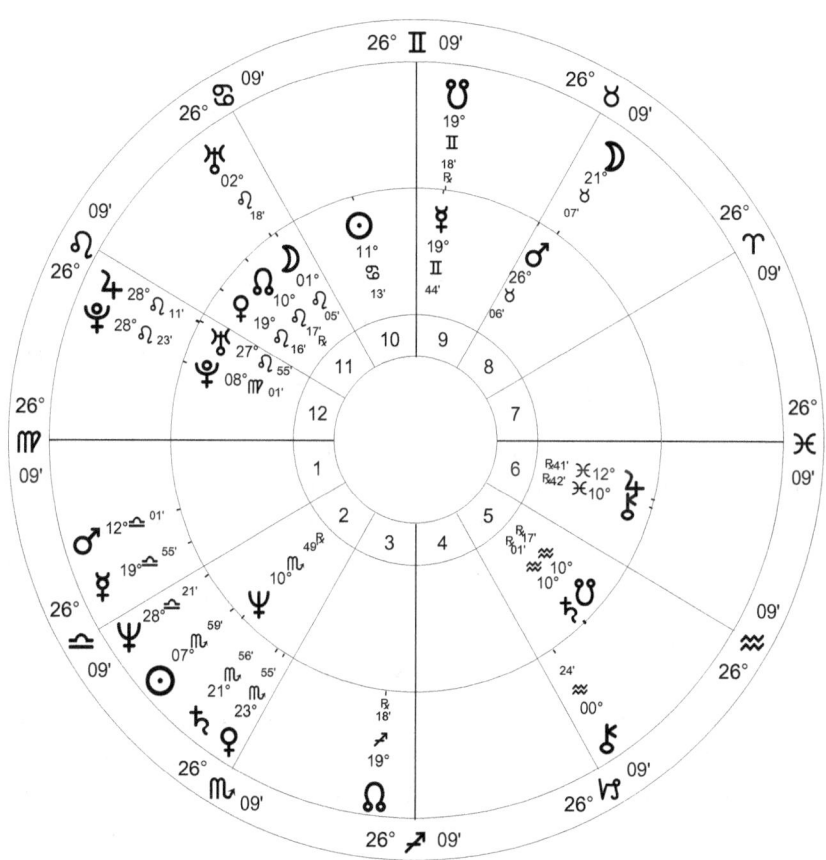

would want to write about his experiences is shown with the Mercury of the war conjunct within a degree of Kovic's Jupiter. At one point in the film, Kovic's mother says to her young son that she had a dream that he was standing on a stage saying great things to many people – she just could not have known that these great things would have been about the misery of an awful war in a faraway land. That Stone might want to make a movie about the war (he also directed *Platoon*) shows with his Jupiter conjunct the Neptune of the war. Cruise's Sun is within three degrees of the war's Neptune and his heart-breaking portrayal of the ruined life of a Vietnam veteran is one that stays with the audience long after the movie has finished.

The film was nominated for Best Picture and Best Actor and won Golden Globes in the same categories.

ERIN BROCKOVICH

Erin Brockovich: 22 June 1960, no time, Lawrence, Kansas.
Source: Wikipedia
Julia Roberts: 28 October 1967, 00:16, Atlanta, Georgia. AA: RR
Release date: 17 March 2000

Single mothers are often treated with derision, even in the modern world. So when single mother Erin Brockovich – who was acting as an unqualified researcher and assistant attorney – almost singlehandedly brought down the Pacific Gas and Electricity Company (PG&E) for a cool $333 million, the world just may have started looking at things a little differently.

After being injured in a car accident, the character Erin Brockovich tries to sue the other driver. In court, however, she lashes out aggressively when the crossexaminer expresses shock that none of her children had the same father. Subsequently, solely due to her reaction to the affront rather than any sense of legal justice, she loses the case. It is this sense of outraged unfairness that establishes the theme of *Erin Brockovich*.

Scorpio is the sign of the zodiac associated with hidden treasures. Pluto, the modern ruler of Scorpio, lived in the Underworld where his assets were well hidden from the world of the living. The character Erin Brockovich counts what is left in her bank account and evades the cockroaches of her infested home by spending the last of her precious

Favourites 265

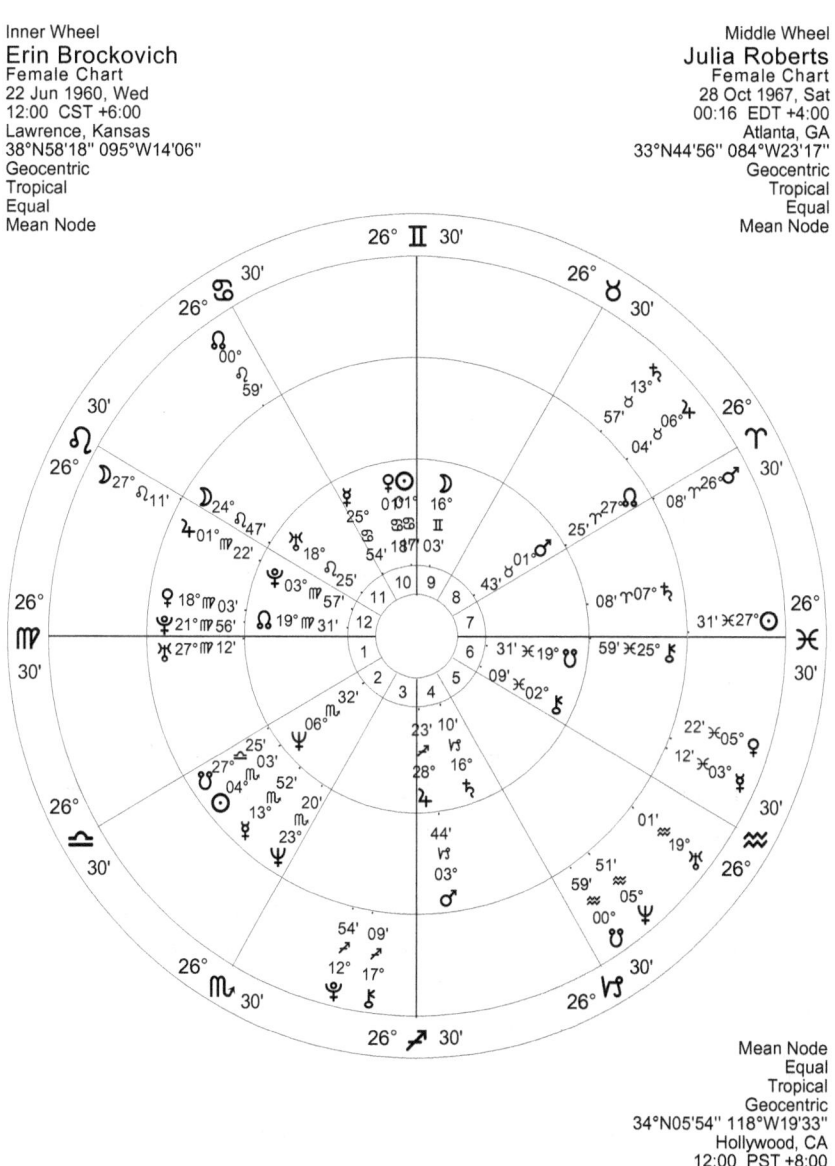

dollars taking her children to the safety of a local restaurant. By the time the film was made, the real Erin Brokovich had escaped the hell that must have been her desperate situation as a single mother. She makes a cameo appearance as the waitress, asking Roberts (who is in character) if she would like to order anything for herself.

The stereotype of the single mother may be the soft, desperate, unkempt sort – to which neither Roberts nor the real life Brockovich conform. Backed into a corner, Brockovich comes out fighting – with miniskirts, low cut tops and immaculately filed fingernails. She is a very different sort of heroine. She browbeats her lawyer into giving her a job and even persuades him to give her a cash advance for the weekend.

The other women who work in her office seem to despise Brockovich out of jealousy. And why not? They are qualified to do their jobs whereas Brockovich appears to have arrived at her job solely through sexy good looks that have somehow charmed their boss.

Whilst looking through some files, Brockovich discovers the illegal activity of PG&E. The company have been contaminating the groundwater of Hinckley, California with carcinogenic hexavalent chromium. Local people were being diagnosed with various forms of rare cancers and PG&E had been paying their medical expenses, presumably to offset any subsequent legal claims.

Brockovich returns to the law office with this news only to discover that her female colleagues have removed her possessions from her desk, and gleefully inform her that she has been fired because she didn't show up for work.

It would seem Brockovich is back to square one as an unemployed single mother with no job prospects. However, her boss visits her at home to ask for the papers she has discovered and the ever resourceful Brockovich not only gets her job back, but is also given a pay raise and benefits.

Julia Roberts, of course, makes the title role her own with her sassy, uncompromising style and overtly sexual manner. Natally, she is a Scorpio Sun with the Neptune of the real life Brockovich conjunct to its position within two degrees. Roberts effortlessly tapped into the glamour of the character – no doubt a factor of the movie's appeal. Brockovich is a "fallen" beauty queen but used her good looks to her advantage in order to uncover information.

Roberts' Venus in Virgo is conjunct Brockovich's North Node so there is real sense of destiny in the exchange. The keywords of Virgo are "service" and "dedication" and it doesn't take too long to see the extent to which Brockovich would go to ensure her family is taken care of. After all, the ruling planet of Virgo is Mercury and Brockovich's Mercury is conjunct Roberts' ascendant in Cancer.

The sign of Virgo also represents health. The Jupiter/Pluto conjunction in Virgo between actress and character also represents the higher knowledge acquired by the lawyers and the depths to which Brockovich is prepared to go in order to secure justice. She begins forming relationships with the local people and so gains their trust. She knows their personal histories, their diseases and other confidential data. Brockovich has the talent to talk to the local people in a way out of town lawyers, who are later hired to assist with the case, cannot. She asks the lawyers who put a price tag on their health to put the terms of compensation into perspective.

Chiron in Pisces of the real-life Brockovich opposes this conjunction of Jupiter/Pluto. Chiron is the "wounded healer" and though it is most unfortunate that the water has made the local people so ill, a payout is unlikely to be of much comfort. However, because of her hard work, empathy for the situation and persistence, the people of Hinckley receive one of the highest legal payouts in US history. And of course, in the process, Brockovich is transformed from a single, destitute mother into a very wealthy one.

On the night of the film's premiere, transiting Mercury was on this Chiron and Jupiter/Pluto opposition. Perhaps more than the financial gain, Erin Brockovich would be remembered as the underdog who bit back.

Roberts won an Academy Award, a BAFTA, a Critics' Choice Movie Award, a Golden Globe Award, a National Board of Review, and a Screen Actors Guild Award for Best actress, becoming the first actress to win so many awards for a single performance.

CAPOTE

Truman Capote: 30 September 1924, 15:00, New Orleans. B: RR
Philip Seymour Hoffman: 23 July 1967, no time, Fairport, New York. Source: Wikipedia
Harper Lee: 28 April 1926, 17:25, Monroeville, Alabama.
AA: CAH
Catherine Keener: 23 March 1959, no time, Miami, Florida.
Source: Wikipedia
Release date: 2 September 2005

A wealthy wheat farmer, his wife and their two young children were found shot to death today in their home. They had been killed by shotgun blasts at close range after being bound and gagged. The father, 48-year-old Herbert W. Clutter, was found in the basement with his son, Kenyon, 15. His wife Ennis, 45, and a daughter, Nancy, 16, were in their beds. There were no signs of a struggle and nothing had been stolen. The telephone lines had been cut. "This is apparently the case of a psychopathic killer," said Sheriff Earl Robinson.

In the film *Capote*, the acclaimed writer Truman Capote (played by the marvellous Philip Seymour Hoffman), reads the above article in 1959 just after this terrible crime was committed and decides he wants to document the story for a magazine. To help him, he invites his childhood friend Harper Lee to help him.

Intending to interview friends of the Clutter family, the pair meet the lead detective on the case and Capote is able to charm his wife with tales of film stars to the point that she invites the pair to dinner. During this dinner a news report reveals that Perry Smith and Richard Hickock have been apprehended for the murders.

Through his connections and with the help of bribes, Capote is able to visit the prisoners in their cells. Capote is particularly interested in Smith and becomes emotionally attached to him as Smith reveals his difficult life. As the killers face execution, Capote helps them to access more robust legal counsel. However, this makes the case drag on for years and doesn't convince Smith to reveal what really happened on the night of the murders. Eventually though, Smith tells Capote everything. Smith's detailed confession gives Capote what he wants but he feels guilty he cannot share in Harper's joy at her book *To Kill a Mockingbird* being turned into a film. He starts to drink heavily and when Smith begs

Favourites 269

Inner Wheel
Truman Capote
Male Chart
30 Sep 1924, Tue
15:00 CST +6:00
New Orleans, LA
29°N57'16" 090°W04'30"
Geocentric
Tropical
Equal
Mean Node

Middle Wheel
Philip Seymour Hoffman
Male Chart
23 Jul 1967, Sun
12:00 EDT +4:00
Fairport, NY
43°N05'55" 077°W26'32"
Geocentric
Tropical
Equal
Mean Node

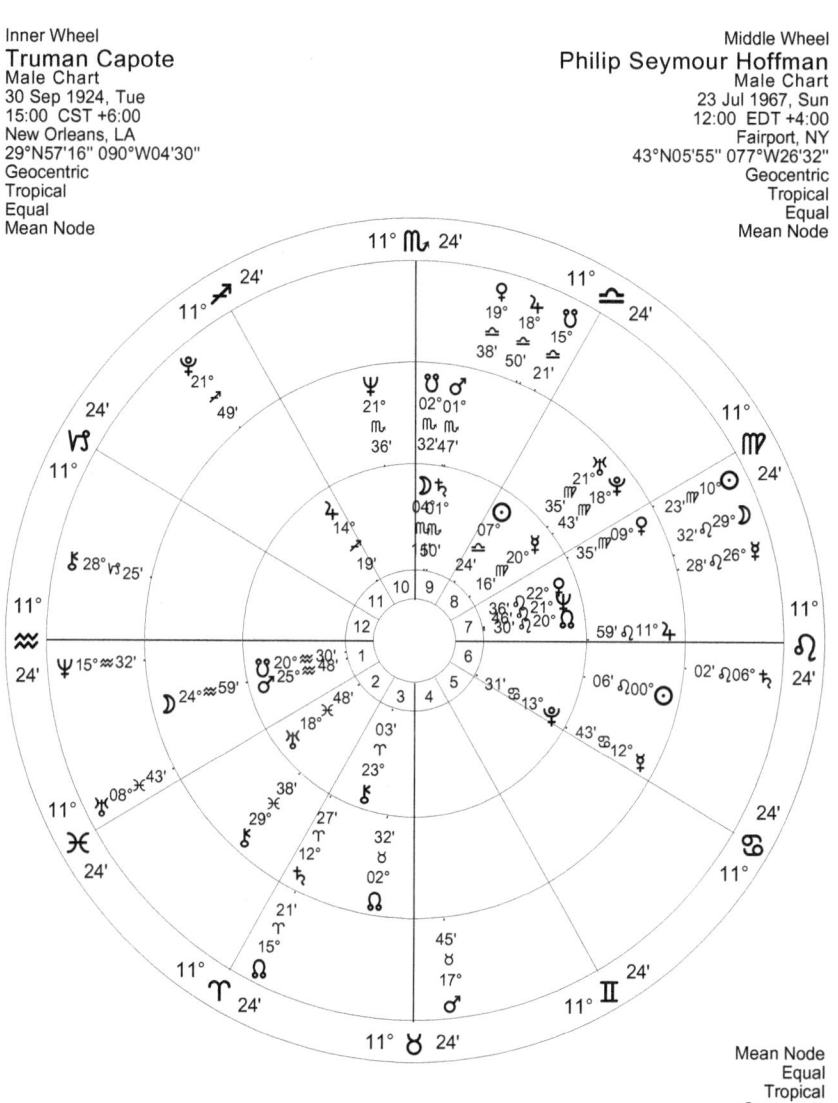

Mean Node
Equal
Tropical
Geocentric
34°N05'54" 118°W19'33"
Hollywood, CA
12:00 PDT +7:00
2 Sep 2005, Fri
Event Chart
Capote release
Outer Wheel

270 Mirror Mirror

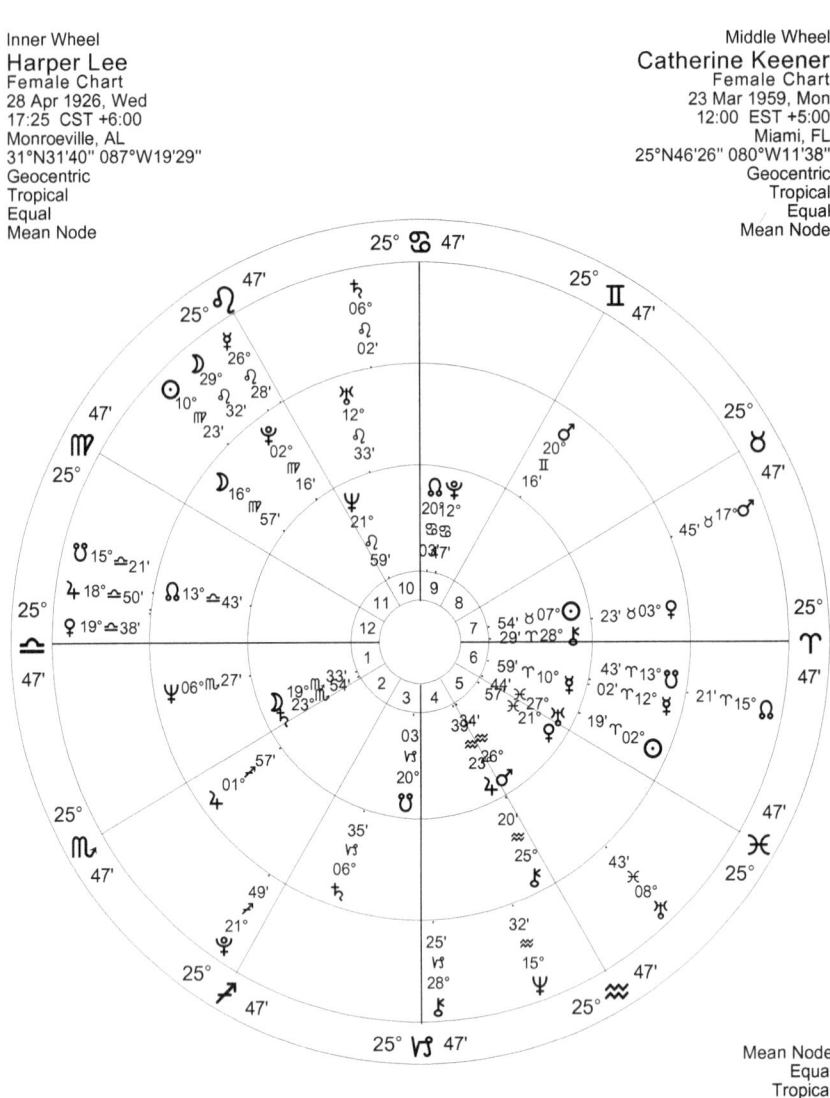

him to say goodbye, he cannot do it. Capote eventually relents and is an eyewitness to the executions.

Catherine Keener and Harper Lee both have Mercury in Aries within a couple of degrees of each other which comes in handy when portraying a writer. Additionally, Keener's Chiron in Aquarius is conjunct the writer's Jupiter/Mars conjunction. The film depicts a well-known author taking an unusual career detour via the investigation of grisly murders and the impending executions of the culprits. Keener plays the role with the sympathy necessary to support a childhood friend through this gruesome task.

Philip Seymour Hoffman's Pluto/Uranus conjunction in Virgo is conjunct Capote's Mercury. As he portrays a writer, it would be important to understand how he would communicate and the depths to which the actor was prepared to go is apparent. From the focus on the grisly murders to the continual probing of the perpetrators to being a witness to their executions, Hoffman's performance was on point.

His South Node/Mars conjunction in Virgo on Capote's Moon tell us how meticulously he researched the author. Additionally, Hoffman's Jupiter in Leo is exactly conjunct Capote's descendant indicating an understanding of the author's relationships which were crucial for the film. Filming would have taken place as transiting Neptune in Aquarius passed over Capote's ascendant, therefore forming a connection to that point.

The film won an Academy Award, a BAFTA, a Golden Globe and several other awards for Best Actor for Hoffman and Capote was also nominated for Best Picture.

GREAT BALLS OF FIRE!
Jerry Lee Lewis: 29 September 1935, 03:00, Ferriday, Louisiana.
AA: RR
Dennis Quaid: 9 April 1954, no time, Houston, Texas.
Source: Wikipedia
Myra Gale Brown: 11 July 1944, no time, Ferriday, Louisiana.
Source: Wikipedia
Winona Ryder: 29 October 1971, 11:00, Rochester, Minnesota.
AA: Clifford
Jimmy Swaggart: 15 March 1935, 01:35, Ferriday, Louisiana.
AA: Pace
Alec Baldwin: 3 April 1953, no time, Amityville, New York.
Source: Wikipedia
Release date: 30 June 1989

Jerry Lee Lewis aka "The Killer" is a good example of a man who threw away his career for love. A piano prodigy who was way ahead of his time, his romance and ultimate marriage to his thirteen-year-old first cousin brought an abrupt end to the trajectory success (that had threatened to eclipse Elvis) of the talented pianist. In *Great Balls of Fire*, we get a *tour de force* performance from Dennis Quaid (who learned to play the piano for the part) in the leading role, with Winona Ryder playing his young wife, and Alec Baldwin as another of Lewis' cousins and future televangelist Jimmy Swaggart.

The subplot of this film is Lewis' awkward relationship with another cousin, a future highly successful Bible thumper who had taken every opportunity to condemn his cousin for playing "the Devil's music". In real life, both men were highly accomplished pianists and singers with similar styles yet completely different purposes.

Born nearly nineteen years apart, Lewis and Quaid have the nodal axis to within two degrees of each other, making it seem as if fate had played a hand in the casting for this film. Quaid's Venus is conjunct Lewis' Uranus: the film focuses on the very odd, and what many have indicated as the incestuous, relationship between Lewis and his young cousin Myra. With Quaid's Jupiter on Lewis' Chiron, the harm this did to the singer's career is astrologically very clear. Quaid's Neptune is conjunct Lewis' Moon in Libra, further emphasizing the focus on Lewis'

Favourites 273

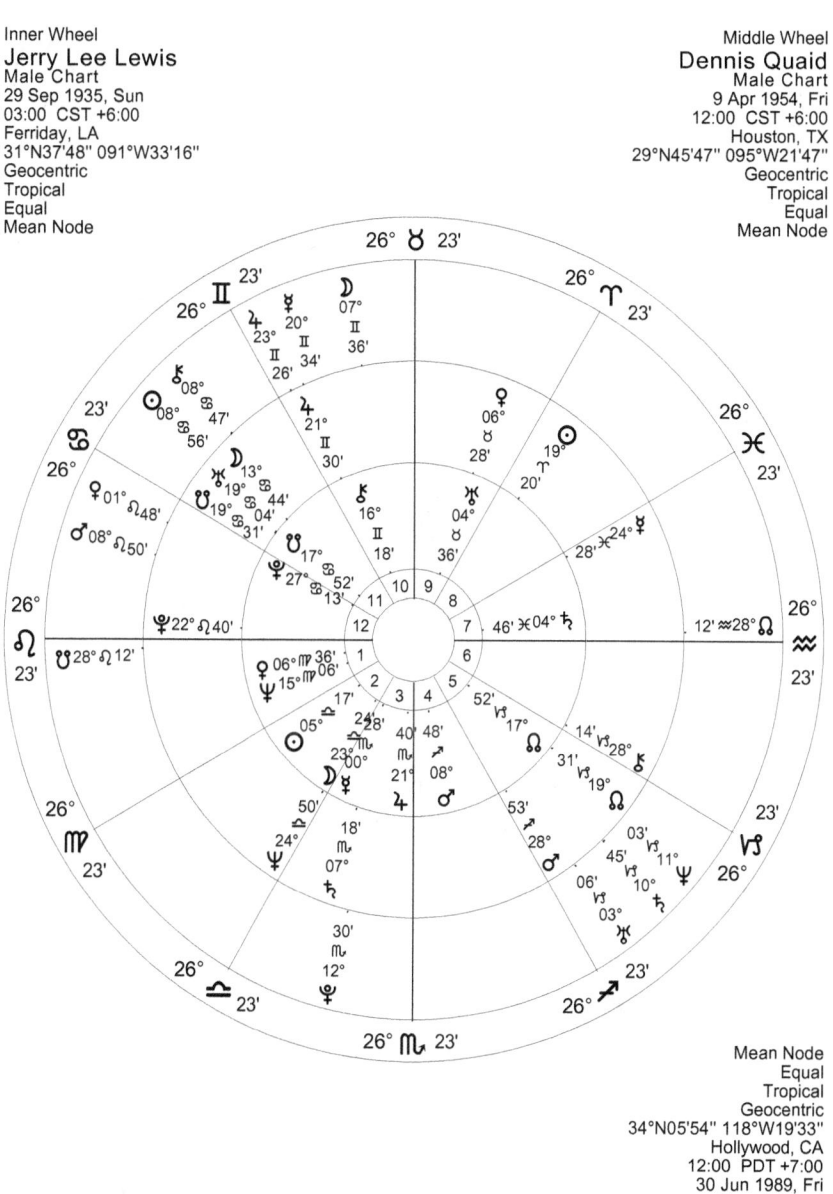

274 Mirror Mirror

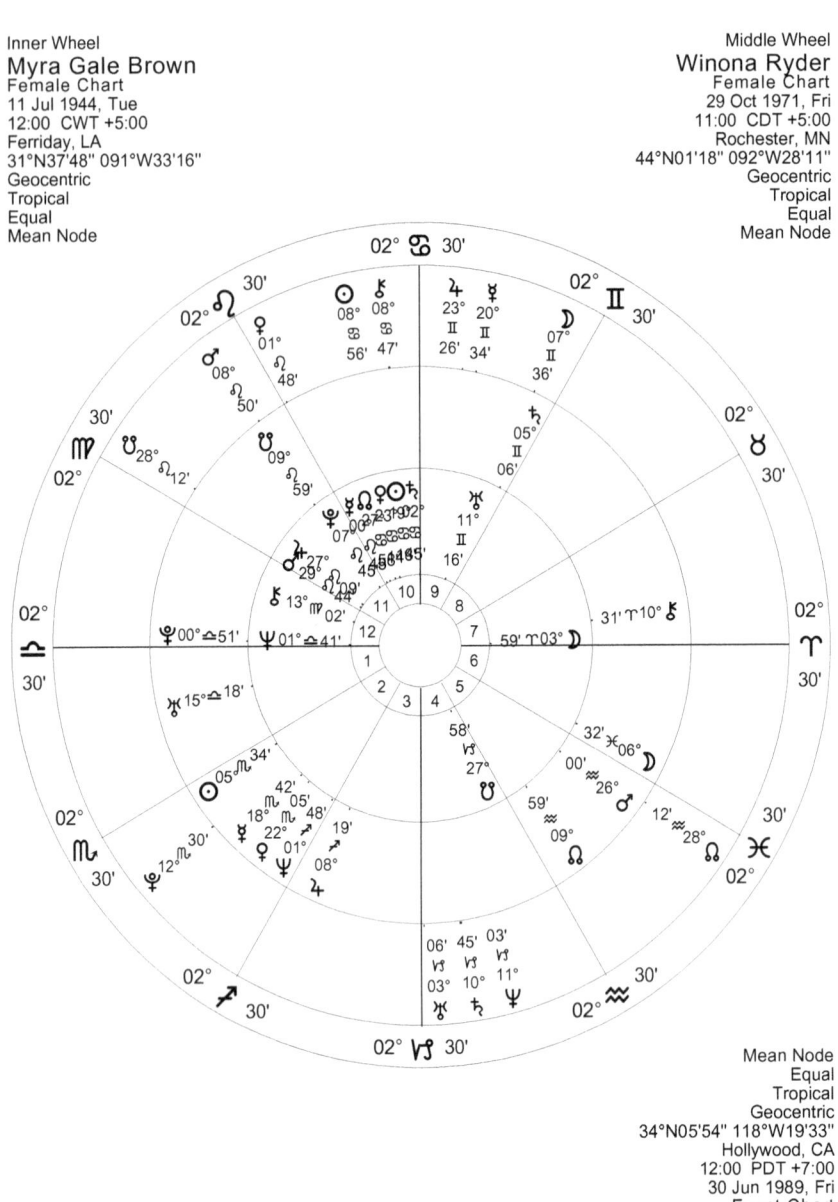

Favourites 275

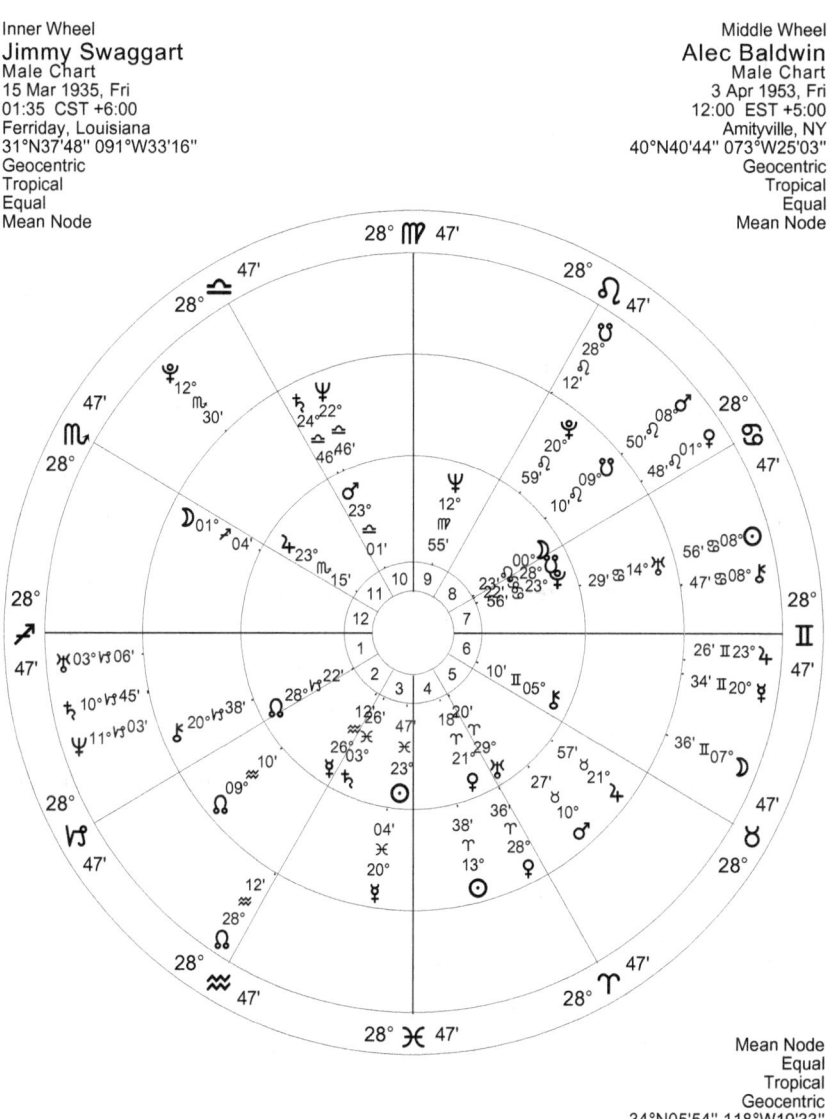

marriage, finances and the subsequent disintegration of his career. The film was released on Quaid's Jupiter Return.

Baldwin's Saturn/Neptune is conjunct Swaggart's Mars in Libra. When Saturn, representing order structure and stability, and Neptune, representing idealism, imagination and flights of fancy, are conjunct, there is a better ability to put good ideas into good practice: dreams are able to become reality. Mars is our drive, it's what we do and how we put up the fight to do it. In the sign of Libra, these tendencies usually manifest through relationships. Just prior to the making of *Great Balls of Fire*, Swaggart was deeply embroiled in a sex scandal involving prostitutes that would eventually lead him to being defrocked from his church and television ministry. The film, released on 30 June 1989, made little, if any at all, allusion to the scandal. Though the filmmakers could not have possibly known this, transiting Jupiter of the film release was trine to Swaggart's Mars as well as trine to Baldwin's Saturn/Neptune conjunction. Transiting Venus was conjunct Swaggart's Moon, and Baldwin's South Node was being transited by Mars in Leo: it wasn't what was said or done that drew attention to the scandal, it was what *wasn't* said or done. The audience of the time would have known about the preacher's sex scandal as it was in every single newspaper in the United States. What juicy irony it was to see Swaggart imploring his cousin to renounce the devil and join him at the pulpit!

Within about two degrees, Myra Gale Brown's Pluto was conjunct Winona Ryder's South Node in Leo. Ryder had simply been able to portray a young girl who was on a more equal footing (North Node in Aquarius) with Lewis than Brown had been in real life. *Great Balls of Fire* was based on the book of the same name written by Myra Gale Brown. She has said in interviews that, "They were looking to stick a knife in rock-n-roll and Jerry gave them the opportunity. And he paid the price." At the time of the movie's release, transiting Mars had passed over her Pluto and during the actual filming transiting Saturn had opposed her natal Saturn.

The film wasn't well received and did not win any awards but the film critic Roger Ebert praised Quaid and Ryder for their work with a limited screenplay, and Ryder won an accolade for best young actress starring in a motion picture.

HITCHCOCK

Alfred Hitchcock: 13 Aug 1899, 03:15, London. DD: RR
Anthony Hopkins: 31 Dec 1937, 09:15, Port Talbot, Wales. A: RR
Alma Hitchcock: 14 Aug 1899, no time, Nottingham, England.
Source: Wikipedia
Helen Mirren: 26 July 1945, 02:00, London. B: Scholfield
Ed Gein: 27 August 1906, no time, LaCrosse, Wisconsin.
Source: Wikipedia (Chart not shown)
Anthony Perkins: 4 April 1932, 09:00, New York. C: Penfield
James D'Arcy: 24 August 1975, no time, Amersham, England.
Source: Wikipedia
Janet Leigh: 6 July 1927, 14:15, Merced Falls, California.
AA: RR
Scarlett Johansson: 22 November 1984, 07:00, New York.
C: Scholfield
Filming of the shower scene: 17-23 December 1959, no time
Release date: 1 November 2012

The movie *Psycho* is deeply embedded in the imagination of fans of film. Based on the life of the notorious killer and necrophile Ed Gein, the plot is terrifying even before the main actress (played by Janet Leigh) is killed as she enjoys a shower after a tense day, just minutes into the movie. It was on the making of this film that the movie *Hitchcock* is based.

According to the film, Hitchcock, played by Welsh actor Anthony Hopkins, had alternatives to making *Psycho*: he turned down directing *Casino Royale* as well as *The Diary of Anne Frank*, much to the chagrin of his wife Alma (played by Helen Mirren). With colleagues equally unsupportive of his interests, Hitchcock funded his own project. They could not have known that Hitchcock's Sun and Venus conjunction was in turn conjunct Gein's three-point stellium (Mercury, Mars and North Node) in Leo. Hitchcock, it seemed, was intent on making Gein a ghoulish star. Although Alma was born the day after her husband, the inner planets had shifted enough to make the connections between her planets and Gein's less potent.

Further tension in the Hitchcock's marriage was shown as Alma collaborated with another writer on a different project behind Alfred's back. Hitchcock accused her of having an affair but the couple eventually reconciled and agreed to work together on improving *Psycho*.

278 Mirror Mirror

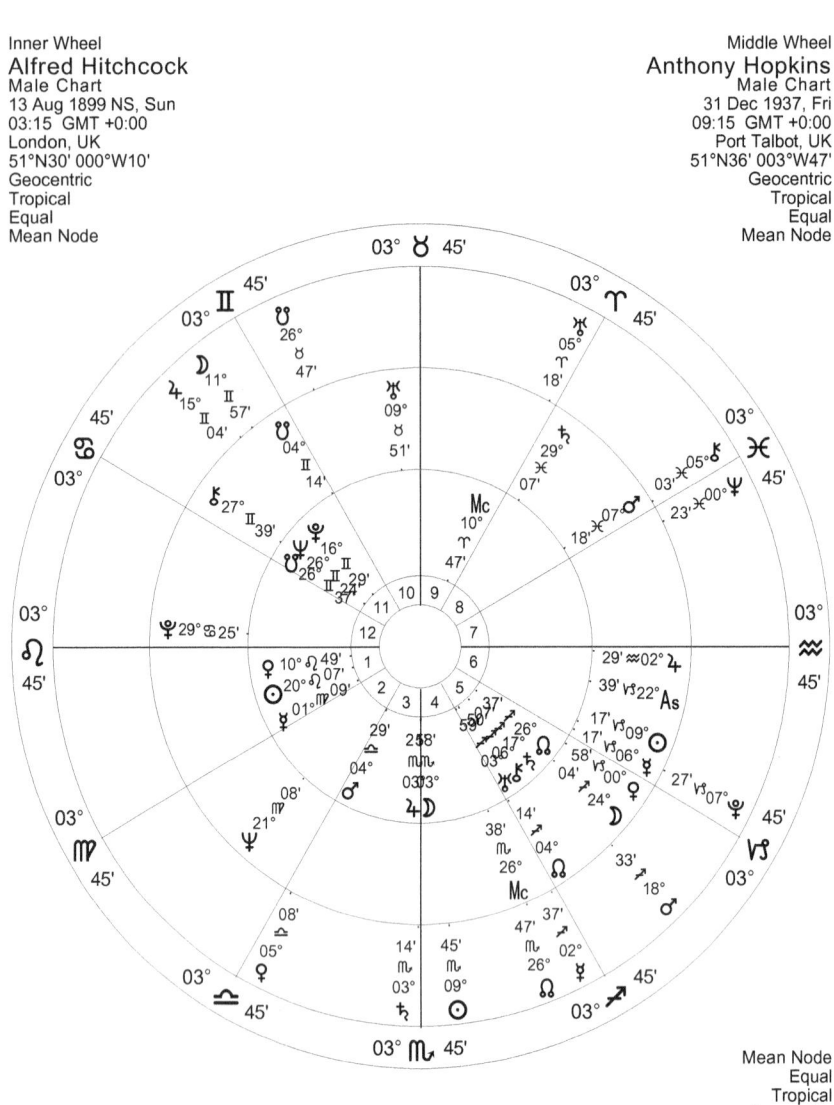

Favourites 279

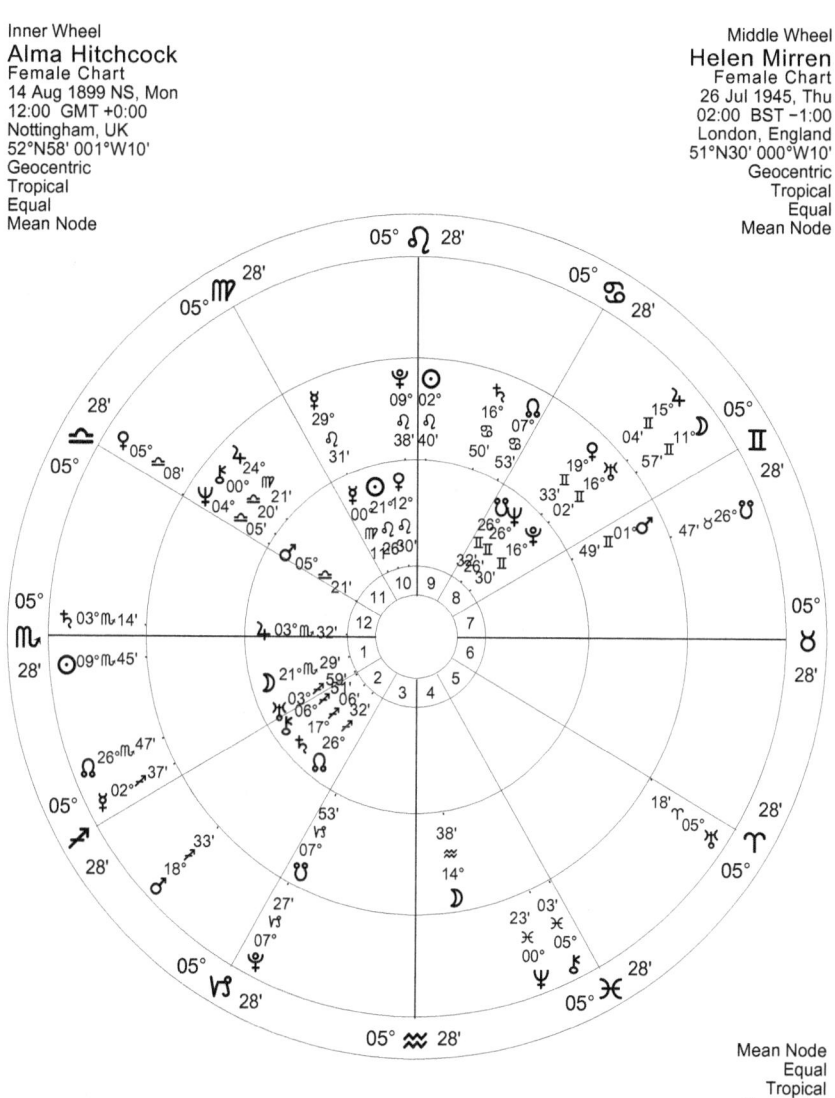

280 Mirror Mirror

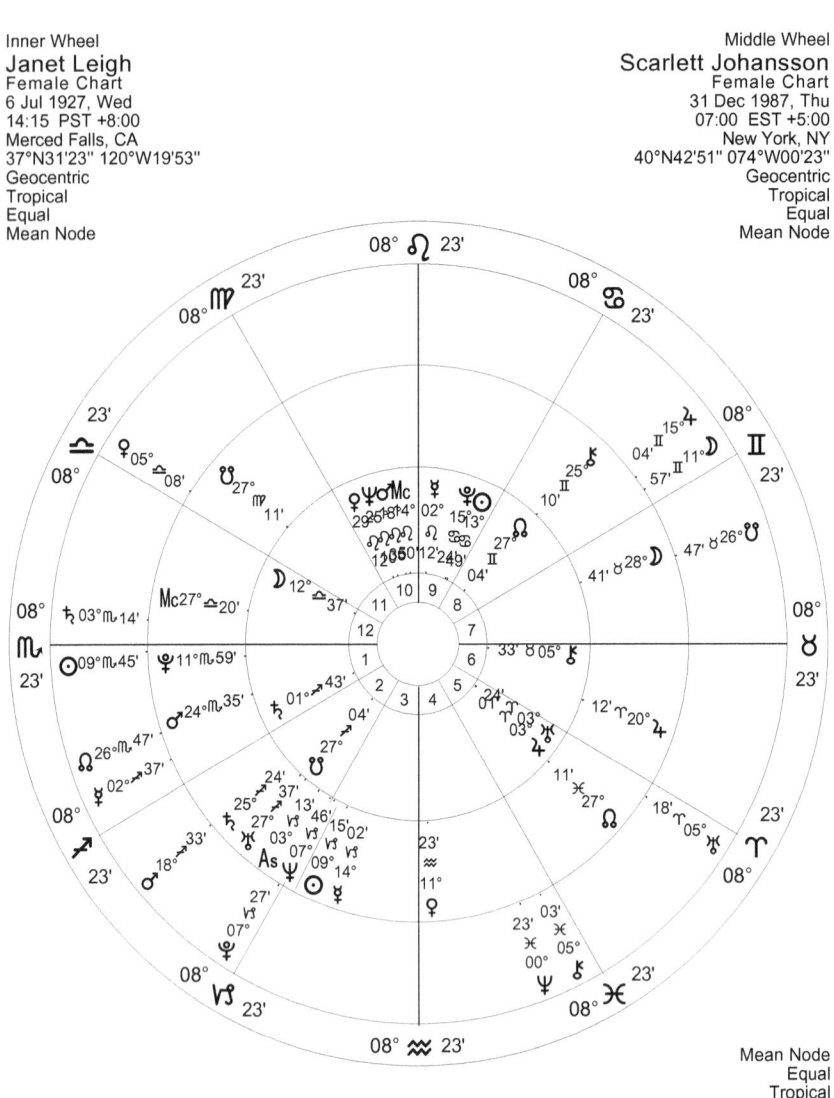

Favourites   281

Inner Wheel
Anthony Perkins
Male Chart
4 Apr 1932, Mon
09:00 EST +5:00
New York, NY
40°N42'51" 074°W00'23"
Geocentric
Tropical
Equal
Mean Node

Middle Wheel
James D'Arcy
Male Chart
24 Aug 1975, Sun
12:00 BST −1:00
Amersham, UK
51°N40' 000°W38'
Geocentric
Tropical
Equal
Mean Node

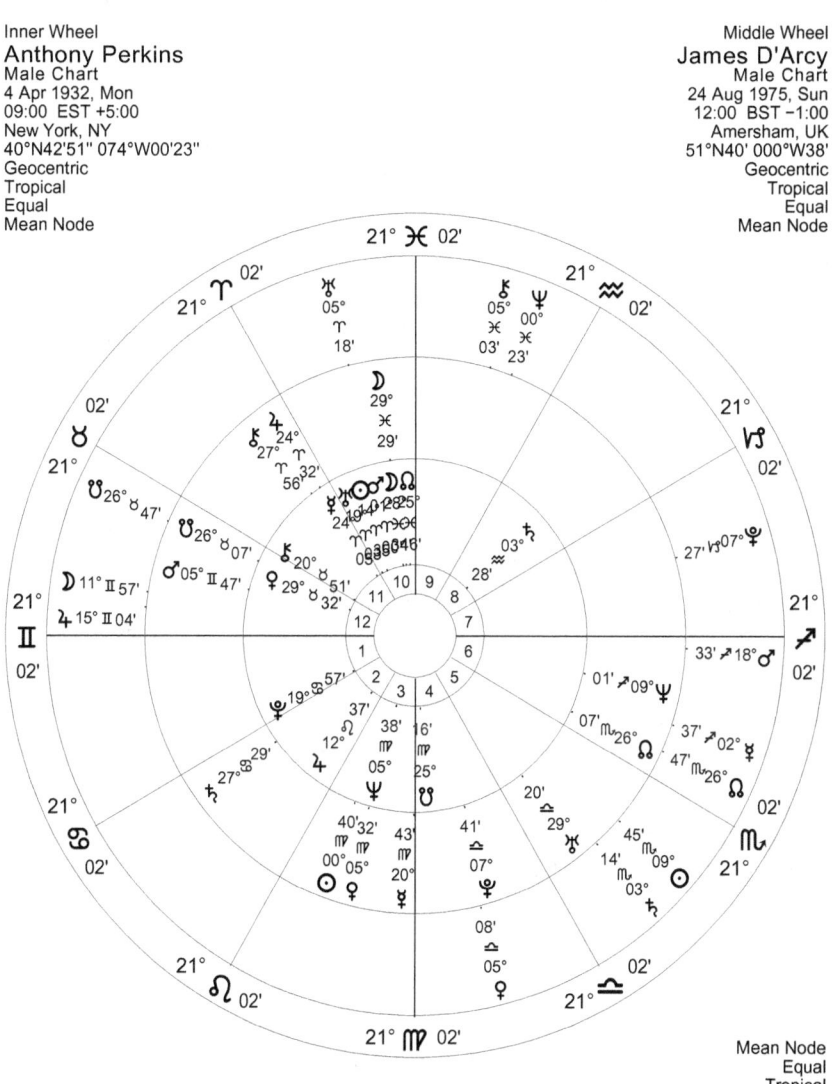

Mean Node
Equal
Tropical
Geocentric
34°N03'08" 118°W14'34"
Los Angeles, CA
12:00 PDT +7:00
1 Nov 2012, Thu
Event Chart
Hitchcock Release
Outer Wheel

Hopkins' Moon in Sagittarius is opposite his Chiron natally, with this opposition being on Hitchcock's nodal axis. This is a film about the vulnerabilities and foibles of a well-known director who tended to work behind the camera (although he did often address his audiences directly).

Mirren's Moon in Aquarius is opposite her Pluto in Leo which is in turn conjunct Alma's Venus in Leo. This film is also about a woman who is torn between supporting her husband's rather unpleasant project or doing her own project with someone else. It is also worth noting that Mirren and Alma have Mercury within 41 minutes of conjunction although in different signs (29 Leo for Mirren and 0 Virgo for Alma). Finally, Mirren's Neptune is also conjunct Alma's Mars in Libra. Libra is a sign usually associated with diplomacy in relationships so it should be no astrological surprise that the film depicts Alma returning to her husband to do as he wishes.

In the original film *Psycho*, playing a twitchy yet seemingly gentle (at first), cross-dressing killer based on the life of a real maniac would have been a challenge. Added to this is the controversy of addressing issues that had never been publically discussed in "decent" company of the time and just one of the reasons why executives were nervous about the film's release. Anthony Perkins however, had Gein's Pluto within a two-degree orb of his ascendant in Gemini. He also had Jupiter in Leo conjunct Gein's Mercury and North Node. With these connections, Perkins had a very good insight into the killer's mind (astrologically at least) and delivered a performance that not only had audiences covering their eyes and screaming in their seats but was just too good to keep concealed. James D'Arcy played Anthony Perkins in the film. His Jupiter in Aries was exactly conjunct Perkins' Mercury. But most incredibly, D'Arcy's Venus in Virgo was exactly conjunct Perkins' Neptune and this conjunction was within two degrees of Gein's Sun. Mercury was transiting this conjunction at the date of the film's release, thus connecting all three and enabling them to unleash a fear of taking a shower onto the audience – and this also included Janet Leigh who claimed she went through great lengths to avoid taking showers for the rest of her life.

Of the famous shower scene, Janet Leigh has said she shared the audiences' horror: "I believed that knife went into me. It was real, that horrifying. I could feel it!" As Leigh's ascendant was conjunct the Neptune of the filming of the famous shower scene, it is easy to imagine her terror. Her husband, Tony Curtis, later related that the only thing people wanted to talk to her about was the shower scene. It drove his wife to drink, he said. It led to her breakdown and ultimately their divorce.

Scarlett Johansson, who played Leigh in *Hitchcock*, has her Saturn in Sagittarius conjunct Leigh's South Node and Chiron conjunct Leigh's North Node in Gemini. Johannson's perplexed and terrified face in *Hitchcock* after the filming of that shower scene is one that stays with you for a long time. She seems to be silently asking him "How could you?" How appropriate it is then that the Pluto of the filming of the shower scene in *Psycho* is conjunct Johannson's Neptune and transiting Venus of the filming of the famous shower scene is conjunct her Pluto in Scorpio. Just about perfect for the most shocking scenes of the horror genre involving the murder of a young woman.

During filming at the end of 1959, transiting Jupiter in Sagittarius was opposite Scorpio's ruler, Pluto, in Gemini in Alfred Hitchcock's chart. As the most famous scene, the iconic shower scene, was filmed 17-23 December 1959, the opposition was exact. Also active during this time was a Saturn square to Hitchcock's natal Mars, co-ruler of the sign of Scorpio, in Libra. Funnily enough, the scene that most upset the censors at the time was the sight of money being flushed down the toilet. Until *Psycho*, no-one had ever seen a toilet flushing at the cinema.

Helen Mirren was nominated for several major awards but did not win.

I, TONYA

Tonya Harding: 12 November 1970, 20:22, Portland, Oregon.
C: RR
Margot Robbie: 2 July 1990 no time, Dalby, Australia. **X: Scholfield**
Allison Janney: 19 November 1959, 12:44, Boston, Massachusetts.
AA: McEvoy
Release date: 8 September 2017

When we think of women's figure skating, we imagine grace, poise and beauty. We never think of deathly competition and jealousy, and it never occurs to us that one day a female skater might resort to violence to put an end to a rival's skating career. *I, Tonya* tells the story of Tonya

284   Mirror Mirror

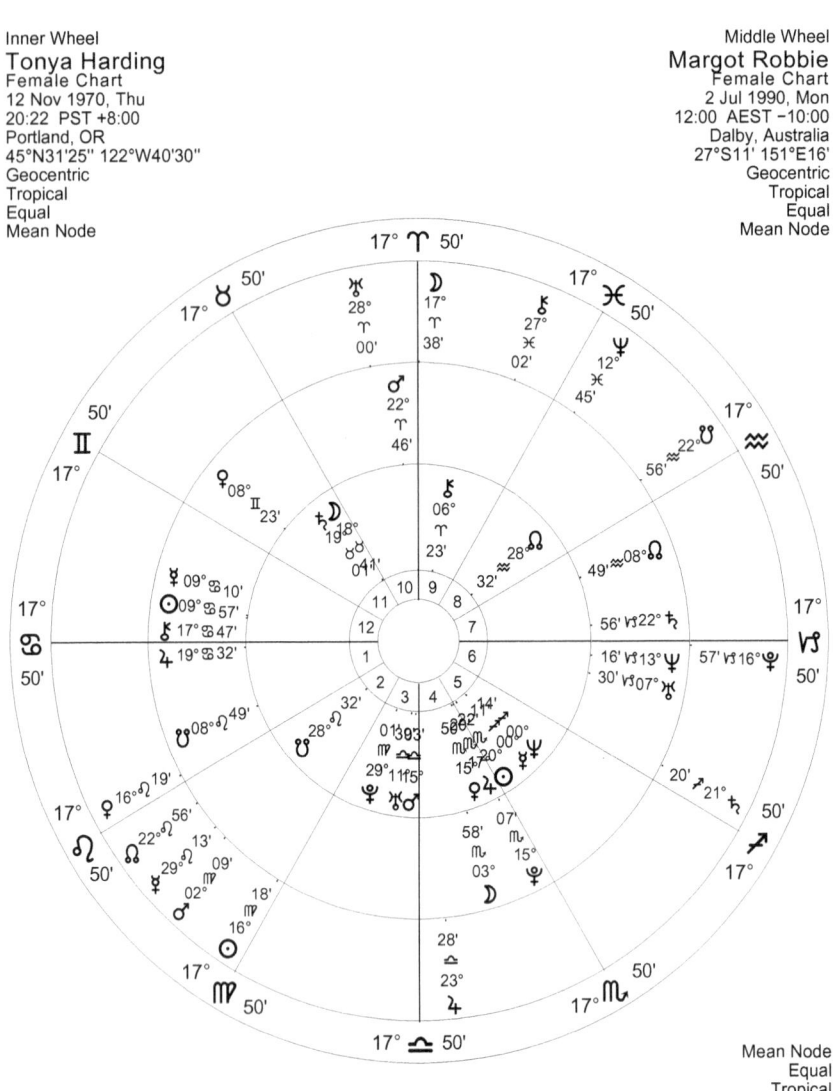

Favourites 285

Inner Wheel
Tonya Harding
Female Chart
12 Nov 1970, Thu
20:22 PST +8:00
Portland, OR
45°N31'25" 122°W40'30"
Geocentric
Tropical
Equal
Mean Node

Outer Wheel
Allison Janney
Female Chart
19 Nov 1959, Thu
12:00 EST +5:00
Boston, Massachusetts
42°N21'30" 071°W03'37"
Geocentric
Tropical
Equal
Mean Node

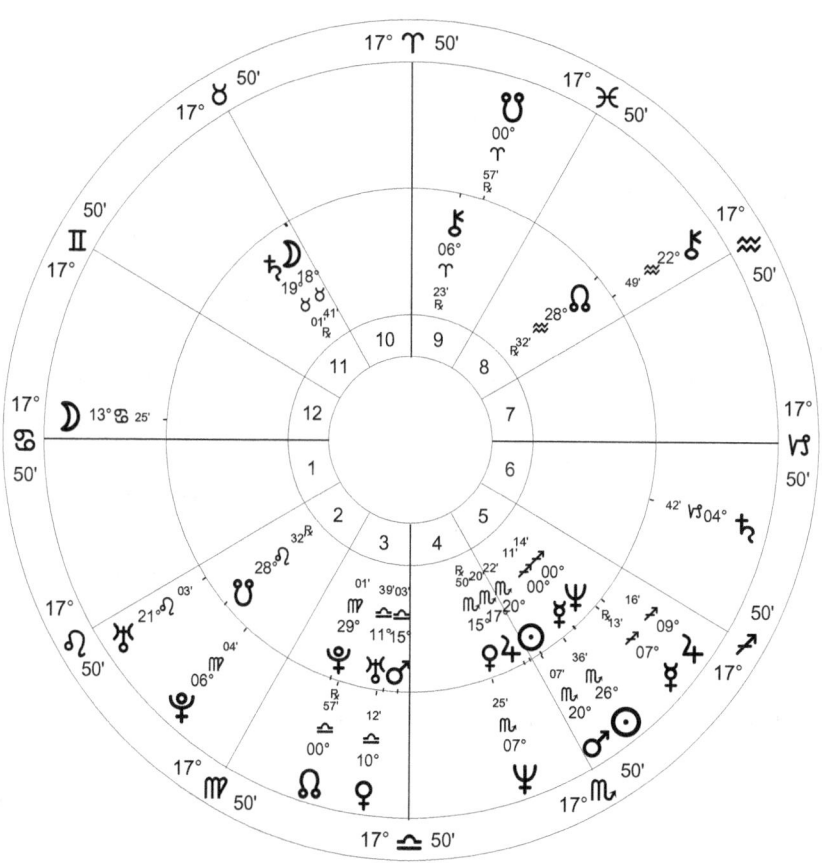

Harding's dizzying successes as well as the events leading up to the attack on her competitor, Nancy Kerrigan. The story is told through a series of interviews and flashbacks and, unusually, characters breaking the fourth wall by addressing the audience directly.

Tonya's upbringing was difficult with an aggressive and abusive mother as well as grinding poverty. She developed a "trailer trash" reputation and did herself no favours by being rude and confrontational with skating judges. Despite this, she becomes the first woman figure skater to land a triple-axel in a competition. Her husband, Jeff Gillooly, alternates between being supportive and being abusive with serious control issues. They split and reconcile several times.

One of Gillooly's friends hires two thugs to carry out an attack on Kerrigan which forces her to drop out of an upcoming competition with Tonya. The thugs are quickly arrested. Eventually both Tonya and Kerrigan, once recovered, are selected to compete in the Olympic Games. However, Gillooly and Tonya are implicated in the attack on Kerrigan but the court hearing is postponed until after the Olympic Games. During this time, Tonya is visited by her mother and when asked about her involvement in the attack, she discovers her mother is wearing a wire. After a poor performance at the Olympics, Tonya is banned from competitive figure skating for life and instead becomes a boxer.

Natally, Harding has a stellium of planets in Scorpio (Sun, Jupiter and Venus) all traditionally ruled by Mars in Libra and opposing the Moon and Saturn in Cancer. This difficult opposition can account for her abusive and critical mother as well as the intensive work she put into her skating.

Margot Robbie, who portrayed Harding in *I, Tonya*, has Pluto exactly on Harding's Venus in Scorpio, pulling in all the planets in Harding's opposition. Robbie practised skating for several hours a day to pull off convincing ice skating performances. Transiting Pluto crossed Tonya's descendant in Capricorn and opposed Robbie's Chiron in Cancer when the film was released.

Incidentally, the attack on Nancy Kerrigan happened on 6 January 1994 in Detroit which means the Sun of this chart (1994) was also transited by Pluto when the film was released. This conjunction was on Tonya's descendant which would generate an interest in her relationships with other people.

Alison Janney, who played Tonya's mother in the film, portrayed a monstrously abusive mother, thus creating much sympathy and understanding for the Tonya of the film. Like Robbie, Janney had a personal planet, in her case Mars in Scorpio, picking up the energy of Tonya's Sun opposite Moon/Saturn.

For her efforts, Robbie became the first actress to be nominated for an Academy Award for Best Actress for playing a real-life athlete.

Hollywood could not have invented a better plot for a movie.

Robbie won Best Actress and Janney won Best Supporting actress at Australia's version of the Oscars and the Critics Choice Movie Awards. Janney won an Academy Award for best supporting actress for her portrayal of Harding's cruel mother. At the Golden Globe, Robbie was nominated for Best Actress and Janney won an award for Best Supporting Actress. Both were nominated for Outstanding performances at the Screen Actors Guild Awards and The Academy Awards. Janney won the Oscar for Best Supporting Actress.

JULIE & JULIA

Julia Child: 15 August 1912, 23:20, Pasadena, California.
AA: CAH
Meryl Streep: 22 June 1949, 08:05, Summit, New Jersey.
AA: Steinbrecher
Paul Child: 15 January 1902, no time, Montclair, New Jersey.
Source: Wikipedia
Stanley Tucci: 11 November 1960, no time, Peekskill, New York.
Source: Wikipedia
Julie Powell: 20 April 1973, no time, Austin, Texas.
Source: Wikipedia
Amy Adams: 20 August 1974, 00:00, Vicenza, Italy. C: Lepoivre
"The Moment of Sensual Delight": 3 November 1948, 14:30, near Rouen, France. C: Trenoweth (time approximated from details in *My Life in France*)
Release date: 7 August 2009

In August 2002, a young creative writing pupil by the name of Julie Powell began writing her now famous blog, *Julie and Julia: 365 days, 534 Recipes and 1 Tiny Kitchen Apartment*. Julie's blog chronicles her attempts

288 Mirror Mirror

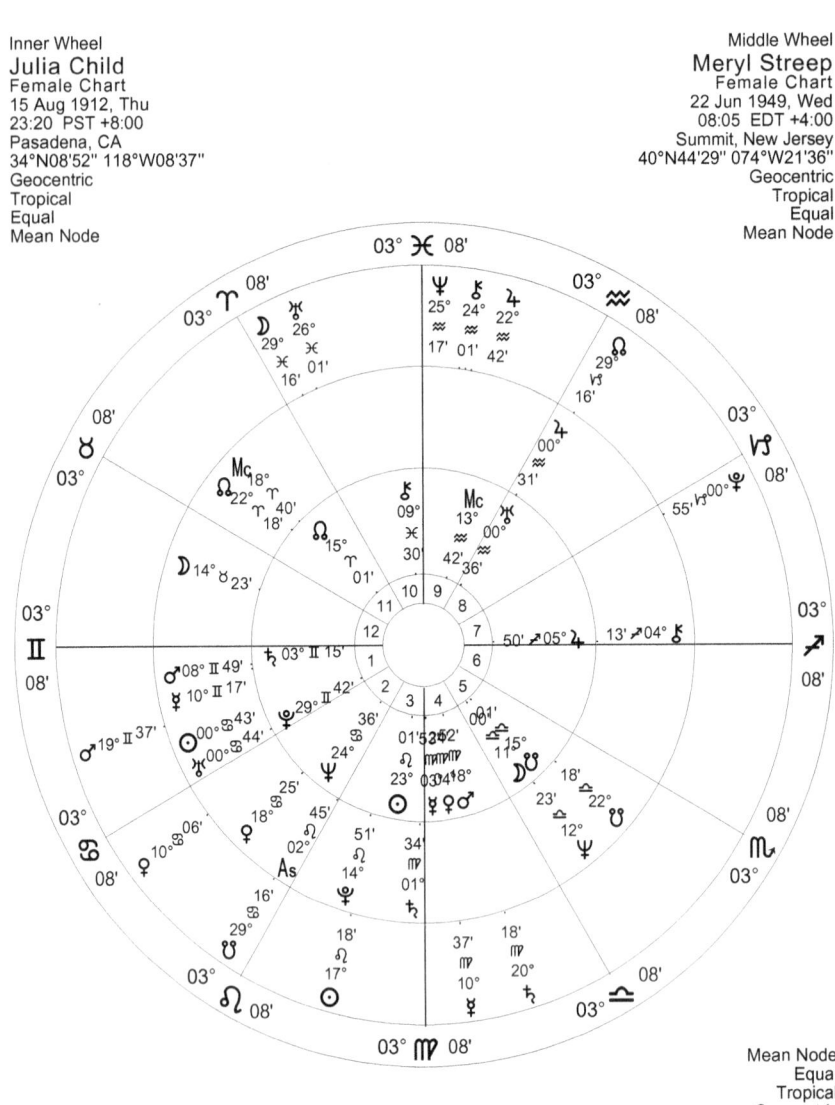

Favourites 289

Inner Wheel
Paul Child
Male Chart
15 Jan 1902, Wed
12:00 EST +5:00
Montclair, NJ
40°N49'33" 074°W12'34"
Geocentric
Tropical
Equal
Mean Node

Middle Wheel
Stanley Tucci
Male Chart
11 Nov 1960, Fri
12:00 EST +5:00
Peekskill, NY
41°N17'24" 073°W55'15"
Geocentric
Tropical
Equal
Mean Node

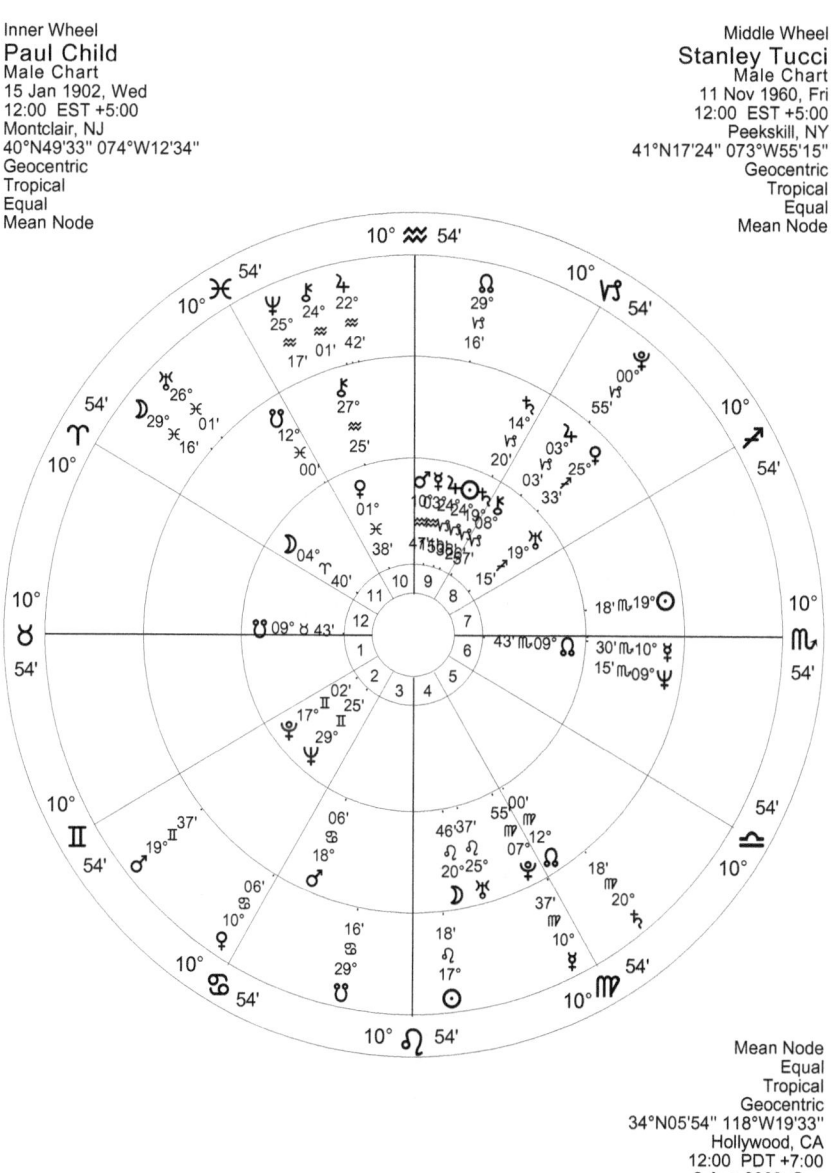

Mean Node
Equal
Tropical
Geocentric
34°N05'54" 118°W19'33"
Hollywood, CA
12:00 PDT +7:00
9 Aug 2009, Sun
Event Chart
Julie & Julia released
Outer Wheel

290 Mirror Mirror

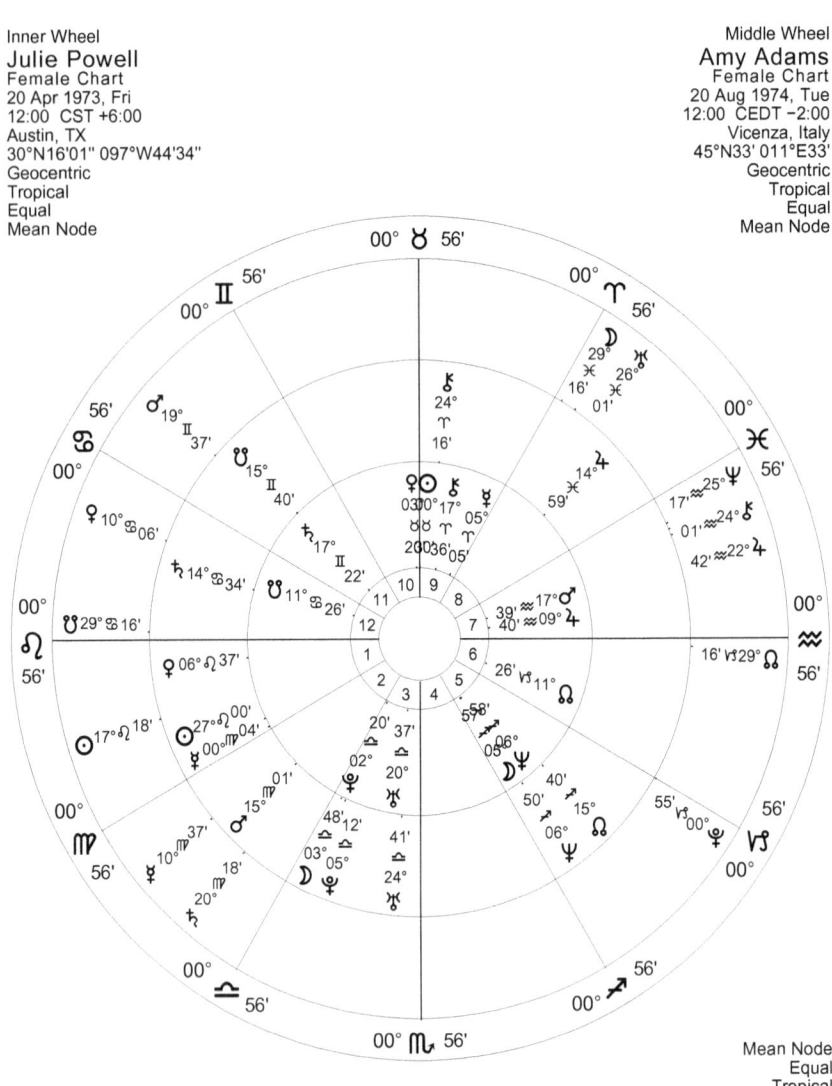

Favourites

Inner Wheel
Julia Child
Female Chart
15 Aug 1912, Thu
23:20 PST +8:00
Pasadena, CA
34°N08'52" 118°W08'37"
Geocentric
Tropical
Equal
Mean Node

Outer Wheel
Moment of Sensual Delight
Event Chart
3 Nov 1948, Wed
14:30 CET −1:00
Rouen, France
49°N26' 001°E05'
Geocentric
Tropical
Equal
Mean Node

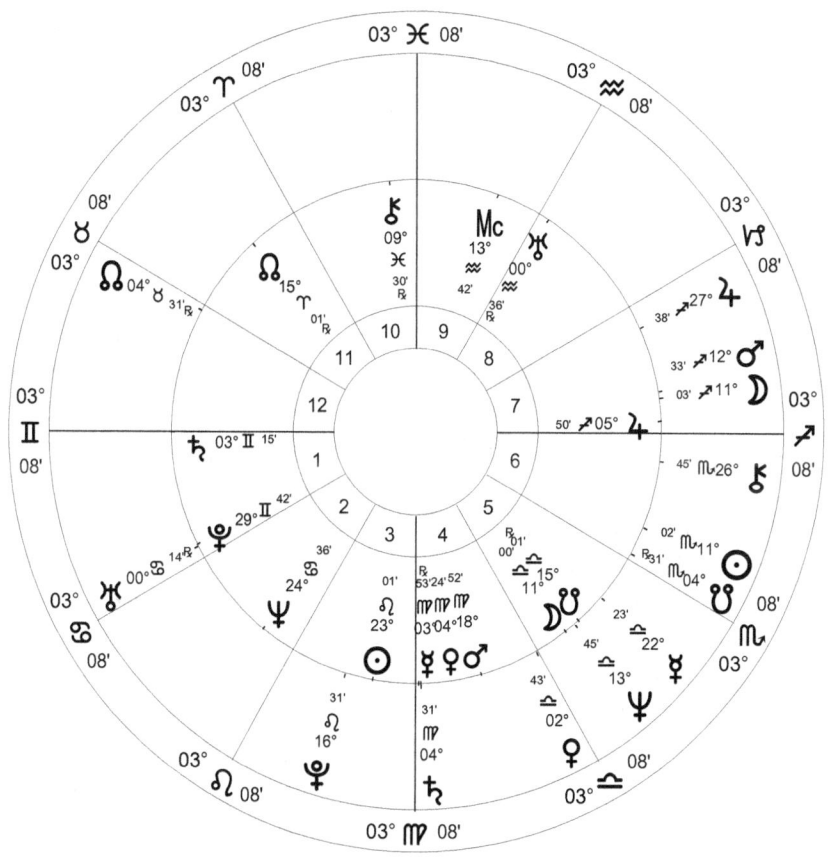

to complete all the recipes in her seminal work *Mastering the Art of French Cooking*. The film alternates between Julie's life in the present time in New York and Julia's time in Paris just after World War Two. *Julie & Julia* was filmed as Jupiter transited Julia's MC and was released in August 2009 as the North Node passed over her Uranus and transiting Neptune opposed her natal Sun – all fairly good arguments for the validation of posthumous transits.

Streep's Mars/Mercury conjunction is very nicely conjunct Julia's Saturn in Gemini. Although Streep is known for her mastery of accents, her delivery of Julia's voice was a pure class act: she managed to do it without taking the proverbial mick and even made Julia's voice endearingly normal yet interesting. Perhaps more impressive is that the actress, with the help of clever camera angles, was able convey Child's formidable height.

Meryl Streep's Saturn is conjunct Julia's Venus/Mercury in Virgo. Streep is portraying an author who is translating French recipes into not only English but to the imperial measurement system. Streep's Neptune is on Julia's Moon in Libra and the touching interpretation of a loving marriage between Julia and her husband Paul (played by Stanley Tucci) was the perfect mix of marital playfulness, subtle naughtiness and loving devotion that are a delight to watch. Streep's Jupiter (natally conjunct her descendant) is conjunct Julia's Uranus. Streep turned Julia's quirkiness to her very great advantage. Of her performance, the notoriously difficult to please movie critic A. O. Scott of *The New York Times* said: "By now [Streep] has exhausted every superlative that exists and to suggest that she has outdone herself is only to say that she's done it again. Her performance goes beyond physical imitation, though she has the rounded shoulders and the fluting voice down perfectly."

There is one final point worth looking at. On 3rd November 1948, just after her marriage to Paul, Julia travelled to France for the first time and experienced French cooking: sole meuniere and oysters. She described it as the "moment of sensual delight". Occurring at about 14:30 near Rouen, transiting Saturn was conjunct her natal Venus: Julia had permanently fallen in love with French cuisine. This moment in the film was beautifully conveyed: a French waiter removes the lid of the dish with a flourish and as the fragrance wafts towards Streep's/Julia's nostrils, a look of pure bliss crosses the character's face. One just knows a transformation has taken place.

What is it in Streep's chart that could pick this moment out so well? Streep was born about six months after the actual event so no surprises for matching outer planets and progressions. Instead, this "moment" deserves its own birth chart. And it is absolutely, completely satisfying that Streep's Sun is conjunct the Uranus of this chart. Small wonder then that even posthumously, Streep made Julia Child a star all over again.

Paul Tucci's Mercury in Scorpio is within one degree of Paul Child's North Node. Paul's words had a powerful effect on Julia both in the film and in real life – and he bought the book that was the inspiration for both of the main characters of the film. Amy Adam's Pluto in Libra was in exact opposition to Powell's Mercury in Aries and the actress' South Node in Gemini was within two degrees of Powell's Saturn. Powell's work on her blog, which involved cooking all of Julia's recipes in one year, had a negative effect on her marriage. Mars transited this point of Powell's Saturn and Adams' South Node in the weeks leading up to the film's release.

The film was released as transiting Pluto was opposing Julia's natal Pluto and was opposing Streep's Uranus. Transiting Neptune hovered over Julia's natal MC so no one should have been surprised that the blog would become a movie.

Streep won a Golden Globe for Best Actress and was nominated for Best Actress in the Screen Actors Guild Awards.

LA VIE EN ROSE
Edith Piaf: 19 December 1915, 05:00, Paris, France. AA: Geslain
Marion Cotillard: 30 September 1975, 04:50, Paris, France.
AA: Geslain
Release date: 8 February 2007

The film opens with Edith as a small child watching her mother busking for change in 1918. The mother writes to Edith's father to tell him she is leaving her daughter with her mother so she can pursue a living as an artist. The father returns from the trenches to take the sickly child to his own mother who was a madam of a brothel in Normandy. The

294 Mirror Mirror

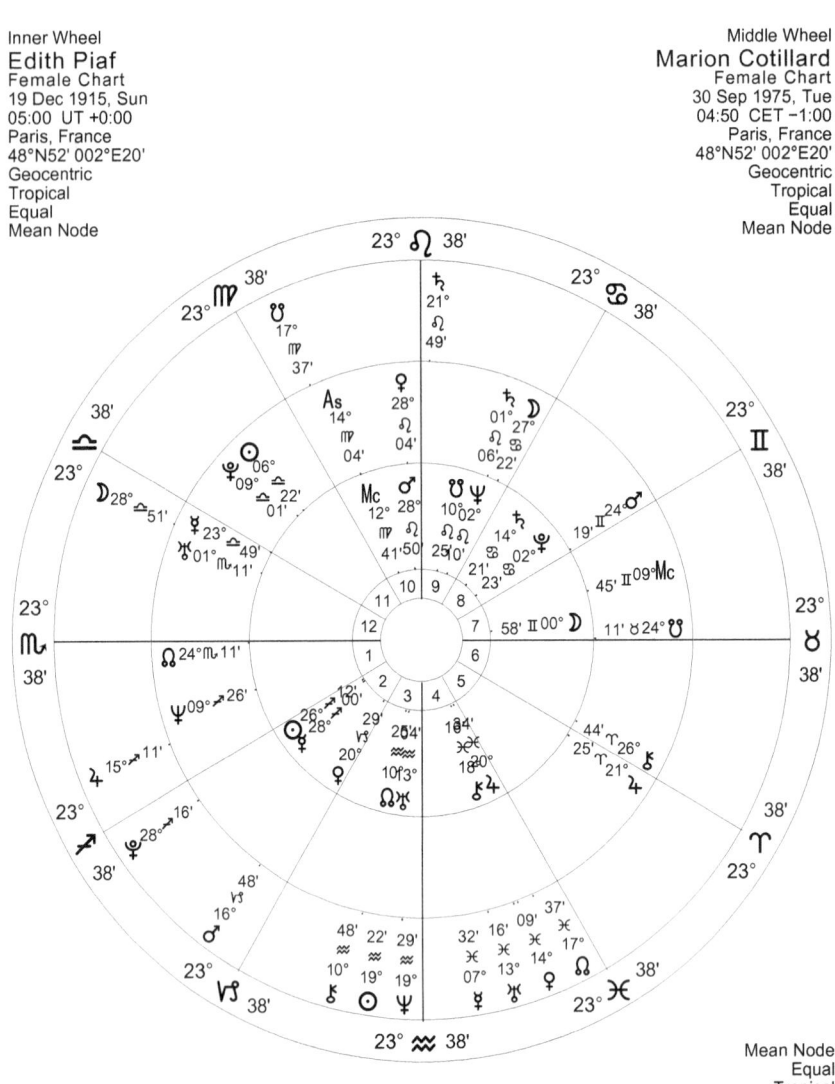

prostitutes also live a difficult life but they look after young Edith, one even singing to her when the girl is temporarily blinded by illness.

Edith's father eventually returns for her and against her will, makes her join him as he works as a circus acrobat. One night she sees a vision of St Theresa in the flames of a fire eater and she comes to believe the saint will always look after her.

After an argument with the circus manager, Edith's father takes to the street to perform his acrobatic skills. The crowds are unimpressed with him so they ask the young girl to do something. She obliges with a song that mesmerises them.

Eventually Edith is invited to sing at a night club by its manager but he is shot dead. The police suspect the cause to be Edith's connections to the Mafia through the pimp who takes a percentage of her earnings from singing on the streets.

Edith gets other work at a rundown cabaret but the audience is hostile. She meets a songwriter and accompanist who bullies her into improving her performances and consequently she gets a place at a music hall, becoming well known for her passionate style of singing.

In New York, she meets another French national, a boxer competing for a championship title, and she falls in love with him. They begin an affair, but he has to return to France to his wife. Edith begs him to come back to her; he agrees and she wakes up to his kiss the following morning. Ecstatic, she goes to her kitchen to get him a cup of coffee and to give him the watch she has bought for him. The friends who had been staying over with her in her home are sullen so she shouts at them to liven up. It is then they reluctantly inform her that the boxer has died in a plane crash. Confused, she runs through her flat screaming her lover's name, but she realises that she must have seen his ghost that morning.

After developing arthritis, she becomes addicted to morphine and enters rehabilitation in California with her new husband. When she recovers, she is driven around in a convertible and insists on taking the wheel – and promptly crashes into a Joshua tree. Uninjured, she gets out of the car and pretends to hitchhike. The scene is a metaphor for her life with her attempts to be happy and her need to entertain others.

The rest of the film intermingles various memories of past performances, in various states of age and health, in particular her singing her signature song, *Non, je ne regrette rien*. Edith died at the age of forty-seven.

Quite remarkably, Piaf's Mars in Leo is exactly conjunct Cotillard's Venus. Here the actress puts her energy into exploring how the singer searches for happiness. Cotillard's Saturn in Leo conjunct the singer's Neptune indicates a portrayal of the singer's aging and increasing decrepitude at such a relatively young age. The actress' nodal axis is conjunct the singer's ascendant-descendant, giving the performance a certain 'fated' feeling. Sometimes you just know an actor has completely absorbed the essence of their role and this is the case with this film.

The film was released as transiting Pluto in Sagittarius passed over Piaf's Sun/Mercury conjunction and Uranus/Venus passed over the Cotillard's descendant.

Cotillard won an Academy Award for Best Actress, the first French language film to receive such an accolade. The film also won several other awards in other categories.

LAWRENCE OF ARABIA
T.E. Lawrence: 16 August 1888, 05:00, Tremadoc, Wales. C: RR
Peter O'Toole: 2 August 1932, 00:15, Wicklow, Ireland. A: RR
Release date: 10 December 1962

The film begins with the death of Lawrence, who was killed in a motorcycle accident. A reporter tries to gain information about the mysterious man at his memorial service at St Paul's Cathedral.

The film then moves back to trace Lawrence's life from his days as a highly educated yet insolent lieutenant in the British army during World War I, and his assignment to observe the leader of the Arab Revolt, Prince Faisal, in North Africa.

Lawrence is provided with a Bedouin guide, and the pair trek across the desert on camels to find Faisal. Out of water, they stop to refill their bottles but the guide is shot and killed by Sherif Ali for drinking from his well without permission. When Lawrence eventually arrives at his destination, he meets Faisal and advises him to launch a surprise attack on the settlement of Aqaba, which will help the British replenish their depleted supplies. The town is heavily fortified by sea but barely defended on land. However, there is a very important reason why the town is

Favourites 297

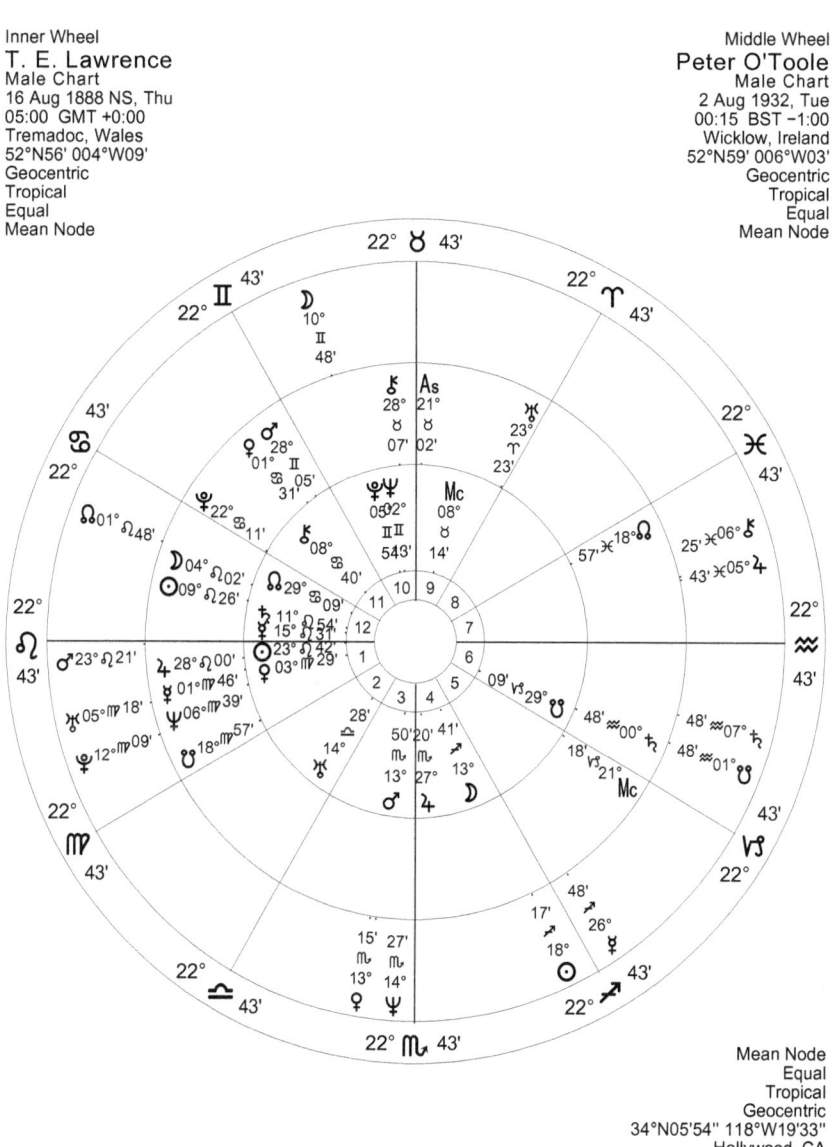

not defended by land: the only approach by land is through the Nefud desert which is considered impassable by even the most experienced Bedouin guides. After convincing Faisal to provide fifty men, Lawrence and the appointed (and very sceptical guide), Sherif Ali, plan to lead the trek across the Nefud Desert to Aqaba on the other side. During preparations, Lawrence appoints two young orphans, Duad and Farraj to be his servants. They have only a very limited time to pass through the desert or the unrelenting daytime sun will kill them.

As dawn approaches, Lawrence realises one of the men, Gasim, is missing. Against all advice, Lawrence turns back to find the unseated man. His successful mission to return with Gasim and bring him to Aqaba results in Lawrence being gifted with Arab robes and a title by an impressed Sherif Ali.

During his victory celebration Lawrence meets the leader of a rival tribe, Auda abu Tayi, who tells him his tribe are siding with the Turks. Lawrence manages to persuade Auda to side with his men against the Turks but the alliance is nearly ruined when one of Sherif Ali's men shoots and kills one of Auda's men owing to a long standing feud. Understanding that retaliation would ruin the mission, Lawrence volunteers to execute the murderer as he is not a part of either tribe. The culprit is Gasim, the man Lawrence had rescued in the desert, but he shoots him as he had promised.

The following morning, the Arabs defeat the Turkish garrison but with the only telegraph broken, Lawrence has no way of telling his superiors of the victory. Taking Duad and Farraj, Lawrence treks across the desert again to Cairo on camelback. During a sandstorm Duad falls off his camel and becomes trapped in quicksand. Lawrence is unable to save him and the devastated pair continue on to Cairo.

Filthy and exhausted, they arrive at headquarters where Farraj is treated as an enemy. Lawrence defends the boy and is able to secure food and lodgings for him in spite of the protests from the British Army.

Lawrence is promoted to major for his feats, but is haunted by the shooting of Gasim. When he asks if the British had plans to take advantage of Arabia, Lawrence is assured by his general that the rumours are untrue.

Lawrence launches a guerrilla-style war on the Turks and is made a famous war hero by an American journalist who takes photos of the skirmishes. While attempting to detonate a railroad line, Farraj is severely injured. Knowing that the Turks will torture him as he dies, Lawrence is forced to shoot the boy.

Still reeling from shock, Lawrence accompanies Sherif Ali to scout the Turkish-held city of Deraa. Lawrence is captured then stripped and molested by the Turkish Bey (local chieftain). Unable to tolerate the threat of further indignity, Lawrence lashes out and is subsequently severely beaten as the Bey looks on.

Humiliated and injured, Lawrence goes back to Cairo and attempts to return to life as a British officer. He is re-assigned to Jerusalem to lead a small army to overtake Damascus but the men are more interested in money than in the cause. When they see a group of Turkish soldiers who have just massacred the residents of Tafas, one of the men charges into the Turks and is killed. Lawrence leads the rest of the men in the ensuing slaughter but later regrets his actions.

After securing Damascus, an attempt to set up an Arab council is made but the desert tribesmen argue so much that the Arabs abandon the city, leaving it to the British.

As his usefulness comes to an end, Lawrence is promoted then ordered to return to Britain.

O'Toole's Sun in Leo is conjunct Lawrence's Saturn within an orb of two degrees. If ever there was an indicator of a man putting the spotlight on the accomplishments of another man then that has to be it. O'Toole's Saturn in Aquarius is one degree from Lawrence's South Node, making this role of a lifetime one of destiny. The understanding of Lawrence's intellectual accomplishments shows with O'Toole's Mercury in Virgo within two degrees of the officer's Venus. Uranus transited this conjunction when the film was released. Further, transiting Mars in Leo was exactly conjunct Lawrence's Sun and within an orb of one degree from his ascendant when the film was released. Transiting Saturn in Aquarius opposed Lawrence's Saturn in Leo as well as O'Toole's Sun and Moon, as audiences all around the world saw this epic film for the very first time. With Saturn connections, you are in it for the long haul and some sixty years after the film's release, *Lawrence of Arabia* still leaves you stunned by the adventures of a man who helped change the course of World War I. It is worth noting that 2021 marks the second Saturn return of this masterpiece.

Lawrence of Arabia is ranked as the 7th greatest film by the AFI and 3rd greatest film by the British Academy of Film and Television. It won a BAFTA, an Academy Award and a Golden Globe for Best Picture and although Peter O'Toole didn't win an Academy Award for Best Actor (it went to Gregory Peck as Atticus Finch in *To Kill a Mockingbird*), it is widely recognised as his greatest role.

MASK

Rocky Dennis: 4 December 1961, 10:03, Downey, California.
AA: RR
Eric Stoltz: 30 September 1961, no time, Whittier, California.
Source: Wikipedia
Florence "Rusty" Dennis: 29 May 1936, no time, Brooklyn, New York. Source: Wikipedia
Cher: 20 May 1946, 07:25, El Centro, California. AA: CAH
Release date: 8 March 1985

We generally think of someone in the movies as being unusually attractive and popular. The use of makeup, both to enhance natural features as well as disguise or even hide unattractive attributes is often used to increase audience appeal.

But occasionally makeup is used for different purposes, as in the case of Eric Stoltz, who was completely unrecognisable beneath the heavy prosthetics required to turn him from an average teenage boy into the tragically deformed Rocky Dennis, the central figure in the award-winning film *Mask*.

Despite his physical deformities, Rocky is intelligent, compassionate and has a good sense of humour. He is adored by his mother Rusty, who is determined that her son will live a life free of pity and she fights to secure Rocky's placement in a mainstream school rather than a school for special needs. However, Rusty is far from conventional. She is part of a motorcycle gang (who all accept Rocky as he is), has addiction issues and has a strained relationship with her more conservative parents. Thinking she is doing the right thing, she also hires a prostitute for Rocky, which offends him.

With his optimism and good sense of humour, Rocky quickly becomes popular with his classmates and even tutors them – for a price. For

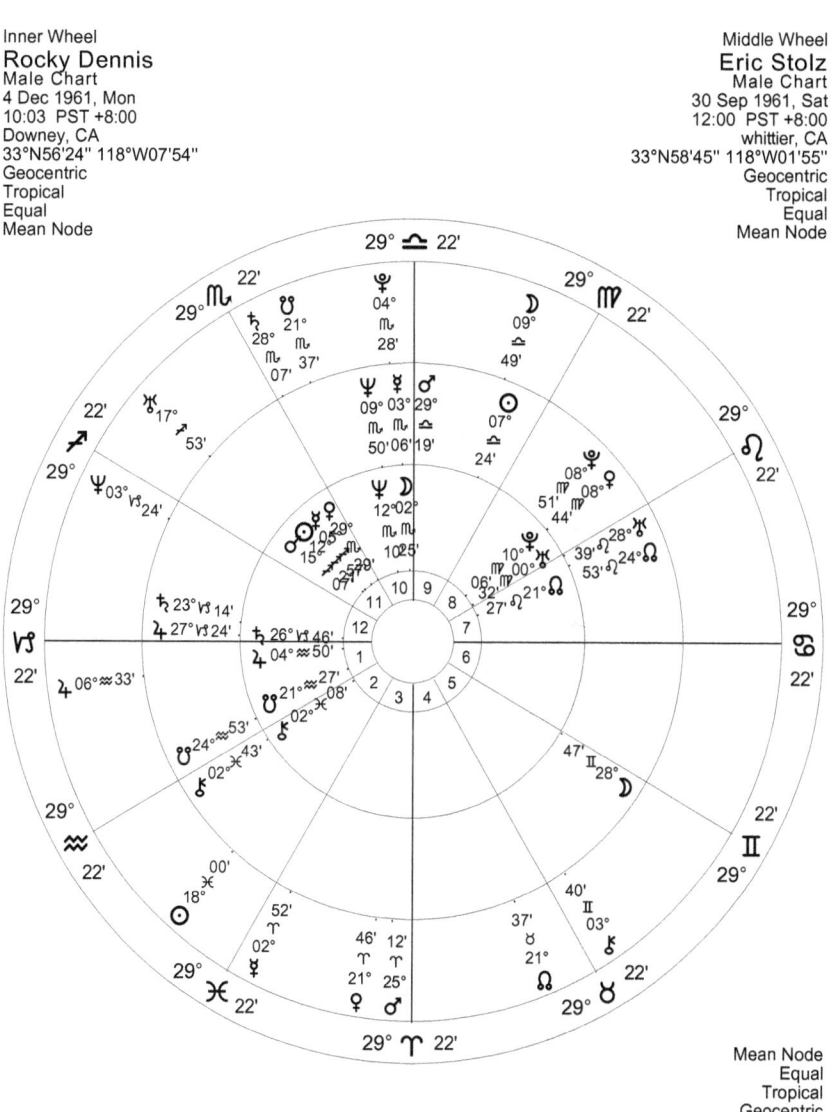

302 Mirror Mirror

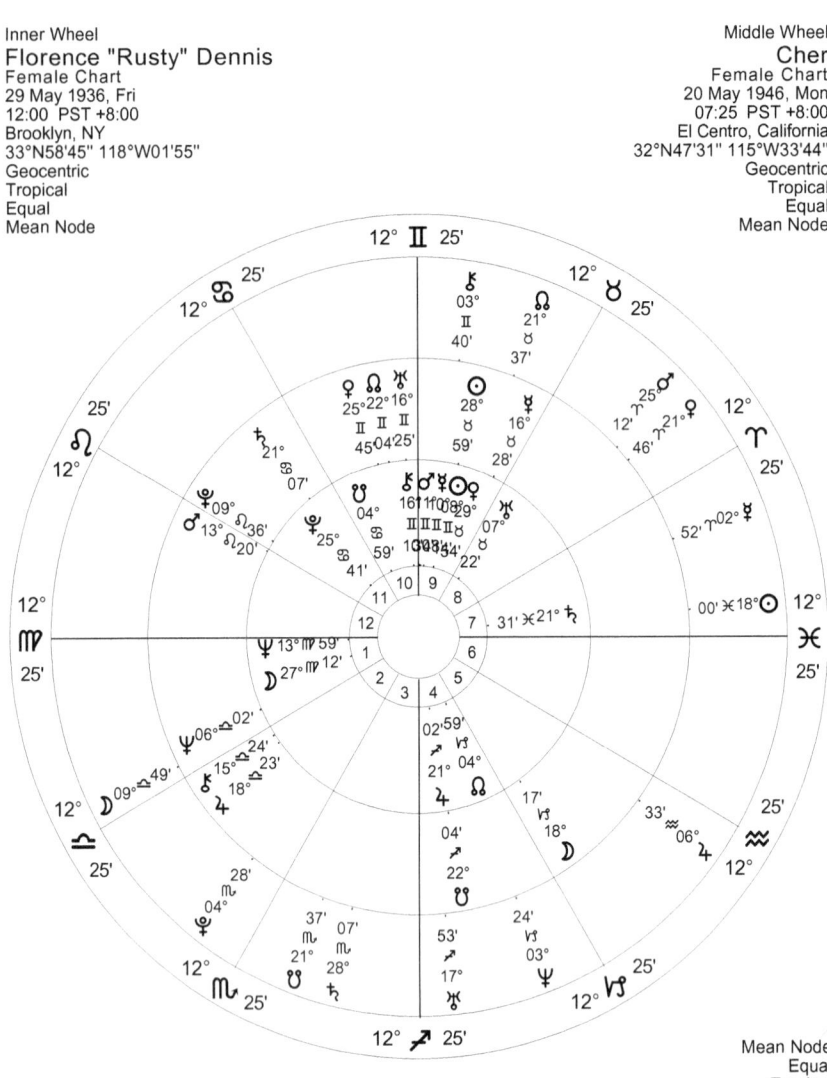

graduation from junior high, where he takes several academic prizes, his mother's friends pool money together to buy him a suit. However, Rocky has frequent headaches which his mother can cure by singing to him and she scoffs when a young doctor tells her that her son only has six months to live.

Rusty's frequent drug-taking leads Rocky to decide he needs to give his mother space to pull herself together. He goes to a summer camp where he meets a blind girl who is enthralled by his intelligence and kindness. Though she is aware that Rocky does not look like everyone else, she introduces him to her parents. Her parents do not want them to spend any further time together and prevent her from receiving Rocky's phone calls.

Rocky's first days of high school are frustrating because his best friend has told him he is moving out of state and that their dream of motorbiking across Europe won't happen. Uncharacteristically, Rocky berates his friend. He later takes a bus trip to visit the girl he has fallen in love with. Although they clearly have feelings for each other, she tells him she is being sent to a private school for the blind and they can't be together any more.

When Rocky returns home, he takes the tacks from his map of Europe and goes to bed with a severe headache. The next morning Rusty tries to wake him up for school but she realises he has died in the night. She sees his map and replaces the tacks saying, "Now you can go anywhere you want, baby".

Roy "Rocky" Dennis was born with Jupiter in Aquarius and Saturn in Capricorn, in loose conjunction and straddling the ascendant. The condition of the ascendant can sometimes describe a person's physical appearance and in Rocky's case, craniodiaphyseal dysplasia seems to fit the astrological significators of abnormal calcium (Saturn) build up (Jupiter) causing disfigurement to the facial features.

Eric Stoltz was born with Jupiter and Saturn in conjunction in Capricorn. Because they were born within months of each other, there is not much difference in the positions of the planets from Jupiter outward in their charts, but the inner planets tell a very interesting tale. With both Mercury and Mars on Rocky's Moon in Scorpio, as well as his Venus conjunct Rocky's Pluto, Eric was able to convey the character's early sexual awakenings to great effect. The scene where Rocky falls out with his mother because she hired a prostitute for him is a good example of this tension.

It is Rusty's determination to ensure her child receives a "normal" education that reflects Rocky's and Eric's Saturn opposition to Cancer. Cher, who played Rusty, had Saturn in Cancer widely opposite Moon in Capricorn (almost the same degrees as Rocky's Saturn) and thus was nicely able to understand Rocky's dilemmas: she was a troubled mother with addictions but fought for her son's rights to be treated the same as any other child. The real life Rusty had her Venus on Cher's Sun and Cher's Uranus was on the mother's Chiron in Gemini. Cher did a marvellous job portraying a mother's unconventional love for her son as he fought the physical as well as the emotional pain of his deformities.

Mask was met with great reviews and high praise for Cher and Eric Stoltz with both receiving nominations for Golden Globes awards.

The film is listed in AFI's list of 100 years. . .100 cheers.

MILK

Harvey Milk: 22 May 1930, 01:30, Woodmere, New York. A: RR
Sean Penn: 17 August 1960, 15:17, Burbank, California. AA: RR
Dan White: 2 September 1946, 08:13, Bellflower, California.
AA: Shaw
Josh Brolin: 12 February 1968, 10:22, Santa Monica, California.
AA: Taglilatelo
Release date: 28 October 2008

From the very beginning of the film, it is very difficult not to like the character of Harvey Milk, wonderfully portrayed by Sean Penn, an actor known for his rough-around-the-edges outsider roles and political activism. Open, honest, intelligent and exuding warmth, the audience can't help but root for Milk and hope that the inevitable assassination will somehow be averted.

The film opens with archived footage of police raiding gay bars in the '50s and '60s and the announcement of Milk's assassination along with the mayor of San Francisco, George Moscone. The film then flashes back to Milk's 40th birthday and his meeting his boyfriend for the first time. The pair decide to move to San Francisco to find more acceptance for their relationship. Milk becomes a gay activist and although his

Favourites 305

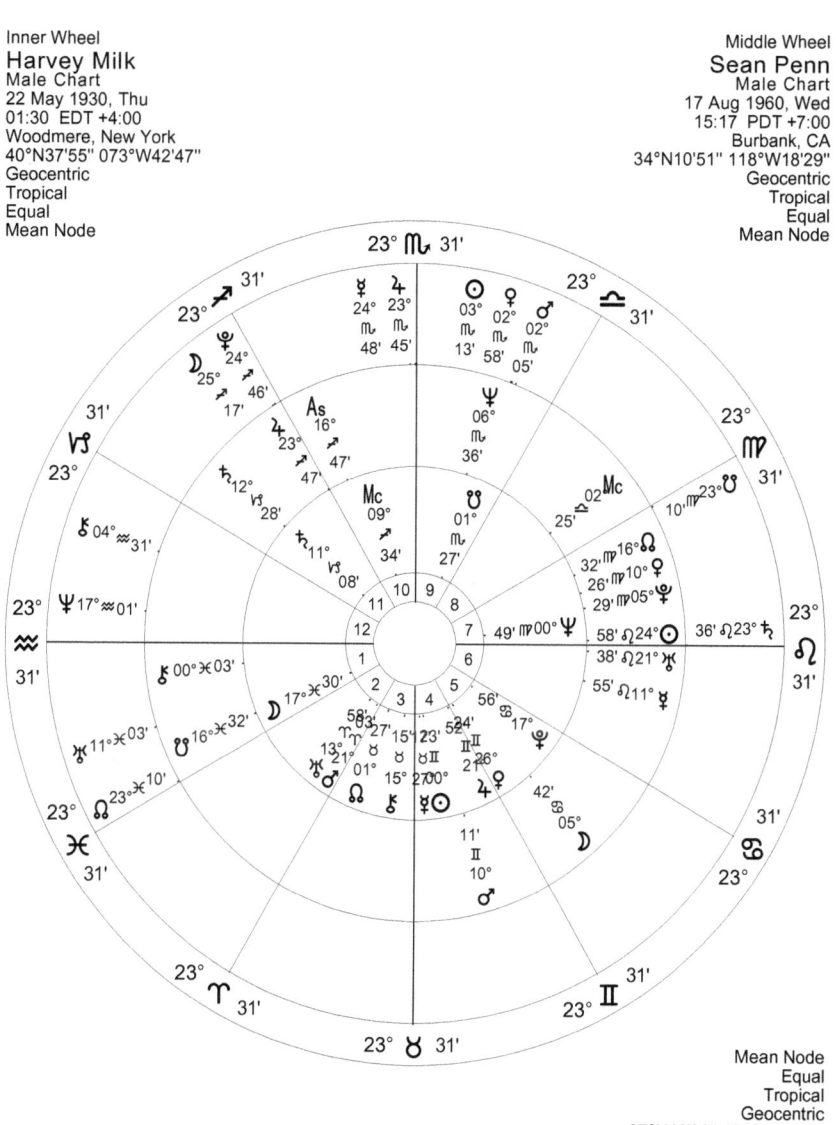

306 Mirror Mirror

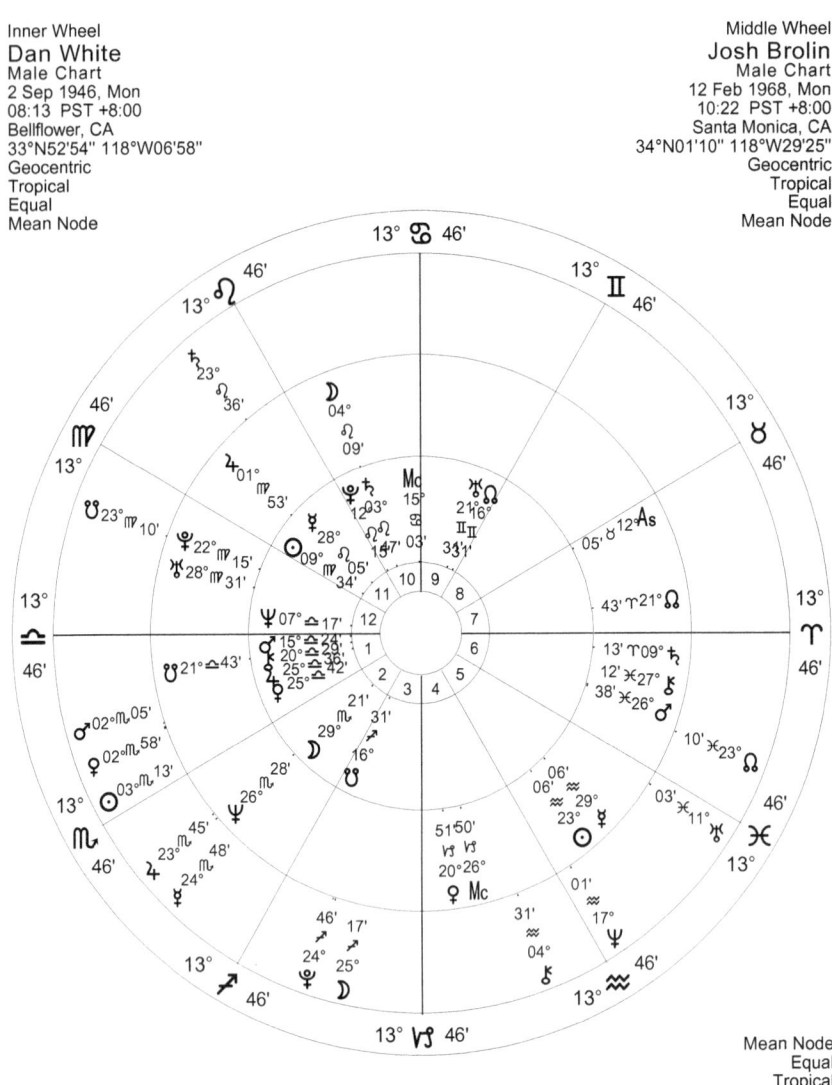

boyfriend is his campaign manager, he becomes frustrated with Milk's devotion to politics and leaves him. Milk meets someone else, but this boyfriend is far more sensitive and sadly hangs himself because he feels Milk isn't paying him enough attention.

Milk finally wins a vote to be in a major public office and becomes one of the few openly homosexual politicians in the United States. He begins working with Dan White; the pair seem to have opposite opinions on many issues and White grows more resentful every time Milk opposes his proposals. Eventually they find themselves at loggerheads on a proposal to ban homosexuality, an initiative that is defeated. White resigns from the Board over a pay dispute then asks to be reinstated. The request is denied and White shoots both Moscone and Milk.

Sean Penn and Harvey Milk were born with Saturn within one degree, in the sign of its dignity, Capricorn. Although born nearly thirty years apart, this karmic connection helped to build credibility that a straight man was a gay politician who fought for LGBT rights in a time when it was not fashionable to do so. It may have helped that Penn's Sun and Uranus were both conjunct Milk's descendant. Not everything you see is what you're going to get. Penn's sensitivity to Milk can also be seen with his South Node conjunct Milk's Moon in Pisces. Incidentally, it is pure astrological genius that Penn received so many accolades for his portrayal of Harvey Milk as his Moon is in Cancer, the sign associated with mothers!

Josh Brolin plays the part of Milk's assassin, Dan White. Actor and real life character had opposing Mercurys within one degree, Brolin's in Aquarius and White's in Leo. If they were real life friends, this would be a challenging aspect because it suggests polar opposite views and ways of thinking. Additionally, Brolin's Moon in Leo was conjunct White's Saturn, also within one degree. This is hardly a comfortable position had this been a relationship in the real world, but on the silver screen it may have given the edge to Brolin in portraying such an unlikeable antagonist. Helping to set aside discomfort in playing the villain, Brolin's Neptune is conjunct White's Moon in Scorpio which may have also helped remove the sting of being unpopular.

In real life, Milk's Jupiter and White's Uranus were in conjunction in Gemini so it's not surprising they would have such extreme political differences. Milk's Pluto is also conjunct White's MC in Cancer. Whilst it would be a long shot to suggest such a combination would drive White to murder Milk, it is indicative of deep-seated issues being played out in a public arena.

Penn and Brolin of course are not enemies, let alone political ones. One can imagine Brolin pulling the trigger on Penn for the big screen and then the pair retreating to some quiet bar to share a beer or two. Brolin's Jupiter in Virgo is conjunct Penn's Pluto in Virgo within an orb of three degrees. Mythologically, Jupiter was known for his shape shifting abilities so Brolin may have been able to adjust his personality to offset his villainy as well as the intensity of Penn's emotions off-camera.

Transiting Saturn was conjunct Penn's Sun in Leo within one degree, and Brolin's Neptune was transited by the Mercury/Jupiter conjunction on the day of the movie's release. A transiting Venus/Mars conjunction in Scorpio was also on Milk's South Node. In sharp contrast, transiting Jupiter and Mercury was conjunct to within a few degrees of White's Moon in Scorpio: it as if his treachery is not only exposed but magnified and talked about.

Sean Penn was nominated for a Golden Globe, a Screen Actors Guild and won an Oscar for Best Actor.

MONSTER

Aileen Wuornos: 29 February 1956, no time, Rochester, Michigan.
Source: Wikipedia
Charlize Theron: 7 August 1975, 08:23, Benoni, South Africa.
Rectified time C: RR Craft
Tyria Moore: 3 August 1962, no time, Tampa, Florida.
Source: Wikipedia
Christina Ricci: 12 February 1980, 18:30, Santa Monica, California. AA: Schoflield
Date of execution: 9 October 2002 09:47 Florida
Release date: 16 November 2003

The most well-known biopic about the serial killer Aileen Wuornos was the Academy Award-winning *Monster* starring an unrecognisable Charlize Theron. The film chronicles Aileen's series of seven murders – from a brutal sexual assault and subsequent shooting in self-defence, to increasingly desperate attempts to gain money and power in a male-dominated world where a woman can be bought, used and then discarded like the weekly trash for a relatively small sum of cash.

The film opens with a series of flashbacks to Aileen's childhood. Her first words (in Charlize Theron's voice) are: "I always wanted to be in the movies," as a series of clips play of a young girl standing before a mirror playing at dressing up and revealing her dreams of being rich and beautiful. The viewer can't help being charmed by the little girl as she tries on elaborate costume jewellery and the type of play clothes that could indicate she is playing a Queen. It is a perfect montage for a child with Jupiter in Leo, and Charlize's stellium in Leo beautifully brings out the theme of a Queen who never ascended to a throne.

And then Pluto starts to kick in.

Aileen, who had Pluto conjunct her Jupiter in Leo, reveals that she believes people don't yet know yet who she is going to be. "One day," she says, "they will all see." Aileen's North Node is conjunct Charlize's Neptune and this factor echoes through the fantasy life that is revealed in the opening credits.

But the viewer can see that Aileen is rejected by her female peers and she believes that, like Marilyn Monroe, someone will discover who she really is and give her the opportunity to be the movie star she feels she should be. She is shown flashing her breasts to boys (presumably in exchange for cash, food or cigarettes as she had to do in real life) or allowing herself to be picked up. All the while she believes one of these men will be the one to take her away to a new life. Unfortunately, the men Aileen come into contact with buy her at a far lower price than she thinks she is worth.

One day, she has to face up to the fact that she's not going to be discovered. And that's the day she decides to end it all. It is later revealed, after she has met the female lover who will ultimately betray her, the only reason she didn't kill herself was that she had five remaining dollars to spend. If she didn't spend those five dollars, then she would have "sucked him off for free" (her last customer).

Aileen's Sun in Pisces is opposite Charlize's Venus in Virgo within a degree and, if the rectified chart is correct, the opposition is on the ascendant/descendant axis of the actress. Charlize had to embrace unattractiveness and the ugly nature of a serial killer to pull off this role.

310 Mirror Mirror

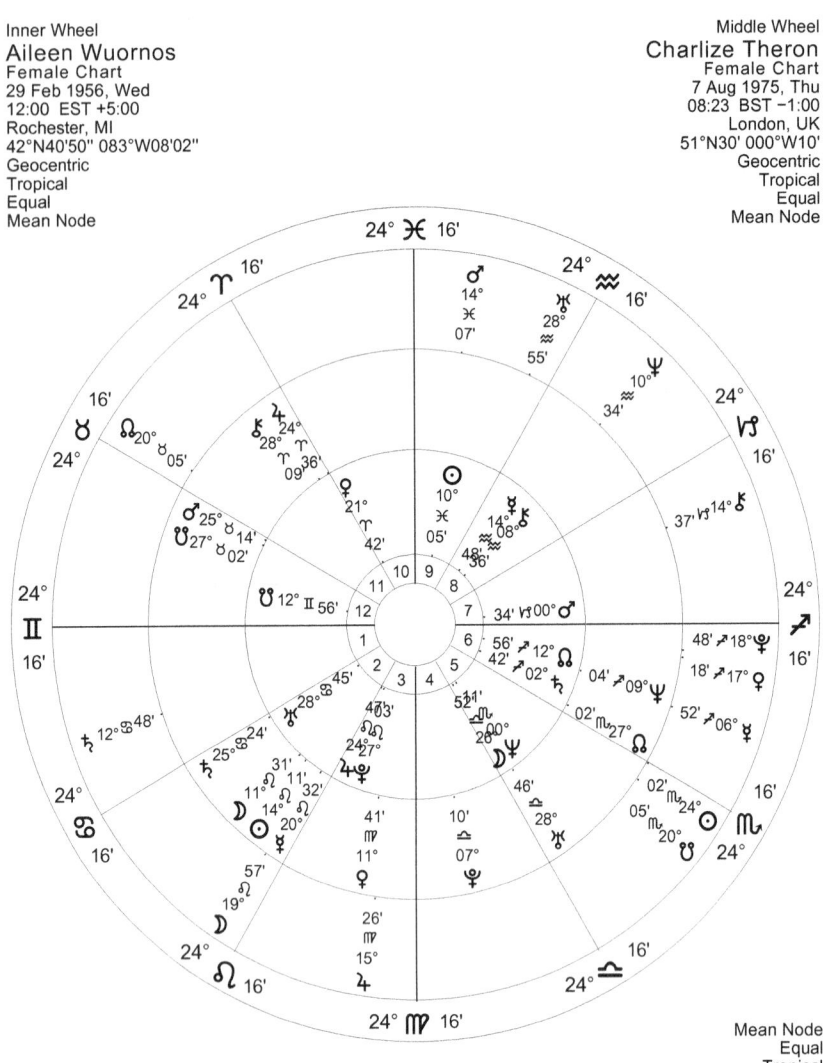

Favourites 311

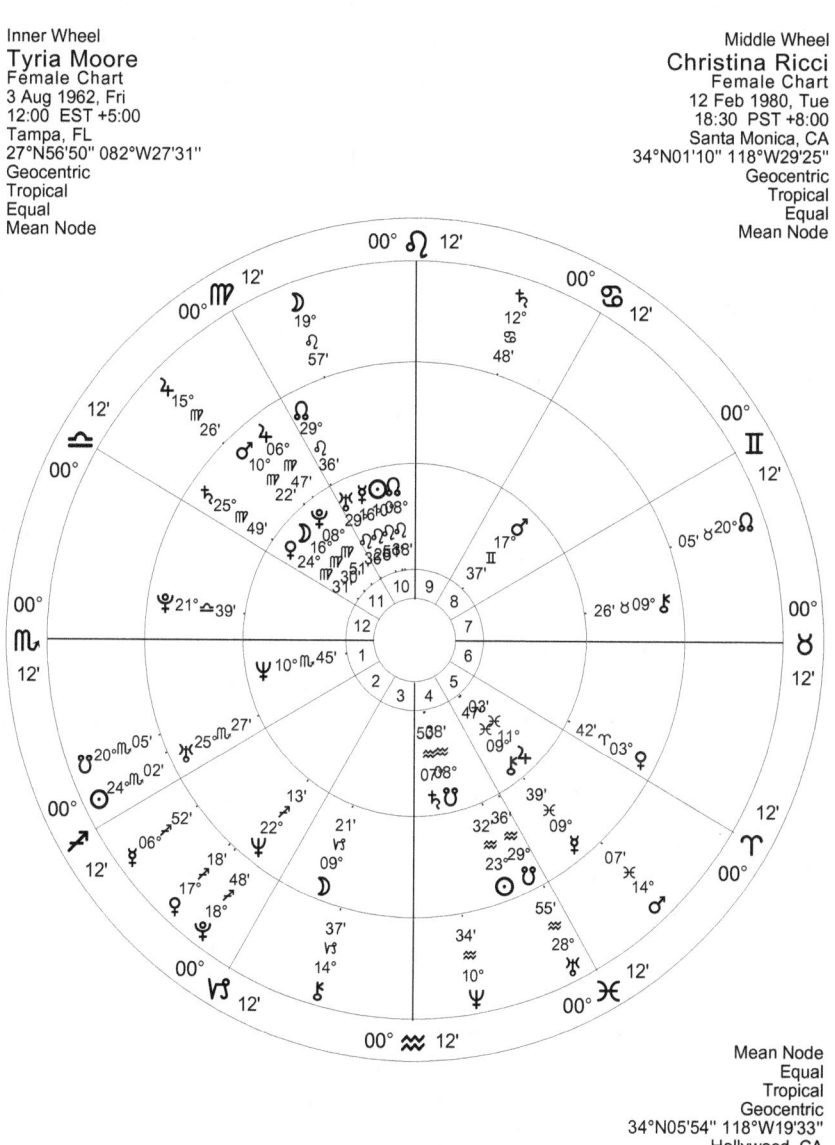

A good starting point for understanding Aileen's character may have been her natal Jupiter/Pluto conjunction in Leo, in turn conjunct Charlize's natal Mercury as a ruling planet. This is not difficult to see when it is considered that Aileen became, through an unfortunate series of perfect storms, a prostitute who was a very rare example of a female serial killer. Charlize was the vessel through which Aileen's tawdry story was told.

Theron is an incredibly attractive woman but it must be pointed out that her South Node and Mars are within one degree of the fixed star Algol which is "the demon star" located at the third eye of the beheaded Medusa in the Perseus tableau. Historically, Algol was associated with violence and in particular, decapitations. Modern astrologers tame this association and tend to pair it with female intensity, obsession and jealousy. Theron pulled off this side of Aileen's character with aplomb.

The role of Selby, Aileen's female lover, was portrayed by Christina Ricci who was criticized for her banal acting. This role was heavily fictionalized to avoid legal action from Tyria Moore who was Aileen's lover in real life.

Moore's Pluto in Virgo is conjunct the ascendant and Jupiter of Ricci, enabling the actress to convey a sense of being taken to the underground through association with Wuornos. In opposition to this placement is a conjunction of Ricci's Mercury and Moore's Chiron in Pisces. Despite criticisms of her acting ability, Ricci was able to draw out the lost innocence of a young girl hopelessly in love with a serial killer. There is also desperation in this character. After all, she had to frame her lover in order to gain immunity from prosecution, represented by a Venus/Saturn conjunction in Virgo between actress and real life character. On the day of Aileen's confession, which would exonerate Moore, Jupiter was transiting Moore's Sun in Leo by exact conjunction. Within two degrees, Jupiter was conjunct her North Node as well. It was a lucky escape indeed. Within a few degrees orb of conjunction, on the day of Aileen's execution by lethal injection, both Mars and Mercury were transiting this Venus/Saturn conjunction.

Neptune was transiting Aileen's natal Mercury and Chiron on the day of the release of *Monster* on 16 November 2003, just over a year after her execution. The film makes it difficult to avoid being sympathetic to

Aileen and it's easy to forget that she had committed crimes that would earn her the death penalty.

Jupiter in Leo was transiting Theron's Sun and Moon on the day of Aileen's execution (chart not shown). This is perhaps appropriate for the role of an actress that would win an Oscar. Both Jupiter and Mars were transiting Theron's ascendant-descendant axis when *Monster* was released. Bearing in mind this transit also highlights the actor's and the real life character's Venus/Sun opposition, it seems highly appropriate the film would bring the sad story of Aileen Wuornos to life.

Theron won an Academy Award, Golden Globe Award and the Screen Actors Guild Award for her performance.

In 2009, Ebert named it the third-best film of the decade.

ROCKETMAN

Reginald Dwight (Elton John): 25 March 1947, no time, Pinner, England. Source: Wikipedia
Taron Egerton: 10 November 1989, no time, Birkenhead, England. Source: Wikipedia
Bernie Taupin: 22 May 1950, no time, Sleaford, England. Source: Wikipedia
Jamie Bell: 14 March 1986, no time, Billingham, England. Source: Wikipedia
John Reid: 9 September 1949, no time, Paisley, Scotland. Source: Wikipedia
Richard Madden: 18 June 1986, 07:40, Paisley Scotland.
AA: Gerard
Release date: 22 May 2019

The opening scene of *Rocketman* shows Elton John bursting through the doors of a rehab clinic dressed in a flamboyant devil's outfit as if he has just stepped off the stage. He recounts his life in a series of flashbacks as a young boy named Reginald, starting with his relationship with his unhappy mother, doting grandmother and absent father. Each time a flashback finishes and returns to Elton in the rehab clinic, he removes a piece of his outfit.

Rocketman is very much about Elton John's search for love. First there is the heart-breaking rejection from his father. As Elton grows into a man, he begins to explore his homosexuality and enters into a relationship with his manager John Reid. At several points in the film Elton rages at Reid, accusing him of never loving him and insinuating he is taking advantage of him. Clearly the relationship between Elton and Reid lacked the equilibrium Elton needed. It is fascinating to watch this being played out between actors who have personal planets conjunct Pluto in Scorpio.

Elton (born Reginald Dwight) began taking piano lessons from a young age and eventually makes his way to the Royal Academy of Music on a scholarship. His home life is unhappy – culminating in his mother having an affair, at which point his father leaves for good. Reginald's stepfather takes more of an interest in Reggie and encourages his interest in rock and roll. As he grows older, he begins performing in pubs and eventually joins a soul band as a backup musician. To put his old life behind him, he changes his name to Elton John and begins writing music with a manager. However, Elton has to admit that while he can write music, he can't write lyrics. After being introduced to lyricist Bernie Taupin, the two begin writing hit songs together and soon Elton becomes very successful.

At a party after a performance Elton meets John Reid, who eventually becomes his lover and manager. Reid insists that Elton tell his parents that he's gay so Elton re-connects with his father and new family who still take no interest in his son. Hurt by the rejection, Elton then tells his mother who responds by saying that she had known for years and that as a consequence he will never be loved. Elton's unhappiness leads him to becoming addicted to alcohol, cocaine, cannabis, sex and shopping to numb his pain. After discovering Reid has been having an affair, Elton attempts suicide by taking an overdose and falling into his pool. He is rushed to the hospital, treated, then pushed onto the stage at Dodger Stadium a few days later.

His life continues its downward spiral and he has a short marriage to a close female friend. His mother is seen showing her scepticism on their wedding day. The marriage doesn't last.

After an argument with his mother, then with Bernie, and suffering a drug and alcohol-induced heart attack, then a nosebleed from too much cocaine use, Elton looks at himself in the mirror – in his flamboyant devil costume – and realizes he needs help. He gets up and walks away from the stadium where he is due to perform and checks in to rehab.

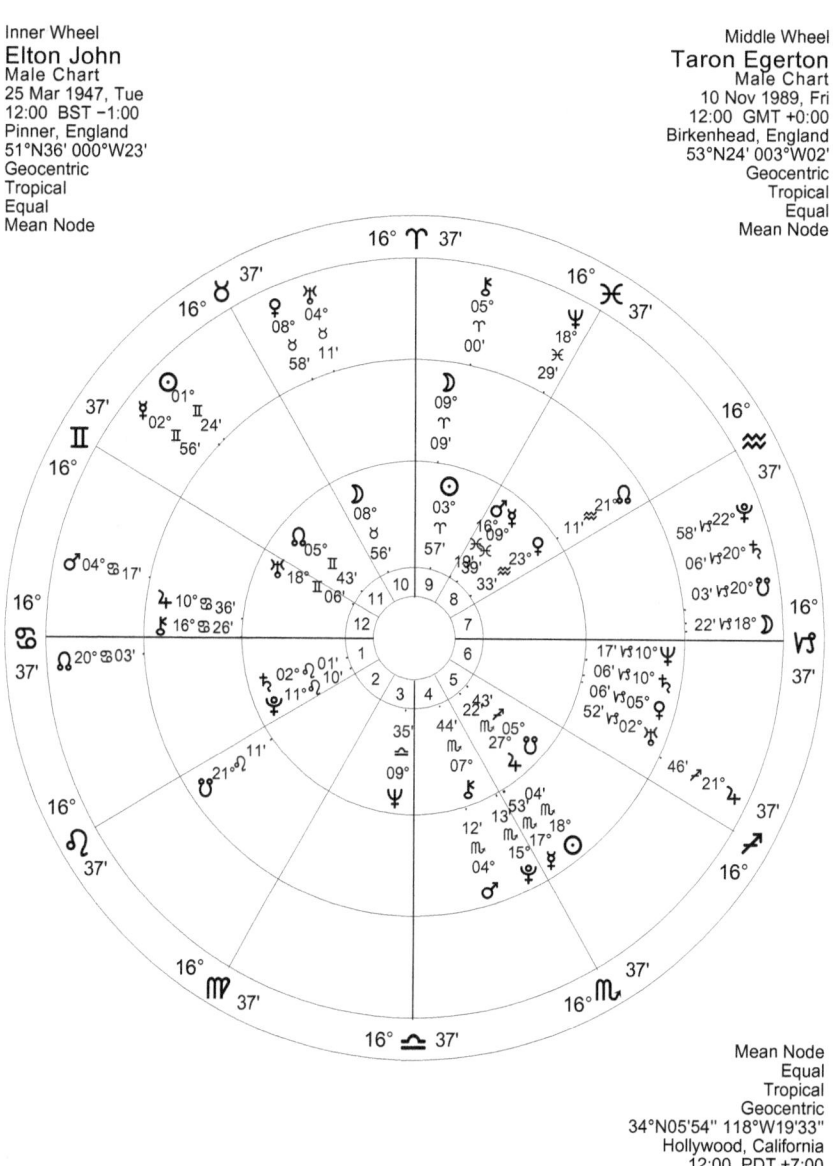

316   Mirror Mirror

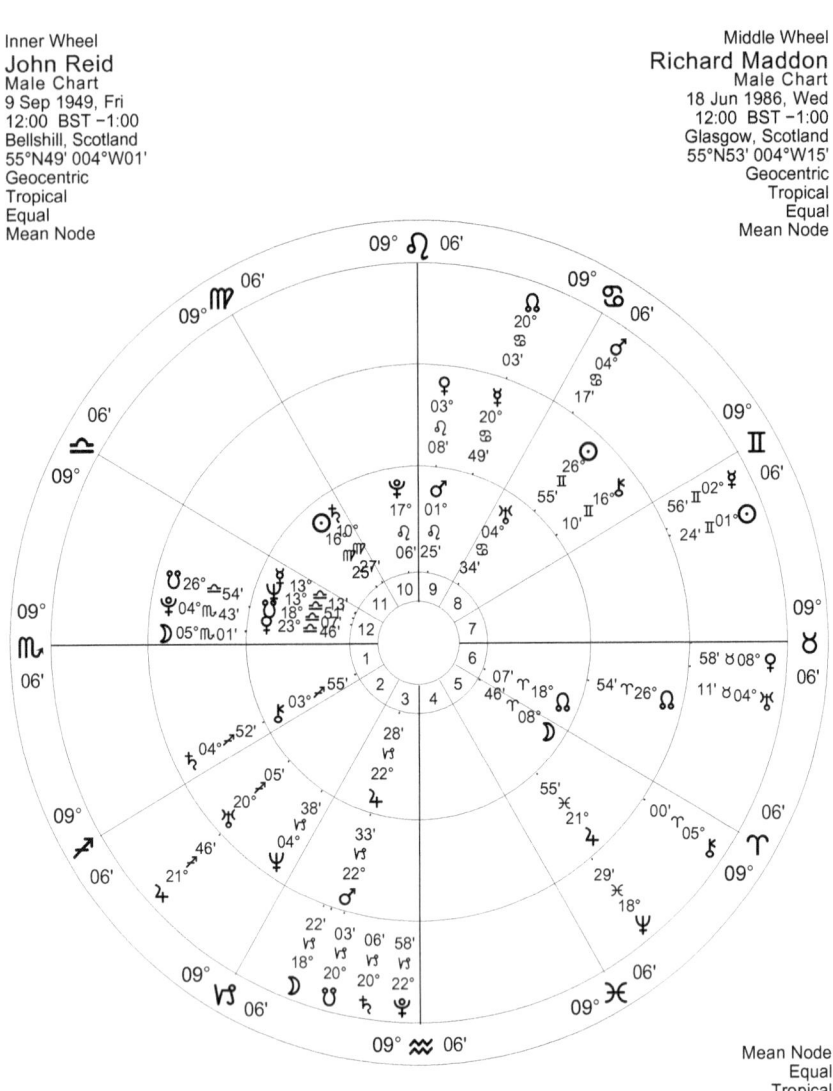

Favourites 317

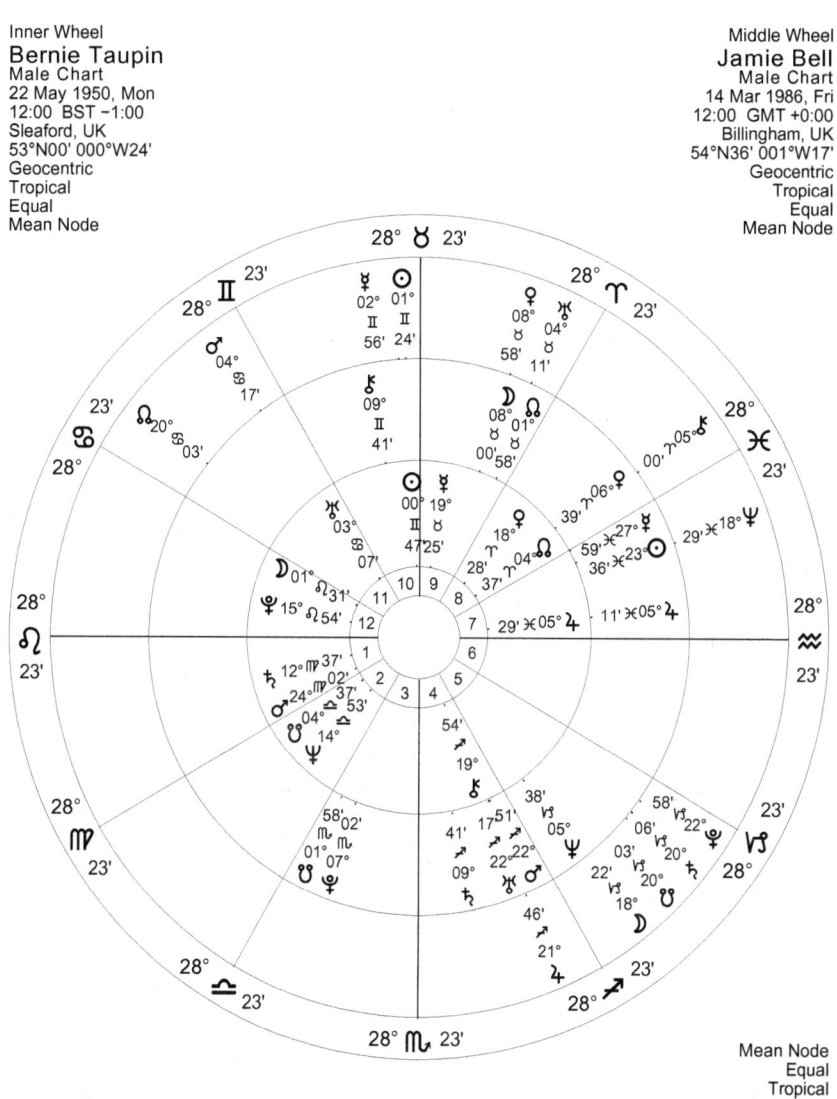

The movie ends with Elton being confronted with his demons from the past. He looks like any other ordinary person as he is no longer hiding behind his stage persona. He checks out of rehab with a performance of *I'm Still Standing*.

The epilogue notes that Elton has been sober for over 28 years but still has issues with shopping, is married to David Furnish and has two children with him. He is finally loved properly.

Looking at the charts of the individuals, we can see that the actor, Taron Egerton, has Saturn conjunct Neptune in Capricorn opposite Jupiter in Cancer, all three at ten degrees. This shows great imagination with a heavy dose of reality: he would have the ability to step into a role, have great fun playing it but also be able to walk out of it as required.

Elton John has the Sun in Aries and Moon in Taurus, both luminaries in their exaltations. He also has Saturn in Leo, a placement that may find it difficult to contend with the spotlight. Indeed throughout the film, several references are made to Elton's shyness and his admission that his elaborate stage costumes allow him to "borrow" a different persona to bring to the stage.

Although the time of Egerton's birth is not known, he has the Moon in Aries which matches Elton's Sun in Aries. Aries is an energetic, impulsive sign that can aggressively pursue its desires until it get what it wants. And then it is likely to lose interest once the chase is over. A Sun/Moon conjunction is pretty ideal when it comes to stepping into the role of a real life person. Taron does a very impressive job of reflecting Elton's personality as well as his singing voice back to us. With his North Node conjunct Elton's Venus, Taron is effectively able to tap into Elton's desires and values and incorporate them as a part of his own soul's journey. Through understanding the things that Elton values (equality, independence, teamwork and collaboration), the actor can find a way to express the singer's destiny. Elton's Venus in Aquarius is square to his Jupiter in Scorpio. This explains the singer's legendary indulgences and as the actor's North Node is implicated, it can explain how he was able to portray the intense (but abusive) relationship Elton had with John Reid.

Reid had Mars in Leo conjunct Elton's Saturn. Elton was essentially shy unless he could hide behind his stage persona. Reid's demand that a reluctant Elton reveal his sexuality to his parents is a good example of how this aspect might work. Elton's Mars/Mercury conjunction in Pisces is opposite Reid's Sun/Saturn conjunction in Virgo. Elton alleged that Reid never understood him and this opposition seems to confirm it. Reid's Chiron in Sagittarius conjunct Elton's South Node is an indication they may have been drawn together to work out issues from Elton's past. Indeed this is exactly what the film shows us: Elton working through his relationship with Reid by understanding the dynamics of his family. This is also quite brilliantly summarised when Elton says to Reid (during rehab) "I gave up everything to keep something I never even had in the first place".

Richard Maddon's Mars in Capricorn is conjunct Reid's Jupiter which seems appropriate for the role of a businessman involved in a sexual relationship with one of his clients. Transiting Mars in Cancer was conjunct Reid's Uranus and opposite Maddon's Neptune which may account for the controversy generated for the first male-male intimate sex scene in cinema history. The scene in question, as well as obvious references to Elton's sexuality, were censored in some countries.

Bernie Taupin and Jamie Bell have several astrological connections worth exploring. Taupin provided Elton with a constant presence and much-needed stability. His support was central in Elton's recovery from addiction. The singer and lyricist have Jupiter and Mercury within four degrees of each other in Pisces. Jamie Bell, who portrayed Taupin in the film, has Jupiter exactly conjunct Taupin's own Jupiter. Bell has Venus in Aries and this is conjunct Taupin's North Node with both planets conjunct John's Sun. Chiron in Aries was transiting this conjunction when the film was released.

The production of *Rocketman* was shelved a few times before the movie was finally unveiled at Cannes Film festival on 16 May 2019. Chiron, the wounded healer was transiting Elton's Sun. The film was a culmination of the highs and lows of his life – as well as the healing of his wounds.

Egerton won a Golden Globe for Best Actor for his performance and several other major nominations.

THE DOORS

**Jim Morrison: 8 December 1943, 11:55am, Melbourne, Florida
AA: Steinbrecher
Val Kilmer: 31 December 1959, 07:58, Los Angeles,
California. AA: RR
Pamela Courson: 22 December 1946, 11:10am, Weed,
California. AA: Young
Meg Ryan: 19 November 1961, 10:36, Fairfield,
Connecticut. AA: RR
Release date: 1 March 1991**

Jim Morrison's Jupiter in Leo was in mutual reception with his Sun in Sagittarius. This is an indication of a person who could be described as "larger than life". A better description of a man who is best remembered for the drama that surrounded his life (and death) would be difficult to find. His overtly sexual nature (and those skin tight leather trousers) ensured that women swooned and his daring antics on and off the stage gave men someone to look up to. He was a guru to the many disillusioned youths who packed concert halls to see him perform with the band he led and founded, The Doors.

Morrison's childhood was perhaps befitting of his stellium in Sagittarius. As is typical of military families, his early life is described as semi-nomadic and his parents had agreed that corporal punishment would not be used on their children. Instead, they opted for "dressing down", which consisted of yelling at and berating the children until they broke down and acknowledged their shortcomings. As Morrison had Saturn in Gemini (unaspected except by using very wide orbs to Jupiter and Sun), he discovered that words can be very painful indeed. As an adult, he broke off all ties to his family and even falsely claimed to be an only child of deceased parents.

Val Kilmer, who played Morrison, has both the Sun and its ruling planet Saturn in Capricorn, an indication he may need time to periodically withdraw from the spotlight. A stellium in Sagittarius may have also helped loosen him up. It isn't uncommon for actors to extensively prepare for their roles and Kilmer is no exception: he lost weight and took six months out of his busy acting career (he had a role in *Top Gun* in 1986 alongside Tom Cruise) to perfect Morrison's voice and he spent

Favourites 321

Inner Wheel
Jim Morrison
Male Chart
8 Dec 1943, Wed
11:55 EWT +4:00
Melbourne, Florida
28°N04'43" 080°W36'10"
Geocentric
Tropical
Equal
Mean Node

Middle Wheel
Val Kilmer
Male Chart
31 Dec 1959, Thu
07:58 PST +8:00
Los Angeles, CA
34°N03'08" 118°W14'34"
Geocentric
Tropical
Equal
Mean Node

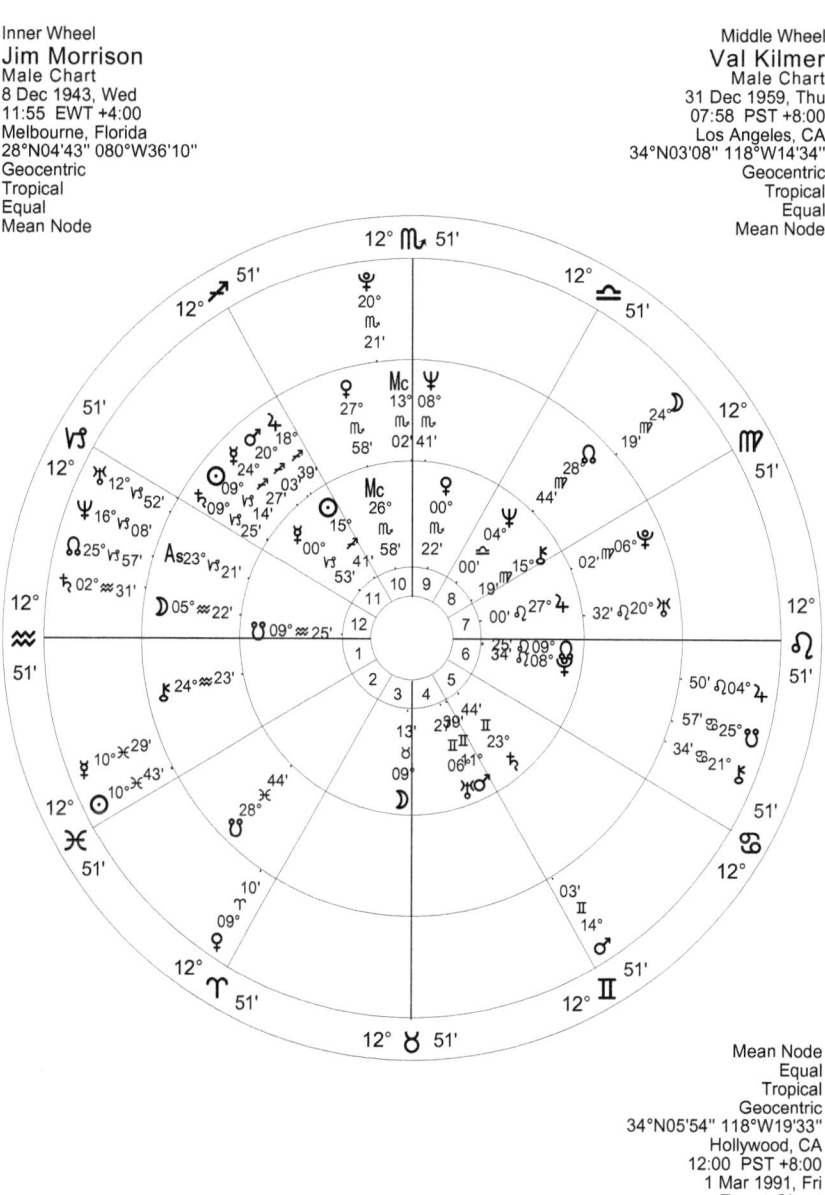

Mean Node
Equal
Tropical
Geocentric
34°N05'54" 118°W19'33"
Hollywood, CA
12:00 PST +8:00
1 Mar 1991, Fri
Event Chart
The Doors release
Outer Wheel

322 Mirror Mirror

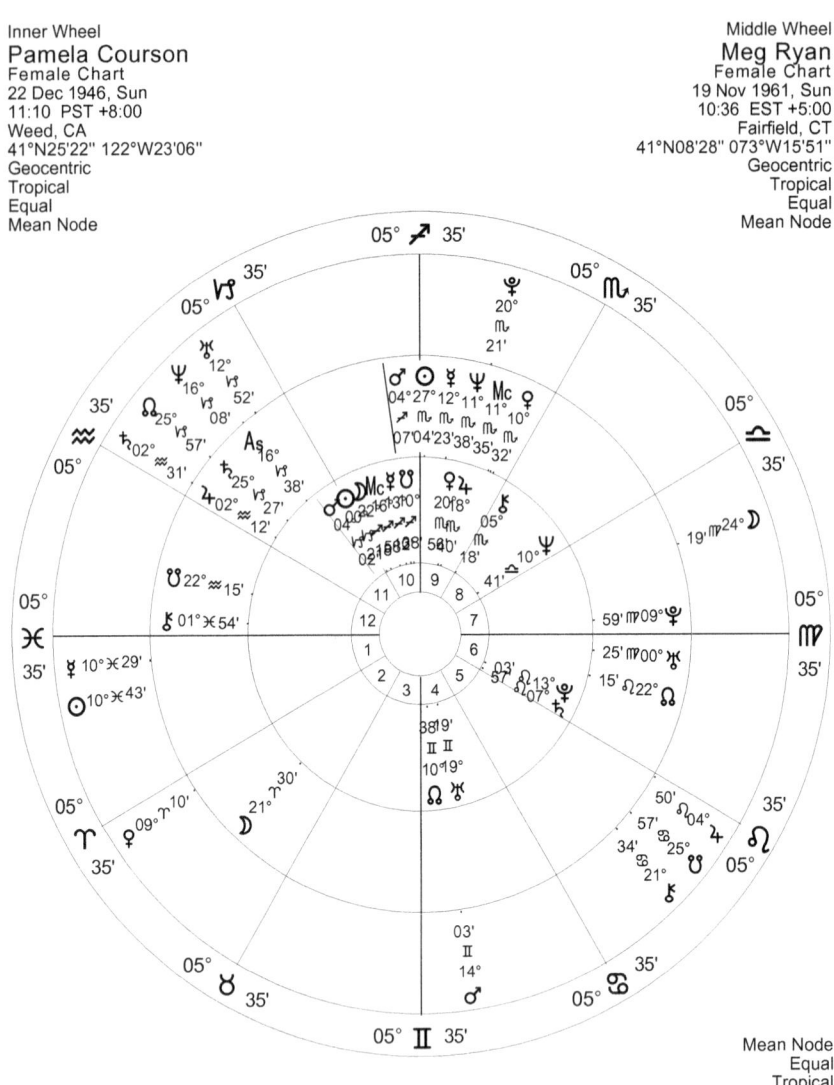

several thousand dollars of his own money in order to make a video of himself singing and looking like the singer at various ages. He learned fifty of Morrison's songs and actually sang fifteen of them in the film, no doubt aided by his natal Neptune in Scorpio conjunct his MC. Kilmer not only got Morrison's voice right, he may just have improved on it. Without this extensive hard work and practice, Kilmer would not have been a convincing "Lizard King".

Astrology of course helped too. Kilmer's Venus in Scorpio was within one degree of Morrison's MC in Scorpio. Coupled with his weight loss and this sexy connection, Kilmer fitted those famous leather trousers just right. Morrison's Sun was conjunct Kilmer's Jupiter in Sagittarius within a few degrees which helped the actor step into the role.

Morrison's love interest (amongst many others), Pamela Courson, was with him when he died. In the film, he refers to her as his muse: is it a coincidence that her Sun was conjunct his Mercury in Capricorn and that her Mercury was conjunct (to within two degrees) his Sun in Sagittarius? Courson's Saturn was conjunct Morrison's Pluto/North Node conjunction and her Uranus is conjunct his Saturn. Small wonder then that they seemed to dismantle each other and descend into tumultuous arguments that centred around infidelities on both sides.

Meg Ryan, who played Morrison's girlfriend Pamela Courson, was fresh from her role as Sally Albright in *When Harry Met Sally* (1989). Already dubbed "America's Sweetheart", there were plenty of doubters when it was announced Ryan had emerged triumphant from a list of sixty other auditioning actresses and would be playing the role of the troubled Courson. Even she admitted she was unfamiliar with Morrison's music and had to re-examine her own perceptions of the '60s. With her Uranus exactly trine to Courson's Sun, this is perfectly understandable. Ryan brought an unexpected sweetness and a certain doomed sadness (as well as a good dose of slapstick comedy) to the role. Her Sun was conjunct Kilmer's Venus, and both of these planets were conjunct Morrison's MC.

The Doors was released to the general public on 1 March 1991, and during filming, transiting Uranus has passed over Kilmer's Sun/Saturn conjunction in Capricorn. Kilmer had gone to extreme lengths to understand Jim Morrison including memorising all of his music and poetry as well as studying the way the singer spoke and dressing like him. Kilmer put his Saturn to work and Uranus helped to make it pay off.

Transiting Saturn in Aquarius was conjunct Ryan's natal Jupiter and transiting Neptune in Capricorn was passing over her ascendant when the film was released. The actress was criticised for turning Courson into a shallow caricature. It can be difficult to have clarity with Neptune transits.

Pluto transited Courson's natal Venus/Jupiter conjunction in Scorpio when the film was released. The sign of Scorpio is often associated with life or death situations so it is interesting indeed that Jupiter transited its ruler, Pluto and North Node in Leo in Morrison's chart, thus magnifying these themes when the film was released.

THE IMITATION GAME
Alan Turing:, 23 June 1912, 02:15am, London. A: RR
Benedict Cumberbatch, 19 July 1976, 12:00, Hammersmith, England. B: Scholfield
Joan Clarke: 24 June 1917, no time, West Norwood, England.
Source: Wikipedia
Keira Knightly: 26 March 1985, no time, London. X: Astrodienst
Release date: 28 November 2014

After a break-in at his home, university professor Alan Turing is visited by two bobbies who have come to the scene of the crime to search for clues. They see an odd machine and Turing on the floor clearing up what he says is cyanide which has been knocked over during the robbery. Because he dismisses the officers, declines their help and claims nothing has been stolen, one of the officers becomes suspicious that there is more to the situation than Turing is letting on. Upon investigation, it's discovered Turing's military records are classified, causing further suspicion.

Back in his boarding school days, Turing was very unhappy and was bullied by the other boys because, as his mother told him, he was an "odd duck". Turing was unable to decipher the meaning of what people were saying to him. However, he developed a close friendship with Christopher Morcom, who taught him to how to deal with the bullying he had to endure but not give the reaction the bullies were looking for. It was Christopher who gave Turing a cryptology book saying, "Sometimes it's the very people who no one imagines anything of who do the things that no one can imagine." Turing realised he was in love with him but Christopher died from tuberculosis before he had a chance to tell him.

A few years later when Britain declares war on Germany, Turing travels to Bletchley Park to join the cryptology team. They are trying to decode the Enigma machine which the Nazis are using to send secret messages. Because he is difficult to work with, Turing doesn't get along with his colleagues, and the funding to construct a machine is denied. Turing writes directly to Winston Churchill, who not only funds the machine but also puts Turing in charge. Turing immediately fires two of his colleagues and places difficult crosswords in newspapers to find replacements from the people who can solve them. Joan, a young female Cambridge graduate, passes Turing's tests but her parents refuse to allow her to work with an all male cryptology team. Turing arranges for her to live and work with the female secretarial team and with her help, he begins forming better relationships with the other code breakers.

Turing eventually builds a machine (which he names "Christopher") that works but not quickly enough, because the Germans change the code settings each day. Because the machine is useless for its purpose, it is under threat of destruction and he is threatened with dismissal. Turing is sharply reminded that while the team works without success, people are dying. However, as he has become more popular and respected with Joan's help, his other colleagues threaten to quit if he is fired. Joan also reveals she has to leave on the wishes of her parents so Turing proposes to her. Inspired by a conversation at his engagement party, Turing realises he can re-program his machine more quickly and after re-calibrating it, the machine quickly decodes a message. However, Turing realises that if they act on every decoded message, the Germans will realise the Enigma code has been broken.

Turing had disclosed to a colleague that he was a homosexual. When Turing discovers this colleague is a Russian spy, the colleague threatens to inform the others about Turing's sexuality. An MI5 agent threatens Joan so Turing reveals that they have a Russian spy working with them. The agent said he knew about this and he is using the spy to leak messages for the benefit of the British. Fearing for Joan's safety, Turing tells her he is homosexual so she will leave Bletchley Park. She tells him she had suspected as much, but insists they would have been happy together. To persuade her to leave, Turing replies that he never cared for her and he

326 Mirror Mirror

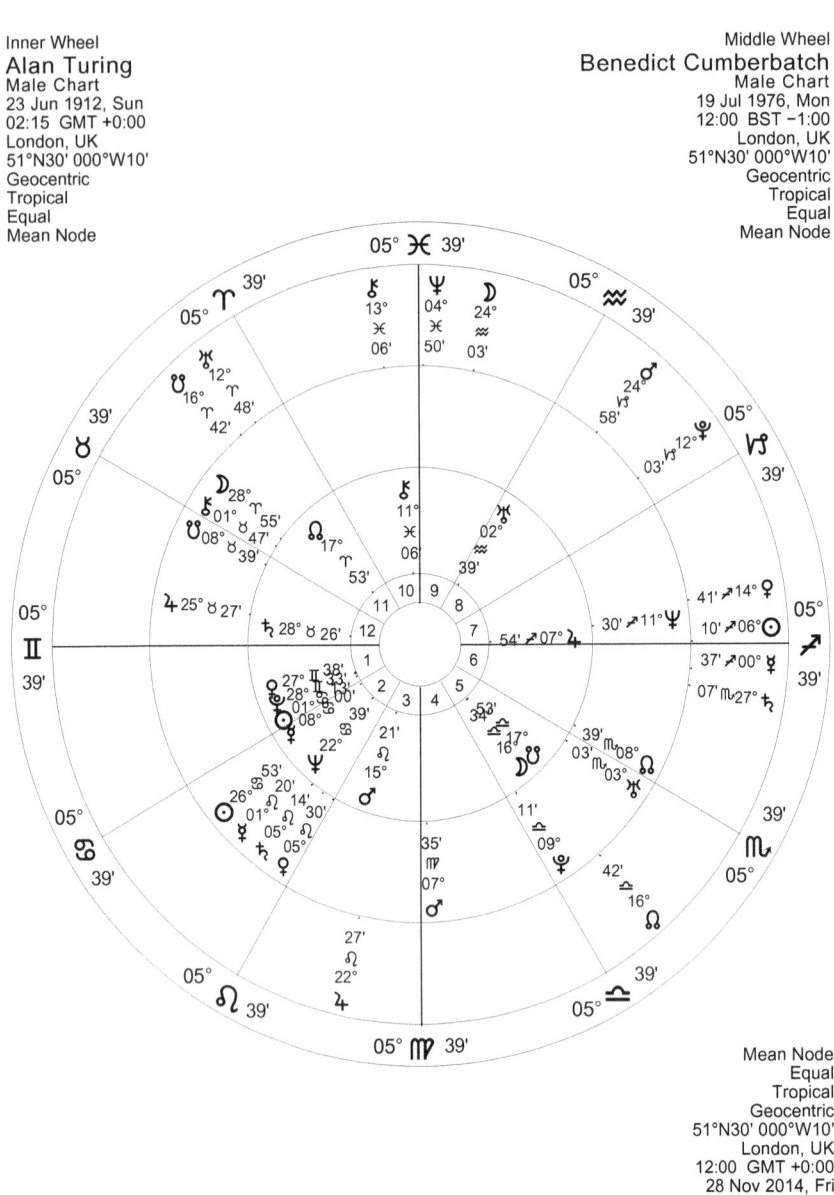

Favourites 327

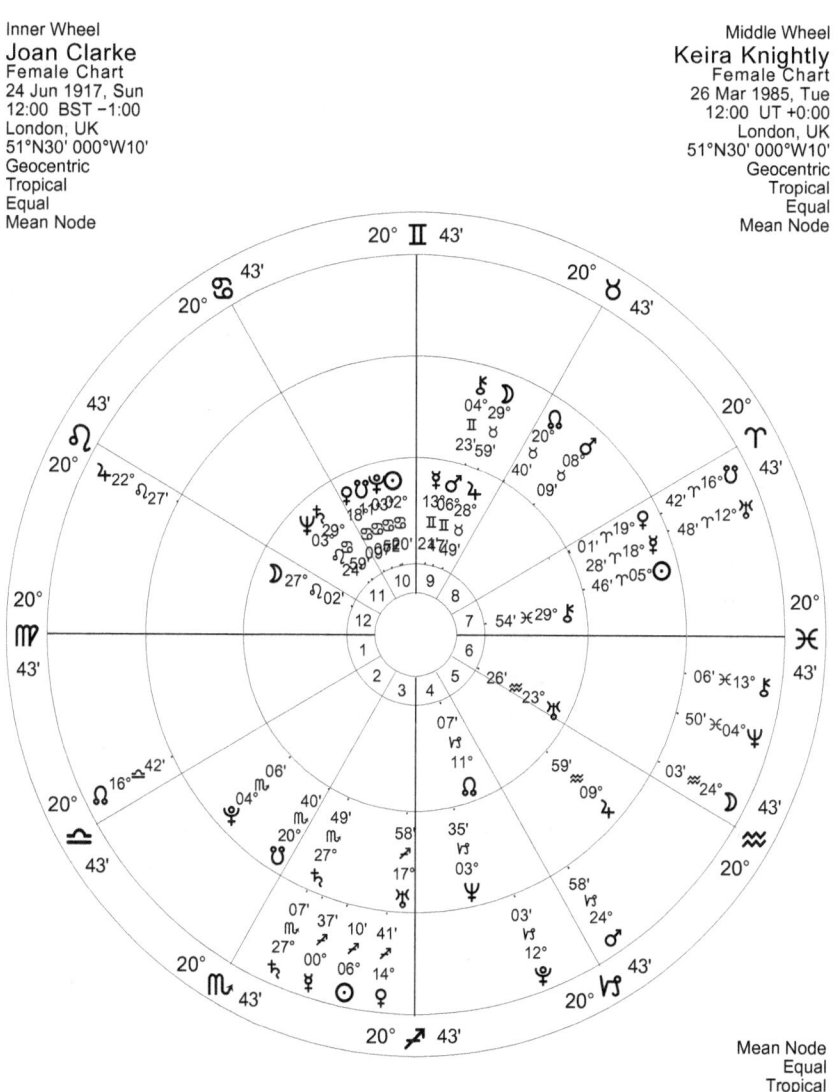

has only been using her for her cryptology skills. In defiance of her family and Turing, she decides to stay and complete what she considers to be the most important thing she will ever do. Shortly afterwards, the team are informed that they must destroy all their work and never speak to each other or reveal what they have achieved.

Turing returns to civilian life as a professor, and the policeman who was investigating the robbery at his home discovers Turing was not a spy but was trying to conceal he was a homosexual. As homosexuality was considered a crime in Britain in the 1950s, Turing was convicted of gross indecency and in lieu of a jail sentence he agrees to be chemically castrated. Years later, Joan visits him and witnesses his obvious physical and mental deterioration. When she offers to help him, he tells her that the authorities will take Christopher, which he has been storing in his home, away from him. Joan consoles him by telling him he saved millions of lives. The end notes reveal that Turing committed suicide and that he received a posthumous pardon from the Queen in 2013 as well as an honour for his achievements.

Uranus is the planet that represents inventions, breakthroughs and rule breaking. In Turing's chart, Uranus is exactly conjunct his MC in Aquarius (its modern rulership) with Cumberbatch's Venus/Saturn opposing it within a three degree orb. Jupiter in Sagittarius (also in its rulership) is the planet of higher learning and it is conjunct Turing's descendant. The descendant is what we project out into the world and therefore the kind of people we attract. Turing was noted for attracting both mavericks and big thinkers who cracked very important codes.

Turing's intense love life could be seen as Venus conjunct Pluto in Gemini, an aspect often linked to jealousy, feeling victimised or obsessed with the objects of one's love. Cumberbatch's Jupiter was conjunct Turing's Saturn as well as conjunct Algol so he was able to project those feelings freely.

The movie was released as the Sun was transiting Turing's descendant and Jupiter.

Clarke's Mars in Gemini was conjunct Keira Knightly's Chiron. The actress was criticised for over-dramatizing Joan's relationship with Turing. Turing's family also thought Knightley was inappropriately cast as Joan was "rather plain". However, transiting Pluto was conjunct Clarke's North Node in Capricorn which brought her brilliance to light, aided of course by the actress. It was Knightly's Saturn return (exactly) when the film was released and so the film represents a coming of age for her.

Although the film was criticised for downplaying Turing's homosexuality, it grossed over $233 million from its worldwide audience, and received numerous prestigious nominations for awards.

THE KING'S SPEECH

George VI ("Bertie"): 14 December 1895, 03:05, Sandringham, England. AA: RR
Colin Firth: 10 September 1960, no time, Greyshott, England. Source: Wikipedia
Elizabeth Bowes Lyon: 4 August 1900, 00:30, London. DD: McEvoy
Helena Bonham Carter: 26 May 1966, no time, London. X: RR
Lionel Logue: 26 February 1880, no time, Sydney, Australia. Source: Wikipedia
Geoffrey Rush: 6 July 1951, 12:00, Toowoomba, Australia. X: RR
Release date: 6 September 2010

Like the Duke of Sussex (Prince Harry, the son of Charles and Diana), Prince Albert, affectionately known as Bertie, was the "spare" to the British throne. No one really considered that one day he would become King, so essentially he was unprepared for the role when his brother abdicated in order to marry the American divorcee Wallis Simpson.

Future kings and queens are typically given years of training and preparation for their roles. Whilst Bertie undoubtedly had the privileges of growing up in a royal household, he felt safe in his older brother's shadow. From this position, he could hide his pronounced stutter from the rest of the world.

Natally, Bertie had Chiron, the Wounded Healer, rising in his birth chart. Although otherwise physically sound and clearly well bred, it was obvious his manner of speaking was going to be a problem. He also had Mercury conjunct the Sun in Sagittarius with Neptune in opposition. Although out of orb to make a solid opposition to the Mercury/Sun conjunction, Pluto was also conjunct Neptune.

330 Mirror Mirror

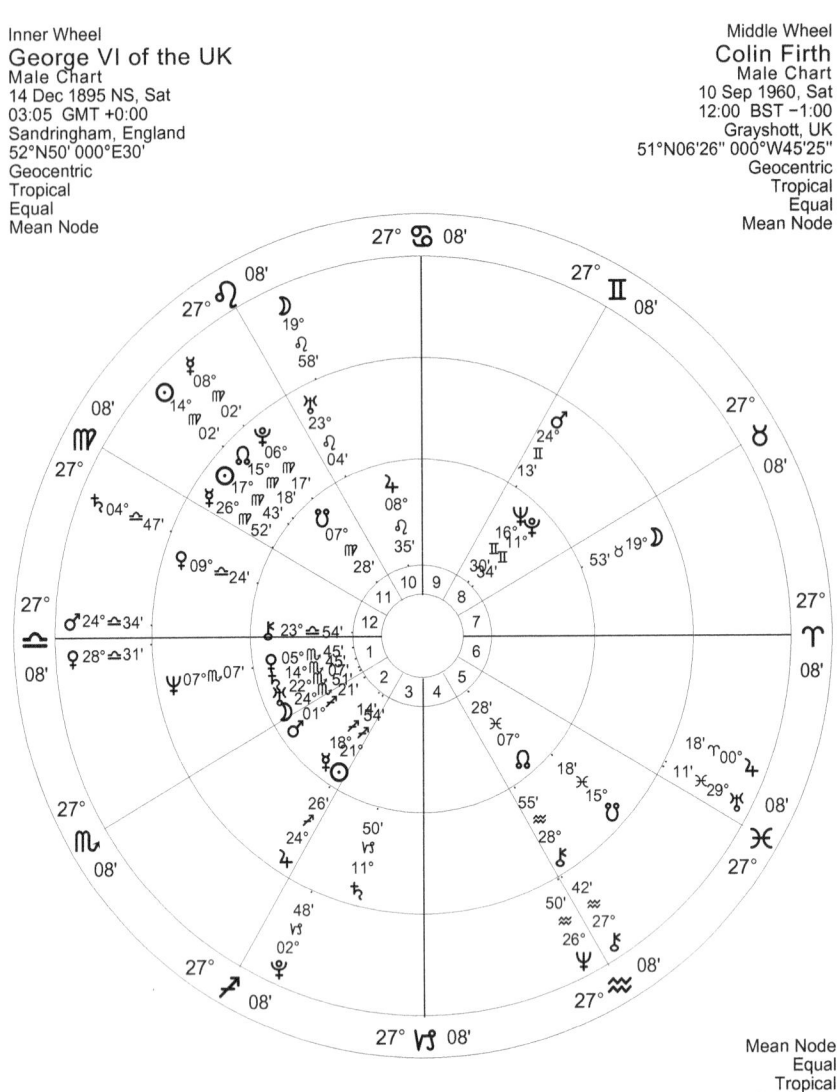

Favourites 331

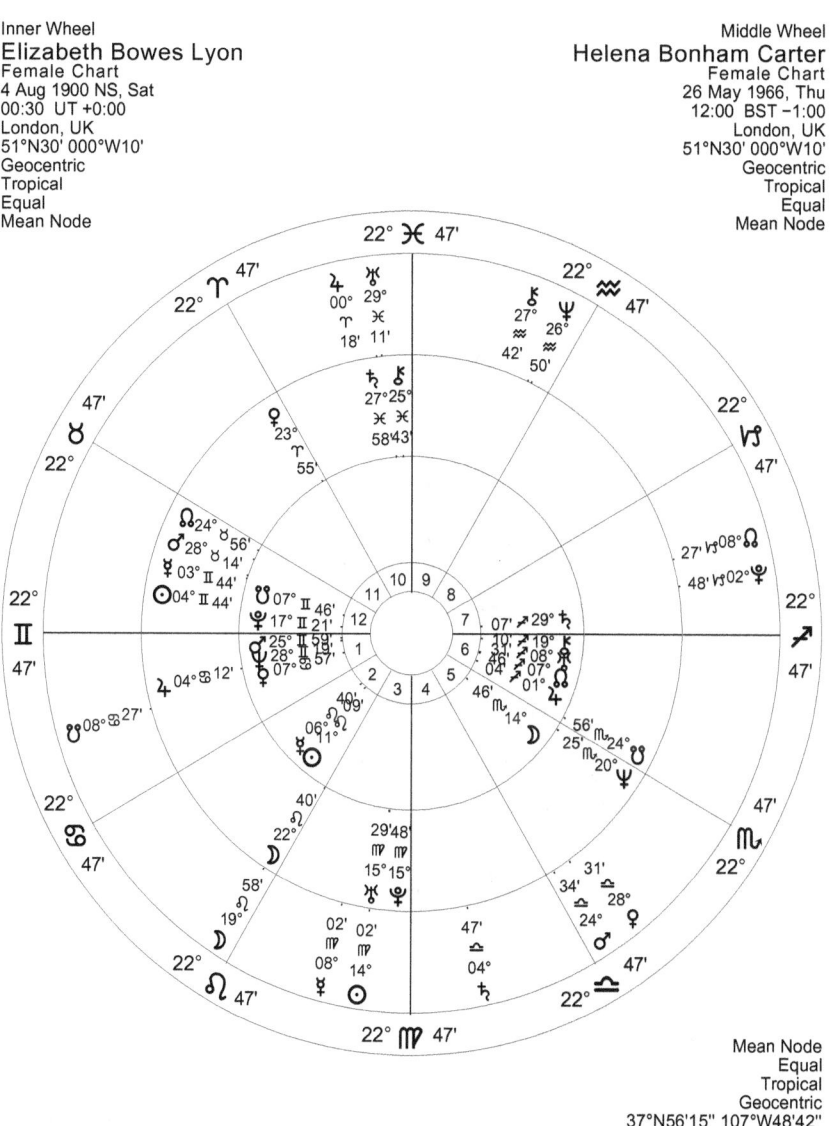

332 Mirror Mirror

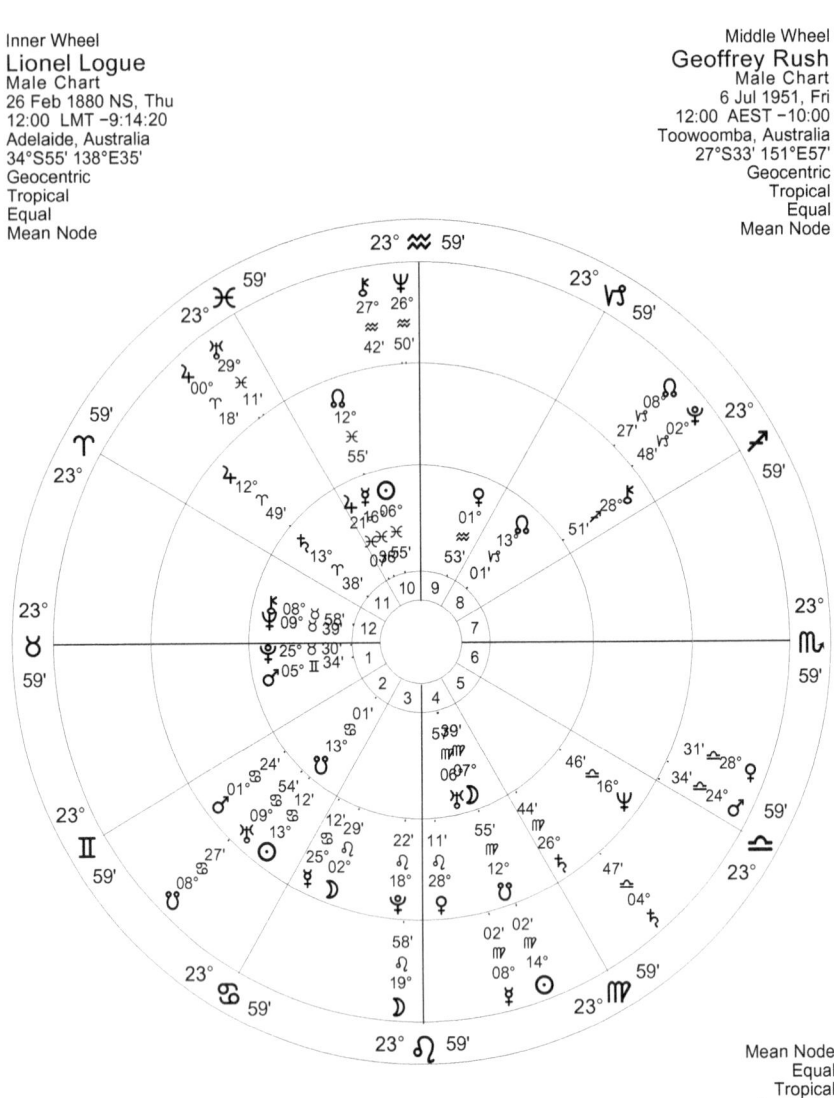

Colin Firth, who portrayed Bertie, had a Jupiter/Mars opposition that very nicely astrologically matched Bertie's opposition. There really can be no better actor to real-life character aspect than Firth's Pluto on Bertie's South Node. Firth's portrayal of the King's frustration as he struggled to communicate with his subjects was so good it earned him a Best Actor Oscar in 2011.

Helena Bonham Carter played Elizabeth Bowes-Lyon, the wife of Bertie and mother to Queen Elizabeth II. Bonham-Carter's role was a supportive but important one. Like her husband, Bowes-Lyon never expected to be on the throne or the mother to a Queen. The shock of the abdication on this family must have been extremely difficult. Like Bertie, both the Queen Mother (as Bowes-Lyon became known) and Bonham-Carter have Mercury conjunct the Sun.

The Queen Mum's Moon in Scorpio quite beautifully protects Bertie's Saturn on the same degree. Bonham-Carter's South Node is exactly conjunct Bertie's Moon in Scorpio too. Here we have two beautiful, strong women supporting a King: one from the past and the other, the future. Bonham Carter's Uranus/Pluto conjunction is sextile the King and Queen's Moon/Saturn.

The influence of Lionel Logue, the King's voice coach, cannot be under-estimated. Geoffrey Rush, who portrayed Logue in the film, had his Jupiter in Aries within a one degree orb of Logue's Saturn. Rush, portraying an authoritative voice coach, has his Saturn exactly on Firth's Mercury. Natally, Logue's Sun was on the King's North Node in Pisces and his Uranus on the King's South Node in Virgo. This is a man who changed the course of a King's reign. Remarkably, this degree of Virgo is Firth's placement of Pluto. Venus was transiting this within a couple of degrees of orb when the King made his address to the nation on 3 September 1939.

The King's Speech premiered on 6 September 2010. Mercury transited at eight degrees Virgo on that day, thus bringing together the King, the actor, the voice coach and the King's speech. As Mercury is the god of communication, it should be no wonder *The King's Speech* won the Oscar for Best Picture.

WALK THE LINE
Johnny Cash: 26 February 1932, 07:30, Kingsland, Arkansas.
A: RR
Joaquin Phoenix: 28 October 1974, 02:55, San Juan, Puerto Rico.
X: RR (rectified)
June Carter Cash: 23 June 1929, no time, Gate City, Virginia.
Source: Wikipedia
Reese Witherspoon: 22 March 1976, no time, New Orleans, Louisiana. Source: Wikipedia
Release date: 4 September 2005

The film focuses on Johnny Cash's early life and career, the disintegration of his family (both with his parents and his wife and children), and his infatuation with June Carter, who Cash liked to listen to on the radio as a child. Like many families during the depression, the Cash family endured extreme financial hardship. He was the fourth of seven children and began working on the family's cotton plantation when he was five years old. Many of the struggles they experienced became themes of Cash's famous songs.

When Johnny was twelve years old, his older brother was pulled into a circular saw and nearly cut in half. The brother suffered for a more than a week before succumbing to his horrific injuries. Just before he died, he said he had visions of singing angels. Cash said decades later that he was looking forward to meeting his brother in heaven.

Eventually Johnny marries his first wife and they struggle to raise a family whilst he tries to break into the music business. Eventually he gets his lucky break and goes on tour with his band. He meets June Carter and falls in love with her, though she objects to his developing drug and alcohol problem. Watching him spiral out of control, she writes *Ring of Fire*. Eventually Johnny's wife discovers his attraction to June and the couple divorce. Johnny buys a big house to prove to June that he has cleaned up from his addictions but when she visits him with her family, it is clear he hasn't. After encouragement from her mother, June gets Johnny into detox and when he recovers, she tells him they have been given a second chance.

Johnny proposes to June on stage and she accepts.

Favourites 335

Inner Wheel
Johnny Cash
Male Chart
26 Feb 1932, Fri
07:30 CST +6:00
Kingsland, Arkansas
33°N51'30" 092°W17'38"
Geocentric
Tropical
Equal
Mean Node

Middle Wheel
Joaquin Phoenix
Male Chart
28 Oct 1974, Mon
12:00 AST +4:00
San Juan, Puerto Rico
18°N28'06" 066°W06'22"
Geocentric
Tropical
Equal
Mean Node

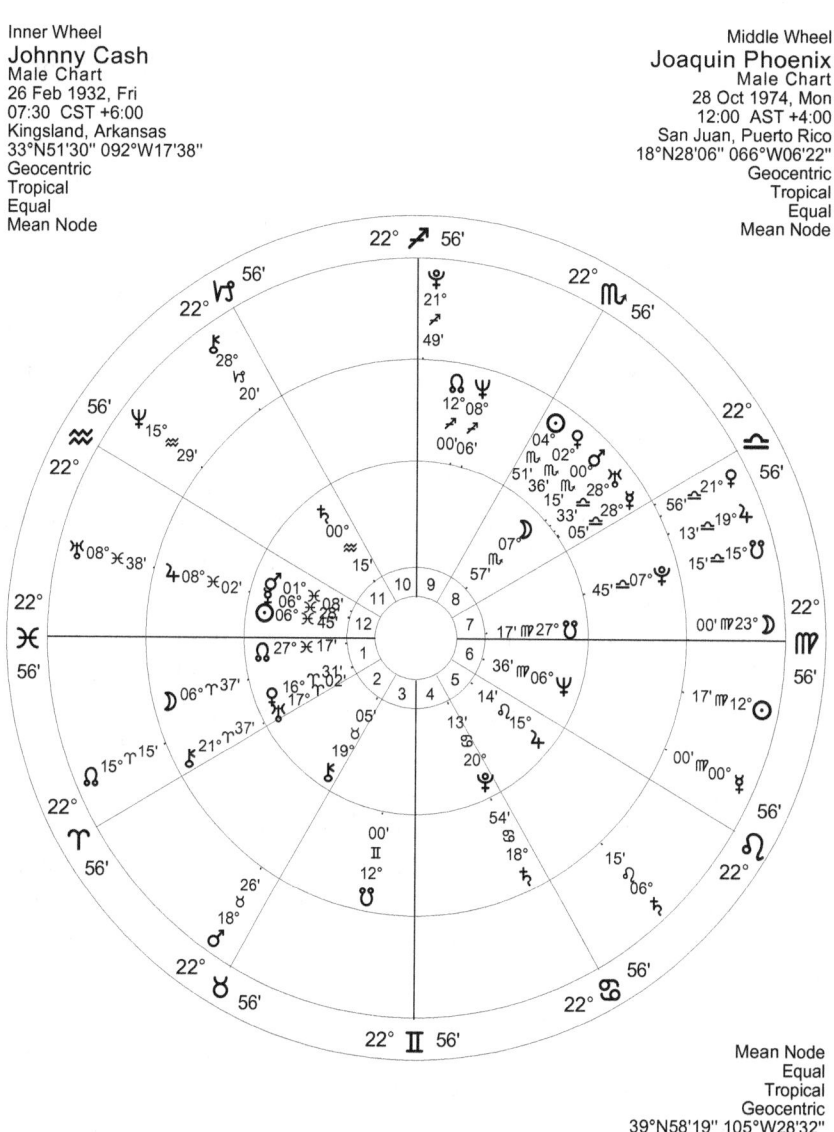

Mean Node
Equal
Tropical
Geocentric
39°N58'19" 105°W28'32"
Tungsten, Colorado
12:00 MDT +6:00
4 Sep 2005, Sun
Event Chart
Walk the Line Release
Outer Wheel

Johnny Cash had a natal three-planet stellium (Sun, Mercury and Mars) in the sign of Pisces in the twelfth house and all opposing Neptune (with the opposition between Neptune and Mercury/Sun being exact to the same degree). Whilst different people in different circumstances might handle this in completely different ways, Cash channelled this energy into his music as well as his dependency on drugs and alcohol. Despite all this, he is widely regarded as one of the most influential musicians of the twentieth century, even though he is remembered mostly for contributing to the genre of country music.

Over half a Uranus cycle in time separates Cash and Joaquin Phoenix, the actor who would portray him in *Walk the Line*. Strikingly both have an unaspected Saturn which would have intensified their work ethic. Cash's stellium of planets in Pisces are within conjunction of Phoenix's natal Jupiter and descendant.

Cash had Uranus conjunct Venus in Aries natally and as there are only a few years' age difference between him and June Carter, it isn't too surprising that June's Uranus was also conjunct this point. Cash's Jupiter in Leo is trine to this point.

In mythology, both Uranus and Jupiter were sky gods known for their fecundity. According to the poet Hesiod, Uranus' inability to love and accept his children led to his wife encouraging one of their children to castrate him. The severed genitals of Uranus were cast into the sea and from the foam of blood, Aphrodite, who would become the goddess of love, was born. Jupiter was not particularly known for his faithfulness to his wife and his long-suffering spouse frequently vented her frustration to anyone who would listen. *Walk the Line* picks up these themes of marital strife, jealousy, and children who felt betrayed and rejected (although the similarities stop well short of actual castration).

Other notable connections include Cash's Chiron on Carter's North Node in Taurus and her Saturn on his MC in Sagittarius. Throughout their relationship, she took care of Cash and spent time keeping her man on the straight and narrow by flushing his stash of pills down the toilet.

Carter's Sun conjunct Witherspoon's Mars in Cancer beautifully encapsulated the singer's sensitivity and ability to hold on to what she regarded as her own. Further enhancing this tendency is Carter's stellium

Favourites 337

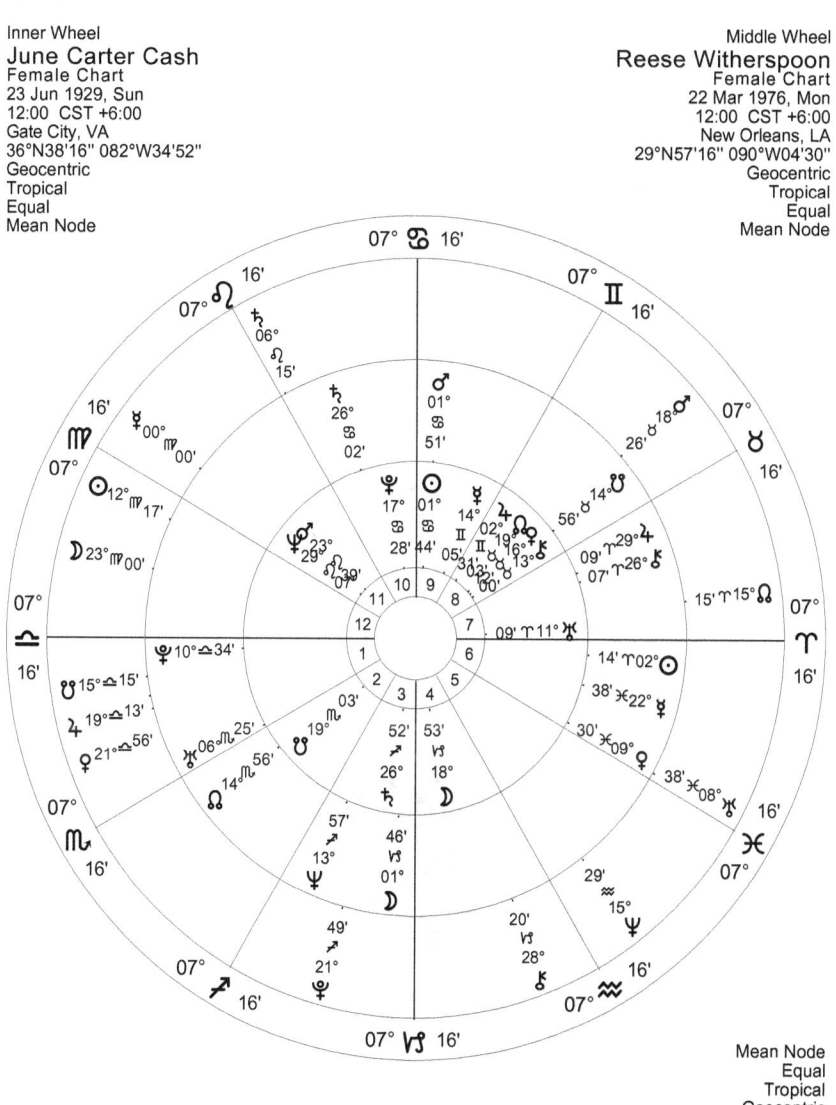

in Taurus (Chiron, Venus and North Node) conjunct Witherspoon's South Node. *Walk the Line* was released as Uranus transited Phoenix's Jupiter and Cash's stellium in Pisces. Phoenix would receive his second nomination for best actor at the academy awards for his portrayal of the Man in Black, Johnny Cash.

Transiting Mars was passing over Carter's stellium in Taurus and Witherspoon's South Node when the movie was released. Witherspoon would win Best Actress at the Academy Awards as well as several other major awards for her portrayal of June Carter Cash.

Johnny Cash and June Carter Cash, their love immortalized in *Walk the Line*, both died in 2003, just four months apart.

In addition to the accolades poured upon the actors, their story would also win the Golden Globe Award for Best Motion Picture. Witherspoon's performance is particularly noteworthy as it won a BAFTA, Oscar and Screen Actors Guild Award for Best Actress, and many others.

GROWING

PAINS

Astrology in Adolescence

Growing Pains: Astrology in Adolescence has been an indispensable resource for parents who are struggling with home schooling during the worldwide pandemic. Alex's insights as both an astrologer and schoolteacher have helped parents better understand how their children learn through their Jupiter signs. The Saturn signs, says Alex, are for the parents and teachers to help them understand how they function as role models and authority figures.

Here is the Introduction from *Growing Pains* with the chapter for Jupiter in Aquarius.

Introduction

As a teacher of adolescents, I wanted to use my skills and knowledge as an astrologer to enhance my career and yet at the same time be accessible to my colleagues as well as the parents of my pupils. I also wanted to challenge my history pupils to embrace the cyclic patterns of events by using the thematic approach of astrology. Although my astrology colleagues help people from all walks of life and almost all ages, they tend to avoid adolescents, who need the most guidance. And so this book is for adolescents, the people who love and care for them and anyone who is curious about how to get the most out of life. I've used celebrity examples, not because I think celebrity is a measure of success but because beneath every Hollywood fairytale, there is a person who has been 'lucky and has worked hard enough to achieve success. This book can help you to work with your natural talents and time your own cycles of growth and development for satisfaction and accomplishment.

Astrologically, Jupiter and Saturn are the planets associated with opportunity and discipline. The placement of Jupiter in the birth chart indicates where and how we are confident and, therefore, where we are likely to take risks. By contrast, the placement of Saturn indicates where and how we fear making mistakes. In the human life cycle, Jupiter is activated first followed by Saturn. The effect is that new opportunities introduced into our lives are followed by a period of honing and developing the skills we have learned.

Usually your Jupiter and Saturn sign will be different to your Sun sign and will take a little time and effort to locate in charts. This is because their cycles around the earth (from our point of view) take far longer than that of the Sun. To find where Jupiter and Saturn are in your chart, it is easiest to start with the year of your birth, referring to the tables at the back of the book, and at the beginning of each chapter.

For example, if you were born in 1990, you would find that Jupiter was in the sign of Cancer from January to August 1990 and in Leo from August 1990 to September 1991. If you then add your date of birth, say for example 2 April, 1990, you would then know Jupiter was in the sign of Cancer at your birth. It works in exactly the same way for finding the sign of Saturn. Once you have worked out the signs of Jupiter and Saturn, it is important to remember that these planets don't stop moving. They continue to revolve and make connections known as transits.

Connections between planets are described as aspects. The conjunction aspect is when planets are close together in the zodiac. The opposition aspect is when planets are in opposite signs in the zodiac. A square is when they are at 90° angles to each other and a trine is when they are at 120° angles to each other.

The planets don't always move in a forward motion from our point of view. Sometimes they appear to move backwards in a motion known as retrograde.

Jupiter and Saturn working together

Imagine laying brick or stone work. We all know bricks and stones are useful for building anything from walls to castles. But there is a skill to laying these materials and it is not as easy as throwing a bit of cement or mortar around and slamming them together. Bricklayers/stonemasons use tools such as levellers to ensure the bricks are even, and they understand the quality of the materials they are using. They know that certain types of bricks and/or mortar are not suitable for a very wet climate whilst others wouldn't suit a very hot one.

In the laying of bricks metaphor, Jupiter represents the bricks and stones and Saturn represents the mortar. Jupiter is used to expand; Saturn is used to hold the bricks together. In the learning process, if the quality of the bricks (Jupiter) is understood, then the suitability of the mortar (Saturn) can be adjusted to ensure a long-lasting finished product. Admire the beauty of cathedrals which have stood for hundreds of years.

Like brickwork, learning is a step by step process. The first time we do anything seldom results in a perfect product. Repeated practice and an understanding of consequences are the keys to improving. A child's first Jupiter opposition at the age of six and the return at about the age of twelve, as well as the first Saturn square at seven and the opposition at about the age of fourteen and a half, are crucial stages of learning. In learning, as in brickwork, the foundation is often the key to ensuring how well a structure will hold up. As parents and teachers, we can help children to understand how they learn. We can help with the process of learning if we understand the material with which we are working. We can look on our children's work and can see if their foundations are wobbly. We can correct and encourage without dictating. In fact, we all have a natural way of doing this via our own Jupiter and Saturn. We, as mature and experienced adults, are continuing to build our fortresses and cathedrals.

The global castle

Although this book is written to be used as a guide to help individuals tap into their learning processes, it is worth bearing in mind that Jupiter and Saturn play a collective role for the whole world. From the point of view of ancient celestial observers, the orbits of Jupiter and Saturn took the most time to complete a cycle (12 and 30 years respectively). Their orbits provided a method of measuring time over a number of years rather than days (the orbit of the sun) or months (the orbit of the moon). Approximately every twenty years, Jupiter and Saturn meet in the sky in an alignment that eventually became known as a Great Conjunction (when these planets are near to the same degree in the same sign).

Great Conjunctions were noted for heralding important events or the birth of important people. For example, it has been theorised that the Star of Bethlehem was a great conjunction.

Although visually less spectacular than solar or lunar eclipses, Great Conjunctions caught the imagination of later astronomers such as Tycho Brahe and Johannes Kepler, who indicated such conjunctions were auspicious. Galileo, who, building on the work of Brahe and Kepler, eventually helped to convince a disbelieving world that the earth revolved around the Sun, was born during a Great Conjunction. Shakespeare, whose work is littered with astrological references, was also born during a Great Conjunction.

The Great Conjunction, fascinating in itself, is a part of measuring even longer periods of time. Early observers of this cycle noted that successive Great Conjunctions took place about 120° later in the zodiac in a sign of the same element.* From any given starting point, every third great conjunction would occur about 9° ahead of its starting point. This time frame of 60 years was known as a trigon. The period of time it takes for Great Conjunctions entering a new element to entering the next element is a period of about 200 years.

After about 800–960 years, Great Conjunctions begin a new cycle and return to similar degrees. Appendix 2 shows a full cycle of Great Conjunctions from the years 1007–2199. Continued research on this cycle will be addressed in future publications.

Recently, the shift changed from conjunctions occurring in earth signs to those occurring in air signs. In 1981, for the first time in centuries, the conjunction took place in Libra, edging the world into a whole new element (although in May 2000 a single conjunction took place in the earth sign Taurus). The Jupiter/Saturn conjunction in Libra coincided with our global focus on the lifestyles of the rich and famous as depicted in TV shows such as *Dallas* or *Dynasty*. Furthermore, the focus was on how the rich played, not on how hard they worked or the price they paid to get there. When the next Jupiter/Saturn conjunction occurred once again in earth signs in 2000 we, as a collective, were able to giggle at the eighties and see it for what it was – a vain attempt to portray life as we might like to think it could be if we only had the right friends and moved in the right social circles. The next Jupiter/Saturn conjunction will occur in the sign of Aquarius in 2020, perhaps launching our understanding of technology into the stratosphere. In schools, technology is changing so quickly that teachers are beginning to acknowledge they are training pupils for jobs that don't even exist yet.

Our current educational system is based on factory-model schools from the 19th century, which are no longer appropriate for the needs of today's students. Astrology can be enormously beneficial in streamlining resources - keeping within budgetary constraints - so that the education we offer our children is more focused on their individual needs rather than our guesswork or what the latest thinking is. It also can help parents and teachers become more effective authority figures. The following pages give an indication of how this might be achieved.

---

* Each sign of the zodiac is associated with an element:
  Fire: Aries, Leo and Sagittarius   Air: Gemini, Libra and Aquarius
  Earth: Taurus, Virgo and Capricorn   Water: Cancer, Scorpio and Pisces

Jupiter in Aquarius

7 January 1926	–	18 January 1927
21 December 1937	–	14 May 1938
31 July 1938	–	29 December 1938
12 April 1949	–	27 June 1949
1 December 1949	–	15 April 1950
16 September 1950	–	2 December 1950
16 March 1961	–	12 August 1961
4 November 1961	–	25 March 1962
23 February 1973	–	8 March 1974
6 February 1985	–	20 February 1986
22 January 1997	–	4 February 1998
5 January 2009	–	18 January 2010
20 December 2020	–	13 May 2021
29 July 2021	–	29 December 2021

Aliens in the classroom

It's finally happened. That thing you never thought would ever happen is happening right now. You don't know where it came from, you don't know what to do with it and words fail you for the first time in your life. Behold, the Jupiter in Aquarius pupils.

To say Jupiter in Aquarius pupils march to the beat of a different drum is a bit of an understatement. These pupils seem to have an internal beat that is completely off whack to fellow pupils or to yourself and indeed seems to have no logical rhythm at all. Teaching them to read will be impossible if you have them sitting in a circle reciting the sounds of every letter the way children usually do. These pupils appreciate inventiveness, experimentation and doing what has never been done before. Stumped for ideas? Ask the pupils. Their creativity will astound, inspire and worry you all at the same time

Through creative play, Jupiter in Aquarius pupils search for ways to ensure that everyone benefits – in their own way – from educational opportunities. Of course, these pupils can't vocalise this premise, but watch them. They excel in teams where they all understand how to take turns being leader. They strive for equality and really do seem unable to differentiate between the genders. In being eccentric, they are calling attention to themselves but give them the attention they seem to want and they run off and hide.

This group of learners requires structure, but only just enough to prevent lessons from becoming a free-for-all. Make sure everyone has the chance to be the teacher and they will appreciate your ability to play the game of fairness. At around the age of six, these pupils will take enormous pride in learning how to read and they will demonstrate their new skills anytime and anywhere – although their choice of reading material can be a little odd (you might want to keep them away from the conspiracy theory sections of the library). These pupils tend to be science-fiction fans so if you have reluctant readers, try anything involving deep space, astronomy or crop circles and you should be able to win them over.

Most pupils enter secondary school determined to follow every rule. Their uniforms are neatly prepared, their books are fresh and their pencils sharpened. Not the Jupiter in Aquarius pupils. They arrive at secondary school determined to break every rule, re-vamp the national curriculum and overturn every tradition. They want revolution.

Once exam time rolls around, all the teachers are tearing out their collective hair because this group is just not interested in changing their ways. They've become beatnik hippies reciting Walt Whitman (who also had Jupiter in Aquarius) and singing Bob Dylan songs. They're organising protest marches and are talking about overthrowing the government. And they're eating everything in sight.

If you're a parent or a teacher and the Jupiter in Aquarius pupils start manifesting these signs during exam season, take a deep breath. The more you push, the more they dig in. Relax. These are smart pupils who do everything a little differently. As exams loom ever closer, you will discover that they have found ingenious ways of looking like they don't care, but they are actually studying like hard core academics. Getting them to surrender their mobile phones might still pose a few problems however.

If you're a teacher with Jupiter in Aquarius, chances are that you have found your way to the House of Commons on more than one occasion. Your teaching methods are questionable, but all your pupils are progressing at the same rate, so everyone is happy. In your free time (which you ensure is plentiful), you scan the night sky for your alien friends, play on the internet all night and join so many groups and have so many affiliations that not even you can keep track of your schedule. As a result of being on the internet so often, your hair has taken on a curiously electric look and your facial expressions seem to have frozen. The kids call you Mr Spock behind your back (even if you're a woman) but they like your eclectic taste in ties and socks – even if you don't wash them very often. By the time you're thirty, you really do live on your own little planet, and by the time you're sixty, you may just want to come home and see what all the earthlings are up to.

Fine-tuning the role of Jupiter

Jupiter in Aquarius is ruled by Saturn, the planet of responsibility and restriction. However, Aquarius is co-ruled by Uranus, the planet of experimentation and innovation (either or both planets can be used). It is often difficult to merge hard-working Saturn with free-wheeling Uranus. It is important to note that Uranus works on a collective basis: Jupiter in Uranus reaches and affects the masses. The interpretations below reflect how a person works towards personal freedom within the confines of society.

Saturn/Uranus in Aries – These pupils naturally work towards independence, perhaps sensing a strong urge to do something to change the status quo. Teachers and other authority figures may be prime targets of mistrust. Those who operate on the edge of society are trusted allies in the fight towards independence.

Saturn/Uranus in Taurus – These pupils naturally work towards stabilising major structures; perhaps sensing huge changes are imminent. Teachers and other authority figures may be relied upon to offer support during times of crisis. Banks and building societies may be viewed as catalysts for change.

Saturn/Uranus in Gemini – These pupils naturally work towards innovating communication systems, perhaps sensing it is imperative to communicate faster and more efficiently. Teachers and other authority figures may be seen as facilitators of this process. Friends and social groups are used to network and distribute information.

Saturn/Uranus in Cancer – These pupils work naturally towards reforming the way society views family values, perhaps sensing that this basic tradition is on the verge of revolution. Teachers and other authority figures are viewed as an intrinsic part of preventing change. Friends and social groups begin to take the place of family.

Saturn/Uranus in Leo – These pupils work naturally toward avant-garde creativity and self-expression, particularly through vehicles such as mass media. High technology begins to replace traditional authority figures. Youth starts to overtake experience.

Saturn/Uranus in Virgo – These pupils work naturally towards reforming work ethics and innovating health care. This generation, when they came of age led the New Age into alternative medicines. Teachers and other authority figures are seen as dirty or contaminated and as such are rejected.

Saturn/Uranus in Libra – These pupils work naturally towards uniting people by equalising their status. Unusual marriages or new laws regarding marriage are now more acceptable than traditional views. Teachers and other authority figures are seen as allies who try to enforce equality.

Saturn/Uranus in Scorpio – These pupils work naturally towards reforming attitudes towards sexuality and other forms of subtle power. Teachers and other authority figures are seen as abusing their power on a collective level.

Saturn/Uranus in Sagittarius – These pupils work naturally towards reforming attitudes concerning religion, education and law. Teachers and other authority figures are seen as those who will not follow conventional law and order as accepted by society.

Saturn/Uranus in Capricorn – These pupils work naturally towards reforming business and government practices. Teachers and authority figures are viewed as those who prevent innovation.

Saturn/Uranus in Aquarius – These pupils work towards changing society. Teachers and other authority figures are viewed as innovators and leaders towards change.

Saturn/Uranus in Pisces – These pupils work towards collectively accepting those who have been marginalised in society. Teachers and other authority figures may be viewed as unexpected martyrs to the harshness and unfairness of society.

Case study – Marilyn Monroe

1 June 1926, 9:30 PST
Los Angeles, California 34°N03'08"118°W14'34"
Rodden rating: AA; Collector: Rodden
Jupiter in Aquarius, Uranus in Pisces
Saturn in Scorpio, Pluto in Cancer
First Jupiter return: April, August, December 1938
Time between first Jupiter return and last Saturn opposition: 3 years, 2 months
First Saturn opposition: April and June 1941
First Saturn return: October 1955

Jupiter conjunct the Moon in Aquarius usually indicates a chaotic childhood and, more specifically, an erratic mother. Norma Jean Baker lived with foster parents until her mentally unstable mother (who had earlier attempted to smuggle her away from her foster parents in a duffle bag) bought a house and brought her daughter back to live with her in 1933, as transiting Saturn made a series of three oppositions to her descendant. Norma Jean (Marilyn) recalled that her mother had several episodes of screaming and laughing fits which led to her being institutionalised.

Norma Jean was made a ward of the state, with her mother's best friend becoming her guardian. Her guardian told the young Norma Jean

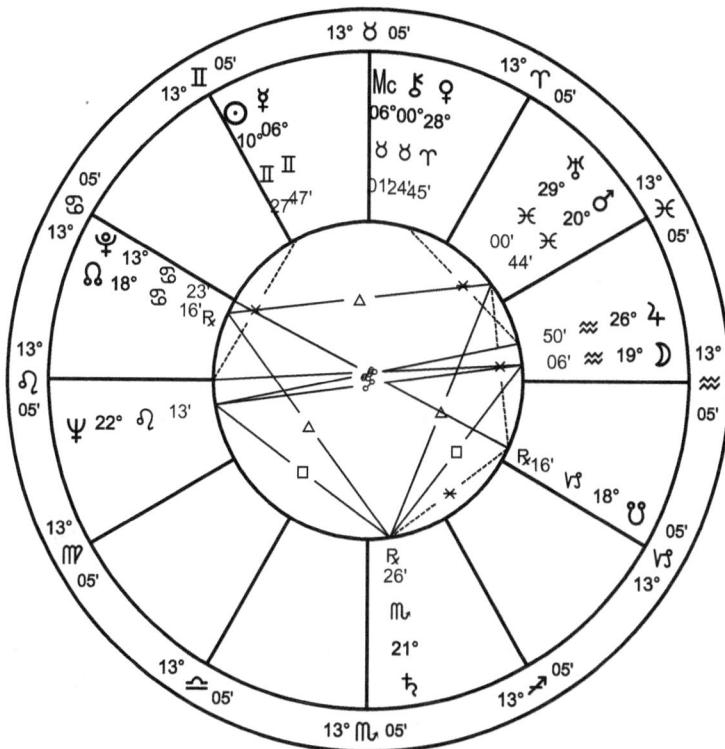

Marilyn Monroe – 1 June 1926

that one day she would become a film star and this stage of her childhood was filled with visits to the cinema and appointments to have her hair curled. When Norma Jean was nine however, the guardian married a man who later made several attempts to sexually assault the young girl; this was in 1937, just after Saturn made a series of conjunctions to her natal Mars in Pisces. Both transiting Saturn and Jupiter made a number of conjunctions to Norma Jean's natal planets in 1942 when she met and married her first husband, James Dougherty. This was probably the only stable time of her life even though, at fifteen, she was under the legal age for marriage.

In 1944, transiting Jupiter in Leo made a series of conjunctions to her natal Neptune and shortly afterwards, she was talent-spotted and the first photographs of her were taken. It was during her time as a model, after some experimentation, that she changed her name to the alliterative Marilyn Monroe. In 1946, as transiting Jupiter was opposite her Venus, her divorce was finalised. In 1947, as she searched for film work, she posed nude for pictures as transiting Jupiter in Scorpio was conjunct her Saturn.

As Saturn in Leo was conjunct her natal Neptune in 1947, she had her slight overbite corrected and later that year, when Jupiter made contact, she was persuaded to have a minor nose job. In March 1952, Jupiter made two squares to her natal Pluto and she was forced to explain her nude photos to the public. Fortunately, the public was sympathetic. Later that year, as Jupiter was conjunct her natal Venus her career really began to take off. She appeared in *Life* magazine and began dating the baseball player Joe DiMaggio.

In September 1954, transiting Saturn opposed her MC at the time when DiMaggio objected to what would become one of her most celebrated scenes, her skirt blowing upwards as a subway train passed. In 1955, just before transiting Jupiter crossed over her ascendant in Leo, the movie *The Seven Year Itch* was released to the public, but by this time she had already divorced DiMaggio.

In 1956, as Jupiter in Leo was conjunct her natal Neptune, she admitted that her marriage to James Dougherty had made her consider suicide[10]. It was also the year she converted to Judaism in order to marry the playwright Arthur Miller. In 1961, as both transiting Saturn and Jupiter made numerous squares to her natal planets, they divorced. Jupiter made its last conjunction to its natal place as Marilyn performed *Happy Birthday, Mr President* for JFK.

Marilyn died during a series of three transiting Jupiter squares to her Moon in Aquarius.

AUTHOR BIO

Alex Trenoweth, MA (CAA), DFAstrolS, is an astrological researcher; she is a professional schoolteacher in London as well as running a thriving consultancy specialising in families. In 2015, she was awarded "International Astrologer of the Year" by the Krishnamurti Institute of Astrology (KIA) in Kolkata India for her ground-breaking and innovative research on Astrology and Education based on her book *Growing Pains: Astrology in Adolescence* (The Wessex Astrologer). Since then, she has spoken at astrology conferences around the world and has contributed to major astrological magazines and publications. She has also recently authored *The Adolescent Astrology Report* which was created to help parents and teachers understand the children they care for and is available from her website.

Alex is now President of the board for Certified Astrological Professionals for the International Society of Astrological Research (CAPISAR) and has recently started her own astrology school, Rohini Academy of Astrology. Her website is www.alextrenoweth.co.uk.

www.ingramcontent.com/pod-product-compliance
Lightning Source LLC
Chambersburg PA
CBHW051108230426
43667CB00014B/2489